History of Intellectual Culture

History of Intellectual Culture

International Yearbook of Knowledge and Society

Edited by
Charlotte A. Lerg, Johan Östling, and Jana Weiß

Advisory Board:
Peter Burke, University of Cambridge
Tristan Coignard, Université Bordeaux Montaigne
Heather Ellis, University of Sheffield
Tiffany N. Florvil, University of New Mexico
Adam Kola, Nicolaus Copernicus University, Torun
Suzanne Marchand, Louisiana State University
Pierre-Héli Monot, Ludwig Maximilian University, Munich
João Ohara, Federal University of Rio de Janeiro
Swen Steinberg, Queen's University, Kingston, and German Historical Institute, Washington, DC
Emily Steinhauer, Royal Holloway, University of London
Eugenia Roldán Vera, Center for Research and Advanced Studies (CINVESTAV), Mexico
Christa Wirth, University of Agder

History of Intellectual Culture

Volume 3
2024

—

Experimental Spaces: Knowledge Production
and its Environments in the Long Nineteenth Century

Edited by
Charlotte A. Lerg, Johan Östling, and Jana Weiß

Thematic section edited by
Anne Kwaschik and Claudia Roesch

DE GRUYTER
OLDENBOURG

This book has been kindly supported by the Thora Ohlsson Foundation and the Knut and Alice Wallenberg Foundation.

ISBN 978-3-11-129090-4
e-ISBN (PDF) 978-3-11-129138-3
e-ISBN (EPUB) 978-3-11-129164-2
ISSN 2747-6766
DOI https://doi.org/10.1515/9783111291383

This work is licensed under the Creative Commons Attribution-NonCommercial-NoDerivatives 4.0 International License. For details go to https://creativecommons.org/licenses/by-nc-nd/4.0

Creative Commons license terms for re-use do not apply to any content (such as graphs, figures, photos, excerpts, etc.) not original to the Open Access publication and further permission may be required from the rights holder. The obligation to research and clear permission lies solely with the party re-using the material.

Library of Congress Control Number: 2024940880

Bibliographic information published by the Deutsche Nationalbibliothek
The Deutsche Nationalbibliothek lists this publication in the Deutsche Nationalbibliografie; detailed bibliographic data are available on the internet at http://dnb.dnb.de.

© 2024 the author(s), editing © 2024 Charlotte A. Lerg, Johan Östling, Jana Weiß, Anne Kwaschik and Claudia Roesch, published by Walter de Gruyter GmbH, Berlin/Boston
The book is published open access at www.degruyter.com.

Cover image: Word Cloud generated with WordArt.com.
Typesetting: Integra Software Services Pvt. Ltd.

www.degruyter.com

HIC Preface for Vol. 3

While this is our third volume as editors of the yearbook *History of Intellectual Culture* (*HIC*), it is also our first volume to feature guest editors for Section 2. We are excited to present a thematic section on "Experimental Spaces: Knowledge Production and its Environments in the Long Nineteenth Century," and we would like to sincerely thank Anne Kwaschik and Claudia Roesch for their dedicated work in bringing together five excellent papers exploring intentional communities, colonial gardens, agricultural colonies, and artistic colonies as experimental spaces.

Moreover, our Section 1 showcases the plethora of topics in the history of knowledge and intellectual culture, stretching from the U.S. patent system in the 1930s and anti-intellectualism in interwar Britain to the cultural translation of knowledge in the wake of the Holocaust, the circulation of economic knowledge in postwar Sweden, and an interrogation of the memoirs of exiled academics through the lens of postmemory.

As always, Section 3 engages the field with several theoretical, historiographical, and methodological interventions and reflections, including a conversation on decolonizing knowledge in academia and beyond. In our view, the style of a conversation allows for multiple perspectives and offers a fruitful way of discussing scholarly and contemporary issues. Needless to say, the views and opinions expressed are those of the individual authors. In addition, Section 3 also contains an investigation of early examples of histories of the humanities as well as a presentation of an analytical framework of socio-epistemic networks.

May 2024

Charlotte A. Lerg, Ludwig Maximilian University, Munich
Johan Östling, Lund Centre for the History of Knowledge (LUCK), Lund University
Jana Weiß, The University of Texas at Austin

Contents

HIC Preface for Vol. 3 — V

Section I: **Individual Articles**

Tomás Irish
"Abhorrent to English Ears": Anti-Intellectualism and the League of Nations in Interwar Britain — 3

Victoria Van Orden Martínez
Survivors of Nazi Persecution, Refugees, Knowledge Actors: The Cultural Translation of Knowledge in an Effort to Document Nazi Atrocities, 1945–1946 — 25

Isabelle Strömstedt and Adam Bisno
Defending the Knowledge Monopoly: The U.S. Patent Office, Propaganda, and the Centennial Celebration of the Patent Act of 1836 — 49

Rasmus Fleischer
Pathologizing the Economy: "Baumol's Cost Disease" and the Circulation of Economic Knowledge in Sweden — 73

Katherine Arens
Memoirs as Postmemory: Adorno, Lazarsfeld, and the US Radio Project — 97

Section II: **Experimental Spaces**

Anne Kwaschik and Claudia Roesch
Experimental Spaces: Knowledge Production and its Environments in the Long Nineteenth Century — 125

Claudia Roesch
Talking about the Weather: Producing Climate Knowledge as Colonial Practice in Intentional Communities in the Americas, 1820s–1840s — 137

Anne Kwaschik
Experimental Discourse and Fourierist Settlements in the 1840s and 1850s —— 159

Alina Marktanner
Experimenting for Empire: Plant Health as an Agricultural Problem in German East Africa, Togo and Cameroon, 1905–1914 —— 181

Gilberto Mazzoli
Climates of Migration: Science, Race, and Agricultural Diplomacy between Italy and the United States, 1895–1916 —— 205

Anne-Sophie Reichert
Knowledge in Motion: Research and Experimentation at Hellerau's School for Rhythmik —— 227

Section III: Engaging the Field

Aleksandra Kaye, Raphael Schlattmann, Malte Vogl, Bernardo S. Buarque, Jascha Schmitz, Lea Weiß, and Laura von Welczeck
Socio-Epistemic Networks: A Framework for History of Knowledge —— 253

Hampus Östh Gustafsson
R. S. Crane and the Invention of the Humanities: The Formation of Historical Narratives of Knowledge in the Mid-Twentieth Century —— 275

HIC Conversation with Tiffany N. Florvil, Madalitso Zililo Phiri, and Vanessa D. Plumly, edited and introduced by Jana Weiß
Interrogating Epistemologies: Decolonizing Knowledge in Academia and Beyond —— 295

Contributors —— 323

Section I: **Individual Articles**

Tomás Irish
"Abhorrent to English Ears": Anti-Intellectualism and the League of Nations in Interwar Britain

Abstract: As noted by Gilbert Murray in 1931, the League Committee of Intellectual Cooperation (CIC) faced skepticism in Great Britain, thus highlighting a prevalent mistrust of abstract ideas among English audiences. This article explores Britain's engagement with intellectual cooperation, arguing that it reflected broader tensions regarding the role of intellectuals in British society and a resistance to transnational cultural cooperation. Two main points are discussed: (1) the negative perception of intellectuals in interwar Britain and the prevailing anti-intellectual discourse; and (2) the British reluctance to fully embrace projects such as the CIC, evidenced by the tepid reception of the British National Committee on Intellectual Cooperation. This reluctance provided some opportunities for Wales to align itself more favorably with the League's cultural initiatives. Debates concerning intellectuals were crucial in the discussions leading up to the establishment of UNESCO during the Second World War.

Keywords: intellectuals, anti-intellectualism, interwar, League of Nations, Britain

Introduction

"The League Committee of Intellectual Cooperation, or CIC, has never attracted much sympathy in Great Britain. The name has about it something priggish, something that sounds to our prejudiced ears 'Latin and not Anglo-Saxon.' It rouses, until it can explain itself, all the Englishman's instinctive mistrust of abstract ideas." These were the words of Gilbert Murray, chair of the International Committee on Intellectual Cooperation (CIC), writing to *The Times* in 1931. Murray's remark is an important starting point in seeking to understand Britain's relationship with the intellectual work of the League of Nations and its associated bodies, namely the CIC and the International Institute for Intellectual Cooperation (IIIC). This is important because it reveals a great deal regarding attitudes toward intellectuals in the interwar period while also providing important insights into the contours of British anti-intellectualism.

Britain's relationship with the idea of "intellectual cooperation" was defined by a pronounced public cynicism throughout the 1920s and 1930s. There were two major reasons for this. First, the discourse surrounding the idea of "intellectual cooperation" in Britain revealed a wider tension regarding the role of the intellectual in British society and the characteristics of intellectuals more generally. The term "intellectual" was often deployed in a negative and pejorative sense where anti-intellectualism was prominent in public discourse and "denialism" was part of the English national identity.[1] Contemporary discourse often emphasized the "foreignness" of the idea of "intellectual cooperation" and frequently asserted that to be an "intellectual" was not a British quality but one that came from elsewhere. Second, Britain's relationship with intellectual cooperation was illustrative of a wider disinclination in British political and cultural life to "buy into" a project that presupposed a degree of transnational cultural coherence, especially when this encroached on longstanding imperial connections. At a more practical level, administrators in cultural organizations were often resistant to fully engage with projects initiated by the Geneva-based CIC as these were perceived as threatening similar projects that had already been initiated within the setting of the British Empire.

This article explores anti-intellectualism in British public life through an analysis of British attitudes to and relationships with the CIC. It shows that the Geneva-based organization was emblematic of wider anti-intellectual attitudes in British interwar society precisely due to its "foreignness." Britain's interactions with intellectual cooperation are measured in three ways: with an analysis of British attitudes toward the idea of "the intellectual," through public discussions of the concept of "intellectual cooperation" and via a brief exploration of the activities of the British National Committee on Intellectual Cooperation (BNCIC). The article concludes during the Second World War when Anglo-American planning discussions for what would become UNESCO self-consciously reflected upon interwar anti-intellectualism in order to ensure greater longevity for the successor organization to the League of Nations.

This article juxtaposes Britain's relationship with the League of Nations and its own anxiety regarding intellectuals as both issues were based on similar ideas. The League of Nations was the world's first intergovernmental organization. First and foremost, it brought countries together to pursue methods such as international arbitration to avoid war but also for a swathe of ancillary purposes, from the prevention of drug trafficking to the standardization of labor legislation. The League, with varying degrees of success, sought to normalize and institutionalize

---

[1] Stefan Collini, *Absent Minds: Intellectuals in Britain* (Oxford: Oxford University Press, 2006), 69; David Edgerton, *The Rise and Fall of the British Nation: A Twentieth-Century History* (London: Penguin, 2018), 153.

international cooperation in many spheres, including intellectual cooperation. While the League progressed tentatively and incrementally in many areas, this was often seen as having the potential to encroach upon national sovereignty, which meant that the League's growing influence was sometimes perceived as being at odds with national or imperial policy.[2] Similarly, Britain's relationship with its intellectuals was also based on a sense of international connectedness as the idea of "the intellectual" was commonly seen as a foreign import that did not align with British qualities. In this way, the issue of Britain's relationship with intellectual cooperation rested upon competing visions of internationalism, both in how it was imagined and how it was informed.[3] This article demonstrates that interwar anti-intellectualism could take a number of forms, which, in turn, mirrored the different meanings of the term intellectual in the same period.

Intellectuals in Britain

There is a broad literature on intellectuals and anti-intellectualism in modern Britain.[4] It is generally accepted that anti-intellectualism and the idea that Britain had no intellectuals was part of the British or, more specifically, English national

---

[2] One area in which sovereignty was often invoked was in the League's desire to influence teaching at school. Kaiyi Li, *Transnational Education between the League of Nations and China* (Cham: Palgrave Macmillan, 2021), 56.
[3] On internationalism, see Glenda Sluga and Patricia Clavin, eds., *Internationalisms: A Twentieth-Century History* (Cambridge: Cambridge University Press, 2016); Daniel Gorman, *International Cooperation in the Early Twentieth Century* (London: Bloomsbury, 2017), Daniel Laqua, ed., *Internationalism Reconfigured: Transnational Ideas and Movements between the World Wars* (London: Bloomsbury, 2011), Glenda Sluga, *Internationalism in the Age of Nationalism* (Philadelphia, PA: University of Pennsylvania Press, 2013).
[4] Collini, *Absent Minds*; John Carey, *The Intellectuals and the Masses: Pride and Prejudice among the Literary Intelligentsia, 1880–1939* (London: Faber, 1992); Noel Annan, *The Dons: Mentors, Eccentrics and Geniuses* (London: Harper Collins, 1999); Frank M. Turner, *Contesting Cultural Authority: Essays in Victorian Intellectual Life* (Cambridge: Cambridge University Press, 1993); William C. Lubenow, *Learned Lives in England, 1900–1950: Institutions, Ideas and Intellectual Experience* (Woodbridge: The Boydell Press, 2020); John Rodden, "On the Political Sociology of Intellectuals: George Orwell and the London Left intelligentsia of the 1930s," *The Canadian Journal of Sociology/Cahiers canadiens de sociologie* 15, no. 3 (1990): 251–273; T. W. Heyck, "Myths and Meanings of Intellectuals in Twentieth-Century British National Identity," *Journal of British Studies* 37, no. 2 (1998): 192–221; Guy Ortolano, *The Two Cultures Controversy: Science, Literature and Cultural Politics in Postwar Britain* (Oxford: Oxford University Press, 2009).

identity.⁵ The idea that Britain did not have any intellectuals emerged in the nineteenth century in tandem with the emergence of the term "intellectual." The noun intellectual was originally imported from France during the Dreyfus Affair and was derived from the French *intellectuel*, meaning that it was frequently seen as something "foreign" and "other" in Britain.⁶ In a French context, the term *intellectuel* was synonymous with interventions in politics, but this function was not widely accepted in early twentieth-century Britain.⁷ Being an intellectual was frequently portrayed in a negative light *because* the term was seen as one emanating from continental Europe. This was bolstered by certain qualities being associated with the national identity; England was frequently seen as valuing qualities such as pragmatism, empiricism, and understatedness, whereas France (and the European continent) was by contrast seen as valuing characteristics such as abstract rationalism, rhetoric, and exaggeration. An additional manifestation of this could be seen in the idea that Britain valued character over intellect.⁸

While there were many individuals who performed the function of intellectuals in early twentieth-century Britain, this was framed by a discourse that denied their existence in those terms and saw this as something other or foreign. Examples of this anti-intellectual discourse can be found in a range of publications. Speaking in 1913, William Inge, the dean of St. Paul's Cathedral claimed that there was an "ingrained contempt" for intellectual life in England.⁹ An editorial in the *Yorkshire Post* in 1930 claimed that the term "intellectual" was "a word of fear" in Britain. It was written in response to a conference of the International Federation of Intellectual Workers being held in London. At this conference, the British delegation refused to recognize the title "intellectual," instead opting for the title of "professional or non-manual workers." The editorial suggested that "a Frenchman or a German is flattered by being called 'intellectual' while a true Englishman regards this epithet with a particular uneasiness, if not as a veiled insult." Intellectual qualities could only be tolerated when concealed by something else, such as lightheartedness, or when mixed with "other qualities more tradi-

---

5 Heyck, "Myths and Meanings," 192–221; Collini, *Absent Minds*; Philip Nind, "British Industry and the Anti-Intellectual Tradition," *Journal of the Royal Society of Arts* 133, no. 5345 (1985): 329–340.
6 Ruth Harris, *The Man on Devil's Island: Alfred Dreyfus and the Affair that Divided France* (London: Penguin 2011); Christophe Charle, *Birth of the Intellectuals 1880–1900* (Cambridge: Polity, 2015).
7 Collini, *Absent Minds*, 49–50; Christophe Charle, *The Birth of the Intellectuals: 1880–1900* (Cambridge: Polity, 2015), 2.
8 Collini, *Absent Minds*, 69; Heyck, "Myths and Meanings," 200.
9 "Anti-intellectualism," *The Globe*, 16 October 1913, 2.

tionally British."[10] It was notable that while unions of intellectual workers were being formed across Europe in the early 1920s, their equivalent in Britain was called the National Federation of Professional, Technical, Administrative and Supervisory Workers.[11]

There was a widespread view that to be an intellectual was foreign and that the label was pejorative. Alfred Zimmern, a classicist and pioneer in the study of international relations who worked closely with the League and its Institute for Intellectual Cooperation, wrote in 1928 that "Englishmen delight, indeed, in proclaiming their distrust of the things of the mind" and claimed that one of their "traditional pleasures," almost "a national sport," was "to fling darts of good natured irony against the lover of ideas."[12] Zimmern contrasted this to how ideas were valued in Continental Europe, where "To be illogical [. . .] is to be convicted of social lapse and, in the case of a hardened offender, to qualify for the asylum. In England it is the apostle of logic who is considered a fit subject for confinement: he belongs to the study or the sanctum where the tides of real life cannot penetrate." In Zimmern's words, this was all an "islander's device," as Britain had brought together intellect and practical life at many points in its history, most notably during the Industrial Revolution and the Great War.[13]

Until the 1930s, to be an intellectual in Britain did not always have a clear meaning but typically entailed an individual with a qualification or eminence in a particular field "speaking out" to a wider audience.[14] The term came into greater usage and took on greater clarity in the 1930s against the polarizing backdrop of the "culture wars" and writers and scholars engaging in political ideologies such as communism or political issues such as the Spanish Civil War. Starting in the 1930s, being an intellectual thus took on greater political connotations, and people frequently spoke of "left-wing" or "right-wing" intellectuals.[15] When a group of writers including Leonard and Virginia Woolf, Norman Angell, J.B.S. Haldane, E.M. Forster, and Gilbert Murray wrote to *The Times* in August 1936 to declare their sympathy for the democratic Spanish government during the civil war, they were criticized as not representative of the British people *because* they were "self-styled intellec-

---

10 "Intellectual," *Yorkshire Post*, 17 September 1930, 8.
11 Tomás Irish, *Feeding the Mind: Humanitarianism and the Reconstruction of European Intellectual Life, 1919–1933* (Cambridge: Cambridge University Press, 2024), 205.
12 Alfred Zimmern, *Learning and Leadership: A Study of the Needs and Possibilities of International Intellectual Cooperation* (London: Oxford University Press, 1928), 70–71.
13 Zimmern, *Learning and Leadership*, 70–71.
14 Collini, *Absent Minds*, 28–33, 47–48.
15 Rodden, "Political Sociology," 253–254; Collini, *Absent Minds*, 33.

tuals."¹⁶ This polarization of intellectuals in the 1930s was famously criticized by George Orwell in his 1940 essay "Inside the Whale," where he concluded that the history of the 1930s "seems to justify the opinion that the writer does well to keep out of politics."¹⁷

Historian and theorist of international relations E.H. Carr offered a further critique of intellectuals by the end of the 1930s that centered on what he felt was their failure to prevent Europe's slide into conflict. In *The Twenty Years' Crisis* (published in 1939), Carr discussed the role of intellectuals in politics and, in particular, the League of Nations. He argued that this represented one of the greatest examples of the League's utopianism and "insistence on general principles." He contrasted the intellectual to the bureaucrat, who, he argued, thought empirically. The failings of intellectuals were the same as the failings of utopianism, namely their inability "to understand existing reality and the way in which their own standards are rooted in it."¹⁸ Speaking that same year, philosopher Bertrand Russell argued that the problem was that intellectuals and experts were not listened to concerning matters of international importance, citing as evidence the Paris Peace Conference of 1919, where teams of academic experts had been brought to the French capital to advise the politicians. Russell claimed that the group able to make a difference in the modern world were not the intellectuals but those whom he termed the "technicians," such as those who could invent "an adequate defense against airplanes."¹⁹ Russell blamed anti-intellectualism on "some very strong passion which is [. . .] incapable of being gratified," meaning that "people take an irrational point of view in order not to see that it can't be gratified."²⁰ By the outbreak of the Second World War, anti-intellectualism in Britain had taken on a number of forms deriving from either an association with other countries, engagement with (left-wing) politics, or involvement in international affairs.

---

[16] "To The Editor of The Times," *The Times*, 19 August 1936, 6; "The Manifesto on Spain," *The Times*, 7 September 1936, 8.
[17] George Orwell, "Inside the Whale," in *The Collected, Essays, Journalism and Letters of George Orwell. Volume 1: An Age Like This, 1920–1940* (London: Secker and Warburg, 1968), 518.
[18] E.H. Carr, *The Twenty Years' Crisis: An Introduction to the Study of International Relations*, 2nd ed. (London: Macmillan & Co. Ltd., 1946), 14.
[19] Bertrand Russell, "The Role of the Intellectual in the Modern World," *American Journal of Sociology* 44, no. 4 (1939): 491–498.
[20] Russell, "Role of the Intellectual," 494.

The League of Nations and the CIC

Following Carr's paradigmatic polemic in the *Twenty Years' Crisis*, the League of Nations became synonymous with failure in the historiography that developed over much of the remainder of the twentieth century. However, there has been a substantial reappraisal of the League in recent decades. The realist-inspired focus on the failure of the League in terms of preventing the outbreak of war in 1939 has been replaced by an exploration of the work done by the international body in a myriad of fields, including humanitarianism, economic and financial work, mandates, and beyond, as well as identifying continuities between the League and subsequent international organizations.[21] This new approach to the life of the League has opened up new and fresh approaches to understanding the ways in which individual states interacted with the Geneva-based organization. Within this new historiography, the League's work on intellectual cooperation has received growing attention in the works of scholars such as Daniel Laqua, Jean-Jacques Renoliet, Corinne Pernet, and others.[22] Allied to this new interest in the institution of the League of Nations, scholars have also begun to explore civic internationalism, or the "grassroots" national organizations intended to buttress

---

[21] Patricia Clavin, *Securing the World Economy: The Reinvention of the League of Nations 1920–1946* (Oxford: Oxford University Press, 2013); Nicholas Mulder, *The Economic Weapon: The Rise of Sanctions as a Tool of Modern War* (New Haven, CT: Yale University Press, 2022); Bruno Cabanes, *The Great War and the Origins of Humanitarianism 1918–1924* (Cambridge: Cambridge University Press, 2014); Mark Mazower, *Governing the World: The History of an Idea* (London: Penguin, 2012); Susan Pedersen, *The Guardians: The League of Nations and the Crisis of Empire* (Oxford: Oxford University Press, 2015); Jay Winter and Antoine Prost, *René Cassin and Human Rights: From the Great War to the Universal Declaration* (Cambridge: Cambridge University Press, 2013); Zara Steiner, *The Lights that Failed: European International History, 1919–1933* (Oxford: Oxford University Press, 2005).

[22] Jo-Anne Pemberton, "The Changing Shape of Intellectual Co-operation: From the League of Nations to UNESCO," *Australian Journal of Politics and History* 58, no. 1 (2012): 34–50; Jean-Jacques Renoliet, *L'UNESCO oubliée: La Société des nations et la coopération intellectuelle, 1919–1946* (Paris: Publications de la Sorbonne, 1999); Daniel Laqua, "Transnational Intellectual Cooperation, the League of Nations, and the Problem of Order," *Journal of Global History* 6, no. 2 (2011): 223–247; Jimena Canales, "Einstein, Bergson, and the Experiment that Failed: Intellectual Cooperation at the League of Nations," *MLN* 120, no. 5 (2005): 1168–1191; Corinne A. Pernet, "Twists, Turns, and Dead Alleys: The League of Nations and Intellectual Cooperation in Times of War," *Journal of Modern European History* 12, no. 3 (2014): 342–358; Tomás Irish, "The 'Moral Basis' of Reconstruction? Humanitarianism, Intellectual Relief and the League of Nations, 1918–1925," *Modern Intellectual History* 17, no. 3 (2020): 769–800; Irish, *Feeding the Mind*.

the main body at Geneva and build an international public opinion favorable to the peaceful resolution of international disputes.[23]

The idea of "intellectual cooperation" was first proposed by the Belgian delegation at the Paris Peace Conference of 1919 but was not included in the final settlements due to the fact that, in the words of one commentator, "it seemed to be rather a decoration than a vital part of the new organization."[24] The International Committee for Intellectual Cooperation was formed in 1922 and met annually in Geneva, home of the League. It was followed in 1925 by an Institute for Intellectual Cooperation (IIIC), established in Paris with financial backing from the French government.

According to an official report written by the French historian and politician Gabriel Hanotaux, members of the International Committee on Intellectual Cooperation were "appointed in consideration of their personal ability and their reputation in learned circles, and without any discrimination as to nationality."[25] Membership was based on (an undefined) cultural authority rather than nationality. At its first meeting in August 1922, the committee was comprised of a group of eminent scholars and writers, including the chair, Henri Bergson (France), as well as figures such as Gilbert Murray (Britain), Marie Curie (France), and Albert Einstein (Germany).[26] The report of the CIC's first meeting identified specific areas for attention – bibliography, scientific, and university cooperation – but also noted the potential for its work to expand. "It immediately became evident," an official report noted, "that there would be very considerable material for discussion and that the principal difficulty would be to sort the material received and to arrange and select the subject-matter."[27] Over the course of its existence, the League's intellectual cooperation bod-

---

23 Helen McCarthy, *The British People and the League of Nations: Democracy, Citizenship and Internationalism, c. 1918–45* (Manchester: Manchester University Press, 2011), Donald Birn, *The League of Nations Union, 1918–1945* (Oxford: Clarendon Press, 1981), Sakiko Kaiga, *Britain and the Intellectual Origins of the League of Nations, 1914–1919* (Cambridge: Cambridge University Press, 2021).
24 Kathleen Gibberd, *The League in Our Time* (Oxford: Basil Blackwell, 1933), 189.
25 Cited in Laqua, "Transnational Intellectual Cooperation," 224.
26 The other members of the inaugural CIC meeting were Jules Destrée (Belgium), George Ellery Hale (United States), D.N. Bannerjea (India), Gonzague de Reynold (Switzerland), Kristine Bonnevie (Norway), A. de Castro (Brazil), F. Ruffini (Italy), L. de Torres Quevedo (Spain). Both Einstein and Hale were prevented from attending the first meeting in August 1922. Hale was later replaced by the US-American physicist Robert Millikan. "The Progress of Science: International Cooperation in Intellectual Work," *The Scientific Monthly* 15, no. 1 (1922): 89; "League's Intellectual Committee," *The Times*, 25 July 1923, 11. League of Nations Archives (LNA), Committee on Intellectual Co-Operation, First Session, held at Geneva from August 1st to 5th, 1922, Report of the Committee to the Council. C-559-1922-XII, 2.
27 LNA C-559-1922-XII, 3.

ies expanded their interests and would take on a vast number of projects encompassing issues such as international education for world peace, the protection of museums and cultural sites, the scientific study of international relations, radio broadcasting, inquiries into unemployment among university graduates, and much beyond.[28] And while the CIC ended up receiving much criticism by the 1930s, the value of its pioneering work can be seen in it providing much of the template upon which UNESCO would later be founded. However, despite all this work, it never successfully defined precisely what it meant by "intellectual cooperation."

Intellectual Cooperation and Othering

"It is a pity," began a newspaper article in July 1938, "that the International Committee on Intellectual Co-operation suffers from the handicap of an unwieldy name. Otherwise more would be known about the way in which the League of Nations brings together eminent men of letters, scientists and other savants of many nationalities in the cause of peace."[29] With some exceptions, British newspapers were broadly sympathetic to the League of Nations in the 1920s and 1930s.[30] The work of the CIC was often reported upon in a mundane and matter-of-fact manner in local and national newspapers. At the same time, these same publications often featured acerbic commentaries about the CIC that tended to fixate on its name. Newspapers variously described the intellectual cooperation bodies as having a "somewhat cumbrous title,"[31] being "abhorrent to English ears,"[32] "very little known, perhaps because of the appalling name!",[33] having an

---

28 Susannah Wright, "Creating Liberal Internationalist World Citizens: League of Nations Union Junior Branches in English Secondary Schools, 1919–1939," *Paedagogica Historica* 56, no. 3 (2020): 321–340; Ken Osborne, "Creating the 'International Mind': The League of Nations' Attempts to Reform History Teaching, 1920–1939," *History of Education Quarterly* 56, no. 2 (2016): 213–240; Jan Stöckmann, *The Architects of International Relations: Building a Discipline, Designing the World, 1914–1940* (Cambridge: Cambridge University Press, 2022); Annamaria Duci, "Europe and the Artistic Patrimony of the Interwar Period: The International Institute of Intellectual Cooperation at the League of Nations," in *Europe in Crisis: Intellectuals and the European Idea, 1917–1957*, eds. Matthew d'Auria and Mark Hewitson (Oxford and New York: Berghahn, 2015), 227–242.
29 "First Class Brains at Geneva," *Ashbourne Telegraph*, 8 July 1938, 6.
30 Birn, *League of Nations Union*, 132–133.
31 "The Best Books," *The Scotsman*, 10 April 1925, 6.
32 "Professors at Geneva," *Daily Echo*, Northampton, 25 July 1928, 2.
33 "Work at Geneva," *Daily Echo*, Northampton, 9 July 1929, 2.

"unattractive name!",[34] being "clumsily" named,[35] and having a "terrifying name" that made the "average man fight shy of it."[36] In 1927, *The Times* made reference to the "so-called" International Committee for Intellectual Cooperation.[37]

British hostility to the idea of intellectual cooperation was often traced back to its origins when British delegates unanimously voted against the establishment of the committee. In 1926, the League of Nations Union president Robert Cecil tried to explain British indifference toward intellectual cooperation by citing different national cultural traditions. He argued that "the Latins" sought to apply a general principle to problems, whereas the British sought to deal with "the actual difficulty before them." Cecil claimed that Britain was initially hostile toward the CIC because it was seen as something "vague and 'high falutin.'"[38] Writing in 1929, Gwilym Davies, a Welsh Baptist minister and supporter of the League, recalled the same hostility on the occasion of the establishment of the CIC. The only instance, he argued, in which the seven British member states of the League had been "enthusiastically unanimous" on an issue was when they decided not to grant any further support to intellectual cooperation.[39]

Criticism of the idea of "intellectual cooperation" in English-language sources predates the intellectual controversies of the 1930s and seemed to derive primarily from the "foreignness" of the term and the institution itself. These criticisms also assumed that to be an intellectual was a European phenomenon and suggested that Britain did not possess any of its own. This was not true: Britain had many figures who might be considered intellectuals with regard to their public function.[40] Indeed, the chair of the CIC between 1928 and 1939 was Gilbert Murray, Regius Professor of Greek at the University of Oxford and one of Britain's leading intellectuals.[41] As the term "intellectual cooperation" was never defined by the League of Nations or the CIC, there were many scurrilous attempts to satirize the terminology. In a broadcast on the BBC in 1930, Murray noted that the

---

[34] "Professor Gilbert Murray Declares the League is Doing its Job," *Daily Herald*, 10 November 1930, 8.
[35] "A League of Brains," *Bexhill-on-Sea Observer*, 8 September 1934, 2.
[36] "League of Nations Notes," *The Whitstable Times and Tankerton Press*, 28 January 1928, 2.
[37] "The League and the Schools," *The Times*, 1 August 1927, 11.
[38] "Lord Cecil on the League: 'Unity in Diversity'," *The Times*, 7 January 1926, 7.
[39] Gwilym Davies, "Wales and the World," *Welsh Outlook* 16, no. 12 (1929): 376.
[40] Collini, *Absent Minds*, 46–52.
[41] Christopher Stray, *Gilbert Murray Reassessed: Hellenism, Theatre & International Politics* (Oxford: Oxford University Press, 2008); Gilbert Murray, *An Unfinished Autobiography: With Contributions by his Friends* (London: George Allen and Unwin Ltd., 1960); Peter Wilson, "Gilbert Murray and International Relations: Hellenism, Liberalism, and International Intellectual Cooperation as a Path to Peace," *Review of International Studies* 37 (2011): 881–909.

term "intellectual cooperation" sounded "absurd" in English but was "all right in French or Italian." Murray argued that since the foundation of the CIC intellectual cooperation had been "taken to mean two different things: first a general co-operation of nations in thought and mind as well as in act; secondly, a special co-operation among what are called the 'intellectuals' of different nations – the teachers, writers, artists, men of science and learning."[42] The fact that intellectual cooperation itself was a translation from French – a language and political culture in which being *un intellectuel* was imbued with greater clarity and carried with it different functions than was the case across the Channel – surely also led to feelings that it was not quite British. This was especially the case by the late 1920s when the publication of Julien Benda's *La trahison des clercs* caused a major debate in France concerning the rectitude of intellectual engagements in political matters. When the book was translated for a British audience in 1928, it was titled *The Great Betrayal*.[43] The distinctions between the different meanings and implications of the term intellectual cooperation were never adequately cleared up in the 1920s and 1930s.

The League of Nations published a vast range of publicity materials in order to explain its purpose and the functions of its subsidiary bodies to a wide audience, from adults to children. These works are revealing in how they attempted to explain the importance of intellectual cooperation for a general reader. One book, published by the League as a guide to teachers, argued that "intellectual activity affects what is most intimate and profound in the life of peoples" and that "the Committee on Intellectual Co-operation in itself represented an act of rapprochement between the nations and a valuable jumping off ground."[44] Still, evidence from public discussions in Britain suggests that a great deal of uncertainty remained regarding the purpose, scope, and necessity of intellectual cooperation.

British criticisms of the CIC represented an opportunity not only to assail the League but also the idea of the intellectual. A satirical piece by "Derso" in the *Illustrated London News* in August 1930 lampooned the CIC at length and highlighted the apparent absurdity of an individual with learning in a particular niche area being able to comment intelligently upon international relations. Here, "Derso" held a conversation with an intellectual who was "an expert in oriental carpets and a philosopher" and concluded that while the man may have been "an expert in Ori-

---

42 Gilbert Murray, "Intellectual Cooperation," BBC Broadcast, 5 March 1930, Bodleian Library Oxford (BLO) MS Murray 277/97.
43 Collini, *Absent Minds*, 288.
44 *The Aims, Methods and Activity of the League of Nations* (Geneva: Secretariat of the League of Nations, 1935), 155–157.

ental carpets [. . .] he knew nothing about statesmen."[45] The piece suggested that it was absurd that men and women with no specific expert knowledge in the field of international relations would apply their learning to the problems of the world based on learning in a particular, and often unrelated, area. By bringing together intellectuals of widely differing backgrounds, this was more or less what the CIC claimed to do.

While the CIC attracted criticism from afar, often fixating on its name or the mystery surrounding what it actually did, those who observed it up close were often no more generous in their appraisals. These first-hand accounts frequently highlighted an opposition between the British way of doing things and the approaches adopted by non-British members. In September 1923, for example, a journalist for a newspaper in the British midlands attended a session of the CIC in Geneva and wrote somewhat flippantly about its multilingualism. It was reported that "one could not enthuse muchly over the proceedings. Professor Bergson spoke charmingly in perfect French, a Swiss professor declaimed in imperfect Swiss-French, and an Italian savant tickled the ears of his audience in somber Italian-French; and we all, to show our master of these foreign tongues, applauded most adequately."[46] In 1929, the words of Mary Agnes Hamilton, a member of parliament who was part of the British delegation to the League Assembly, received wide coverage in British newspapers. On her return from Geneva, she said that "this committee is a joke to everybody except itself; but, having taken it up, we must make a serious effort to make a job of it and take it out of it [sic] atmosphere of slight hilarity which now exists."[47] And, writing in December 1929, Gwilym Davies, a keen supporter of the CIC, argued that as newspapers were conducting their end-of-year stocktaking, "it is likely that, amongst ourselves, little will be said of the intellectual side. Abroad British people are not considered to be much concerned with the things of the mind."[48]

---

45 "'Derso' on the Institute of Intellectual Cooperation," *Illustrated London News*, 30 August 1930, 364.
46 "Other 'innocents' abroad," *Leamington Spa Courier and Warwickshire Standard*, 21 September 1923, 7.
47 "Mrs Hamilton M.P., on Geneva Politeness," *Lancashire Evening Post*, 18 October 1929, 9.
48 Gwilym Davies, "Wales and the World," *Welsh Outlook* 16, no. 12 (1929): 376.

Defending Intellectual Cooperation

Accounts of the work of the CIC were not overwhelmingly negative. Newspapers frequently presented accounts of the committee's many activities. In July 1924, *The Mercury* wrote that "Intellectual Co-operation is at all events, no experiment. Its place in the history of learning assures of its value."[49] In February 1929, the *Nottingham Journal* claimed that its establishment was "one of the most important and statesmanlike decisions of the League in its earlier stages" since "intellectual opinion all over the world is in a key position to influence public opinion."[50] Meanwhile, in September 1929, the under-secretary of state for foreign affairs, Hugh Dalton, referred to the "great conception of intellectual cooperation."[51]

Even allowing for some positive coverage of the efforts of intellectual cooperation, the Geneva-based committee and its advocates frequently found themselves having to defend or advocate for its work in public, as did supporters of the League of Nations more generally by the mid-to-late 1930s. The most strident defenses of intellectual cooperation unsurprisingly came from Gilbert Murray. As chair of the CIC and a prominent public figure in Britain, it was understandable that Murray would become a firm and enthusiastic proponent of its importance.

In 1936, Murray sparred with the novelist H.G. Wells in a public debate that played out in the pages of a national newspaper. In a public letter to *The Times* in 1936, Murray wrote of his support of the CIC. He argued that if "the goal of British policy is the appeasement of Europe," this required cooperation between governments of different sorts, especially those that could "outside politics, have the power of both guiding and interpreting the currents of thought and feeling in their respective countries." Murray claimed that the CIC's inclusiveness was key to its effectiveness, with even non-League members participating in different ways.[52] He also asserted that the British government had adopted an attitude of philistinism while at the same time noting with some sarcasm that many British politicians were "badly tainted with the virus of intellect."[53]

Wells, a supporter of the League in its early days who later became a staunch critic, launched a strident criticism of the efforts of intellectual cooperation in re-

---

49 "Co-operation among the intellectuals," *The Mercury*, 18 July 1924, 6.
50 "The New International Brotherhood," *The Nottingham Journal*, 12 February 1929, 6.
51 "Chinese Resolution to League Assembly Opposed," *Belfast News-letter*, 23 September 1929, 5.
52 "Appeasement in Europe: The Intellectual Links," *The Times*, 25 September 1936, 10.
53 Ibid.

sponse to Murray's letter.⁵⁴ He wondered whether the committee even existed in reality, sarcastically asking whether it was "anything more than a phantom with a postal address" and disingenuously claiming that he had been "trying to find out what were its activities" for years.⁵⁵ In a telephone reply given to the *Daily News*, Murray claimed that Wells' comments were "perfect nonsense" and that he "always refused to know anything about the committee."⁵⁶ He elaborated on these comments in a piece in another letter to *The Times* a few days later, claiming that Wells was ignorant regarding the CIC because he was opposed to it. "He does not know about it because he does not like it. It is like a famous person's reason for not knowing foreign languages: he does not know them because he does not like foreigners."⁵⁷

George Bernard Shaw's *Geneva*, a satirical play about the League of Nations published in 1938, began at the International Committee for Intellectual Cooperation. Written at a time when the League was increasingly sidelined in international affairs and subject to widespread criticisms for its inability to stem the tide of international aggression, it was significant that the lampoon began with the CIC. Its Geneva office was equipped with "secondhand furniture, much the worse for wear" where a young English secretary, hitherto working on a card index, put her feet up on the table while smoking a cigarette.⁵⁸ The scenes that followed painted the CIC as underfunded and understaffed, its work "mere compilation" rather than anything meaningful or substantial. A German-Jewish character asked how "the intellectual giants who form your committee bringing the enormous dynamic force of their brains, their prestige, their authority, to bearing the destinies of the nations?" and was told that the extent of their involvement in terms of practical work was to have "their names on our notepaper."⁵⁹

Cumulatively, the criticisms of the CIC took aim at an institution and its activities while portraying it as thoroughly European and irreconcilable with British life. They emphasized not only the general "foreignness" of intellectuals to Britain, but also a set of bureaucratic practices such as the accumulation of information and a belief in the power of rational intellect to solve international problems. George Or-

---

54 Simon J. James, *Maps of Utopia: H.G. Wells, Modernity, and the End of Culture* (Oxford: Oxford University Press, 2012), 164; John S. Partington, *Building Cosmopolis: The Political Thought of H.G. Wells* (London: Taylor and Francis, 2016), 105.
55 "The C.I.C. in Paris," *The Times*, 28 September 1936, 13.
56 "Two Famous Peace Men in War of Words," *Daily News*, 29 September 1936, 3.
57 "The C.I.C. in Paris," *The Times*, 30 September 1936, 8.
58 G.B. Shaw, *Geneva, Cymbeline Refinished, & Good King Charles* (London: Constable and Company, 1946), 29.
59 Shaw, *Geneva*, 31.

well in his 1940 essay "Inside the Whale" spoke of many writers utilizing "Geneva language," which he implied was impersonal, detached, and cold. This idea permeates many of the anti-CIC polemics of the preceding decades.[60] However, as demonstrated in the following section, there was a sharp distinction between the idea of intellectual cooperation as embodied by the CIC and its practice away from Geneva.

Intellectual Cooperation in Practice

By 1938, Gilbert Murray had served as president of the International Committee for Intellectual Cooperation for almost a decade. He reflected on his experiences as Britain's best-known advocate of the League of Nations' cultural and educational policies in a letter published in *The Times*. "It has always seemed to me an odd thing that, though an Englishman has for several years been president of the organization," as well as the widespread involvement of British scholars and administrators in its work, "the committee has never been invited to meet in England and the British Government has never made any contribution to the work of the institute." "I can hardly believe," Murray wrote, "that it can be permanently cold-shouldered simply on the ground that the British people take no stock in mere moral and intellectual values."[61]

Murray claimed that not only was there a general skepticism surrounding the work of intellectual cooperation, but also that there had been a pronounced reluctance to work with it on certain issues. The potential vastness of the field of intellectual cooperation meant that it theoretically encompassed a great deal, and there is substantial evidence that supporters of the League in Britain engaged with many of the initiatives emanating from Geneva in different ways. The League of Nations Union, for example, was a mass movement whose membership peaked at 406,000 people in 1931 and which was responsible for the Peace Ballot, which mobilized almost twelve million British individuals in 1935.[62]

There is a great deal of evidence suggesting that British people engaged with the efforts of intellectual cooperation but only when it was labelled in other ways. The best example of this is the work undertaken with schoolchildren. Helen McCarthy has argued that "if there was one place in interwar Britain

---

60 Orwell, "Inside the Whale," 497.
61 "Good Will Among Nations," *The Times*, 31 December 1938, 8.
62 Birn, *League of Nations Union*, 131; Martin Ceadel, "The First British Referendum: The Peace Ballot, 1934–5," *English Historical Review* 95, no. 377 (1980): 810–839.

where the fact of the League's existence was hard to miss, it was the classroom."[63] The civic culture that emerged around children and youth was premised upon the idea that the next generation would need to be educated to understand the League and work with it in order to avoid conflict. Youth questions generally became part of the remit of the CIC, which formed an Advisory Committee on League of Nations Teaching and oversaw a project to revise school textbooks in order to excise belligerent narratives relating to the war.[64] As education in Britain was decentralized, it was often up to individual schools or teachers to engage with the League in their teaching ethos, something that many did, with Wales being prominent through its enthusiastic engagement with the League.[65] Engagement with an aspect of the intellectual cooperation agenda could also be seen in the efforts of the League of Nations Union Junior Branches. Often established at schools, Junior Branches constituted forums through which children and young people could continue their internationalist formation. While their activities varied from case to case, Junior Branches put on an array of activities including lectures by visiting speakers, mock assemblies, exhibitions, pen-pal schemes, and competitions to win a trip to Geneva.[66]

Evidence of a reluctance and hesitation to work with the CIC was the most apparent in instances involving direct relationships between the committee and its counterparts in Britain. This was especially the case when it came to issues such as gathering information for inquiries undertaken by the League, such as the 1923 CIC investigation into international intellectual life.[67] The key source of tension on that occasion – and others – seems to have stemmed from the fact that the CIC dealt with the Universities Bureau of the British Empire (UBBE), established in 1912 to bring together universities in an imperial setting.[68] The interactions between the UBBE and CIC suggested that the former saw the latter as not only encroaching into its sphere of operation but also fundamentally misunderstanding the nature of British higher education.[69] Alex Hill, the secretary of UBBE, as well as several university vice-chancellors, received many requests for statistical information from Geneva, and many seemed to quickly grow weary of

---

63 McCarthy, *British People*, 104.
64 Osborne, "Creating the 'International Mind'," 213–240.
65 National Library of Wales, NLW V/5/28–60; Stuart Booker, "Wales and the League of Nations, c.1918–1945", PhD Dissertation, Swansea University, 2023.
66 Wright, "Creating"; McCarthy, *British People*, 103–131.
67 Irish, "Moral Basis," 796–799.
68 Tamson Pietsch, *Empire of Scholars; Universities, Networks and the British Academic World 1850–1939* (Manchester: Manchester University Press, 2013), 100–103.
69 Hill to Halecki, 23 February 1923, National Archives of the UK, Kew (NAUK), ED 25/1.

these requests. In December 1925, Hill wrote to all vice-chancellors and principals of universities and colleges in Britain to explain that he had informed the CIC that "the heads of the universities of Great Britain and Ireland do not welcome questionnaires," instructing them to refer to the UBBE's yearbook for future inquiries.[70] Hill was less restrained in private. For instance, he wrote to Joseph Wells, the vice-chancellor of the University of Oxford, that the League's requests for information had put "various people, especially myself, to a great deal of trouble" and doubted whether the information served "any useful purpose," speculating flippantly – in a manner that emphasized the association of the League with bureaucracy – that "it is in a pigeon-hole in Geneva."[71] Gilbert Murray wrote privately that "the attitude taken by the Bureau of Universities has shown no particular cordiality."[72]

The most striking evidence of a reluctance to engage institutionally with the CIC can be seen with the establishment of a British National Committee on Intellectual Cooperation (BNCIC). Starting in 1923, the CIC asked member nations to set up national committees, which were intended to enable the Geneva-based committee to decentralize and outsource some of its work. National committees could serve as points of contact for the various intellectual cooperation initiatives taking place and could both gather information and disseminate it as necessary.[73] Committees had been set up in eighteen countries by 1924, most of which were located in Europe and many of which were new states set up in the aftermath of the First World War.[74] This number had grown to thirty-eight by 1937, of which fourteen were situated outside of Europe.[75]

Britain was slow in terms of setting up its national committee. In 1927, as he planned the establishment of the committee, Gilbert Murray wrote to Julien Luchaire of his progress: "we must somehow convince British opinion, which no doubt tends to be over-practical, that the CIC and the Institute are achieving definite and useful results. We have to overcome a good deal of criticism and prejudice."[76] Despite the misgivings of Hill and others, a British Committee for Intellectual Cooperation was set up in 1928, with its first meeting chaired by historian H.A.L. Fisher.[77]

---

70 Hill to Vice Chancellors and Principals, 30 December 1925, NAUK, ED25/5.
71 Hill to Wells, 5 January 1925, NAUK, ED25/5.
72 Murray to Luchaire, 14 November 1925, UNESCO Archives, Paris (UNESCO), A.I.35.
73 "Suggestions relative to the Organisation of National Committees on International Co-Operation," 5 December 1923, C.L.20.1924,XII, Annex II. International Committee on Intellectual Co-operation, NAUK, ED 25/1.
74 BLO, MS Murray 266/122–123.
75 *National Committees on Intellectual Cooperation* (Geneva: League of Nations, 1937), 3–4.
76 Gilbert Murray to Luchaire, 25 February 1927, UNESCO Archives, A.I.12.
77 Minutes of Meeting of LNU of May 17, 1928, NAUK, ED25/2; BLO, MS Zimmern 86.

The BNCIC was populated with figures drawn from learned societies, such as the Royal Society and the British Academy. For much of its existence it was chaired by Sir Frederic Kenyon, a former president of the British Academy. By the mid-1930s, the BNCIC received a paltry annual £150 from the British government, which, unlike other national governments, also refused to make a financial contribution to the work of the International Institute on Intellectual Cooperation in Paris.[78]

Even once established, the British National Committee was not an especially enthusiastic or active body. In fact, when the British Council was established in 1934, newspapers noted that it would perform much of the same task as that for which the League's national committee had been established.[79] An editorial in the *Manchester Guardian* noted that the establishment of the British Council should draw attention to the fact that the CIC had been "morally and materially starved of official British support. Yet its purpose has always been to accomplish on international lines much of what the British Council now proposes to attempt nationally."[80] By 1935, H.R. Cummings, who worked for the British League of Nations Union, wrote to the CIC secretary, Jean Daniel de Montenach, that "no one ever hears anything" of the British national committee.[81] It had, however, been prominent in supporting the International Studies Conference that took place in London in 1935 as well as initiatives relating to moral disarmament.

The establishment of the British Council brought tensions to a head as both the BC and BNCIC seemed to step on each other's toes in promoting international mobility of teachers and students. As the BC developed and the BNCIC continued to struggle for funds, relations deteriorated, and by the late 1930s, leading figures at the Foreign Office such as Rex Leeper proposed that the BC should take over the BNCIC. Charles Bridge, the secretary of the BC, stated that "there is no doubt at all that it is the wish of the Foreign Office that the British Council shall take over the functions of the British National Committee on Intellectual Co-operation." Moreover, he bluntly stated that the FO wanted to get rid of Gilbert Murray who had made everything "a one-man show." Bridge claimed that "the Foreign Office would be glad to see him go."[82] As war broke out in 1939, the BNCIC continued to operate under the presidency of Sir Frederic Kenyon, thus leaving the conflict unresolved.

---

78 Undated account of the work of the BNCIC, NAUK, BW/2/163.
79 Alice Byrne, "'A Sound Investment'? British Cultural Diplomacy and Overseas Students: The British Council's Students Committee, 1935–1939," *Contemporary European History* 30, no. 2 (2021): 265–283.
80 "Intellectual Co-operation under the League," *Manchester Guardian*, 23 March 1935, LNA R3992, 5B/17724/1137.
81 Cummings to Montenach, 20 March 1935, LNA R3992, 5B/17724/1137.
82 Memorandum of the Sec. Gen. of the British Council, 10 August 1938, NAUK, BW/2/163.

Towards UNESCO

The outbreak of the Second World War in 1939 brought a great deal of internationalist activity to a halt. The CIC held its final meeting in July 1939 while the Paris-based Institute ceased operation after 1940, with many of its key members fleeing Europe and seeking to continue the work of intellectual cooperation in other parts of the world, notably in Latin America.[83] Meanwhile, the League's buildings in Geneva were operated by a skeleton staff. In Britain, hostile attitudes remained toward intellectuals: in a famous wartime essay, George Orwell reasserted the idea that compared to other parts of Europe, the English people were "not intellectual."[84] And yet, by the end of 1945, the constitution for a body – the United Nations Educational, Scientific and Cultural Organization (UNESCO) – had been agreed upon at a conference in London. The creation of UNESCO served as an important coda that elucidates how Britain's experiences of interwar intellectual cooperation played a prominent role in wartime discussions.

During the Second World War, Gilbert Murray drafted a memorandum for the Conference of Allied Ministers of Education (CAME). Populated by ministers and educationalists in exile, CAME first met in London in late 1942. Murray's memorandum set out the background and achievements of intellectual cooperation and presented suggestions for the future. Murray reflected that "the publicity of the CIC was bad. Perhaps real savants are not apt to advertise themselves. Perhaps this country is less well-informed than others about the whole movement." He went on to suggest that if the movement had been better funded, it could have achieved greater success.[85] In an influential 1943 pamphlet, Gwilym Davies wrote that "on intellectual cooperation, it owed nothing to the British as emphasis on the intellectual is not regarded as their strong point [. . .] all along there was a tendency amongst the British to think of 'Intellectual Co-operation' as French for 'high-brow'."[86] British planning for UNESCO was premised upon learning the lessons of interwar intellectual cooperation, which meant changing the elitist emphasis and the name.

The debate over the name of the new organization played out at the London Conference in November 1945. The proposal that emerged through CAME, in con-

---

[83] Pernet, "Twists, Turns," 342–4.
[84] George Orwell, "The Lion and the Unicorn," in *The Collected Essays, Journalism and Letters of George Orwell, Volume II*, eds. Sonia Orwell and Ian Angus (London: Secker and Warburg, 1968), 58.
[85] Gilbert Murray, "Intellectual Cooperation," UNESCO Archives, Conference of Allied Ministers of Education, London 1942–45. Vol VII: Drafting the UNESCO Constitution, 9.
[86] Gwilym Davies, *Intellectual Cooperation Between the Two Wars* (London: Council for Education in World Citizenship, 1943), 4.

junction with collaborators in the United States, called for the creation of an "Educational and Cultural Organization," while a separate French proposal, written in close collaboration with the recently-revived International Institute for Intellectual Cooperation, instead sought a "United Nations Organization of Intellectual Co-operation."[87] The British delegates were supported by the US-Americans in their opposition to a name including the term "intellectual cooperation"; one account of the discussions in London claimed that there was a reluctance to use the term "intellectual" in the name as this constituted "one word in French and quite another in English."[88] The decision to adopt the name UNESCO demonstrated a determination not only to develop a distance between the initiatives of the League and the new United Nations, but also to distance the organization from the anti-intellectualism having undermined British interaction with the League's educational and cultural initiatives.

Conclusion

British anti-intellectualism was not merely a phenomenon of the interwar years. Speaking in the run-up to the Brexit referendum in 2016, Michael Gove – a government minister and advocate that Britain leave the European Union – argued that "people in this country have had enough of experts."[89] He was speaking about the fact that no economists had backed Brexit and that the vast majority of economists argued that it would not be in Britain's economic interests to do so. While Gove did not specifically refer to "intellectuals," his comments brought to mind much older debates suggesting that intellect and learning were associated with other places – and not Britain. And while the League of Nations is not the European Union, some parallels are noticeable in the language used to describe the activities of both.

Britain's engagement with the League of Nations and intellectual cooperation in the 1920s and 1930s epitomized salient characteristics in British attitudes toward intellectuals. Antipathy toward intellectual cooperation stemmed from the related ideas that Britain itself had no intellectuals and that "intellectuals" were

---

[87] "Conference for the Establishment," 1–9. The US and China favored the name UNESCO, whereas India preferred the French proposal for an "Intellectual Organisation" of the United Nations.
[88] "Summary and Analysis of the United Nations Educational, Scientific and Cultural Organization," *'The Defences of Peace': Documents Relating to UNESCO: The United Nations Scientific and Cultural Organisation*, Part II (Washington, DC: United Sates Government Printing Office, 1946), 13.
[89] https://www.ft.com/content/3be49734-29cb-11e6-83e4-abc22d5d108c.

something foreign and other. The twin bases for intellectual cooperation – Paris and Geneva – seemed to confirm this sense of otherness to British observers, while the term "intellectual cooperation," imported from French and with different connotations in the translation, provided further evidence of this. The cynicism aimed at the CIC differed in terms of roots and themes compared to that aimed at the left-wing intellectuals of the 1930s, thus demonstrating that as much as there were many definitions of the word intellectual in this period, there were also many manifestations of anti-intellectualism.[90] From a British perspective, the creation of UNESCO from the ashes of the League of Nations did not represent a distinct change in attitudes *per se*, but a desire to learn the lessons of the interwar period and to circumvent latent anti-intellectualism. It certainly did not mark the end of British skepticism regarding intellectuals and experts but rather demonstrated how the builders of international institutions sought to address it.

Tomás Irish is an associate professor of modern history at Swansea University, Wales. He has published on the cultural history of Europe during the First World War and the interwar period, with a focus on universities and intellectual life. His most recent book, *Feeding the Mind: Humanitarianism and the Reconstruction of European Intellectual Life, 1919–1933*, was published in 2023.

---

90 On the intellectual divisions of the 1930s, see E.P. Thompson's famous essay (and riposte to Orwell), "Outside the Whale," *The Poverty of Theory and Other Essays* (London: Merlin Press, 1978), 1–33.

Victoria Van Orden Martínez

Survivors of Nazi Persecution, Refugees, Knowledge Actors: The Cultural Translation of Knowledge in an Effort to Document Nazi Atrocities, 1945–1946

Abstract: Objects smuggled out of Nazi concentration camps and brought to Sweden by liberated prisoners have served as valued museum objects in Sweden for almost 60 years. They and the written testimonies given by survivors represent not only the suffering experienced by the victims of the Nazis and their resistance against dehumanization but also how these aspects of the Second World War and the Holocaust were culturally transferred from the epicenter of Nazi atrocities to a nominally neutral country in the immediate postwar period. What has been overlooked is that the former prisoners coming to Sweden as "repatriates" brought with them more than just objects and stories. They also brought knowledge. They carried this knowledge to Sweden, where it was culturally translated into a new context. Unlike the objects, however, there has been limited focus on the knowledge brought to Sweden by survivors of Nazi persecution and the significance of this knowledge. This article seeks to rectify this by arguing that many of the survivors whose objects and testimonies are now in Swedish museums and archival collections were not merely passive contributors to our knowledge of Nazi atrocities but were also knowledge actors who carried and culturally translated knowledge that helped enable the collection of this material.

Keywords: survivors of Nazi persecution, Holocaust documentation, migrant knowledge, cultural translation, knowledge actors

Introduction

Soon after arriving in Sweden as "repatriates" – refugees expected to stay for a limited period – in the spring and summer of 1945, Jewish and non-Jewish Polish survivors of Nazi persecution became involved in an initiative to document the Nazi atrocities for the sake of justice and history. They embarked on this work in an unofficial capacity while in quarantine facilities, emergency field hospitals,

---

Victoria Van Orden Martínez, Linköping University, e-mail: victoria.martinez@liu.se

and other assembly points established for refugees in Sweden. Their efforts were facilitated and organized by Dr. Zygmunt Łakociński, a Polish art historian who had settled in Sweden in 1934 and then worked as a foreign language assistant at Lund University. The institute – best known today as the Polish Research Institute in Lund, Sweden (hereafter abbreviated as PIZ) – continued this work in an official capacity between October 1945 and November 1946, during which time it was funded by the Swedish government. Nine survivors were employed as part of this formal workgroup and many other survivors contributed to the efforts in more unofficial ways.[1]

By the end of 1946, when government funding for PIZ ended, the survivors had collected hundreds of eyewitness testimonies from survivors of Nazi persecution, mostly through interviews between a survivor-interviewer and a survivor-witness, as well as an abundance of documents, photographs, paintings and drawings, poetry and other literary expressions, and additional material evidence that had been smuggled out of the concentration camps by former prisoners. For nearly 20 years, the material was carefully safeguarded in two primary locations: the witness testimonies in the United States and the material evidence in the Lund apartment of survivor Ludwika Broel-Plater, a PIZ workgroup member who dedicated the rest of her life to the institute.[2]

In 1964, Łakociński donated the material that had been kept by Broel-Plater to Lund University, where it could then be utilized by researchers. Two years later, some of this material was presented as a long-term loan to *Kulturen*, a museum in Lund.[3] The collected evidence almost immediately started to fulfill the long-term ambition of Łakociński and the survivors that the material should be available to future generations. In 1966, *Kulturen* opened an exhibition called *Att överleva* (To Survive) that featured many of the objects brought to Sweden by the survivors of Nazi persecution and collected by PIZ. The exhibition still to this day informs the public about Nazi atrocities.[4] In 1972, the testimonies were returned from the United States and were made available to researchers in the 1990s. The

---

[1] This article is adapted from Chapter 5 in Victoria Van Orden Martínez, "Afterlives: Jewish and Non-Jewish Polish Survivors of Nazi Persecution in Sweden Documenting Nazi Atrocities, 1945–1946" (PhD diss., Linköping University, 2023).
[2] Victoria Van Orden Martínez, "An Eternally-Grateful Refugee? Silences in Swedish Public Discourse and the (De)Historicization of Polish-Swedish Activist Ludwika Broel-Plater," in *Forced Migrants in Nordic Histories and Historiographies*, eds. Johanna Leinonen et al. (Helsinki: Helsinki University Press, forthcoming).
[3] "The Polish Research Institute in Lund (PIZ) archive" (Lund University Library, Sweden), 44:3 g, Memorandum dated November 11, 1966, signed by Łakociński, p. 1.
[4] "Att överleva – Röster från Ravensbrück," accessed September 28, 2023, https://www.kulturen.com/utstallningar/att-overleva-roster-fran-ravensbruck/.

bulk of these testimonies have since been transcribed and translated from Polish into English and are available online along with images and scans of other material from the PIZ collection.[5]

Although this is not always explicitly stated, there is little doubt that the survivors associated with PIZ contributed knowledge of the events of the Second World War and the Holocaust. They themselves, the items they smuggled out of the concentration camps, and the witness testimonies they provided served as evidence in the early postwar trials of Nazi perpetrators, represent valuable sources for researchers, and have educated the public in museums and digitized collections. However, it is worth noting that how the survivors contributed knowledge to the efforts to document and collect this valuable material has never been studied.

Previous research has situated Sture Bolin, a professor of history at Lund University, and Łakociński as the primary contributors of knowledge to this effort. Some scholars have even argued that the method used by PIZ to collect survivor witness testimonies was invented by one or both of these men. Conversely, the role of survivors in the PIZ initiative has been under-studied, and the historically important PIZ archive and the *Kulturen* exhibition are still described as if the primarily female Polish survivors were little more than passive contributors to the collection.[6] Although the survivors involved with PIZ were considered intellectuals, their knowledge contributions have almost entirely been overlooked, and the rich histories of knowledge they would have been familiar with have not been associated with the PIZ effort in the immediate postwar period to document Nazi persecution.

This article studies how Jewish and non-Jewish Polish survivors of Nazi persecution arriving in Sweden in 1945 as repatriates and associated with PIZ were knowledge actors who, along with Bolin and Łakociński, were part of a cultural translation of knowledge. I argue that driven by a dedication to gathering evidence and testimonies from other survivors for the sake of history and justice, the survivors not only brought knowledge of persecution and suffering under the Nazis to the PIZ initiative but also knowledge of scholarly and popular methods developed in Eastern Europe before and during the Second World War. By using previously overlooked migrant knowledge as an analytical tool, I shed new light on how survivors of Nazi persecution living in Sweden as refugees in the early postwar period contributed with previously unrecognized forms of knowledge to postwar efforts to document the Second World War and the Holocaust.

---

5 "Witnessing genocide," accessed September 28, 2023, https://www.ub.lu.se/hitta/digitala-samlingar/witnessing-genocide.
6 For instance, Katrine Tinning, "Courage, Resistance and Vulnerability in Memory Culture: Swedish Museum Education and the Representation of the Holocaust Survivor at the Turn of the Twenty-First Century," *Memory Studies* online first (September 15, 2022): 1–24, doi:10.1177/17506980221122227.

Survivors and Knowledge Actors

The historically significant involvement of survivors of Nazi persecution as political subjects while living as refugees during the postwar period is a burgeoning but still under-served area of research.[7] Several recently published works focus on survivors living in particular geographical settings to better understand how they not only existed but also *acted* in social and political processes during the early postwar period.[8] In their analyses, these scholars inherently, if not always overtly, consider the knowledge these forced migrants carried with them and applied in their particular circumstances. Other scholars use migrant knowledge as their point of departure.[9] This area of research includes studies concerned with the knowledge carried by survivors of Nazi persecution into new settings as displaced persons in the aftermath of the Second World War and the Holocaust.[10]

---

7 Recent scholarship includes Kata Bohus et al., eds., *Our Courage: Jews in Europe 1945–48* (Berlin: De Gruyter Oldenbourg, 2020); David Cesarani et al., eds., *Survivors of Nazi Persecution in Europe after the Second World War, Landscapes after Battle: Volume 1* (London: Vallentine Mitchell, 2010); Anna Holian, *Between National Socialism and Soviet Communism: Displaced Persons in Postwar Germany* (Ann Arbor, Michigan: University of Michigan Press, 2011); Margarete Myers Feinstein, *Holocaust Survivors in Postwar Germany, 1945–1957* (New York: Cambridge University Press, 2014); Avinoam J. Patt and Michael Berkowitz, eds., *"We are here": New Approaches to Jewish Displaced Persons in Postwar Germany* (Detroit: Wayne State University Press, 2010).

8 For instance, Jochen Lingelbach, *On the Edges of Whiteness: Polish refugees in British Colonial Africa during and after the Second World War* (New York: Berghahn Books, 2020); Emma Kuby, *Political Survivors: The Resistance, the Cold War, and the Fight against Concentration Camps after 1945* (Ithaca and London: Cornell University Press, 2019); Michael Fleming, *In the Shadow of the Holocaust: Poland, the United Nations War Crimes Commission, and the Search for Justice* (Cambridge: Cambridge University Press, 2021). See also Katarzyna Nowak, "'We Would Rather Drown Ourselves in Lake Victoria': Refugee Women, Protest, and Polish Displacement in Colonial East Africa, 1948–49," *Immigrants and Minorities* 37, no. 1–2 (2019), doi:10.1080/02619288.2019.1677467.

9 Simone Lässig and Swen Steinberg, "Why Young Migrants Matter in the History of Knowledge," *KNOW: A Journal on the Formation of Knowledge* 3, no. 2 (2019), doi:10.1086/704617; Simone Lässig and Swen Steinberg, "Knowledge on the Move: New Approaches toward a History of Migrant Knowledge," *Geschichte und Gesellschaft* 43, no. 3 (2017); Simone Lässig, "The History of Knowledge and the Expansion of the Historical Research Agenda," *Bulletin of the GHI Washington* 59 (Fall 2016).

10 For instance, Kijan Espahangizi, *Der Migration-Integration-Komplex: Wissenschaft und Politik in Einem (Nicht-)Einwanderungsland, 1960–2010* (Konstanz: Konstanz University Press, 2022); Matthias Springborn, "Some Challenges for Knowledge Transfer in Jewish Displaced Persons Camps after World War II," in *Migrant Knowledge*, eds. Andreas Greiner et al., The German Historical Institute Washington (GHI), April 15, 2021, accessed September 28, 2023, https://migrantknowledge.org/2021/04/15/knowledge-transfer-jewish-dp-camps/; Stephanie Zloch, *Das Wissen der Einwanderungsgesellschaft: Migration und Bildung in Deutschland 1945–2000 Moderne Europäische Geschichte* (Göttingen: Göttingen University Press, forthcoming 2023).

Historians of the circulation of knowledge are increasingly examining previously ignored peoples and groups – such as migrants, women, colonized peoples, etc. – while encouraging scholars to think beyond traditional sources and approaches.[11] Historians Simone Lässig and Swen Steinberg, for instance, argue that migrant knowledge has traditionally been overlooked or ignored but also that the "category of knowledge can function as the chemical reagent that renders legible a history written in invisible ink."[12] This statement highlights that the problem regarding a lack of overall empirical materials and/or empirical materials that do not speak to the history and knowledge of migrants may be overcome by using knowledge as an analytical tool.

This method is useful in an examination of the PIZ archival material, which, while relatively abundant, does not explicitly record the knowledge that the survivors arriving in Sweden as refugees carried with them and could contribute to the PIZ documentation and collection efforts. The result is that some scholars have assumed that the survivors did not contribute any knowledge to the methods and practices of PIZ and have instead vested all credit and responsibility for the initiative with Łakociński and Bolin.[13] For instance, Swedish historian Kristian Gerner has asserted that "Lakocinski [sic] carried out 500 interviews,"[14] even though Łakociński did not conduct any of the interviews. Rather, all interviews were conducted by the survivors. Similarly, Gerner and Klas-Göran Karlsson have claimed that Bolin was solely responsible for designing the PIZ initiative to collect survivor witness testimonies.[15] However, the archival documents indicate that Bolin only offered methodological guidelines and support.

Most directly related to knowledge circulation are the assertions that no scholarly efforts to collect survivor testimonies were undertaken until Bolin "pio-

---

11 For instance, Peter Burke, *What is the History of Knowledge?* (Cambridge and Malden: Polity Press, 2016); Lässig, "History of Knowledge"; Johan Östling et al., eds., *Knowledge Actors: Revisiting Agency in the History of Knowledge* (Lund, Sweden: Nordic Academic Press, 2023); Johan Östling et al., eds., *Forms of Knowledge: Developing the History of Knowledge* (Lund, Sweden: Nordic Academic Press, 2020); Johan Östling et al., eds., *Circulation of Knowledge: Explorations in the History of Knowledge* (Lund, Sweden: Nordic Academic Press, 2018).
12 Lässig and Steinberg, "Knowledge on the Move," 320.
13 Kristian Gerner, "The Holocaust and Memory Culture: The Case of Sweden," in *Historicizing the Uses of the Past*, eds. Helle Bjerg et al. (Bielefeld: Transcript Verlag, 2011), 94. See also Kristian Gerner and Klas-Göran Karlsson, *Folkmordens historia: Perspektiv på det moderna samhällets skuggsida* (Stockholm: Atlantis, 2005), 189.
14 Gerner, "The Holocaust," 95.
15 Gerner, "The Holocaust," 94. See also Gerner and Karlsson, *Folkmordens historia*, 189.

neered" the "groundbreaking" method utilized by PIZ.[16] Contrary to these claims, such efforts had been made by Polish Jews, including by many professional historians, during and immediately following the Second World War and the Holocaust. As demonstrated in this article, the "bottom-up" approach to research characterizing these efforts – known as *khurbn forshung* (destruction research)[17] – in which the voices of the "common people" are sought out by researchers and contextualized alongside other sources, have deep roots in modern Polish and Polish-Jewish historiographical and sociological practices. This article views this history of knowledge, which has thus far not been contextualized in relation to PIZ, as the "chemical reagent" in this analysis.

Since the majority of participants in the PIZ efforts were women, gender cannot be dismissed as a possible reason for "selective ignorance" regarding the knowledge contributions made by survivors to PIZ.[18] Scholars of the feminist history of science have noted that, although the Second World War increased the opportunities for women intellectuals and scientists to engage in their professions at high levels and contribute with important knowledge in various initiatives, their contributions were not necessarily recognized or appreciated in their own time and often remain obscure today.[19] However, recent research implicitly and explicitly demonstrates how the knowledge and experience gained by women before and after the Second World War and the Holocaust were carried into their work with the postwar historical commissions. In addition to their documentation and collection efforts, they also influenced and established methods and methodologies for interviewing, collecting, and archiving, while also in various ways

---

16 Gerner, "The Holocaust," 94; Gerner and Karlsson, *Folkmordens historia*, 189; Artur Szulc, *Röster som aldrig tystnar: Tredje rikets offer berättar* (Stockholm: Prisma, 2005), 24.
17 Laura Jockusch, *Collect and Record! Jewish Holocaust Documentation in Early Postwar Europe* (Oxford: Oxford University Press, 2012), 19.
18 Peter Burke, *Ignorance: A Global History* (New Haven: Yale University Press, 2023), 12, 244–45.
19 Hannah Wills et al., eds., *Women in the History of Science: A Sourcebook* (London: UCL Press, 2023), 329–89. See also, for instance, Natalia Aleksiun, "Female, Jewish, Educated, and Writing Polish Jewish History," in *Polin: Studies in Polish Jewry Volume 29*, eds. Natalia Aleksiun et al., *Writing Jewish History in Eastern Europe* (Liverpool: Liverpool University Press, 2017); Bethany G. Anderson and Kristen Allen Wilson, "Remembering Women Scientists: The Case for Proactively Documenting Women in Science," *Collections* 18, no. 4 (2022), doi:10.1177/15501906221129436; Susan Cohen, "In Defence of Academic Women Refugees: The British Federation of University Women," in *In Defence of Learning: The Plight, Persecution, and Placement of Academic Refugees, 1933–1980s*, eds. Shula Marks et al., *Proceedings of the British Academy* (New York: Oxford University Press, 2011).

combatting bureaucracy, lack of funding, and public and academic disinterest in continuing to collect, preserving existing collections, and so forth.[20]

Since the survivors associated with PIZ have rarely been considered historical actors, I analyze them as knowledge actors who "within a given historical context, contributed to the production and/or circulation of knowledge."[21] As knowledge actors, their agency is brought to the forefront of the analysis, transforming them from supposedly passive bearers of knowledge concerning the Second World War and the Holocaust into active contributors of knowledge on how to document these atrocities. Along with other scholars, however, I recognize that this cannot be accomplished in a vacuum since knowledge is always produced and circulated among a variety of actors and through different layers of power.[22] Hence, I view the survivors as knowledge actors alongside Bolin and Łakociński to reflect the pluralities of knowledge that helped shape PIZ through what Lässig and Steinberg refer to as "the cultural translation of knowledge."

Lässig and Steinberg argue that the transfer of knowledge carried out by migrants to "host" countries involves "the processes and practices of the cultural translation of knowledge."

---

20 See, for instance, Boaz Cohen, "Rachel Auerbach, Yad Vashem, and Israeli Holocaust Memory," in *Polin: Studies in Polish Jewry Volume 20: Making Holocaust Memory*, eds. Gabriel N. Finder et al. (Liverpool: Liverpool University Press, 2007), 220; Sharon Geva, "Documenters, Researchers and Commemorators: The Life Stories and Work of Miriam Novitch and Rachel Auerbach in Comparative Perspective," *MORESHET Journal for the Study of the Holocaust and Antisemitism* 16 (2019): 57–58; Johannes Heuman, "In Search of Documentation: Nella Rost and the Jewish Historical Commission," in *Early Holocaust Memory in Sweden: Archives, Testimonies and Reflections*, eds. Johannes Heuman and Pontus Rudberg (Basingstoke and New York: Palgrave MacMillan, 2021), 36, 47; Christine Schmidt, "'We Are All Witnesses': Eva Reichmann and the Wiener Library's Eyewitness Accounts Collection," in *Agency and the Holocaust: Essays in Honor of Debórah Dwork*, eds. Thomas Kühne and Mary Jane Rein (New York: Springer International Publishing, 2020).
21 Johan Östling et al., "Introduction: Revisiting agency in the history of knowledge," in *Knowledge Actors: Revisiting Agency in the History of Knowledge*, eds. Johan Östling et al. (Lund, Sweden: Nordic Academic Press, 2023), 12. See also Marian Füssel, *Wissen: Konzepte, Praktiken, Prozesse, Historische Einführungen* (Frankfurt: Campus, 2021); Philipp Sarasin, "Was ist Wissensgeschichte?" in *Internationales Archiv für Sozialgeschichte der deutschen Literatur* 36, no. 1 (2011), doi:10.1515/iasl.2011.010; Zloch, *Das Wissen der Einwanderungsgesellschaft*; Stephanie Zloch, "Migrationswissen: Das Beispiel der Bundesrepublik Deutschland aus zeithistorischer Sicht," *Aus Politik und Zeitgeschichte* 71, no. 3–4 (2021).
22 Maria Bach, "Positive Discourse Analysis: A Method for the History of Knowledge?" in *History of Intellectual Culture*, eds. Charlotte A. Lerg et al. (Berlin: De Gruyter Oldenbourg, 2022), 203–04; Lässig, "History of Knowledge," 43; Lässig and Steinberg, "Knowledge on the Move," 322; Zloch, "Migrationswissen," 33.

> Cultural translation took place before, during, and after migration and on different but often interconnected levels: between generations; between and within ethnic or religious communities; between migrant groups and the state or receiving society; between migrants and their former compatriots. [. . .] In the process of cultural translation, new knowledge can be created, already existing knowledge can take on new meaning or significance, and, consequently, knowledge orders can be transformed.[23]

This article studies how the PIZ efforts to document the Nazi atrocities in the early postwar period were the result of a cultural translation of knowledge in which the survivors, Łakociński, and Bolin were all knowledge actors.

Wartime Efforts to Document the Nazi Atrocities

Following the invasion of Poland by Soviet and Nazi forces in 1939, the Polish government-in-exile, with assistance from the Polish underground resistance movement, began gathering material and evidence related to the Nazi occupation of Poland.[24] Zygmunt Łakociński, working at Lund University, took similar action. Subsequently, he and two other Poles who also worked as foreign language assistants at Swedish universities – Józef Trypućko at Uppsala University and Zbigniew Folejewski at Stockholm University – then responded to a request by the Polish legation in Stockholm that Poles working as teachers in Swedish universities should collaborate to gather information in support of the Polish authorities, resulting in the formation of PIZ in January 1940.[25]

The fact that the PIZ efforts to document the Nazi atrocities were intended for history and inspired by a deep sense of patriotism is clear when reading a PIZ memorandum written in 1946, stating that for Poles, "the historical tradition has been and is the foundation of the struggle for the existing [sic] of the state."[26] As a national project, the wartime efforts of PIZ mirrored those of the Polish government-in-exile in that they were both concerned with documenting the Nazi occu-

---

23 Lässig and Steinberg, "Knowledge on the Move," 330.
24 Michael Fleming, "The Polish Government-in-Exile: The United Nations War Crimes Commission and the Holocaust," *Holocaust and Genocide Studies* 36 (2022), doi:10.1093/hgs/dcac012.
25 Eugeniusz Stanisław Kruszewski, *Polski Instytut Źródłowy w Lund (1939–1972): Zarys historii i dorobek* (London and Copenhagen: Polski Uniwersytet na Obczyźnie; Instytut Polsko-Skandynawski, 2001), 16–18.
26 PIZ 44:2 o, Memorandum in English dated October 13, 1946, and signed by Zygmunt Łakociński, p. 1.

pation of Poland and the persecution of Polish citizens generally, which they understood as including Polish Jews.[27]

The archives of PIZ and Zygmunt Łakociński, both held at the Lund University Library,[28] reflect the extent of the ongoing communications between PIZ and a variety of Polish governmental and other organizations in Sweden and elsewhere, both directly and indirectly, including the Polish government-in-exile in London.[29] Łakociński is thus likely to have known about the efforts made by members of the Polish underground to pass on intelligence to the government-in-exile and the efforts of the latter to establish legal charges using this evidence.[30] However, PIZ operated independently of the Polish government-in-exile during the war and was essentially a grassroots effort. In the spring of 1944, Łakociński in two memoranda summarized the purpose, aims, and methods used by PIZ up to that point, as well as what had been collected by the institute.

In the first, titled "Memorandum on collecting the war archive,"[31] he explains that the war archive is divided into five sections: 1. War library, 2. War archive, 3. War bibliography, 4. Registration of cultural losses, and 5. Polish-German relations. The document emphasizes that much of the material collected up until that point consisted of newspaper clippings (mainly in Swedish and German), propaganda (mainly in German), and photographs. Even though the aim had initially been to focus on the situation in Poland and for the Polish people, this changed to include a more general focus on the war since "at present few Poles have the possibility of collecting the kind of collections to which scientists-historians have already given the importance of first-class historical documents."[32] In the subsequent memorandum, he emphasizes that the main task of PIZ was to research and document the current state of Polish ethnicity and Polish-German relations and to process the collected materials objectively.[33]

Concurrent with the PIZ efforts, there were also initiatives to document Nazi persecution of Jews in Poland and elsewhere. As historian Laura Jockusch has observed in her comprehensive account of Holocaust documentation efforts: "German

---

27 Michael Fleming, "Geographies of obligation and the dissemination of news of the Holocaust," *Holocaust Studies* 23, no. 1–2 (2017), doi:10.1080/17504902.2016.1209834; Fleming, "The Polish Government-in-Exile."
28 PIZ; "Zygmunt Łakocińskis arkiv," (Lund University Library, Sweden).
29 This material is dispersed throughout the ZL and PIZ archives; for example, in several volumes of the ZL archive containing personal letters (e.g., volumes 5–7) and in PIZ volumes 46–50.
30 Fleming, "Geographies of obligation"; Fleming, "The Polish Government-in-Exile."
31 PIZ 44:1 a, "Pro memoria w/ sprawie zbierania archiwum wojennego," dated February 26, 1944, signed by Łakociński, p. 1. All translations made by the author unless otherwise indicated.
32 PIZ 44:1 a, p. 1.
33 PIZ 44:1 b, "Wytczene [sic] organizacyjne i Zadania," dated March, 25, 1944, p. 1.

persecution and extermination policies elicited widespread and multifaceted individual and collective Jewish documentation efforts across Europe."[34] What is today known as the Wiener Holocaust Library in London began in 1933 when Dr. Alfred Wiener, a German Jew fleeing Nazi persecution, established the Jewish Central Information Office in Amsterdam to collect material on the Nazis and their actions against Jews.[35] Starting in 1940, clandestine archives were created in several Polish ghettos, most notably the *Oyneg Shabes* (Oneg Shabbat) archive in the Warsaw Ghetto in Poland, which was founded by Polish-Jewish historian Emmanuel Ringelblum to "capture the experiences of Polish Jews under German occupation."[36] In France, the *Centre de Documentation Juive Contemporaire* (Contemporary Jewish Documentation Center) was established in 1943.[37]

Many of the Jewish efforts to document the Holocaust as it was happening were influenced by grassroots efforts originating among Eastern European Jews in the late nineteenth century as well as by Polish sociological practices developed during the interwar period. The former, known as *khurbn forshung* (destruction research), has been described by Jockusch as "a distinct 'historiography of trauma'" that originated in the late nineteenth century and was further developed in the early twentieth century to document pogroms against Jews in Eastern Europe.[38] From the beginning, this approach included gathering testimonies from eyewitnesses and victims. After the First World War, *khurbn forshung* was developed further as a scholarly method used to objectively document the history of Jewish persecution and destruction "from below" that prioritized the experiences and perspectives of the eyewitnesses and victims without neglecting perpetrator sources.[39] In the interwar period, a variety of groups and organizations were established by Jewish historians in Poland that "combined historical scholarship with political and social activism for the Jewish community."[40]

One of these organizations was the Yiddish Scientific Institute (YIVO), established in 1925 with its headquarters in Vilno, Poland. One of the founders of YIVO

---

34 Jockusch, *Collect and Record*, 33.
35 Schmidt, "We Are All Witnesses," 125–26. Ben Barkow, *Alfred Wiener and the Making of the Holocaust Library* (London: Vallentine Mitchell, 1997).
36 Jockusch, *Collect and Record*, 34.
37 See, for instance, Johannes Heuman, "The Quest for Recognition: The Holocaust and French Historical Culture, 1945–65" (PhD diss., Stockholm University, 2014).
38 Jockusch, *Collect and Record*, 19.
39 Laura Jockusch, "Chroniclers of Catastrophe: History Writing as a Jewish Response to Persecution Before and After the Holocaust," in *Holocaust Historiography in Context: Emergence, Challenges, Polemics and Achievements*, eds. David Bankier and Dan Michman (New York and Oxford: Berghahn Books, 2008).
40 Jockusch, *Collect and Record*, 31.

was Russian-Jewish historian Simon Dubnow, a pioneer of the "from below" or what he called a "sociological" approach to Jewish historiography.[41] One aspect of the *khurbn forshung* tradition introduced by Dubnow and further developed at YIVO was the role of collectors (*zamlers*), whose job was to gather documents and evidence and conduct interviews with witnesses.[42] Sociological methods were also embraced by Russian-Jewish scholar Max Weinreich, who, in his capacity as director of YIVO, was one of the academics working in Poland to adopt a new method called "social memoir," which he utilized to collect hundreds of memoirs written by young Jews. This method was pioneered in the early 1920s by Polish sociologist Florian Znaniecki, building on his previous collaboration with US-American sociologist William I. Thomas, which "promoted close analysis of 'personal documents' such as letters, diaries, and autobiographies" of Polish immigrants to the United States.[43] After returning to Poland, Znaniecki initiated competitions to solicit personal stories from members of the public on specific topics, which eventually came to include a variety of social and political issues such as unemployment, healthcare, the plight of peasants, etc. The approach was further developed by Znaniecki and other Polish sociologists up until the Nazi occupation and became known outside Poland as the "Polish method."[44]

The significance of institutions such as YIVO training young scholars in these practices became evident following the Nazi occupation of Poland and the establishment of Jewish ghettos in Poland and elsewhere beginning in 1940.[45] In the ghetto established in Riga, Latvia, Simon Dubnow encouraged the Jews imprisoned there to record the atrocities carried out against them.[46] Such documentation efforts were initiated in several Jewish ghettos in Poland.[47] One of the most

---

[41] Philip Friedman, "Polish Jewish Historiography between the Two Wars (1918–1939)," *Jewish Social Studies* 11, no. 4 (1949): 375; Jockusch, *Collect and Record*, 32.
[42] Samuel D. Kassow, *Who will write our history? Emanuel Ringelblum, the Warsaw Ghetto, and the Oyneg Shabes Archive* (Bloomington, Illinois: Indiana University Press, 2018), 51–52. See also: Jockusch, *Collect and Record*, 32–33.
[43] Katherine Lebow, "Autobiography as Complaint: Polish Social Memoir Between the World Wars," *Laboratorium: Russian Review of Social Research* 6, no. 3 (2014): 16.
[44] Katherine Lebow, "The Conscience of the Skin: Interwar Polish Autobiography and Social Rights," *Humanity: An International Journal of Human Rights, Humanitarianism, and Development* 3, no. 3 (2012): 298, doi:10.1353/hum.2012.0027.
[45] Havi Dreifuss, "Jewish Historiography of the Holocaust in Eastern Europe," in *Polin: Studies in Polish Jewry*, ed. Natalia Aleksiun (Liverpool: Liverpool University Press, Littman Library of Jewish Civilization, 2017), 220; Jockusch, *Collect and Record*, 34–36.
[46] Annette Wieviorka, "The Witness in History," trans. Jared Stark, *Poetics Today: International Journal for Theory and Analysis of Literature and Communication* 27, no. 2 (2006): 386, doi:10.1215/03335371-2005-009.
[47] Jockusch, *Collect and Record*, 33–34.

significant of these efforts was the Oneg Shabbat secret archive established in the Warsaw Ghetto in November 1940 by Emanuel Ringelblum, who had worked in the historical section of YIVO. This effort included gathering witness accounts of Jewish persecution inside and outside the ghetto as well as collecting diaries and distributing questionnaires on life in the ghetto. Ringelblum brought to this initiative his previous experience of gathering witness testimonies in 1938 and 1939 from Polish Jews in a refugee camp in Poland.[48] There is also evidence that social memoir competitions were being held in the Warsaw Ghetto, reflecting Ringelblum's close association with Weinreich at YIVO and the continued adaptation of the sociological method pioneered by Znaniecki.[49] The result of these and other cultural translations of knowledge was the development of what has been referred to as "the methodology of witness," which was then further utilized and adapted in the numerous postwar Jewish survivor historical commissions.[50]

Although PIZ and the primarily Jewish documentation efforts of the wartime period were contemporaneous, this brief overview demonstrates that these differed in several important ways. First, the work at PIZ was conducted by individuals who were not subject to persecution, while the Jewish efforts were conducted by people actively being persecuted. Second, whereas the Jewish efforts were developing and utilizing a distinctive method of scholarship from below that drew on diverse grassroots and scholarly practices to collect eyewitness testimonies, the PIZ initiative was primarily a patriotic effort to collect what secondary material it was able to collect in a nominally neutral country. Third, as a national effort, PIZ had a more universalized understanding of Nazi persecution of Jewish and non-Jewish Poles, while the Jewish efforts already at the outset recognized that Jews were subjected to a distinctive form of persecution by the Nazis. These distinctions indicate that Łakociński had little to no knowledge of the Jewish efforts and how their methods and methodologies had been influenced and shaped by prewar Eastern European grassroots and academic practices.

---

48 Joseph Kermish, introduction to "Polish-Jewish Relations During the Second World War," in *The Nazi Holocaust – Part 5: Public Opinion and relations to the Jews in Nazi Europe*, ed. Michael R. Marrus, The Nazi Holocaust: Historical Articles on the Destruction of European Jews (Berlin and New York: K. G. Saur, 1989), 269–70.
49 Lebow, "The Conscience of the Skin," 311.
50 Katherine Lebow, "The Methodology of Witness: Pre-War Polish Sociology and the Jewish Historical Commissions in Poland, 1945–1948" (The Central European University Jewish Studies Program, Budapest, February 11, 2014), Lecture, accessed September 29, 2023, https://nationalism.ceu.edu/events/2014-02-11/js-lecture-series-katherine-lebow-methodology-witnesspre-war-polish-sociology-and. See also, Jockusch, *Collect and Record*, 33.

The Impact of Survivors and Their Knowledge

In late April and early May 1945, survivors of Nazi persecution started to flow into Sweden for medical care and recovery. Poles represented one of the largest national groups, eventually numbering as many as 13,000 with the majority being women. Łakociński recognized that he and PIZ could be of assistance to the Polish survivors, including by serving as an interpreter and collecting and preserving evidence smuggled out of the concentration camps. At the same time, many of the survivors he encountered in quarantine camps and hospitals were activists and intellectuals who were accustomed to acting on their own behalf and that of others.

The encounters between Łakociński and the survivors had an almost immediate impact on PIZ, as revealed in a May 17, 1945, memorandum: "The sudden arrival of a large group of Polish prisoners from Germany [. . .] has significantly updated the entire issue." He continues, highlighting both continuity and rupture between the previous documentation efforts of PIZ and the new direction of the institute:

> The immensely important field of war crimes can now be investigated and documented with the help of thousands of witnesses-victims, who took away documents that constitute an extremely important source for the history of camps, prisons, torture and death not only of Poles but also of other nationalities.[51]

This statement highlights how the arrival of the survivors meant that the PIZ efforts could now move from collecting secondary material to collecting material that could be used in courts of law to prosecute Nazis and other perpetrators. PIZ thus had the potential to achieve justice in a similar way as the Polish government-in-exile. However, another excerpt from this memorandum demonstrates how the method for gathering witness testimonies had also fundamentally been changed by the arrival of the survivors.

> This material must in no way be dispersed; on the contrary, it should be gathered as thoroughly as possible and multiplied by drawing up as precise protocols as possible with each former prisoner, taking advantage of their presence in greater quantity in relatively close proximity and with a fresh memory of the events that took place. This work may be performed only by persons appointed to this type of research.[52]

---

51 PIZ 44:1 c – "Memoriał w sprawie polskiego instytutu źródłowego w Lund /Szwecja/" (Memorandum on the Polish source institute in Lund, Sweden), dated May 17, 1945, p. 1.
52 PIZ 44:1 c, p. 1.

Describing the changing nature of the documentation efforts, Łakociński stressed both the urgency of the work and the need for qualified individuals – historians, doctors, lawyers, and other specialists – to conduct it. In fact, as the memorandum shows, this work was already being performed by "documentation commissions" composed exclusively of female former prisoners having been established by Łakociński at refugee assembly points in and around Lund. He intended that these commissions would eventually come together to form the new "Source Institute," which I refer to as the PIZ workgroup.[53] Significantly, one month later, on June 20, 1945, a memorandum drafted to gain financial support from the Swedish government for the PIZ workgroup describes it as a "Polish female intellectual working group in Lund."[54] Moreover, this memorandum describes the survivor-witnesses as sources: "they themselves constitute first-class witness material."[55]

These memoranda demonstrate how, in less than two months, PIZ was transformed by the involvement of female survivors of Nazi persecution. From a purely documentary initiative inspired by a larger national initiative and undertaken by male émigré academics, PIZ was now more closely aligned with the Jewish documentation commissions operating during the war and continuing to proliferate in the early postwar period. Like these efforts, PIZ was now primarily a survivor-operated initiative utilizing a "bottom-up" approach to research and which recognized victims of violence as credible sources that could be used to supplement perpetrator sources.

Funding for the PIZ workgroup under the terms laid out in the June 20 memorandum was granted by the Swedish government in July 1945. However, it took several months for the work to officially begin. Nonetheless, before the group was formally established in October 1945, many female survivors, including those involved in the documentation commissions, collected evidence and testimonies from survivors, while also contributing to establishing the composition, methods, and practices of the nascent workgroup. Finally, in October 1945, the workgroup officially began its work with funding provided by *Statens Arbetsmarknadskommission* (the Swedish Labor Market Commission) through labor market subsidies and officially operated as a sub-division of *Utrikespolitiska Institutet* (the Swedish Institute of Foreign Affairs). Eventually, seven female and two male survivors were hired as PIZ workgroup members. Even though their duties varied, they were all involved in working and communicating with other survivors to record and collect witness testimonies.

---

53 PIZ 44:1 c, p. 1.
54 44:1 d – "P.M. angående en polsk kvinnlig intellektuell arbetsgrupp i Lund," dated June 20, 1945.
55 PIZ 44:1 d, p. 1.

Łakociński coordinated with Lund University and Swedish historian Sture Bolin to establish methodological rules and an interview process to ensure that the results were acceptable as historical sources. However, contrary to the narratives that have situated Bolin as the "innovator" of the PIZ initiative, other scholars have argued based on extant empirical material that Łakociński already had the working method in place before he met with Sture Bolin.[56] I take these arguments and evidence further to argue that the memoranda from 1944 and 1945 indicate that this method was not in place until *after* the survivors arrived in Sweden in the spring of 1945 and Łakociński came into contact with them. I contend that the early interactions at the assembly points, especially with the female survivors of the documentation commissions, precipitated the cultural translation of the knowledge that the survivors carried with them, including knowledge of the same Polish and Polish-Jewish methods utilized by the Jewish survivor historical commissions and how to apply them.

The Cultural Translation of Knowledge

In the immediate postwar period, most academic historians in Scandinavia and Western Europe did not practice "from below" methods of historical research, as they typically prioritized the nation and politics in their analyses.[57] Moreover,

---

56 Izabela A. Dahl, "Witnessing the Holocaust: Jewish Experiences and the Collection of the Polish Source Institute in Lund," in *Early Holocaust Memory in Sweden: Archives, Testimonies and Reflections*, eds. Johannes Heuman and Pontus Rudberg (Basingstoke and New York: Palgrave Macmillan, 2021), 74; Kruszewski, *Polski Instytut Źródłowy w Lund*, 34; Paul Rudny, "Polski Instytut Źródłowy w Lund (The Polish Research Institute in Lund): A presentation of the archives" (Lund University Library, 2003), 6, accessed September 29, 2023, http://www3.ub.lu.se/ravensbruck/piz-eng-presentation.pdf. See also the work report signed by Zygmunt Łakociński from October 1946 in which he writes: "Before the beginning of the work, the undersigned chairman [Łakociński] had discussed the method of work, [sic] to be adopted in order to comply with all exigencies of history with Prof. Sture Bolin, from Lund." (See: PIZ 44:2 m, "Report for the time: 22/10.1945 – 30.9.1946" written in English and signed by Zygmunt Łakociński, dated October 10, 1946, p. 2.)
57 Simon Larsson, "Scientific historiography and its discontents: Danish and Swedish 'aristocratic empiricism'," in *Making Nordic Historiography: Connections, Tensions and Methodology, 1850–1970*, eds. Pertti Haapala et al., Making Sense of History: Studies in Historical Cultures (New York and Oxford: Berghahn Books, 2017), 130–31; Paul Richard Thompson, *The Voice of the Past. Oral History*, 3rd ed. (Oxford and New York: Oxford University Press), 3–4; Yvonne Maria Werner, "'Weibullarna' – lundahistoriker i takt med tiden," in *Historia och historiker: Om Lunds universitet genom 350 år*, ed. Lars Edgren, Studia historica Lundensia (Lund: Department of History, Lund University, 2018), 82.

few Western European scholars were familiar with the progressive methods developed by Jewish and non-Jewish historians and other scholars in Eastern Europe before the war due to language barriers and other issues concerning access and interest.[58] When the progressive methods developed in Poland before and during the Second World War did appear outside Eastern Europe, it was usually due to the fact they had been introduced by survivors from Poland and other Eastern European countries. Some of the most significant historical commissions launched during or immediately after the war in countries such as France, Germany, and what is now Israel were established by Jewish survivors from Eastern Europe, especially Poland.[59] Thinking of this in terms of migrant knowledge "on the move,"[60] survivors brought the knowledge of *khurbn forshung*, social memoir, and other practices as they had been developed and practiced in Poland during and immediately following the Second World War to other countries and contexts where knowledge of the methods and how they had been adapted and used to document the Nazi atrocities were culturally translated in distinct contexts. I argue that a similar cultural translation of knowledge occurred at PIZ.[61]

The wartime efforts of PIZ reflect that Łakociński was unaware of how the "methodology of witness" had developed and was used during the war by Jewish victims of the Nazis. But even if Łakociński and his colleagues in Sweden had some knowledge of these efforts, they would have had little practical experience with them. Unlike other efforts initiated during the war, PIZ did not gather firsthand intelligence from eyewitnesses, or at least not to the same extent, during the war.[62] Hence, the method and methodology for gathering witness testimonies from survivors had not developed at PIZ to the same extent as the documentation initiatives established during the war, such as the Central Jewish Historical Commission, which started to collect survivor testimonies in August 1944 and became one of the most significant survivor historical commissions in the early postwar period.[63]

---

58 Natalia Aleksiun, "From Galicia to Warsaw: Interwar Historians of Polish Jewry," in *Warsaw: The Jewish metropolis: Essays in honor of the 75th birthday of professor Antony Polonsky*, eds. Glenn Dynner and François Guesnet, IJS Studies in Judaica (Leiden: Brill, 2015), 388; Jockusch, "Chroniclers of Catastrophe," 165.
59 Jockusch, *Collect and Record*, 7.
60 Lässig and Steinberg, "Knowledge on the Move."
61 Lässig and Steinberg, "Knowledge on the Move," 332; Lässig, "History of Knowledge," 32.
62 As Kruszewski (18) points out, PIZ did collect "reports" from individuals who had been in Poland and come to Sweden, such as Daniel Cederberg, a Swedish priest from Lund who had spent some time in Poland and Ukraine and offered an account of what he saw. See also ZL 1, Cederberg, Daniel; ZL 28, Cederberg, Daniel.
63 Jockusch, *Collect and Record*, 84–120.

The arrival of Polish survivors starting in the spring of 1945 meant that PIZ was now able to conduct this work. However, this was not only because they were witnesses to the events in question but also because they were knowledge actors serving as "carriers, cultural translators and creators"[64] of propositional, practical, and situated knowledge regarding the methods and practices described above, which had already been and could be further culturally translated. Not least, they knew *that* and *how* the Nazi atrocities had been documented during the war by those who suffered from them. Accordingly, they were what Lässig describes as "conveyers of a migrant knowledge that was not immediately at the disposal of the host society."[65] Although the survivors involved with PIZ tended to be well-educated individuals having previously engaged in activism, they nonetheless reflect the pluralities of knowledge carried by different knowledge actors. They were what Johannes Westberg refers to as "multifaceted knowledge actors" who play various roles in different contexts and "can support the flow of knowledge, ideas, and practices across social borders and distinctions."[66] Focusing on the latter for this analysis, it is possible to see how the diverse backgrounds and experiences of the survivors enabled them to contribute with some forms of knowledge and to support the flow of others.

Historians involved in PIZ, such as non-Jewish Polish survivors Helena Salska and Wanda Madlerowa, would have been familiar with how historical and other scholarly methods and methodologies were used and adapted in Poland during the interwar period and the war and would thus have contributed this knowledge. Łakociński's awareness concerning the value of the knowledge of these survivors is evident by his early determination that the ones who would be employed by PIZ should be intellectuals. As people who had experienced and witnessed Nazi persecution firsthand and with professional experience in various forms of scientific work, they could contribute to the endeavor in ways that no one else could. During the early period of the formation of PIZ, Salska's involvement was so important that Łakociński described her as "the soul of the whole company."[67] However, the knowledge contributions made by the survivors were not solely limited to what they had gained as professionals.

---

64 Lässig, "History of Knowledge," 32. See also Lässig and Steinberg, "Knowledge on the Move," 322.
65 Lässig, "History of Knowledge," 31.
66 Johannes Westberg, "Multifaceted knowledge actors: Nineteenth-century teachers as authors, researchers, administrators, and politicians," in *Knowledge Actors: Revisiting Agency in the History of Knowledge*, eds. Johan Östling et al. (Lund, Sweden: Nordic Academic Press, 2023), 47.
67 PIZ 46:4 – Letter from Łakociński to Sven Dahl, in Swedish, dated September 1, 1945. In Swedish: "att mgr Helena Salska, själen i hela företaget."

In addition to the knowledge they carried as historians, doctors, lawyers, etc., many of the female survivors in the documentation commissions had been actively involved in Polish underground resistance movements and/or clandestine educational initiatives in the concentration camps, which meant that they brought specific and valuable forms of knowledge gathered from these experiences to the documentation and collection efforts. They would, for instance, have firsthand knowledge of the Polish underground's efforts to gather and transmit intelligence on atrocities against Jews and non-Jews in Nazi-occupied Poland and concentration and death camps. Other forms of knowledge were also carried by survivors who experienced Nazi persecution in distinct ways, such as Jewish survivors. Although the survivors associated with PIZ were primarily non-Jewish, Jewish survivors also contributed evidence and testimony to PIZ and worked for PIZ in official and unofficial capacities. Luba Melchior, for instance, who had been part of the documentation commissions and was the only Jewish PIZ workgroup member, would have been a carrier and cultural translator of knowledge not only regarding the specificity of Jewish persecution but also concerning Jewish documentation efforts during the war, such as from her time in the Radom ghetto, where a documentation initiative was undertaken.[68] While it is unlikely that the non-Jewish survivors involved in PIZ, who were in the majority, had any direct experience with *khurbn forshung*, some of them would have been familiar with the documentation efforts through their work as activists inside and beyond the walls of the concentration camps.

Łakociński's early interactions with the Polish survivors at the assembly points – in particular, the women involved in the documentation commissions – and his ability to communicate with them in their native language meant that he immediately became part of the cultural translation by acting as a facilitator of knowledge, a knowledge actor who "brokers" – arranges and organizes – the circulation of knowledge.[69] This is reflected in the comparison of the memoranda, which I argue reveals how contact with the survivors at the assembly points and in documentation commissions led to the PIZ initiative adopting the same or similar Eastern European traditions and methods having been adapted and developed during the war by the Jewish documentation initiatives. This knowledge was carried by the

---

68 Victoria Van Orden Martínez, "Documenting the Documenter: Piecing Together the History of Polish Holocaust Survivor-Historian Luba Melchior," ed. Wolfgang Schellenbacher *EHRI Document Blog*, December 12, 2022, accessed September 29, 2023, https://blog.ehri-project.eu/2022/12/12/luba-melchior/.

69 Thomas Mougey, "Organizing Knowledge Circulation: Using conference design to engineer the exchange of knowledge," in *Knowledge Actors: Revisiting Agency in the History of Knowledge*, eds. Johan Östling et al. (Lund, Sweden: Nordic Academic Press, 2023); Östling et al., "Revisiting agency," 21.

survivors to Sweden, where it was arranged and organized by Łakociński, as reflected in the 1945 memoranda that conceptualized the PIZ workgroup.

The claims that Sture Bolin pioneered the PIZ method are refuted by empirical material in the archives as well as by the history of knowledge outlined earlier in this chapter, which demonstrates that the postwar efforts of PIZ were similar to the historical commissions and documentation centers established by Jewish victims of the Nazis before and after the war. However, this does not mean that Bolin was not part of the cultural translation of knowledge at PIZ.

Bolin's primary contribution to the PIZ workgroup appears to have consisted of establishing the formal methodological guidelines for the PIZ documentation work.[70] According to Birgitta Odén, Bolin's protégé and scholarly biographer, the methodology reflects Bolin's adherence to the so-called "Weibull school" of source criticism in that it specifies how to extract objective facts from a witness and then authenticate these facts and testify to the credibility of the witness.[71] Named after Swedish historians Lauritz and Curt Weibull, the Weibull method is considered part of a Scandinavian shift in the early twentieth century to a more "radical" form of source criticism that not only critiqued the sources but also the conclusions of previous researchers.[72] For Lauritz Weibull, who was a mentor to Bolin during his early years at Lund University, this not only meant eliminating oral and narrative sources from his analyses but also criticizing other historians using these sources.[73] Bolin utilized the Weibull method in his work as a historian, with Odén describing him as "radically source critical."[74]

As a prominent Swedish historian working at Lund University, he enjoyed a position of authority that made him not only a facilitator of knowledge who organized knowledge but more specifically a *gatekeeper* of knowledge with the power to grant or deny its legitimacy.[75] Considering that one of the primary purposes of the PIZ workgroup was to gather oral and narrative sources, it is remarkable that Bolin as a follower of the Weibull school chose to endorse the effort and apply the Weibull method to it – acts that were almost certainly crucial for gaining government funding for the group. Yet, the methodology attributed to Bolin differed

---

70 PIZ 44:6 a, Minutes of PIZ workgroup dated November 22, 1945, signed by Zygmunt Łakociński and Krystyna Karier, p. 1. The topic was a lecture by Sture Bolin, who presented the methodological guidelines for recording the witness testimonies.
71 Birgitta Odén, *Sture Bolin – historiker under andra världskriget* (Stockholm: Kungl. Vitterhets historie och antikvitets akademien, 2011), 82.
72 Odén, *Sture Bolin*, 57–58; Werner, "Weibullarna," 82.
73 Werner, "Weibullarna," 77.
74 Odén, *Sture Bolin*, 54.
75 Lässig, "History of Knowledge," 44.

little from those utilized in the Jewish documentation efforts developed before, during, and after the Second World War, which also strove for objectivity on the part of both the interviewers and witnesses and utilized similar means of authenticating the facts of the testimonies, establishing witness credibility, and so forth. I suggest that the fact that the methodology Bolin put his name to appears to abandon the radical source criticism of the Weibull school to more closely resemble the "methodology of witness" constitutes further evidence of the cultural translation of knowledge at PIZ.

Conclusion

Survivors of Nazi persecution who came to Sweden as refugees in 1945 have rarely been considered active and agential historical actors in Swedish narratives pertaining to the Second World War, the Holocaust, and the postwar period. Their existence in these narratives has typically been presented as passive recipients of Swedish refuge and relief. Accordingly, the kinds of knowledge they carried to Sweden and how these were of value and significance in the postwar period have also been neglected, both in general and in relation to PIZ. Previous research on PIZ has primarily situated the survivors associated with the institute as subordinate figures to Sture Bolin and Zygmunt Łakociński, who have been situated as the main historical and knowledge actors.[76] By viewing the survivors associated with PIZ as historical actors and – perhaps for the first time – as knowledge actors, this analysis contributes to a growing body of scholarship on the history and circulation of knowledge that has fused migrant knowledge studies with Holocaust aftermath studies. In doing so, it also addresses PIZ as an anomaly of sorts – a survivor historical commission that was composed of both Jewish and non-Jewish interviewers and collectors and which gathered evidence and testimony from Jewish and non-Jewish Poles. This was unusual for the time and has meant that situating PIZ in the larger context of Holocaust documentation efforts represents a challenge that has previously not been taken on by researchers.[77]

---

76 For a fuller discussion, see, for instance, Martínez, "Afterlives," 1–6.
77 But which has been argued for as necessary. See, for instance, Dahl, "Witnessing the Holocaust," 68; Malin Thor Tureby, "Memories, Testimonies and Oral History: On collections and research about and with Holocaust survivors in Sweden," in *Holocaust Remembrance and Representation: Documentation from a Research Conference*, ed. Karin Kvist Geverts (Research anthology from the Inquiry on A Museum about the Holocaust; Stockholm: Swedish Government Official Reports, SOU 2020:21), 73.

I contend that the analytical category of knowledge has been one of the elements missing from previous research.[78] Even though evidence of the survivors' knowledge can be found in extant empirical material, it lacked the necessary context – the "chemical reagent" – needed to make it visible. I have argued that this context is the history of knowledge behind other documentation initiatives related to the Second World War and the early postwar period. By analyzing PIZ in relation to this history of knowledge, I have argued that the survivors of Nazi persecution were knowledge actors who carried knowledge concerning other documentation efforts and the methods and practices utilized in these efforts to Sweden in 1945. Through their work with PIZ, they culturally translated this knowledge together with Łakociński and Bolin, thereby shaping the PIZ initiative to document the Nazi atrocities in the aftermath of the Second World War and the Holocaust. This means that they were not only contributors of important knowledge related to these events but also contributors of knowledge that was essential for documenting and collecting this valuable material for the sake of justice and history.

In the spring of 1945, this cultural translation of knowledge was precipitated when Polish survivors of Nazi persecution in Sweden came into contact with Łakociński at refugee assembly points. In addition to material evidence and their knowledge of the Nazi atrocities, they also brought knowledge of the "methodology of witness," the scholarly practices and methods that influenced it, and how these various practices and methods were utilized before and during the war. A cultural translation of knowledge occurred as both the knowledge of these practices and the practices themselves were not just transferred but also *transformed* in transit – both geographically and culturally – in the context of PIZ. From its founding, PIZ conducted its collection efforts in a way similar to that of the Polish government-in-exile, which gathered material on the Nazi persecution of both Jewish and non-Jewish Poles. This did not change when the survivors became involved in the initiative. Rather, their knowledge of Eastern European scholarly and grassroots efforts became part of the cultural translation of knowledge that fundamentally changed the documentation and collection efforts of PIZ while also retaining aspects of its former approach. As I have argued, PIZ operated along lines similar to the many Jewish survivor historical commissions of the early postwar period as it shared a history of knowledge with these efforts. At the same time, by focusing on both Jewish and non-Jewish victims and by recognizing

---

78 I explore this and other aspects in Martínez, "Afterlives."

the specificity of Jewish persecution, PIZ was also working in line with the postwar justice efforts taking place in Poland. PIZ may thus be understood in relation to both the juridical efforts led mainly by non-Jewish Poles and the primarily Jewish survivor historical commissions and documentation centers.

As knowledge actors in this cultural translation of knowledge, Jewish survivors (of whom more than just Luba Melchior were involved in PIZ in unofficial capacities)[79] were more likely to have direct experiences with *khurbn forshung* and thus the ability to transfer their knowledge in a new context. Non-Jewish survivors associated with PIZ – some of whom were historians – would have had similar practical experiences with the methods and practices that contributed to shaping the methodology of witness, such as *khurbn forshung* and the "Polish Method" of social memoir. However, not only the direct experience of using these scholarly methods would have been transformed but also the knowledge of how these practices and scholarly methods had been used to document the Nazi atrocities before, during, and immediately following the Second World War and the Holocaust. In their different roles as knowledge actors, the survivors associated with PIZ not only contributed with their own knowledge but also supported the flow of other forms of knowledge, ensuring that the methods and practices and how to use them were both part of the cultural translation of knowledge. Łakociński organized these multiple forms of knowledge and conceptualized the new documentation initiative with the support of Bolin, who granted legitimacy to these efforts. Although Bolin was not the mastermind behind the PIZ initiative, his support was essential for gaining government funding and credibility.

In these and other respects, my findings contribute to changing received knowledge regarding the roles of various actors – not just the survivor-refugees – in social and political contexts related to PIZ. In turn, this fundamentally changes how PIZ has been constructed historiographically as an initiative dominated by respected men and their knowledge. It is now possible to see that survivors who came to Sweden as refugees, most of whom were women, and their knowledge were foundational to the transformation of PIZ in the immediate postwar period, how it conducted its work, and how it may be understood in the context of the phenomenon of documenting the Nazi atrocities.

Victoria Van Orden Martínez is a researcher at Linköping University and Lund University in Sweden. Her current research focuses on how survivors of Nazi persecution who came to Sweden as refugees during and after the Second World War and the Holocaust were involved in various social and political processes in the early postwar period, with a focus on the role of gender and other differences. Recent publications include "Witnessing the Suffering of Others in Watercolor and

---

79 See Martínez, "Afterlives."

Pencil: Jadwiga Simon-Pietkiewicz's Holocaust Art Exhibited in Sweden, 1945–46" in *Holocaust and Genocide Studies* (2023), "Monuments Cast Shadows: Remembering and Forgetting the 'Dead Survivors' of Nazi Persecution in Swedish Cemeteries," co-authored with Malin Thor Tureby, in *Fallen Monuments and Contested Memorials* (2023), and her Ph.D. thesis, *Afterlives: Jewish and Non-Jewish Polish Survivors of Nazi Persecution in Sweden Documenting Nazi Atrocities, 1945–1946* (2023).

Isabelle Strömstedt and Adam Bisno

Defending the Knowledge Monopoly: The U.S. Patent Office, Propaganda, and the Centennial Celebration of the Patent Act of 1836

Abstract: During the Great Depression, the increasing dominance of big business over the U.S. patent system attracted attention and controversy, culminating in a congressional investigation of the issue: Had corporations co-opted the patent system to form monopolies, stifle competition, and constrict industries? In response, big business and the U.S. Patent Office used celebrations of the history of the patent system as key opportunities for presenting a more positive counternarrative to the US-American public. The first such opportunity was the hundredth anniversary of the Patent Act of 1836. In the 1936 commemoration, Patent Office officials and patent system stakeholders exploited the figure of the lone inventor, a trope used to help the public associate the patent system with the creative genius of the individual patentee rather than with the monopolistic practices of big business. This essay, a narratological study of the celebratory proceedings in 1936, explains how and why officials embarked on this exercise in peacetime propaganda, even as it ended up contradicting the priorities of President Franklin D. Roosevelt.

Keywords: anniversary, 1930s, 1940s, United States, patent system, inventors, narrative, Great Depression

Introduction

The Centennial Celebration of the U.S. Patent Act of 1836 was lavish. It entailed a programme of lectures, a multimedia Research Parade, national radio specials and exhibitions, and a thousand-seat dinner at the Mayflower Hotel in Washington,

---

Note: The authors thank Eva Hemmungs Wirtén for introducing us under the auspices of her project, "Patents as Scientific Information, 1895–2020" (PASSIM), funded by the European Research Council under the Horizon 2020 research and innovation programme (grant agreement ERC-AdG-741095). We thank PASSIM's participants for their help in refining our argument and improving our approach, especially Johanna Dahlin, Martin Fredriksson, and Johan Larson Lindal. We are grateful to Jana Weiß and Rikard Ehnsiö for several invaluable edits. Finally, we wish to thank our peer reviewers for their careful consideration and collegial advice.

Open Access. © 2024 the author(s), published by De Gruyter. This work is licensed under the Creative Commons Attribution-NonCommercial-NoDerivatives 4.0 International License.
https://doi.org/10.1515/9783111291383-003

D.C. – more events, indeed, than a single study can touch upon. These events are significant as they constituted a concerted propaganda campaign, uncommon in peacetime, originating from a collaboration between big business, on one side, and the U.S. Patent Office and the Department of Commerce, on the other.[1] Together, and to defend the patent system against reform, the National Association of Manufacturers (NAM) and U.S. government officials told stories foregrounding the figure of the lone inventor, a trope central to patent lore. In doing so, they deflected attention from the increasing and apparent advantage enjoyed by corporate R&D over lone inventors. By collaborating with NAM in this way, the U.S. Patent Office and the Department of Commerce took the side of big business in a political debate on the role of corporations in the economic disasters of the 1930s.

Patent system anniversaries are as of yet an unexplored dimension of the public and political debate regarding the patent system in the 1930s, despite the existence of a conspicuous historical and transnational tradition of celebrating the patent system and patent offices.[2] By focusing on the 1936 celebration, which reached farther than previous ones and occurred at a time of intense conflict over patents, we offer a broader understanding of how officials and actors in the patent system used celebrations to deflect attention from the excesses of the system and spin a counternarrative of heroic inventiveness and US-American progress. The organisers of the celebration relied on a stock of characters and themes familiar to US-Americans at the time as well as today: the self-made man, the self-starting inventor of the Industrial Revolution, and the timeless genius of individual enterprise.[3]

In this article, we scrutinise the lone inventor as a narrative, a "social transaction" and "negotiation" of meanings that resulted in the ongoing establishment of a

---

[1] On peacetime propaganda in the United States in a comparative perspective, see Wolfgang Schivelbusch, *Three New Deals: Reflections on Roosevelt's America, Mussolini's Italy, and Hitler's Germany, 1933–1939* (New York: Picador, 2006), 73–80.

[2] An exception is Isabelle Strömstedt, "The Patent Office on Display: Intellectual Property in the Public Eye" (PhD diss., Linköping University, 2023), on the fiftieth anniversary of the Swedish Intellectual Property Office in 1941. On anniversaries at other patent offices, see Austria Patentamt, *100 Jahre Österreichisches Patentamt, 1899–1999: Festschrift* (Vienna: Österreichisches Patentamt, 1999); Ming Tinghua, ed., *A Decade of China Patent System: The Patent Office of the People's Republic of China* ([Beijing]: [China Patent News Office], 1995); "History," Deutsches Patent- und Markenamt, last modified 5 August 2022, https://www.dpma.de/english/our_office/about_us/history/index.html; "Historien vår," Patentstyret (Norway), last modified 7 October 2021, https://www.patentstyret.no/om-oss/var-historie/.

[3] See Larry Owens, "Patents, the 'Frontiers' of American Invention, and the Monopoly Committee of 1939: Anatomy of a Discourse," *Technology and Culture* 32 (1991): 1092.

"canon."[4] In this case, the canon held that the patent system had been created in 1836 for the benefit of the lone inventor, who remained its hero and justification. Over the decades, however, as conditions changed and big business learned to take advantage of patents as state-issued monopolies on scientific and technical knowledge, this canon had come under threat by the critics of big business. To manage this threat, representatives of big business and officials of the U.S. government resorted to narrative propaganda. They attempted to dispel the controversy by renegotiating the social and cultural meanings of patents as well as by shoring up the system against efforts to make sweeping reforms.

Our sources – proceedings of the celebrations and correspondence of the commissioner of patents – directly engage with narratives and counternarratives regarding the patent system during the Great Depression. In this case, the narrative of the heroic lone inventor entailed an important process of self-fashioning for the Patent Office in a culture and society destabilised by the Great Depression and the increasing power of large corporations in the national economy.

The question specific to the 1930s was this: Had the patent system safeguarded democracy by empowering the individual or had it compromised democracy by enabling the formation of monopolies and cartels, which President Franklin D. Roosevelt and others eventually came to see as hallmarks of a fascist political economy?[5] At the centre of this question was the issue of knowledge, especially its use. Publicised upon being granted, a patent disseminated technical knowledge that might otherwise have remained a trade secret. And yet, at the same time, the patent furnished its owner with the ability to restrict the use of knowledge contained in the patent. Anyone coming too close to competing with the patentee was vulnerable to an infringement suit, especially if the patentee was a corporation. The lone inventor, liable or not, stood little chance in court against some of the wealthiest, mightiest formations on earth.

For the most part, such formations were not supposed to exist under U.S. law. In 1890, Congress had passed the Sherman Antitrust Act. Taking aim at the monopolistic practices of large US-American corporations, the act nonetheless left the patent monopoly alone. Hence, starting in the 1890s, corporations and cartels resorted to patents as reliable instruments for creating monopolies. In acquiring masses of patents, corporations exerted monopolistic control over technologies

---

4 Thomas B. Whalen, *Complexity, Society and Social Transactions: Developing a Comprehensive Social Theory* (Abingdon, Oxon: Routledge, 2019), chap. 7 and 8; Anna Linda Musacchio Adorisio, "Organizational Remembering as Narrative: 'Storying' the Past in Banking," *Organization* 21 (2014): 466.
5 Tony A. Freyer, *Antitrust and Global Capitalism, 1930–2004* (Cambridge: Cambridge University Press, 2006), 22. Cf. B. Zorina Khan, *The Democratization of Invention: Patents and Copyrights in American Economic Development, 1790–1920* (Cambridge: Cambridge University Press, 2005), 106–27, 182–83.

and sectors by suing competitors for patent infringement. Corporate lawyers also found ways to extend patent monopolies by taking advantage of the Patent Office's slow administration and Patent Office rules that made it possible to extend the temporary monopoly from the standard 17 years to 44. Corporations and cartels for decades used these measures and the courts to crush independent inventors whose creations posed even the semblance of a threat.[6]

The onset of the Great Depression in 1929 added urgency to the discussion concerning these issues among inventors, economic planners, and consumer advocates. Critics argued that the monopolistic practices of corporations and cartels had hurt productivity and cost the economy jobs and growth, thus contributing to this latest and greatest economic disaster.[7] Anticompetitive practices also increased costs for consumers already struggling to afford necessities as the Great Depression wore on.[8] Nevertheless, during the first half of the Depression, President Franklin D. Roosevelt and his New Dealers tended to work with rather than against big business to try and stimulate economic growth.[9]

Overall economic conditions started to improve in the mid-1930s, despite some setbacks to Roosevelt and his administration, but the uptick was short-lived. As the recovery faltered in 1937, reformers blamed big business for hoarding profits instead of increasing wages and employment. Roosevelt, along with large segments of the US-American public, eventually turned his attention back to monopolies in 1938.[10] The result was the creation, at Roosevelt's insistence, of the Temporary National Economic Committee (TNEC), a congressional committee that would hear evidence, subpoena witnesses, carry out studies, and recommend changes, perhaps fundamental ones, to the rules of the game. The committee was composed of federal lawmakers and representatives from federal agencies (Justice, Treasury, Labor, Commerce, the Securities and Exchange Commission, and the Federal Trade Commission). As part of its work, the committee would conduct the farthest-reaching, deepest-delving investigation of the U.S. patent system to date. Newspapers referred to the TNEC as the "Monopoly Committee" and covered its activities in detail. A great deal of this coverage was negative about patents, the TNEC's first object of study.

---

6 Eric S. Hintz, *American Independent Inventors in an Era of Corporate R&D* (Cambridge, MA: MIT Press, 2021), 139–45.
7 Ellis W. Hawley, *The New Deal and the Problem of Monopoly: A Study in Economic Ambivalence* (Princeton: Princeton University Press, 1966), 12, 137; Stanley Lebergott, *Consumer Expenditures: New Measures and Old Motives* (Princeton: Princeton University Press, 1995), 9–21.
8 David Lynch, *The Concentration of Economic Power* (New York: Columbia University Press, 1946), 77, 243.
9 Hintz, *American Independent Inventors*, 145.
10 Hintz, *American Independent Inventors*, 146. Cf. Hawley, *New Deal*, 390–410.

Our study begins with a discussion on the historiography concerning the lone inventor versus big business. The next section covers the planning of the 1936 commemoration. The actual commemoration forms the subject of subsequent sections. The final sections consider the afterlife of the campaign in the TNEC's patent hearings of 1938–1939 and show how the 1936 propaganda push had laid the discursive groundwork for the triumph of the patent system over its detractors. A coda posits another campaign, the 1940 commemoration of the 1790 patent act, as the entrenchment of the counternarrative spun in 1936.

Lone Inventors Versus Big Business

Scholars have attended to the controversy around the TNEC's patent investigation in detail, as well as to the struggles, real and imagined, between lone inventors and corporations. In his recent book, Eric Hintz tracks these conflicts and myths over several decades. He shows that even though the national conversation pitted lone inventors against corporate R&D laboratories and that even though the pervasive assumption was that lone inventors were on the brink of annihilation, they nonetheless persisted. Although they lacked lasting professional organisations to combat the likes of NAM (National Association of Manufacturers), lone inventors did not disappear, nor was the line between lone inventor and corporate R&D as clear as people assumed. After all, corporations with R&D labs frequently purchased patents from lone inventors, thus suggesting a possible symbiotic relationship obscured by the more spectacularly rancorous one visible to contemporary observers.[11] We do not intend to recapitulate Hintz's work here. Rather, we aim to show how and why the issue of the lone inventor versus corporate R&D in the 1930s became a key site of mythmaking and storytelling for US-American champions of capitalism, under threat as it was in the interwar period and especially during the Great Depression. In our view, it is no accident that the TNEC investigations, intended to combat monopolistic practices throughout the economy, focused their first hearings on patents. Patents were at the heart of the problem of corporate capitalism: how it captured markets and the state to the detriment of individuals and their rights, both as inventors and as consumers.

We find in this story a rare, early instance of the establishment of a peacetime propaganda campaign. Our study thus contributes to the literature on antisocialist

---

[11] Hintz, *American Independent Inventors*, 4–5, 16–19; see also Tom Nicholas, "The Role of Independent Inventions in U.S. Technological Development, 1880–1930," *The Journal of Economic History* 70 (2010): 57–82.

propaganda and shows that even within the executive branch of the federal government, agency leaders such as Coe were able to sanction propaganda campaigns contradicting the priorities of the president himself, Roosevelt, whose New Deal, a series of expansive economic and social reforms intended to revive the U.S. economy, sought to curtail the excesses of corporate capitalism before it was too late.[12] We situate our argument along several lines of scholarship: the history of Depression-era efforts aimed at reforming the patent system, the role of myths in Depression-era political discourses in the United States, and the history and theory of public relations and propaganda, especially as they relate to narratives.

In 1950, historians Fritz Machlup and Edith Penrose accounted for the earliest significant controversy concerning patents, which occurred in Europe between 1850 and 1875. Liberal critics of the patent system called for its reform and even abolition on the basis that patents, as monopolies, were illiberal instruments that frustrated free trade. The resulting debates, which appeared in newspapers and magazines in Great Britain, France, German lands, Switzerland, and the Netherlands, resulted in studies, inquiries, and actions. In the Dutch case, the government eliminated its patent system. For the most part, however, patent systems remained intact.[13]

With regard to the United States, Larry Owens has attributed the staying power of the system to its associations with the pioneer and the frontier spirit. "The myth of the frontier was enormously elastic," he explains, "capable of being turned to a variety of ends," conservative and liberal. Owens shows that interlocutors at the TNEC hearings amplified these historical idioms, which naturally sprang from a discursive repertoire that was well-rehearsed by 1939.[14] Our article supplies a backstory to Owens's insights by uncovering the efforts of big business and the Patent Office to blitz the US-American public with stories associating the

---

12 On public relations, publicity, and propaganda in U.S. politics, culture, and society before World War II, see Inger L. Stole, *Advertising on Trial: Consumer Activism and Corporate Public Relations in the 1930s* (Urbana: University of Illinois Press, 2006); Kevin Stoker and Brad L. Rawlins, "The 'Light' of Publicity in the Progressive Era: From Searchlight to Flashlight," *Journalism History* 30 (2005): 177–83; J. Michael Sproule, "Authorship and Origins of the Seven Propaganda Devices: A Research Note," *Rhetoric & Public Affairs* 4 (2001): 135–36; Cayce Myers, "Reconsidering Propaganda in U.S. Public Relations History: An Analysis of Propaganda in the Popular Press, 1810–1918," *Public Relations Review* 41 (2015): 551–61; Burton St. John III, "Claiming Journalistic Truth: U.S. Press Guardedness toward Edward L. Bernays' Conception of the Minority Voice and the 'Corroding Acid' of Propaganda," *Journalism Studies* 10 (2009): 357; Karla K. Gower, "U.S. Corporate Public Relations in the Progressive Era," *Journal of Communication Management* 12 (2008): 307–11; see also Hintz, *American Independent Inventors*, 163, 293n72.
13 Fritz Machlup and Edith Penrose, "The Patent Controversy in the Nineteenth Century," *The Journal of Economic History* 10 (1950): 1–4, 21.
14 Owens, "Patents," 1089–93.

lone inventor with the heroic pioneer, quintessentially US-American, to better deflect attention from real lone inventors' precarious situation. Following Adrian Johns' *Piracy*, we focus on the tension in the patent system, set up to reward individual inventors while so frequently operating to their detriment.[15]

Planning the Commemoration

By 1936, the Patent Office had a long history of spectacular engagement with the public. In fact, the Patent Office's "National Gallery" had in the early 1840s become the country's first federally funded museum space. It housed patent models, exotic objects, and various relics of the American Revolution.[16] The Patent Office supplemented these offerings with a large-scale commemoration in 1891 to mark the hundredth anniversary (one-hundred-and-first, actually) of the Patent Act of 1790. Speeches to mark the occasion linked the U.S. patent system to the economic and political triumph of the US-American project.[17]

The 1936 celebration was to be no different in this respect: The occasion "must be recognised as belonging to the whole Nation and not merely those who attend," proclaimed the famous engineer and prolific patentee Charles F. Kettering, chief of the Research Division of the General Motors Corporation and the principal organiser of the commemoration.[18] In the spring of 1936, a National Committee had materialised at the last minute to plan the celebrations, created by Commissioner of Patents Conway Coe and the officials at the Department of Commerce.[19] (The Patent

---

15 Adrian Johns, *Piracy: The Intellectual Property Wars from Gutenberg to Gates* (Chicago: University of Chicago Press, 2009).
16 Antony Adler, "From the Pacific to the Patent Office: The U.S. Exploring Expedition and the Origins of America's First National Museum," *Journal of the History of Collections* 23 (2011): 49–74.
17 [National Committee on Centennial Celebration of the American Patent System] and United States Patent Office, *Proceeding and Addresses: Celebration of the Beginning of the Second Century of the American Patent System at Washington City, D.C., April 8, 9, 10, 1891* (Washington, DC: Gedney & Roberts, 1892), 21–23, https://doi.org/10.5479/sil.118606.39088002584530.
18 U.S. Department of Commerce, National Committee on the Centennial Celebration of the American Patent System, *Centennial Celebration of the American Patent System 1836–1936* (Washington, DC: Government Printing Office, 1937), 54, https://hdl.handle.net/2027/mdp.39015011417634 (hereafter: *Centennial Volume*); C. F. Kettering to Coe, letter of 27 August 1936, Folder 3, Box 163, (1925–1966), Records of the U.S. Patent and Trademark Office (Record Group 241), National Archives at College Park, College Park, MD (hereafter: Commissioner's Subject Files).
19 Commissioner of Patents Conway Coe to Assistant Secretary of Commerce Ernest G. Draper, memo of 25 March 1936, Folder 3, Box 163, Commissioner's Subject Files.

Office was and still is a bureau of the Department of Commerce.) On 4 May 1936, a representative of NAM, the interest group for big business, wrote to Commissioner Coe to ask for a role.[20] Other industrialists followed suit and Coe accepted the offer. A draft of a November 1936 press release by NAM on the upcoming commemoration dinner is clear with regard to the implications of the collaboration:

> "The widespread desire of manufacturers to cooperate whole-heartedly with Government for the benefit of this country as a whole will be symbolized by celebrations to be held in Washington and other large cities on November 23," C. M. Chester, President, National Association of Manufacturers and Chairman of General Foods Corporation, announced in New York City today. . . . "In the opinion of my associates in the manufacturing world, an additional significance of these Dinners is that they usher in an era of good feeling between industry and Government."[21]

The draft sits in Coe's files at the National Archives in College Park, Maryland. It was forwarded to him, via a secretary, from the Business Advisory Council of the Department of Commerce with the handwritten instruction: "Please show this to the Comm[issioner] on his return. Ask him if he will write a letter to Chester." Himself already a member of NAM's commemoration planning committee, Coe sent his thanks for such "unselfish labors."[22]

In the late summer of 1936, Coe's office and the office of the secretary of commerce had decided to schedule the dinner for sometime after the national elections in November "in order to assure a maximum amount of public interest and stage a worthwhile celebration." They also decided that only members "of the patent profession" (e.g., top patent attorneys and administrators), the "scientific world" (e.g., heads of R&D labs and presidents of professional associations), and "the industrial groups" (i.e., big business) were to be invited.[23] Only as an afterthought, months later, did Kettering, Coe, and the other organisers include lone inventors in the celebrations – as guests and honourees but not as co-planners.[24] The marginalisation of living lone inventors was curious in light of the 1836 Patent Act, the subject of the 1936 commemoration. This act had reformed the patent system by replacing the registration system with a pre-examination system. In-

---

20 Executive Vice President Robert Lund of Lambert Pharmaceutical Co., St. Louis, to Coe, letter of 4 May 1936, Folder 3, Box 163, Commissioner's Subject Files.
21 Press release ("Centennial Celebration of the American Patent System") of 13 November 1936, Commissioner's Subject Files.
22 Coe to Charles F. Kettering, letter of 28 November 1936, Folder 3, Box 163, Commissioner's Subject Files.
23 Planning document, ca. July 1936, Folder 3, Box 163, Commissioner's Subject Files.
24 Eric S. Hintz has found that inventors lacked "stable professional organizations" to match those of big business; see Hintz, *American Independent Inventors*, 134.

stead of issuing patents regardless of novelty, leaving the courts to hash things out later, the government would issue patents only for inventions it could judge to be novel.[25] Furthermore, the act introduced a commissioner of patents, a patent library, and patent examiners.[26] The effect of these reforms was to strengthen the patent as a form of intellectual property protection by assuring licensees and the courts that a U.S. patent constituted good evidence of bona fide novelty and utility. The impetus behind this transformation had been an individual inventor, Senator John Ruggles of Maine.

Reporters would share the proceedings with the wider public. The message to be broadcast placed "major emphasis on the opportunities to advance even more rapidly under this truly American [patent] system in future."[27] Organisers were going to try and present a positivistic continuity of innovation across the pre-industrial/industrial divide. Absent was any reference to the rise of large corporations with their capital-intensive R&D labs and formidable legal resources. Instead, as an official at the Department of Commerce put it to Coe, the "purpose of marking the anniversary" was to tell people that lone inventors, geniuses availing themselves of patents, had "ushered in the modern miracles of steel, electricity, radio, plastics, air and land transportation through their experiments . . . often struggling against the objections and opposition of their families, friends and business associates until eventual success brought acclaim and in some instances adequate monetary rewards."[28]

Thus began an effort to summon, largely from imagination, the historical examples most likely to deflect attention from the crisis of the US-American patent system and capitalism in the 1930s as people understood it: the victimisation of the lone economic actor by the consolidation of corporate forces.[29] The U.S. patent system and the Patent Office itself were deeply implicated in this process, according to critics, individual inventors, and even President Roosevelt himself.[30] Commissioner Coe, his colleagues at the Department of Commerce, and the industrialists who bankrolled the 1936 celebrations were all on the defensive that year, using a centennial celebration to tell a different, more benign story.

---

25 Pre-examination to determine novelty had been in practice before, from 1790 to 1793, and was then replaced with a registration system.
26 Patent Act of 1836, Ch. 357, Stat. 117 (4 July 1836).
27 Planning document, ca. July 1936, Folder 3, Box 163, Commissioner's Subject Files.
28 Draft of a press release forwarded from Commerce to Coe, 24 October 1936, with a handwritten note reading, "Mr. Commissioner: This story at least serves the purpose of marking the anniversary. Cordially, [illeg.]," Folder 3, Box 163, Commissioner's Subject Files (emphasis in the original).
29 Hintz, *American Independent Inventors*, 9, 137–45.
30 Hintz, *American Independent Inventors*, 137–39.

Commemoration as Propaganda

Propaganda is not the typical term used for the public affairs activities of U.S. government agencies in peacetime, but it is the appropriate term in this case for two reasons.[31] First, we need this term for its descriptive precision as we are studying a state agency colluding with an interest group to launch a PR blitz in an effort to fend off critics and forestall reform. Second, we need it for the context it imparts: In the mid-1930s, in the United States as elsewhere, propaganda was a widespread topic of discussion and debate in the face of the proliferation of authoritarian regimes and their techniques of mass persuasion.[32]

The U.S. Institute for Propaganda Analysis in the November 1937 issue of its magazine published a guide to help people recognise propaganda when they saw it. The guide identified several attributes of propaganda, most of which applied to the patent PR blitz of 1936: (1) *name-calling*: "communist," "fascist"; (2) so-called *glittering generalities*, "virtue words" such as "freedom," "liberty," "democracy," "progress," and the "American way"; (3) *transfer*, whereby "the propagandist" (such as NAM) "carries over the authority, sanction, and prestige of something we respect and revere" (such as the U.S. Patent Office); (4) *testimonial*, where the propagandist speaks through a respected individual (such as Commissioner Coe); (5) *plain folk*, where the propagandist identifies itself with ordinary Americans (e.g., the lone inventor); (6) *card stacking*, "distortions and omissions" that communicate "half-truths"; and, finally, (7) *band wagon*, appeals to ties of "nation, religion, race, sex, or occupation."[33] Through and together with the Patent Office, NAM tried all these moves in the 1936 celebrations, which served as a dress rehearsal for a successful performance at the TNEC hearings of 1938–1939.[34]

In the case of the Patent Office in 1936, the source of the propaganda was somewhat obscured. Coe let big business hide behind the prestige and authority of his office, setting a precedent and proving to big business that it had a winning strategy: Whenever possible, speak through the state rather than at it, using its reach and authority to capture the attention of the masses, change their perceptions, and

---

31 Machlup and Penrose identify concerted efforts in Europe between 1867 and 1877 to counter critiques of the patent system with propaganda in "Patent Controversy," 5–6.
32 Sarah Ellen Graham, *Culture and Propaganda: The Progressive Origins of American Public Diplomacy, 1936–1953* (Burlington, VT: Ashgate, 2015), 7–8; Timothy Glander, *Origins of Mass Communications Research during the American Cold War: Educational Effects and Contemporary Implications* (Mahwah, NJ: Lawrence Earlbaum, 2000), 3.
33 Sproule, "Authorship," 135–36.
34 New Dealers produced their own propaganda; see Schivelbusch, *Three New Deals*, 78–80.

effect a favourable policy outcome.³⁵ The Patent Office celebrations became an additional, more insidious way for NAM to open a new front in opposition to Roosevelt's reforms. Having already attacked policies related to industrial development and labour unions, they now targeted patent reform.³⁶

Orations

The commemoration began on the morning of 23 November 1936 with a symposium in the auditorium of the National Academy of Sciences and the National Research Council in Washington, D.C., and continued with an afternoon ceremony at the Department of Commerce auditorium. This was followed by the Research Parade, an "experimental presentation" by the Science Service, a science advocacy and education organisation. This spectacle combined motion pictures and radio with a stage presentation on the benefits to industry of scientific research. Across the country, local associations of patent lawyers and engineers could follow the celebrations on the radio, and more than thirty museums and libraries countrywide participated in the celebration with special exhibitions on the importance of the patent system. Back in Washington, the public attended film screenings and a special exhibition on rare books and manuscripts related to patent history.³⁷

The morning addresses at the National Academy of Sciences made it clear that the independent inventor and the Patent Office were part of a master narrative, a story, established through repetition, reflecting society's morals and concerns – the master narrative of the American Dream, available in nearly every political context in the United States.³⁸ Just as free land and the free market had given frontiersmen the chance to profit from their toil, so did patents, and the market in licenses gave inventors the chance to profit from their individual ingenuity. For the inventors and the frontiersmen alike, private property and capitalism created the right conditions for upward social mobility. This notion, that

---

35 The decades before and after the 1930s were crucial for the development of corporate PR strategy and machinery. See Richard S. Tedlow, *Keeping the Corporate Image: Public Relations and Business, 1900–1950* (Greenwich, CT: JAI Press, 1979); Roland Marchand, *Creating the Corporate Soul: The Rise of Public Relations and Corporate Imagery in American Big Business* (Berkeley: University of California Press, 1998).
36 Hintz, *American Independent Inventors*, 163.
37 *Centennial Volume*, 63–66.
38 H. Porter Abbott, *The Cambridge Introduction to Narrative*, 3rd ed. (Cambridge: Cambridge University Press, 2021), 52–53; Lawrence R. Samuel, *The American Dream: A Cultural History* (Syracuse, NY: Syracuse University Press, 2012), 13.

anyone could invent and make money on an invention by patenting it, became an important feature in the Patent Office's narrative as well as in the narrative of US-American innovation more generally.³⁹

All morning speakers at the centennial celebration touted individualism. Dexter S. Kimball, dean of the College of Engineering at Cornell University, in his speech declared that "invention is distinctly personal in character."⁴⁰ Progress is made by individuals, he asserted, not the masses, which is why the inventor must have freedom from "restrictive influences" such as the state, church, professional association, and trade union. These institutions were the strawmen in Kimball's argument. In fact, they posed little demonstrable threat to the lone inventor, who faced a different set of adversaries: the corporations with their R&D laboratories and their patent pools, agreements between corporations to share patents among each other, which amounted to cartels. But these received no mention.

Instead, in a previous speech, former Commissioner of Patents Thomas Ewing had spoken of authoritarianism and asserted that nothing good could come of a "dictator" ordering inventions to appear. Rather, inventions resulted from patient experimentation and careful consideration of extant knowledge. Acknowledging the threat to lone inventors posed by merchants, manufacturers, and consumers who resisted new technologies, Ewing asserted that "the democratic patent system" was the only rescue. It offered the chance for individuals to transform their ideas into capital. Through talent and the patent system alone, inventors "starting without friends or money, have raised themselves in the social scale," he claimed, and suggested that this was still the case in the 1930s.⁴¹

Something haunting these assertions and distortions was the spectre of Europe, its past and present. As the antidote to early modern despotism, for example, Ewing and the other speakers conjured the U.S. patent system, which had defeated the guilds and kings and honours and favours that had so impeded the natural progression of technology. But again, the argument went, under Europe's authoritarian regimes, with their central committees (the Soviet Union) and anti-competitive industrial formations (Fascist Italy and Nazi Germany), the situation

---

39 See Wyn Wachhorst, *Thomas Alva Edison: An American Myth* (Cambridge, MA: MIT Press, 1981); Paul Israel, "Inventing Industrial Research: Thomas Edison and the Menlo Park Laboratory," *Endeavour* 26 (2002): 48–50; William Greenleaf, *Monopoly on Wheels: Henry Ford and the Selden Automobile Patent* (Detroit: Wayne State University Press, 2011); Thomas P. Hughes, *Human-Built World: How to Think about Technology and Culture* (Chicago: University of Chicago Press, 2004), 6.
40 *Centennial Volume*, 19.
41 *Centennial Volume*, 9.

had become perilous.⁴² Real and imagined, Europe's example obsessed the celebration and served to divert attention from discussions on the vulnerability of lone inventors to abuses of *American* corporations of the *American* patent system.⁴³ Instead, when America was mentioned at all, it was as a dreamworld of entirely self-made inventors availing themselves of protections from a quintessentially democratic institution, the U.S. Patent Office.

For this story to work, speakers had to minimise the conflict between the lone inventor and corporate innovation. Hence, only one speaker, Robert E. Wilson, vice chairman of the Pan American Petroleum and Transport company, addressed the issue head-on, albeit from the perspective of big business. The lone inventor was all but finished, he declared, because as technologies became more complicated, the chances of a lone inventor improving upon them diminished.⁴⁴ Wilson neglected to mention corporations' using the patent system to crush lone inventors whose patents posed a threat, nor did he seem to realise the implications of his assertion on the validity of the grander narrative at work in the 1936 celebrations. Whither the American Dream in an America lacking space for maximum individual ingenuity?⁴⁵

Ewing and other speakers did acknowledge that the system had become the subject of some controversy, attracting criticism from "every class of people who give it any attention":

> Many object because of the monopolistic character of the grants; many that it throws people out of employment; some manufacturers claim that it operates to the disorganization of their business; inventors, that they cannot find a market for the product of their labors; investors tell of grievous losses; the public complains of high prices and the suppression⁴⁶ of useful inventions; and the expense and burden of litigation is all but intolerable.⁴⁷

Ewing proceeded to dismiss each criticism directly, except for the last, with reference to Western history stretching back to the Greeks. And without quite addressing the issue of costly litigation, he marshalled Social Darwinist logic to the defence of a patent system that pitted the weak against the strong for the sake of technological and economic progress: "Invention is subject to all the difficulties

---

42 *Centennial Volume*, 12.
43 On this discussion, see Hintz, *American Independent Inventors*, 138.
44 *Centennial Volume*, 20.
45 See Samuel, *American Dream*, 13ff.
46 Patent suppression, as difficult to define in the 1930s as it is in the 2020s, referred to an attempt to stop a patented invention from coming to market. A firm might, for example, buy the patents for a competing firm's technology to ensure that it never be licensed for production, or the firm might rush to patent a competing technology first, only to keep it from the market for as long as possible. See Alexander Morrow, "The Suppression of Patents," *The American Scholar* 14 (1945): 210.
47 *Centennial Volume*, 6.

inherent in evolutionary processes," the "destruction of enormous numbers of individuals to the advantage of the few fitted to survive." The process "may be altered by public policy, but the fundamental character of the evolution is not controlled thereby."[48]

The solutions offered by Ewing were fundamentally conservative: only tiny changes, if any. If adjustments to the laws were to be made, he urged that they be made with respect for the system's long history and an awareness of its inherent flexibility. Lawmakers should not be allowed to forget "that 2 million patents have been granted under our statute and that on the whole, it has worked fairly well."[49] After all, he claimed, in all these years, the patent system had "never been a subject of political controversy extensive enough to affect its development."[50]

In fact, controversy has shaped patent law and Patent Office practices since the mid-nineteenth century, when a transnational "patent controversy" broke out. Popular critiques, mostly focused on the difficulty of attaining patents and the use of patents as barriers to enterprise, resulted in the Netherlands abolishing its patent system in 1869 and the United Kingdom lowering its application fee in 1883.[51] In Sweden after 1891, insufficient staffing and overly long waiting times at the patent office attracted constant scrutiny by the press and a series of investigations by the state.[52] And just like its US-American counterpart, the Swedish Patent and Registration Office (PRV) learned to use commemorations for its counternarratives. In order to spin a story about the agency's efficiency and accountability on the occasion of its fiftieth anniversary in 1941, the PRV displayed patents, uniforms, a desk, and a mural of the application process as part of an exhibition at the National Museum of Science and Technology.[53] The lone inventor figured, too, as a beneficiary of a democratic patent system.[54]

---

48 *Centennial Volume*, 6–7. On the treatment of terms such as "economic progress" and "evolution" in Ewing's milieu, see George E. Roberts, ed., *Economics for Executives*, vol. 23, *Economic Progress* (New York: American Chamber of Economics, 1923), 7–11.
49 *Centennial Volume*, 11.
50 *Centennial Volume*, 7.
51 On international exhibitions as an essential aspect of the patent debates, see Megan Richardson and Julian Thomas, *Fashioning Intellectual Property: Exhibition, Advertising and the Press 1789–1918* (Cambridge: Cambridge University Press, 2012), 53–86. On reform and abolition, see Machlup and Penrose, "Patent Controversy," 3, 5.
52 See Nils Avelius, *Patentverket från gamla tider till nu, 1885–1967/68* (Stockholm: Patentverkets tjänstemannasällskap, 1969), 84.
53 Strömstedt, "Patent Office on Display," 1–2, 107–46.
54 Strömstedt, "Patent Office on Display," 131–41.

The U.S. system and its administration had come under official or quasi-official investigation in the living memory of the 1936 speakers, in 1912, 1919, 1926, and 1935.[55] The 1935 investigation, and each of the twentieth-century investigations before it, had in some part been animated by worries over whether the patent system was failing lone inventors, the people it had been designed to protect, and by extension the nation, the beneficiary of the lone inventor's genius.

Pomp and Circumstance

In the afternoon, the Patent Office Society, the professional association of examiners, held its ceremony at the Department of Commerce auditorium and bestowed its gift to the Patent Office, a bust of Thomas Jefferson.[56] Patent Office lore positioned Jefferson as the country's very first patent examiner.[57] In accepting the bust, Commissioner Coe praised Jefferson for his role in building US-American democracy as well. Coe then argued that industrial progress would safeguard Jefferson's legacy by establishing a foundation of prosperity to support the independence of the nation and the liberties of its citizens. A crucial element of this prosperity, he went on to say, was the patent system. By incentivising innovation and, in turn, improving the material living conditions for US-Americans, the patent system helped "maintain and preserve our nationhood against successful attacks from without and from the causes of internal revolution."[58]

The next event in the programme was the Research Parade, which according to the event report was an experimental presentation combining film, music, and stagecraft technologies to demonstrate "scientific and technical principles and achievements which have not yet materialized into industrial applications."[59] The show transported viewers to the Patent Office of the 1840s with a presentation by an actor playing Commissioner of Patents Henry Leavitt Ellsworth and then returned them to the present with demonstrations by representatives from the titans of US-American industry and scientific research: General Electric, Westinghouse Electric, RCA Manufacturing Company, Scott

---

55 "Review of the Investigations of the Patent System and the Patent Office," a confidential report produced for the Commissioner of Patents, ca. 1941, Commissioner's Subject Files.
56 *Centennial Volume*, 29–30.
57 Robert M. S. McDonald, *Light and Liberty: Thomas Jefferson and the Power of Knowledge* (Charlottesville: University of Virginia Press, 2012), 59.
58 *Centennial Volume*, 30.
59 "Centennial Celebration of the American Patent System," *Science* 84:2183 (30 October 1936): 385.

Radio Laboratories, the Smithsonian Institution, and Johns Hopkins University[60]. These large institutions and corporations were the heroes of the Research Parade. In this way, the Research Parade foreshadowed the focus of the celebration dinner that evening.

The dinner took place at the splendid Mayflower Hotel. Kettering, the head of the commemoration committee, served as toastmaster. The programme for the evening, formatted as a patent, began with dense, mock-technical language about the festivities and ended, just as a patent does, in a series of claims that happened to establish the order of events.[61] The tables were decorated with patented flowers (plant patents became available in 1930). As dinner theatre, the organisers treated guests to a series of dramatisations, demonstrations, and stunts. The *Washington Herald* described the experience almost as an assault on the senses: "Lamps more powerful than tropical sunlight, sounds so loud they hurt the ear drums, edible plates and 'fresh' [flash-frozen] foods, prepared months ago."[62] A crystal ball made of patented compounds was supposed to foretell the future, and a voice recording of Thomas A. Edison came through a phonograph as a technological link to the past.[63]

This dinner for more than 1,000 guests, very few of whom were inventors, barred women from entry and excluded their stories from the presentations. The event thus excluded women inventors, patent agents, attorneys, and examiners, as well as the wives of the men attending.[64] This was "a strictly stag affair," as journalist Jane Eads called it. Marie K. Saunders, president of the Women's Patent Law Association, had told Eads that "we were not at all surprised, of course. But frankly we are tired of having men think women never invent anything that amounts to a row of pins."[65] Suffragists had used women's patents to refute the aspersions regarding women's capacity for invention, but the masculinist fantasy of women's inability persisted even after women gained the vote.[66] The stag dinner at the Mayflower reflected this fantasy. Indeed, even as the notion of women

---

[60] *Centennial Volume*, 32.
[61] Patent dinner programme, "One Hundredth Anniversary of the Present Patent System (1936)," Folder 3, Box 163, Commissioner's Subject Files.
[62] "Inventors Eat Patents Here, Plate and All," *Washington Herald*, 24 November 1936.
[63] "Inventors Eat Patents Here"; Watson Davis, "Centennial Celebration of the American Patent System," *The Scientific Monthly* 44, no. 1 (1937): 100.
[64] Henry D. Williams to Coe, letter of 12 November 1936, Folder 3, Box 163, Commissioner's Subject Files; secretary to the commissioner to Williams, letter of 14 November 1936, Folder 3, Box 163, Commissioner's Subject Files.
[65] Jane Eads, "Women Inventors Hit Patent 'Stag' Dinner," *Washington Herald*, 13 November 1936.
[66] See Ruth Oldenziel, *Making Technology Masculine: Men, Women, and Modern Machines in America, 1870–1945* (Amsterdam: Amsterdam University Press, 2004); Kara Swanson, "Inventing the Woman Voter: Suffrage, Ability and Patents," *The Journal of the Gilded Age and Progressive Era* 19 (2020): 559–74.

inventors gained broad public acceptance, the inventions themselves were presented as mundane—useful only on the woman's side of the gendered division of labour.[67]

The stag night ended as it began, with speeches honouring the lone inventor and his timeless genius while turning a blind eye to the conditions of 1936, when the machinations of cartels and their monopolies based on intellectual property increasingly alienated lone inventors from the patent system and the fruits of their creativity. The failure to attend to the serious critiques of the patent system – namely, that it might be enabling monopolies, which, in turn, laid waste to the US-American economy and civilisation, to say nothing of the fortunes of individual inventors – set a precedent and reflected the key purpose of the event: to tell a compelling, if invalid, story about the patent system's championing of the interests of lone inventors rather than large corporations.[68]

With breathless commentary, the most spectacular parts of the evening reached the nation via radio thanks to NBC (National Broadcasting Company). "I have standing back of me four drummers of the United States Army Band," an announcer said, and "as they sound the drum rolls the Voice of Progress, speaking from the Eastern Air Line transport plane high above Washington, will reveal the names" of a secular pantheon of US-American inventors: Alexander Graham Bell, Thomas Edison, Charles Goodyear, Charles Martin Hall, Elias Howe, Cyrus Hall McCormick, Samuel Morse, George Westinghouse, Wilbur and Orville Wright, Eli Whitney, Robert Fulton, and Ottmar Mergenthaler. This was followed by "drums, trumpeters, prolonged fanfare." Several fanfares later, the programme ended with Kettering, "now gazing intently into a synthetic crystal ball" and delivering his final prophesy and benediction: "Human courage, with human faith, and the proper degree of humility knows no end and the boundless future is our territory in which we may work."[69]

Five days later, primetime on the evening of 28 November 1936, the Columbia Workshop Program, an anthology series by CBS (Columbia Broadcasting System), broadcast its own half-hour auditory pageant. Global in scope, the episode flitted from location to location, century to century, inventor to inventor. Its narrator, unlike the Voice of Progress on NBC, made obvious political claims at the outset. "It is significant," he asserted, "that while democratic government is on trial among

---

67 Swanson, "Inventing the Woman Voter," 564.
68 Draft of a press release forwarded from Commerce to Coe, 24 October 1936, with a handwritten note reading, "Mr. Commissioner: This story [of America's greatest lone inventors] at least serves the purpose of marking the anniversary" (emphasis in the original).
69 *Centennial Volume*, 63–64.

other nations of the world, they move to the measure of American genius."[70] By now, the message would have been familiar to many Americans: that the United States, and indeed the world, owed its progress and security to the U.S. patent system. That system, like the democratic system it supported, must be celebrated and, soon enough, defended.

Investigation

The following year (1937), when economic conditions once again deteriorated, President Roosevelt and the New Dealers looked anew at the economic structures that might be impeding growth. Among other things, they were drawn to the patent system. Did the patent monopoly incur social costs that were too high? Did corporations' use of the patent system produce a chilling effect? In the wrong hands, was this system stopping people from using new technical knowledge towards positive economic ends?[71] These questions were sufficiently pressing that when Congress in 1938 formed the TNEC at Roosevelt's insistence, its leaders chose to investigate the patent system before any of the other species of monopoly under consideration.

Coe and his staff prepared evidence and testimony in the summer and autumn of 1938. From within the Patent Office, they gathered information about independent inventors, corporate innovation, and cases of interference (when two or more patent applicants had claims that were too close to each other, so some determination of priority had to be made). Coe's staff also sought information outside the Patent Office. A draft letter of October 1938 to General Electric, for example, asked the corporation to confirm that it possessed between 8,000 and 9,000 unexpired patents.[72] Nearing the winter of 1938 and the TNEC hearings on patents, Patent Office staff collated the data, wrote their reports, and built their case for modest, not sweeping, reform.

Coe and the Department of Commerce were under pressure from their stakeholders to keep the patent system largely unaltered. The TNEC and the Department of Commerce had forwarded Coe a great deal of correspondence from industrialists, patent attorneys, and small-business owners. Most of these letters came as the TNEC's patent hearings were getting underway, just before Coe was to testify, and urged restraint: Keep the patent system fundamentally the same, but make a few

---

70 *Centennial Volume*, 68. The first U.S. patent act was passed in 1790.
71 Hintz, *American Independent Inventors*, 138–39.
72 H. H. Jacobs, Examiner of Interferences, to Justin W. Macklin, First Assistant Commissioner, letter of 9 September 1938, Folder 1, Box 171, Commissioner's Subject Files.

new rules.⁷³ Indeed, Coe and his colleagues at the Patent Office were working in an echo chamber, where arguments for restraint resounded, drowning out outsiders' pleas for a radical curtailment of the patent monopoly right.

In Coe's testimony in January 1939, the heroic lone inventors of 1936 were nowhere to be found. Instead, Coe presented the facts about corporations' increasing control over the patent system and the resulting "displace[ment]" of independent inventors.⁷⁴ The gravity of the problem notwithstanding, Coe insisted on subtle reform. As his recommendations and reasoning made their way to the national press, there was an increase in letters sent directly to the Patent Office. Most of these came from patent attorneys and heads of corporate R&D. They were all congratulatory.⁷⁵ Many touted the positive effects of patents on the U.S. economy and ignored the pitfalls.

The letter from Barton A. Bean Jr. of Bean, Brooks, Buckley & Bean, a patent law firm, is representative. Where the detractors of the patent system saw patented machinery as eliminating jobs, Bean saw that same machinery "enable[ing] our workmen to earn in one hour in usable commodities and goods what it takes workmen in other parts of the world, for example in Russia, up to twenty-six and one-half hours to earn." Without patents, he went on, industrialisation would grind to a halt and everyone would be plunged into a communist misery of incorrigible want (as if this scourge did not obtain in the United States of the 1930s).⁷⁶ Appealing to the fear of communism made sense in the context of the "little" red scares breaking out across the country – less famous than the "big" red scares of

---

73 [James] Alvan Macauley [Sr.], President of Packard Motor Car Co., to Senator Joseph C. O'Mahoney, Chairman, TNEC, letter of 30 December 1938, Folder 3, Box 171, Commissioner's Subject Files. In Folder 3 ("Letters Referred from T.N.E.C. – Special 50"), Box 170, Commissioner's Subject Files: John M. Spellman to Hatton W. Summers, Monopoly Investigating Committee (TNEC), letter of 14 December 1938; J. P. Hubbell to O'Mahoney, letter of 7 December 1938; Harry Pennington to Summers, letter of 15 December 1938; W. P. Deppé to O'Mahoney, letter of 29 December 1938.
74 Owens, "Patents," 1081.
75 In Folder 4, Box 170, Commissioner's Subject Files: George E. Kirk to Coe, letter of 18 January 1939; H. Sherbak to Coe, letter of 19 January 1939; Thomas Griswold Jr. (Dow Chemical Company) to Coe, letter of 19 January 1939; Harry Knight to Coe, letter of 20 January 1939; Henry W. Carter (Owens-Illinois Glass Company) to Coe, letter of 20 January 1939; Milton Tibbetts (Packard Motor Car Company) to Coe, letter of 2 January 1939; Hector M. Holmes to Coe, letter of 24 January 1939; E. G. Ackerman (Glass Container Association of America) to Coe, letter of 25 January 1939; Philip S. Hopkins to Coe, letter of 25 January 1939; Joseph L. Baldwin (Association of American Railroads) to Coe, letter of 27 January 1939; Edward G. Wood to Coe, letter of 27 January 1939; Henry H. Snelling to Coe, letter of 27 January 1939; George H. Houston (NAM) to Coe, letter of 30 January 1939.
76 Barton A. Bean Jr. (Bean, Brooks, Buckley & Bean Patent Counsel) to Coe, letter of 16 January 1939, Folder 4, Box 170, Commissioner's Subject Files.

the 1920s and 1940s–1950s but more pervasive.[77] Rather than a revolutionary transformation, Bean believed, better enforcement of the existing antitrust laws would be enough to curb the excesses of capitalism and the patent system. Others recommended small changes along lines already presented by Coe to tip the balance in favour of lone inventors.[78] Almost everyone opposed the radical option of compulsory licensing, a change that would have compelled patent owners to license their patents to any entity willing to pay a reasonable royalty set by the government.[79] In this way, the government would have control of the patent monopolies it granted. A corporation would no longer be able to patent, or acquire patents for, a technology only to suppress or delay it because its existence on the market might threaten profitability.

The argument for compulsory licensing revolved around the issue of knowledge and the use of knowledge for the benefit of society. Letters to the TNEC had made that link, but none more clearly than the appeal of H. L. Prestholdt, president of a local business in Minneapolis called Monite Waterproof Glue Co.:

> I believe that if the amount of knowledge and information that is now held in the Patent Office, the use of same now denied the general public, was made available . . . it would be of tremendous value and offer a solution to our numerous problems in business and industry and would open up a broad avenue toward true recovery.[80]

By barring the public from using the knowledge contained in unexpired patents, Prestholdt suggested, the Patent Office and patent system were prolonging the Great Depression. His views, like the views of many others in the United States, anticipated the TNEC's conclusions.

The TNEC released its final report on 31 March 1941. It was damning. "No one can read the testimony developed before this committee on patents," it charged,

---

77 Robert J. Goldstein, ed., *Little "Red Scares": Anti-Communism and Political Repression in the United States, 1921–1946* (London: Routledge, 2016), xv; in the same volume, see M. J. Heale, "Citizens Versus Outsiders: Anti-Communism at State and Local Levels," 45–70; and Timothy Reese Cain, "Little Red Schoolhouses? Anti-Communists and Education in an 'Age of Conflicts,'" 105–34.

78 In Folder 4, Box 170, Commissioner's Subject Files: Henry D. Williams to Coe, letter of 2 March 1939; Miller Reese Hutchison to Coe, letter of 16 January 1939; Magnus Björndal to Coe, letter of 19 January 1939; Crosby Field to Coe, letter of 22 January 1939; Henry H. Snelling to Coe, letter of 27 January 1939; Edward G. Wood to Coe, letter of 27 January 1939.

79 Jerome H. Reichman, "Non-Voluntary Licensing of Patented Inventions," *Intellectual Property Rights and Sustainable Development*, a publication of the UNCTAD-ICTSD Project on IPRs and Sustainable Development (June 2003), 1; cf. Paris Convention for Industrial Property, 20 March 1883, rev. Stockholm, 14 July 1967, 25 Stat. 1372, 828 U.N.T.S. 305.

80 H. L. Prestholdt to Leon Henderson, Executive Secretary, TNEC, letter of 25 March 1939, forwarded to Coe, in Folder 3, Box 170, Commissioner's Subject Files.

"without coming to a realization that in many important segments of our economy the privilege accorded by the patent monopoly has been shamefully abused." The use of the word "privilege" here served as a shot across the Patent Office bow, a refusal at the outset even to entertain the possibility that there existed a patent *right*. But the TNEC never got to pull its trigger. Having depended on press coverage for its influence in Congress, the TNEC lost this influence over the course of 1941. The possible U.S. entry into World War II loomed large on front pages right down to 7 December, the attack on Pearl Harbor. The patent system stayed largely the same. The turning point did not turn.

Coda: 1940–1941

In April 1940, for the one-hundred-fiftieth anniversary of the very first U.S. patent act (1790), Coe, Kettering, and NAM teamed up again. Centred in Washington but taking place nationwide, the celebration featured dinners, radio programmes, exhibitions, publications, and a day of speeches praising the patent system.[81] The lone inventor figured once again, but more as an artifact of US-American history, alongside the patriots of the Revolutionary era, the surveyors of the early Republic, and the pioneers of the mid-nineteenth century – important but largely obsolete.[82] Now, speakers more readily acknowledged the ascent of R&D laboratories, which were now given a positive spin. R&D laboratories, the new argument went, stood alongside the patent system as crucial agents of knowledge circulation. Speakers praised R&D laboratories for focusing streams of corporate capital into channels of research that was fundamental to US-American progress, followed by licensing or manufacturing inventions for the good of everyone. When Coe spoke later that day, it was to emphasise how the patent system, by collecting and distributing technical knowledge, had "established a lasting treasury of the most precious of all human products, that is to say, useful conceptions."[83] Sidestepping the issue of abuses of the patent monopoly, Coe insisted that the patent system

---

81 "Patent Office Report for 1940," *Journal of the Patent Office Society* 22 (1940): 3; *United States Patent Law Sesquicentennial Celebration: A Record of the Proceedings Commemorating the One Hundred and Fiftieth Anniversary of the Signing of the First United States Patent Law* (Washington, DC: Government Printing Office, 1941), (hereafter: *Sesquicentennial Volume*).
82 *Sesquicentennial Volume*, 7, 16; Hughes, *Human-Built World*, 6.
83 *Sesquicentennial Volume*, 16. On earlier, alternative notions of intellectual property, see Stuart Banner, *American Property: A History of How, Why, and What We Own* (Cambridge, MA: Harvard University Press, 2011), 23–28.

worked to benefit everyone since patent specifications and illustrations eventually became public goods.[84]

NAM, for its part, decided to honour some of America's most celebrated inventors and research scientists with Modern Pioneer awards in February 1941. The campaign fit neatly into a communications strategy developed by NAM in the 1930s. The objective was to get US-Americans to associate innovation and the patent system with an US-American ideology of individualism – even as NAM continued to fight individual inventors on all possible fronts.[85]

Conclusion

In the context of the national debate on patents that led to a congressional investigation, the 1936 commemorations became a key site of US-American mythmaking, where government officials helped disseminate stories about the heroism of individual US-American inventors. In doing so, these officials assisted big business in its slow-motion takeover of the system. Why did Coe and other officials agree to this? Did they believe in the messaging? How important was their vested interest in the maintenance of the patent system? The answers must be speculative. Coe and his associates were not inventors. They were members of the community of patent attorneys and agents. In many cases, after their tenures in public service were over, they returned to that community. And by the 1930s, more and more of the community's lifeblood issued from corporations, not lone inventors. Under these conditions, the commissioner of patents himself resorted to a series of public relations campaigns using the figure of the heroic lone inventor to obscure the unpopular reality that the system was increasingly favouring corporations.

A recent article by Hyo Yoon Kang (2023) addresses the staying power of what we argue is deflective propaganda, such as the "zany patents" publicised by patent offices on their social media accounts, which associate the patent, an otherwise serious and dry legal document, with playfulness and even inanity.[86] The ploys come and go according to trends and engagement metrics. But the 1936 deflection lives on: the image of the lone inventor, the elaboration of his story, and the combination of

---

[84] The Patent Office published (and the U.S. Patent and Trademark Office still publishes) patents upon being granted. The specifications and illustrations were accessible to all, either by request (for a nominal fee) or in the Patent Office's research facility (free). Several libraries across the United States also collected and made available specifications and illustrations.

[85] Hintz, *American Independent Inventors*, 163–67.

[86] Hyo Yoon Kang, "Patents as Capitalist Aesthetic Forms," *Law Critique* (2023), https://doi.org/10.1007/s10978-023-09349-2.

similar stories into a master narrative of US-American progress. The U.S. Patent and Trademark Office (USPTO) continues to foreground the lone inventor in its *Journeys of Innovation* series, monthly stories at the top of the agency's homepage emphasising the link between individual ingenuity and U.S. patents. The USPTO also funds a private museum, the National Inventors Hall of Fame (NIHF), whose very name and exhibitions do the same.[87] NIHF's summer programming reaches some 250,000 children in the United States each year.[88]

About the Contributors

Adam Bisno is an independent scholar in Stockholm. He is the author of *Big Business and the Crisis of German Democracy: Liberalism and the Grand Hotels of Berlin, 1875–1933* (Cambridge University Press, 2024), a case study in the failure of German liberalism. From the vantage of grand hotels, the book also accounts for the ironies in liberal ideology that made it no match for the fascist onslaught. Between 2020 and 2022, Bisno served as the official historian of the U.S. Patent and Trademark Office.

Isabelle Strömstedt is a lecturer at the Department of Science and Technology, Linköping University. Her research focuses on narratology, communication, visual culture, and popular culture. Strömstedt's dissertation was published in 2023 and is a microhistorical study of the Swedish Intellectual Property Office's fiftieth anniversary in 1941. The dissertation examines how the patent office presented itself to the public by positioning itself in master narratives of the independent inventor and Swedish inventiveness but also established a narrative of the patent office as effective and bureaucratic.

---

87 "Journeys of Innovation," Office of the Chief Communications Officer, United States Patent and Trademark Office, accessed 15 January 2024, https://www.uspto.gov/learning-and-resources/journeys-innovation.

88 "USPTO and National Inventors Hall of Fame Programs," Office of the Chief Communications Officer, United States Patent and Trademark Office, last modified 23 December 2022, https://www.uspto.gov/learning-and-resources/ip-programs-and-awards/uspto-and-national-inventors-hall-fame-programs.

Rasmus Fleischer
Pathologizing the Economy: "Baumol's Cost Disease" and the Circulation of Economic Knowledge in Sweden

Abstract: "Baumol's cost disease" (BCD) is a famous concept in economics, highlighting the reason why personal services tend to become less affordable over time. This article traces the circulation of the notion of BCD in Sweden from 1968 to 1991, showing how this simple piece of economic knowledge was translated into vastly different political agendas. Three such agendas are identified: redistribution, austerity and degrowth. In the context of cultural policy, BCD was seen as justifying public subsidies to the arts. However, for liberal critics of the Swedish welfare state, BCD proved the historical necessity of limiting the responsibilities of the public sector. In an alternative reading, it was used as an argument for degrowth and for a reduction in working hours. The circulation of BCD in the public sphere highlights the importance of rhetoric to economics and in particular the appeal of the medical metaphor of "disease" as key for articulating a sense of social or cultural crisis.

Keywords: cultural policy, degrowth, economic knowledge, economic metaphors, unbalanced growth, welfare state

1 Introduction

In the late 1960s, a hypothesis was developed by a prominent economist. Unlike much of the increasingly mathematized work in this discipline, however, this was a hypothesis simple enough for anyone to understand. The argument centered around the story of a string quartet, highlighting how it needs a certain amount of time to perform a certain piece of classical music. It would not make sense for the musicians to play faster, nor is the quartet able to reduce its workforce to any number smaller than four. The economist then used this string quartet as an analogy in order to characterize a wide range of human activities that all seem unable to keep up with economic demands to become ever more efficient. As a result, such activities tend to become increasingly expensive over time.

I here refer to the so-called "cost disease," usually presented as "Baumol's cost disease,"[1] sometimes "the Baumol effect"[2] or even "Baumol's law."[3] It is commonly presented as a discovery made by US-American economist William Baumol (1922–2017), but as we will soon see, the actual phenomenon had already been analyzed by several economists before him. However, it was only with Baumol that it became a "thing," and variations of the same story – typically with reference to a string quartet – have circulated in the public sphere for over half a century. The same "disease" has been brought up in vastly different contexts to explain the long-term outlook for society and to support a wide range of political agendas.

The fundamental dynamic of the cost disease is indeed very simple. While there is a tendency in every capitalist economy toward rising productivity, this is not to say that productivity may rise at an even pace in each sector of the economy. In certain industries, technological innovation may offer exceptional opportunities to reduce the need for human labor. Accordingly, there must be other economic activities lagging behind the average rate of productivity growth. This lag is particularly apparent in the case of personal services such as childcare where the "product" may hardly be disentangled from the presence of a human. In the words of William Baumol, childcare appears to be "technologically stagnant," just like a string quartet.[4]

The fact that productivity growth is "unbalanced" tends to manifest itself through changes in the relative price of products.[5] As many manufactured goods become more affordable over time, personal services get more expensive in relative terms. Once upon a time, it cost more money to buy a pair of scissors than to visit a barber while the opposite tends to be the case today.

---

[1] Charles M. Gray, "Baumol's cost disease," in *The New Palgrave Dictionary of Economics*, eds. Matias Vernengo, Esteban Perez Caldentey & Barkley J. Rosser Jr (London: Palgrave Macmillan, 2020), online version accessed January 13, 2024; James Heilbrun, "Baumol's cost disease," in *A Handbook of Cultural Economics*, 2nd ed., ed. Ruth Towse (Cheltenham: Edward Elgar Publishing, 2011), 67–75.

[2] "Baumol effect," in *A Dictionary of Climate Change and the Environment*, R. Quentin Grafton, Harry W. Nelson, N. Ross Lambie & Paul R. Wyrwoll (Cheltenham: Edward Elgar Publishing, 2012), online version accessed January 13, 2024.

[3] "Baumol's law," in *Oxford Dictionary of Economics*, Nigar Hashimzade, Gareth Myles & John Black (Cheltenham: Edward Elgar Publishing, 2017), online version accessed January 13, 2024.

[4] William J. Baumol & William G. Bowen, *Performing Arts: The Economic Dilemma: A Study of Problems Common to the Theater, Opera, Music and Dance* (New York: The Twentieth Century Fund, 1966), 164.

[5] This is based on an additional assumption, namely that we live in a more or less capitalist society where there is one single market for the necessities of life and where individuals are able to choose between jobs in different industries. Accordingly, the wage level cannot diverge *too* much between industries.

This is a historical trajectory that can be understood almost intuitively, even by someone without any formal training in economics. It boils down to the simple fact that human time is a scarce resource[6] – something that in itself may hardly be seen as paradoxical or pathological. Yet, the concept of "Baumol's cost disease" has turned out to be very attractive for economists and laymen alike. The metaphor of a "disease" has a long history in Western economic thought.[7] Apparently, it may provide an opportunity to talk about the economic roots of looming social or cultural crises.

In this article, I trace the reception and circulation of "Baumol's cost disease" (BCD) in Sweden, focusing on the period 1968–1991. One reason for choosing Sweden as a case is that much of William Baumol's own work on the cost disease was actually carried out in Sweden. As shown in section 5 below, he spent time as a visiting researcher in Stockholm around 1970 and interacted with Swedish actors both within and outside academia.

Furthermore, Sweden at the time was an expansive welfare state as well as a country where the push for increased productivity was institutionalized by central wage bargaining. The so-called "solidarity wage policy" sought to preclude the growth of a low-wage service sector. Hence, Sweden could in theory be expected to confront the effects of the cost disease earlier and more directly than other countries in which uneven productivity growth was allowed to manifest itself in the form of rising wage inequalities between different industries.[8]

In an influential study on the emergence of different "postindustrial employment regimes," sociologist Gøsta Esping-Andersen compared data from Sweden, Germany and the US from the 1960s until the 1980s. America's postindustrial job growth mostly occurred in the private service sector, particularly in entertainment, restaurants and tourism. On the other hand, "Sweden's postindustrialism lies in the welfare state edifice," as Esping-Andersen concluded in 1991. Most new jobs created in Sweden had gone to women in healthcare, education and other public sector services. This resulted in the Swedish labor market being much

---

[6] Roy Harrod, "The possibility of economic satiety: Use of economic growth for improving the quality of education and leisure," in *Problems of United States Economic Development* (New York: Committee for Economic Development, 1958), Volume I, 207–213; Fred Hirsch, *Social Limits to Growth* (Cambridge: Harvard University Press, 1976), 23–24.

[7] Daniele Besomi, "Crises as a disease of the body politick: A metaphor in the history of nineteenth-century economics," *Journal of the History of Economic Thought* 33, no. 1 (2011): 67–118.

[8] Per-Anders Edin & Bertil Holmlund, "The Swedish wage structure: The rise and fall of solidarity wage policy?" in *Differences and Changes in Wage Structures*, eds. Richard B. Freeman & Lawrence F. Katz (Chicago: University of Chicago Press, 1995), 307–344.

more gender-segregated than the other two cases.[9] Hence, this structural difference between the US and Sweden serves as an important context for the Swedish reception of the "cost disease."

I do not try to answer whether Baumol was right about the cost disease, nor how the cost disease has affected the Swedish economy. In my view, the "cost disease" is not a clearly defined hypothesis and thus cannot be falsified.[10] Here, it is rather understood as a *rhetorical device*. When emphasizing the rhetorical component of economic knowledge, I am taking a cue from Deirdre McCloskey's influential study *The Rhetoric of Economics*.[11] She argues that the use of metaphors is an inherent feature of economics as a science. Not every metaphor merely serves an "ornamental" purpose. Indeed, according to McCloskey, economic models already represent a form of "nonornamental metaphors."[12]

As a rhetorical device, BCD refers to, but is not identical to, the simple fact that productivity does not increase evenly. Starting off from this observation, a two-step operation is required to arrive at the "cost disease." First, a highly simplified model is presented of an economy consisting of two sectors: one in which productivity does increase over time and another where it does not. This is where the above-mentioned analogy of a string quartet is often used to illustrate how some activities cannot be rendered more productive by using new technology. In the second step, the resulting changes in relative prices are said to be a problem or even a pathology. Baumol came to employ the medical metaphor of "disease." This particular combination of a two-sector model and a medical metaphor is what characterizes BCD. Furthermore, every time the "cost disease" is attributed to the famous economist William Baumol, this in itself constitutes a third kind of rhetorical operation, known as the "appeal to authority."[13] In other words, on a closer look, the rhetorical device I study turns out to be a specific combination of several simple devices.

Accordingly, I ask how BCD has *been made relevant* by a variety of actors and how this helped articulate different social and political visions. My focus is not on internal intellectual developments in the discipline of economics but on the circulation and perception of economic knowledge between academia, policymaking and

---

9 Gøsta Esping-Andersen, "Three postindustrial employment regimes," *International Journal of Sociology* 21, no. 2 (1991): 149–188.
10 To see why BCS is *not* a clearly defined hypothesis, we only need to compare the divergent explanations provided by scholarly dictionaries, such as the ones referred to in footnotes 1–3.
11 Deirdre N. McCloskey, *The Rhetoric of Economics*, 2nd ed. (Madison: University of Wisconsin Press, 1998).
12 McCloskey, *Rhetoric of Economics*, 13, 19, 40–44.
13 McCloskey, *Rhetoric of Economics*, 36–37, 170.

the public sphere. "Knowledge" is here understood as something moving and malleable. Importantly, it is not defined in relation to truth: as long as some actors find that a claim is relevant for understanding the world, it counts as knowledge.[14]

My main sources are major Swedish newspapers and governmental committee reports (SOU). Searching this material for the period 1965–2015, I was initially able to identify about one hundred newspaper articles, as well as a few dozen reports.[15] From all these sources, I have also followed references to books, magazine articles and other printed sources, which were subsequently also included in the empirical study.

As mentioned above, my main focus is on the period 1968–1991: a time when the Swedish postindustrialization process took the shape of a growing public sector, coupled with a growing sense of crisis for the welfare state due to the increasing costs of maintaining it. Against this background, it is particularly interesting to examine the appeal of "disease" as a metaphor. For additional context, I have also decided to include a prelude on the 1950s and a postlude covering the period of restructuring the Swedish welfare state, beginning with the financial crisis in the early 1990s.

2 Prelude: Swedish Predecessors in the 1950s

Already in the mid-1950s, one decade before Baumol, a group of Swedish economists were discussing the long-term consequences of unbalanced growth. Ragnar Bentzel, Jan Wallander and Erik Höök all worked at the Swedish industry's economic research institute (IUI), which had just initiated a major study on trends in Swedish consumption.[16] Bentzel soon noticed a decline over time in the volume of personal services consumed by households. He presented this as a curious side

---

14 For a general overview of the history of knowledge and the significance of circulation as a concept for this field, see Johan Östling, "Circulation, arenas, and the quest for public knowledge: Historiographical currents and analytical frameworks," *History and Theory* 59, no. 4 (2020): 111–126.
15 Both these newspapers and the SOU reports have been digitized by Sweden's National Library. The search terms used included the name "Baumol," "cost disease" [*kostnadssjuka*] and other variants. As I identified key phrases and actors in the material, further searches were performed in an attempt to also find implicit references to BCD. Some of the references to William Baumol concerned other elements of his work unrelated to BCD.
16 Ragnar Bentzel, ed., *Den privata konsumtionen i Sverige 1931–65* (Stockholm: Industriens utredningsinstitut, 1957); Jan Wallander, *Livet som det blev. En bankdirektör blir till* (Stockholm: Bonnier, 1997), 288–292.

effect of rising material standards: if a service lags behind the average rate of productivity growth, it will become increasingly expensive until it is priced out of the market.[17]

In a 1956 lecture, Bentzel even illustrated this by means of a kind of science fiction story. In a future Sweden, after a few hundred years of growth, society will be incredibly affluent. Even a simple worker "will be able to afford to throw away his private jet every time it runs out of gas, but he will not be able to afford a domestic servant."[18] Throwing things away instead of repairing them seemed like a rational lifestyle in a world where goods become cheaper, while time remained scarce and expensive. Jan Wallander appeared on Swedish television in 1961 to defend "slit-och-släng" [throwawayism] against its critics, whose arguments he dismissed as just "a moral lag." The notion that it is virtuous to patch up and repair broken goods was, in his view, a relic from "a time when capital goods were expensive and scarce, but cheap labor was plentiful." This situation had now been inverted, something which current morals had to adapt to. What is wasteful, Wallander claimed, was not throwing away goods but to waste expensive time on repairing them.[19] The historical demise of personal services – later to be known as the cost disease – was not yet pathologized but rather affirmed as an inherent feature of modern life.

In his 1962 doctoral thesis, Erik Höök sought to explain the growth of the public sector. To that end, he first presented a simplified model of a two-sector economy, in which only one sector may enjoy increased productivity over time. This is exactly the same kind of model serving as the point of departure for BCD, as I defined it in the introduction. However, Höök did not employ the medical metaphor of disease. He also was quick to point out why such a model in reality is too static, as it ignores the possibility that a service might qualitatively change over time. Interestingly, Höök even pointed to *theatre* as an example of such a malleable service.[20] He most likely was not aware that on the other side of the Atlantic, two colleagues had just initiated a large study focusing on precisely the economics of theatre.

---

17 Bentzel, *Den privata konsumtionen*, 11–12; Ragnar Bentzel, *Samhällsproblem vid ekonomisk expansion* (Stockholm: Svenska bankföreningen, 1962).
18 Ragnar Bentzel, "Tendenser i vår konsumtionsutveckling," *Vårt Ekonomiska Läge* (1956), 87–95.
19 Wallander, *Livet som det blev*, 288–292; Jan Wallander, "Skrotmakarna," *Svenska Dagbladet*, January 17, 1961; Orsi Husz, "The morality of quality: Assimilating material mass culture in twentieth-century Sweden," *Journal of Modern European History* 10, no. 2 (2012): 152–181.
20 Erik Höök, *Den offentliga sektorns expansion: En studie av de offentliga civila utgifternas utveckling åren 1913–58*, diss. (Stockholm: Almqvist & Wiksell, 1962), 28–39.

3 Across the Atlantic: The Pathologization of Unbalanced Growth

Around 1960, William Baumol was commissioned by a think tank to study the economic situation of the performing arts in the United States. His younger colleague William Bowen was put in charge of the vast empirical groundwork. Over several years, data was collected from a large number of theatre companies, opera houses and philharmonic orchestras.[21] The study resulted in a 600-page book, published in 1966 with the title *Performing Arts: The Economic Dilemma*.[22] It received a great deal of publicity, with front-page stories not only in major US newspapers but even in the Soviet *Pravda*. Today, the book is seen as having founded "cultural economics" as a distinct field of study.[23]

Baumol and Bowen were certainly not the first to apply economic analysis to the arts, but the empirical scope of their study made it stand out. It also introduced a potent trope: "Let us imagine an economy divided into two sectors, one in which productivity is rising and another in which it is constant, the first producing automobiles, and the second, performances of Haydn trios."[24] The authors made no claim that this model represented a theoretical innovation. On the contrary, they pointed out: "There is nothing new in these observations on the effects of differential rates of productivity change on costs and prices."[25] Baumol and Bowen explicitly pointed to a 1959 paper by economists Anne and Tibor Scitovsky discussing the same phenomenon of unbalanced productivity growth with regard to its various political, cultural and psychological implications. The performing arts were mentioned by the Scitovskys as one of several fields of human activity where the need for public subsidies would only increase over time.[26]

---

21 William J. Baumol, "On the career of a microeconomist," in *Recollections of Eminent Economists: Volume 2*, ed. Jan Allen Kregel (London: Palgrave Macmillan), 209–335.
22 Baumol & Bowen, *Performing Arts*.
23 David Throsby, "Economic circumstances of the performing artist: Baumol and Bowen thirty years on," *Journal of Cultural Economics* 20, no. 3 (1996): 225–240; Gregory Besharov, "The outbreak of the cost disease: Baumol and Bowen's founding of cultural economics," *New Political Economy* 37, no. 3 (2005): 412–430; Bruno S. Frey & Andre Briviba, "Two types of cultural economics," *International Review of Economics* 70, no. 1 (2023): 1–9.
24 Baumol & Bowen, *Performing Arts*, 167–168. The earliest version of this trope can be found in William J. Baumol & William G. Bowen, "On the performing arts: The anatomy of their economic problems," *The American Economic Review* 55, no. 1–2 (1965): 495–502.
25 Baumol & Bowen, *Performing Arts*, 167; see also Baumol & Bowen, "On the performing arts," 499.
26 Anne Scitovsky & Tibor Scitovsky, "What price economic progress?" *Yale Review* 49, no. 1 (1959): 95–110.

So, while Baumol cannot be said to have made a new discovery, he picked up an existing argument on differential productivity growth and gave it a simple and powerful rhetorical structure. He postulated a binary model of an economy only consisting of two sectors: one sector consisting of "the typical manufacturing industry" and the other sector represented by live performances of a Schubert string quartet. The latter was then said to be "technologically stagnant,"[27] thus destined for a "perpetual crisis."[28] Indeed, Baumol and Bowen had intended to name their book "The Permanent Crisis of the Arts" but were dissuaded by the sponsors of the project who were afraid that the reference to "crisis" would sound too ominous.[29]

A year after the book was published in 1967, Baumol applied the same model on a broader segment of the economy in a paper on "the anatomy of urban crisis." One sector was now defined as "technologically progressive" while the other was defined as "nonprogressive" (i.e., what had previously been referred to as "stagnant"). In the first sector, "labor is primarily an instrument," while in the other sector, "the labor is an end in itself," meaning that "quality is judged directly in terms of amount of labor" and that it is impossible to reduce the number of hours worked without a degradation in quality.[30] Baumol noted that a lot of public services belong to this nonprogressive sector, including schools, hospitals and the police. Even if the level of quality was to be kept constant, providing these services would become increasingly expensive over time. According to Baumol, this could explain much of the financial troubles already experienced by local governments in the US. The conclusion was sobering, almost fatalist: "This is a trend for which no man and no group should be blamed, for there is nothing that can be done to stop it."[31]

Commenting on this paper, economist Alice Vandermeulen coined the term "Baumol's disease,"[32] which William Baumol himself was quick to pick up.[33] The introduction of this metaphor amounted to a *pathologization* of unbalanced

---

27 Baumol & Bowen, *Performing Arts*, 164.
28 Baumol & Bowen, *Performing Arts*, 302.
29 William J. Baumol, "The permanent crisis of the arts," transcript of a speech held at the Stockholm Concert Hall, printed in Konsertföreningen i Stockholm, "Styrelsens berättelse för verksamhetsperioden 1 juli 1972 – 30 juni 1973" (volume B1, Konsertföreningens i Stockholm arkiv, National Archives of Sweden).
30 We may here note that an additional feature of many personal services concerns the fact that it is impossible to make a clear distinction between the quantity and the quality provided.
31 William J. Baumol, "Macroeconomics of unbalanced growth: The anatomy of urban crisis," *The American Economic Review* 57, no. 3 (1967): 415–426.
32 Alice Vandermeulen, "A remission from Baumol's disease: Ways to publish more articles," *Southern Economic Journal* 35, no. 2 (1968): 189–191.
33 William J. Baumol, "Macroeconomics of unbalanced growth: Comment," *The American Economic Review* 58, no. 4 (1968): 896–897.

growth. The implicit suggestion was that a "healthy" economy could only be achieved when productivity grows at an even rate everywhere. Naming it a "disease" also opened the door for recurrent discussions on the possibility of finding a "cure," regardless of the fact that Baumol himself believed that the cost disease was chronic.

4 Economic Eschatology

William Baumol's earliest publications on the cost disease were first presented to a Swedish public in the middle of 1968. "Economic eschatology" was the title of a rather unorthodox essay in the newspaper *Svenska Dagbladet*.[34] It was written by Staffan Burenstam Linder, an economist who only a few weeks later was to be elected to the Swedish parliament for the right-wing Moderate Party. A decade later, he would become minister of commerce.[35]

Eschatology designates the part of theology focusing on the *end*, be it the end of an individual life, the end of an era or the end of the world. Matters of salvation and damnation are at the center of Christian eschatology. Accordingly, Linder's essay discussed the prospects for establishing an "economic heaven" on earth.[36] His proposal that economists should start asking the same kind of questions asked by theologians could be seen as prefiguring the twenty-first century emergence of "economic theology" as a research field[37] with "economic eschatology" as a sub-field.[38] Anyhow, the conclusion reached by Linder in 1968 was that economic growth should *not* be understood as a path leading to "heaven" and that economists need to start questioning growth: which problems it is actually able to solve, which new problems it may cause and whether it is about to come to an end.

---

34 Staffan Burenstam Linder, "Ekonomisk eskatologi," *Svenska Dagbladet*, August 3, 1968.
35 Mats Lundahl, "Ekonomporträtt: Staffan Burenstam Linder – en fritänkare," *Ekonomisk Debatt* 33, no. 3 (2005): 40–54.
36 Linder, "Ekonomisk eskatologi."
37 In a useful review, Enrico Beltramini argues that economic theology is "a somewhat ill-named field" defined differently by different scholars. It may either be framed "in terms of analogies and conceptual exchanges between the two fields of theology and economy" or as a philosophical method for analyzing the liberal order and the deeper causes of its crisis. See "Economic theology: Is economy a subfield of theology?" *Ephemera* 21, no. 3 (2021): 217–227.
38 Sigmund Wagner-Tsukamoto, "Eschatology and eschaton," in *The Routledge Handbook of Economic Theology*, ed. Stefan Schwarzkopf (Abingdon: Routledge, 2020), 28–35.

Linder pointed at two specific limits to growth. The first limit was ecological: finite natural resources. However, he also saw another finite resource, namely "our *time*, our twenty-four hours per day." The essay presented William Baumol's work as an important contribution for understanding the implications of "the rising price of time."[39] Linder did not only see this as affecting the *production* of goods and services – from healthcare to the arts – but he also reflected on the increasing lack of time to spend on *consumption*. In the sphere of leisure, the arts also had to compete with a multitude of other activities that had become more widely available thanks to the mass production of cheap goods.

For these reasons, Linder's 1968 essay criticized the widespread notion of an emerging "affluent society" and the idea that economic growth "brings us ever closer to an economic heaven." The essay ended with a recommendation to policymakers to focus less on economic indicators such as GDP and more on alternative measures of human well-being.[40] It should be noted that this was still several years before the critique of economic growth was popularized, and the concept of "degrowth" was established in 1972.[41] Not only was Linder early to formulate such a critique, he also did so from a political perspective different from that of many left-leaning degrowthers in the 1970s.

In fact, "Economic eschatology" reads like a synopsis of the hugely influential book that Staffan Linder would go on to publish soon after: *The Harried Leisure Class* (1970).[42] Here, he added numerous examples from everyday life so that any reader was able to grasp his main thesis: as we get richer, we also get time poor. In his extensive list of references, Linder presented this analysis as largely being based on the work of two US-American economists: first Gary Becker's household economics followed by Baumol's analysis of the cost disease.[43]

According to sociologist Jiri Zuzanek, *The Harried Leisure Class* represented somewhat of a watershed in the public perception of leisure. The 1960s had been filled with expectations regarding a coming "leisure society," but in the 1970s, the discussion instead started to focus on the lack of time.[44]

---

39 Linder, "Ekonomisk eskatologi."
40 Linder, "Ekonomisk eskatologi."
41 41 "Introduction: Degrowth," in *Degrowth: A Vocabulary for a New Era*, eds. Giacomo D'Alisa, Federico Demaria & Giorgios Kallis. (Abingdon: Routledge, 2014), 1–17.
42 Staffan Burenstam Linder, *The Harried Leisure Class* (New York: Columbia University Press, 1970). This book was originally written in English but first published in Swedish: *Den rastlösa välfärdsmänniskan: Tidsbrist i överflöd – en ekonomisk studie* (Stockholm: Bonnier, 1969).
43 Linder, *Harried Leisure Class*, 9, 45–46, 105–106, 157, 163–165, 168–171.
44 Still to this day, *The Harried Leisure Class* remains widely cited in sociology and business management. For a sociological homage to Staffan Linder as a "cultural rather than economic"

In 1970s Sweden, *The Harried Leisure Class* also helped popularizing the notion of unbalanced growth as a key for understanding long-term social and cultural change. As an example, art critic Ulf Hård af Segerstad wrote an essay in 1973 on the decline of craft-based arts such as pottery and woodwork. He concluded that "it's an ever-increasing price for time, which inexorably displaces those activities that require a lot of time."[45] This was written with reference to Linder, albeit without mentioning Baumol, thus demonstrating how one piece of economic knowledge could take on more than one form, circulating at the same time.

While Linder was heavily influenced by Baumol, he developed his own way of presenting the matter, which mostly did *not* rely on the particular combination of a model and a metaphor by which I have characterized BCD. At times, Linder leaned toward an almost existentialist meditation on the finitude of individual lives, citing being influenced by the novelist Aldous Huxley.[46] Linder's distinctive interpretation of BCD would continue to fascinate readers for a long time, and further examples are presented below in section 7.

5 William Baumol in Stockholm

William Baumol spent the fall of 1968 as a visiting researcher at the Stockholm School of Economics. He returned to Stockholm for a longer stay in the early 1970s and became a personal friend of Swedish economists Bertil Ohlin, Erik Lundberg and Assar Lindbeck.[47]

During his years in Stockholm, Baumol wrote an additional three papers on the cost disease, all printed in Swedish publications. The first one (together with Mary I. Oates) was historical: "On the economics of the theater in renaissance London"; in other words, a study of cultural economics *before* the onset of a serious cost disease. The economic conditions for performing arts were found to in certain ways having been better at the time of Shakespeare – with its much lower levels of productivity and wages – than in modern industrial society. The same paper also included a brief discussion on *The Harried Leisure Class*, concluding on a note very much in line with Linder's critique of growth: "economic prosper-

---

theorist, see Hartmut Rosa & William E. Scheuerman, *High-Speed Society: Social Acceleration, Power and Modernity* (University Park: Pennsylvania State University Press, 2009), 9, 85.
45 Ulf Hård af Segerstad, "Skall konsthantverket överleva?" *Svenska Dagbladet*, May 22, 1973.
46 Linder, *Harried Leisure Class*, 95–96, 145.
47 William J. Baumol, "Erik Lundberg, 1907–1987," *The Scandinavian Journal of Economics* 92, no. 1 (1990): 1–9.

ity does not automatically bring with it all the things that are usually taken to contribute to the 'quality of life'," such as fine arts.[48] The circulation of knowledge clearly went both ways: first by Baumol influencing Linder, followed by Linder influencing Baumol.

Baumol's examination of the cost disease was broadened during his years in Stockholm, and it seems probable that this broadening to some degree was influenced by Linder. The next paper, which Baumol co-authored with W. E. Oates, was titled "The cost disease of the personal services and the quality of life." It was published in 1972, both in English and Swedish, in the quarterly journal of a major Swedish bank. This text was to become the most frequently cited publication in the 1970s Swedish reception of BCD.[49] It has also been referenced by international scholars, but much less frequently.[50]

The core argument here was the same as in Baumol's 1968 paper on "urban crisis." This time, however, the cost disease was discussed within a more sociological framework and with a new emphasis on contingency. For each and every "non-progressive" activity beset by the cost disease, Baumol and Oates identified four possible ways forward. First, the activity may become an increasingly expensive luxury for the few or disappear from the market altogether. Examples included domestic servants, as well as certain crafts, such as making furniture by hand. Second, there are cases in which the quality of a service will be "allowed to deteriorate progressively." This might mean larger classes in schools or shorter rehearsal periods in theatres. Third, a service profession may over time be replaced by unpaid amateur activities, which has not been uncommon in the sphere of culture. Another example mentioned by Baumol and Oates was shaving: cheaper industrial products have allowed people to shave themselves at home instead of visiting a professional barber. Finally, the public may step in with sufficient subsidies to maintain a given service at a constant quantity and quality, even if this will become increasingly expensive.[51]

So even though Baumol and Oates saw "no real cure" for the cost disease, they suggested that there were still different ways of addressing this. If society

---

48 Mary I. Oates & William J. Baumol, "On the economics of the theater in renaissance London," *The Swedish Journal of Economics* 74, no. 1 (1972): 136–160.
49 William J. Baumol & W. E. Oates, "The cost disease of the personal services and the quality of life," *Skandinaviska Enskilda Banken Quarterly Review* no. 2 (1972): 44–54. The journal, including this paper, was also simultaneously published in a Swedish version.
50 Google Scholar includes about one hundred references to the paper by Baumol and Oates, mostly from the twenty-first century. It is worth noting, however, that this paper has never been republished and is still absent from all digital research repositories.
51 Baumol & Oates, "Cost disease," 49; cf. Baumol, "Macroeconomics of unbalanced growth," 422.

could only realize the long-term dynamics at play, it would still be possible to choose between different political visions. This conclusion appears far less fatalistic than the emphasis on "permanent crisis" in Baumol's previous writing on the cost disease.⁵²

As soon as this paper by Baumol and Oates had been published, each of the two morning newspapers in Stockholm dedicated a full editorial to discuss its political implications. According to the right-wing *Svenska Dagbladet*, Baumol and Oates had written "a powerful plea for granting the public sector more resources." Likewise, liberal *Dagens Nyheter* argued that it had proven that in an advanced economy, "a growing public sector is a natural feature." Both newspapers described the argument presented by Baumol and Oates as undisputable in itself. We must learn to accept the rising cost of maintaining a welfare state, *Svenska Dagbladet* argued, but the solution must not be to raise taxes, but rather to accelerate economic growth in order to increase the tax base. If, however, this was still not sufficient, the last resort should be to start charging fees for the use of healthcare and other public services. *Dagens Nyheter* did not go this far but concluded that "it will become necessary for politicians to draw a limit as to which services will be provided by the public sector."⁵³ (Here, it may be noted that ten years prior, *Dagens Nyheter* had presented an identical argument, also in relation to the long-term consequences of unbalanced productivity growth – but this time with reference to Bentzel, not Baumol.⁵⁴)

These examples show how a liberal critique of the Swedish welfare state could be articulated by reference to BCD. However, this critique differed fundamentally from the neoliberal rejection of the welfare state as such represented by thinkers such as Friedrich Hayek, who in 1974, to many people's great surprise, was awarded the Nobel Memorial Prize in Economics. (Someone who had played a decisive role in the choice of Hayek was the chairman of the prize committee, Assar Lindbeck, who at the time had a close personal relationship with William Baumol, as mentioned above.⁵⁵)

The Hayekian critique of the welfare state argued that central planning posed a danger to individual freedom. Instead of public welfare, this critique pro-

---

52 Baumol & Oates, "Cost disease," 52–54.
53 "H Gabler och G Sträng," *Dagens Nyheter*, July 16, 1972; "Tjänstesektorn," *Svenska Dagbladet*, August 1, 1972.
54 "Brigitte Bardots like?" *Dagens Nyheter*, October 30, 1962; cf. Bentzel, "Samhällsproblem," 10–11.
55 Avner Offer & Gabriel Söderberg, *The Nobel Factor: The Prize in Economics, Social Democracy, and the Market Turn* (Princeton: Princeton University Press, 2016), 174–188.

moted the principle of individual consumer sovereignty.[56] But it was not until the late 1970s that this type of neoliberal critique truly started to take hold in Swedish debates.[57]

In the early 1970s, "Baumolian" critique was much more modest. It did not claim that the postwar expansion of the welfare state had been a mistake, nor did it openly call for dismantling it. The liberal opinionmakers quoted above simply argued that due to rising relative costs, the existing welfare state could only be maintained if it did not expand into additional areas. The public sector could only take responsibility for *some* victims of the cost disease (i.e., only provide the most necessary personal services). After all, what Baumol and Oates had demonstrated in their 1972 paper was that public subsidies were just *one* of several possible ways of managing BCD.

6 Baumol and Swedish Cultural Policy

William Baumol's time in Stockholm happened to coincide with the Swedish process of developing a much more ambitious cultural policy. An expert committee appointed by the government began its work in early 1969. Its final report, delivered in 1972, mapped out the need for subsidies in the different arts. On the basis of this, a new set of cultural policies were enacted in 1974.[58]

According to a newspaper report, William Baumol was engaged as a "consultant" by this committee,[59] but it remains unclear which actual contributions he might have made. The final committee report briefly referred to *Performing Arts: The Economic Dilemma* but without explicitly discussing the cost disease.[60] Indeed, it is worth noting that at the very beginning, Sweden's new system for cul-

---

56 Niklas Olsen, *The Sovereign Consumer: A New Intellectual History of Neoliberalism* (Cham: Palgrave Macmillan, 2019).
57 Jenny Andersson, "The Freedom Front and the welfare state counter revolution," *Journal of Political Ideologies* 28, no. 3 (2023): 1–21.
58 Statens kulturråd, "Ny kulturpolitik: 1. Nuläge och förslag," Swedish Government Official Report SOU 1972:66; Tobias Harding, "Nationalising culture: The reorganisation of national culture in Swedish cultural policy 1970–2002" (Diss., Linköping University, 2007), 111–155; My Klockar Linder, "Kulturpolitik: Formeringen av en modern kategori" (Diss., Uppsala University, 2014), 101–107, 131–149.
59 Sigvard Hammar, "Kulturens penningkris – kan bara botas politiskt," *Dagens Nyheter*, February 27, 1973.
60 Statens kulturråd, "Ny kulturpolitik," 499.

tural subsidies was *not* presented as a remedy for problems caused by unbalanced productivity.

However, this would change within a few years, and Baumol would be canonized in the context of Swedish cultural policy. Subsequent committee reports addressing public support for film, theatre and orchestras all emphasized the cost disease as a key concept for understanding the need for public subsidies.[61]

In early 1973, the Stockholm Concert Hall opened its doors once again after several years of renovations. A seminar on cultural economics was organized as part of the opening celebrations with William Baumol giving a keynote speech titled "The permanent crisis of the arts."[62] In front of the king of Sweden and the cultural elite, Baumol first emphasized that he only spoke as a simple economist, without any aesthetic expertise, yet he also recommended a recent article in *Dagens Nyheter* for its "beautiful discussion" regarding the value of opera as an art form.[63] He then proceeded to present the fundamental dynamics of the cost disease and why the artists should not be blamed for the rising costs of art. Baumol mentioned that as an economist, he could "be dependent upon to advocate the use of the market mechanism" but also acknowledged that there was a limit in terms of what the market could achieve, thus also a need for public subsidies for the arts. The final sentence in Baumol's speech was to be quoted frequently by Swedish commentators: "The crisis of the arts is permanent, but there is no reason for that crisis to be allowed to destroy the arts."[64]

Journalists with some surprise reported from this seminar that the US-American expert on cultural economics proved to be an optimist, after all. The message was that in a growing economy, there will always be enough money available for supporting the arts.[65] *Dagens Nyheter* quoted Baumol as saying: "The problem is not economic, but political."[66]

---

61 "Samhället och filmen: 4. Slutbetänkande," Swedish Government Official Report SOU 1973:53, 154; "Teaterkostnadsutredningen. Teaterns kostnadsutveckling 1975–1990 med särskilda studier av Operan, Dramaten och Riksteatern," Swedish Government Official Report SOU 1991:71, 137–142; "Den professionella orkestermusiken i Sverige," Swedish Government Official Report SOU 2006:34, 59–60.
62 Baumol, "Permanent crisis."
63 "Opera – varför?" *Dagens Nyheter*, January 19, 1973. Baumol's reference to this article indicates that he at around this time was probably also well-aware of how his own writings were received by Swedish columnists.
64 Baumol, "Permanent crisis."
65 "Kulturen – vad kostar den?" *Expressen*, December 12, 1972; Leif Aare, "Konsertföreningen firar," *Dagens Nyheter*, January 1, 1973.
66 Sigvard Hammar, "Kulturens penningkris – kan bara botas politiskt," *Dagens Nyheter*, February 27, 1973.

Nils Wallin, a musicologist and director of the Stockholm Concert Hall, would publish several essays stressing the significance of BCD for realizing the need for generous public funding for the arts.[67] Two or three decades later, the same kind of argument, with reference to William Baumol, would still be commonplace in debates on Swedish cultural policy. The bottom line of Baumol's keynote speech was repeatedly quoted by cultural commentators as a slogan in favor of heavy subsidies for cultural activities.[68] In other words, what would echo in discussions on cultural policies was a relatively optimistic interpretation of BCD.

7 The Utopia of Amateurism

Responding to the critique of the Swedish welfare state, some thinkers were apparently attracted to the notion of finding an alternative third way, beyond both state and market. In the 1980s, such visions were thriving in the vicinity of the newly founded Green Party and were articulated in reference to a particular interpretation of BCD.

A leading intellectual in this context was Lars Ingelstam, a mathematics professor and social democrat, who in 1973 had become the first director of Sweden's new Secretariat for Futures Studies. Historians have recently highlighted the conflicts surrounding the establishment of futures studies as a field in both Sweden and elsewhere. Leftists such as Ingelstam objected to the concept of technocratic forecasting, instead envisioning a kind of public science seeking to present a plurality of alternative futures and thus inviting democratic dialogues.[69]

---

67 Nils Wallin, "Konserthuset i konkurs?" *Svenska Dagbladet*, January 14, 1975; Nils Wallin, "Baumols sjukdom – hjärnspöke eller realitet?" *Svenska Dagbladet*, March 21, 1976; Nils Wallin, "Erkänn musiken! Tendenser från 50-talet mot ett musikaliskt systemsamhälle," *Svensk tidskrift för musikforskning* no. 1 (1980): 7–39.

68 Mikael Strömberg, "Konsten att (inte) bygga ett konserthus," *Aftonbladet*, October 10, 1995; Ingrid Elam, "Barnvagnar och principer," *Göteborgs-Posten*, May 11, 1997; Mikael Strömberg, "Det stora blå," *Aftonbladet*, January 21, 1998; Tobias Nielsén, "Vem pinar fiolen?" *Expressen*, May 19, 2000; Mikael Strömberg, "Fattigmansrapporten," *Aftonbladet*, November 11, 2003.

69 Jenny Andersson, "Choosing futures: Alva Myrdal and the construction of Swedish futures studies, 1967–1972," *International Review of Social History* 51, no. 2 (2006): 277–295; Jenny Andersson & David Larsson Heidenblad, "Thinking the human system: The application of humanities and social science reasoning to societal problems," in *The Humanities and the Modern Politics of Knowledge: The Impact and Organization of the Humanities in Sweden, 1850–2020*, eds. Anders Ekström & Hampus Östh Gustafsson (Amsterdam: Amsterdam University Press, 2022), 207–230; Karl Haikola, "Framtidens fragmentering: Sekretariatet för framtidsstudier och välfärdssamhällets dilemman under det långa 1970-talet" (Diss., Lund University, 2023).

Ingelstam would during his years as director of the Secretariat become renowned for his radical proposals, such as reducing the consumption of meat and banning private cars in cities. In 1980, he left the Secretariat after the liberal government had decided to reorganize it. He spent the 1980s at Linköping University as a professor of technology and social change. Here, he also developed an alternative reading of BCS.

Ingelstam identified a great paradox in industrial society: in the long run, no abundance of material goods can pay for essential services like culture, education and healthcare. However, he found no reason for pessimism in this predicament: "Assuming that we want a future economy that accommodates human services and humanistic values, there *must* be a way to trick the market and put reason above the economic 'laws'. I see great opportunities in organized cooperation outside of the monetary economy, cooperation, self-management, perhaps community service."[70]

In other words, Ingelstam's preferred solution to BCD would be to gradually phase out the monetary economy. The future for many of the diseased services would be as unpaid amateur activities. After all, amateurization had been one of the four alternative pathways highlighted by Bauol and Oates in 1972. Ingelstam drew further inspiration from social scientists such as Jiří Skolka and Jonathan Gershuny, who in the 1970s put forth ideas of an emerging "self-service society."[71] While these ideas had focused on ongoing changes in the everyday life of private households, Ingelstam took them further when he proposed the partial amateurization of culture, education and healthcare. To make this possible, he emphasized that it was necessary to reduce the volume of wage labor, starting with the introduction of a 6-hour working day. Some of the responsibilities of the welfare state could then be transferred to what he referred to as "the informal sector."

Economic historian Aaron Benanav has traced how this concept was established in the 1970s. The International Labor Organization played a decisive role here, whose definition of the informal sector included "both workers with insufficient employment and employers with profit-making enterprises."[72] For Ingelstam, however, informality had different connotations. His primary interest was

---

70 Lars Ingelstam, "Varför har vi inte råd med tjänster?" *Stockholms-Tidningen*, June 2, 1982. Bold style has here been changed into italics.
71 Jiří Skolka, "The substitution of self-service activities for marketed services," *Review of Income and Wealth* 22, no. 4 (1976): 297–304; Jonathan Gershuny, *After Industrial Society? The Emerging Self-Service Economy* (London: Macmillan, 1978); Lars Ingelstam, *Arbetets värde och tidens bruk: En framtidsstudie* (Stockholm: Liber, 1980).
72 Aaron Benanav, "The origins of informality: The ILO at the limit of the concept of unemployment," *Journal of Global History* 14, no. 1 (2019): 107–125.

in forms of collaboration and exchange occurring without any money changing hands. The informal sector, in his view, already included things such as childcare cooperatives and various forms of charity work. It just needed to be scaled up to unlock its great potential.

In addition, Ingelstam also proposed a more formalized system of mandatory community service: every member of society should be obliged to work for a certain time in "childcare, elderly care, the simpler forms of healthcare, food production and many other activities."[73] Organized by the state, this would amount to a form of taxation in kind. Instead of raising the tax rate on monetary incomes, every citizen was to contribute equally by working the same number of hours for the common good. This is how the proposal was presented by Ingelstam's close associate Christer Sanne, who in the late 1980s became another public advocate of degrowth.[74] Just like Linder before them, they developed their own set of analogies used to explain the implications of uneven growth. In most of the articles I have found, they are not quoted as explicitly referring to William Baumol or to the metaphor of a disease; in fact, the centrality of BCD for these visions is more apparent in their books.[75]

Particularly in 1980–81, Lars Ingelstam seemed to appear everywhere in the media, presenting his vision of a growing informal economy. To many columnists at the time, this at least seemed like an interesting third way, transcending the old divide between left and right – as far away from socialism as from free-market liberalism.[76] (Whether this was an accurate description of Ingelstam's po-

---

73 Stina Helmersson, "'Vi har bara två vägar att välja!'" *Aftonbladet*, May 23, 1983; see also Lars Ingelstam, "Varför har vi inte råd med tjänster?" *Stockholms-Tidningen*, June 2, 1982; Ingela Björk, "Ingelstams recept för fortsatt välfärd: Tio timmar samhällstjänst," *Statstjänstemannen* 1994, no 10.
74 Christer Sanne, *Hur mycket arbete behövs?* (Stockholm: Statens råd för byggnadsforskning, 1989); Christer Sanne, "Hur vill vi arbeta?" *Aftonbladet*, December 10, 1989.
75 Lars Ingelstam, *Ekonomi för en ny tid: Lärobok om industrisamhället och framtiden* (Stockholm: Carlsson, 1995), 149–156; Christer Sanne, *Keynes barnbarn: En bättre framtid med arbete och välfärd* (Stockholm: Formas, 2007).
76 See, for example, Weje Sandén, "Lars Ingelstam i ny bok: Dags börja räkna med den dolda ekonomin," *Svenska Dagbladet*, October 23, 1980; Kerstin Vinterhed, "Lars Ingelstam, fd framtidsforskare: 'Politiker tänker kortsiktigt, de planerar bara till nästa val'," *Dagens Nyheter*, July 27, 1980; Bertil Ekerlid, "Du är verksamhetslysten och aktiv, säger Ingelstam," *Expressen*, November 3, 1980; Bernicus, "Svepet," *Göteborgs-Posten*, November 9, 1980; Christian Swalander, "Visst finns det en framtid för den svenska ekonomin," *GT*, February 2, 1981; Karl Erik Lagerlöf, "Informell ekonomi och ekonomisk demokrati. Fatta sitt liv," *Dagens Nyheter*, April 22, 1981; Björn Grahm, "Chalmerister diskuterar tjänster och gentjänster," *Göteborgs-Posten*, October 5, 1981; Lars Ingelstam, "Varför har vi inte råd med tjänster?" *Stockholms-Tidningen*, June 2, 1982; Bengt Rolfer, "Den folkliga klokheten – ett vapen mot Storebror," *Aftonbladet*, January 24, 1983; Ann

litical vision is another question.) After the Social Democrats returned to power in 1983, it was even reported that the new deputy prime minister, Ingvar Carlsson, found inspiration in Ingelstam's reassessment of the informal economy.[77]

"The new Swedish model" was the title of a 1986 programmatic article by Ingelstam published in the more theoretical journal of the Social Democratic Party.[78] However, his model for degrowth, described by some as "lingonberry-picking socialism," apparently did not receive any significant reactions from the Social Democrats.[79] There was greater enthusiasm in the Green Party, which had been founded in 1981 and shared Ingelstam's critique of economic growth.[80] Interviewed by the Green Party's journal, Ingelstam argued – without mentioning Baumol's name – that in the formal, monetary economy, "goods become cheaper while services become expensive." For this reason, "economic reason speaks for the further development of the informal sector." Relying on unpaid amateurs would not only provide welfare services at a low cost but also "restore the collective sense of life."[81] After the Green Party was first elected to the Swedish parliament in 1988, Ingelstam was reported to serve as their informal advisor.[82]

One of the early ideologues in the Green Party, Birger Schlaug, has indicated in retrospect that his political evolution was deeply shaped both by Ingelstam and by Linder's *The Harried Leisure Class*.[83] Schlaug also writes that during his

---

Svärding, "Framtidsforskare: Dela både jobben och hushållsmaskinerna," *Dagens Industri*, February 21, 1983; Stina Helmersson, "'Vi har bara två vägar att välja!'" *Aftonbladet*, May 23, 1983; Inga-Lisa Sangregorio, "Bör allt arbete vara lönearbete?" *Dagens Nyheter*, January 21, 1985; Gundel Wetter, "Envise optimisten Ingelstam: 'Det är dags att överge den svenska modellen'," *Göteborgs-Posten*, April 7, 1985; Ulla Herlitz, "Informellt arbete för regional balans," *Göteborgs-Posten*, May 30, 1985; Åke Lundquist, "En spännande berättelse om jobben i framtiden," *Dagens Nyheter*, October 20, 1985.

77 Anders Kilner, "Ny idé från Ingvar C gynnar privat service," *Göteborgs-Posten*, January 31, 1984; Monika Olson, "Obetalt jobb är vanligast," *Dagens Nyheter*, January 31, 1984.

78 Lars Ingelstam, "Arbetstidsfrågan och en ny svensk modell," *Tiden* 1986, no. 5–6, 297–311; cf. Lars Ingelstam, "Sverige är möjligheternas land för delade jobb," *Dagens Nyheter*, January 14, 1986.

79 Lars Ingelstam, "Tillväxtens falska profeter," *Moderna Tider*, October 1993, 30–35.

80 Per Gahrton, "Ökad tillväxt fel väg för Sverige," *Dagens Nyheter*, February 5, 1985.

81 Mats Jacobsson, "Arbetslöshet som en befrielse," interview with Lars Ingelstam, *Alternativet i svensk politik* 1986, no. 29, 6–7.

82 Magdalena Ribbing, "Lösa förbindelser påverkar partiledare," *Dagens Nyheter*, January 21, 1990.

83 Birger Schlaug, "Den rastlösa välfärdsmänniskan," blog post, May 22, 2008. <https://schlaug.blogspot.com/2008/05/grn-vecka-och-vad-gr-vi-nu-d.html>; Birger Schlaug, "Myt 2: 'Skola, äldrevård och omsorg kräver ekonomisk tillväxt. . .'," blog post, May 8, 2013. <https://schlaug.blogspot.com/2013/05/myt-2-skola-aldrevard-och-omsorg-kraver.html>.

many years as a Green Party spokesperson, he struggled to make people understand the real significance of BCD. In this reading, William Baumol was primarily an important critic of economic growth.[84]

8 Postlude: The Reception of BCD since the 1990s

Sweden entered a deep economic crisis in the early 1990s, and the Social Democrats lost the 1991 elections. This marks a shift in the Swedish reception of BCD. The idea of degrowth as a solution to the cost disease, which had been circulating in the 1980s, was soon marginalized. On the other hand, BCD ended up becoming more frequently used by mainstream economists to explain the fiscal crisis of the welfare state. Throughout the 1990s and early 2000s, the Baumolian analogy of a string quartet was commonly referenced in Swedish discussions on the cost of public services. However, a closer look reveals a subtle change in how the cost disease was articulated as a problem.

The focus was no longer on *unbalanced* growth (i.e., the relative difference in productivity growth between sectors). Instead, most references to BCD served to problematize *low* growth in absolute and aggregate terms. BCD had previously often been presented as a "paradoxical" phenomenon characteristic of a rapidly growing economy. Now, it was rather used to explain overall stagnation.[85]

The period 2002–2006 stands out as one of exceptionally high concern regarding BCD among Swedish opinionmakers. In various reports, economists speculated that municipal tax rates might have to double in the future as a result of both BCD and an aging population.[86] During these years, Baumol's old example of

---

84 Birger Schlaug, "DN har upptäckt nåt. . .," blog post, January 21, 2014. <https://schlaug.blogspot.com/2014/01/dn-har-upptackt-nat.html>; Birger Schlaug, "Tankegångar som kan mota kortsiktighet och stuprörstänkande," blog post, February 26, 2021. <https://schlaug.blogspot.com/2021/02/tankegangar-som-kan-mota-kortsiktighet.html>.

85 This is particularly apparent in the case of Klas Eklund, author of the most influential Swedish economics textbook. Here, BCD is mostly presented as a way to explain fiscal crises. Students are also presented with the doubtful claim that William Baumol was "the first to observe" how personal services tend to become more expensive over time. See Klas Eklund, *Vår ekonomi: En introduktion till samhällsekonomin*, 13th ed. (Lund: Studentlitteratur, 2013), 199.

86 Torben M. Andersen & Per Molander, eds., *Alternativ i välfärdspolitiken: Hur möter vi en åldrande befolkning och internationalisering?* (Stockholm: SNS, 2002); *Kommunala framtider: En långtidsutredning om behov och resurser till år 2050* (Stockholm: Svenska kommunförbundet, 2002); "Alternativ finansiering av offentliga tjänster," Swedish Government Report SOU 2003:57, 19–23; "Långtidsutredningen 2003/04," Swedish Government Report SOU 2004:19, 11–13; "Sveriges ekonomi – utsikter till 2020," Swedish Government Report SOU 2004:11, 77, 100–102; cf. Rianne

a string quartet was frequently invoked in the Swedish press, mostly to support a right-wing critique of the Social Democratic government. Liberal opinionmakers typically concluded that due to BCD, citizens must over time accept a form of access to healthcare that is less equal in a more privatized system.[87] According to the above-mentioned economist Assar Lindbeck, such a dismantling of the welfare state should not be understood as an ideological choice but as a necessity following from "fundamental economic mechanisms, such as Baumol's Law."[88]

In the 2006 elections, the Social Democratic government lost to a liberal/conservative alliance. From that point and onwards, references to BCD in the Swedish press suddenly became much less frequent.

9 Concluding Remarks

The Swedish reception of Baumol's cost disease demonstrates the significance of rhetorical devices in the circulation of economic knowledge and how the same rhetorical device could be used in support of vastly different political agendas. What the different uses have in common is the articulation of some sense of crisis, one which does not strike suddenly but rather constitutes a long-term process that will force society, or some parts thereof, to rethink the conventional way of organizing the economy.

For some commentators, BCD appeared as the key for presenting a radical critique of economic growth. Others arrived at the opposite conclusion: that economic growth must accelerate in those sectors where growth is possible to enable a redistribution of resources to the diseased sectors. In relation to cultural policy, appealing to the authority of Baumol is routinely done when arguing for a strong and expansive public funding of the arts. In the wider context of the future of welfare services, however, BCD has mostly been referenced by those arguing that the public sector must reduce its responsibilities.

The fact that we can identify a plurality of "politics of the cost disease" should not come as a surprise, considering that the rhetorical device in question depends

---

Mahon, "Swedish model dying of Baumols? Current debates," *New Political Economy* 12, no. 1 (2007): 79–85.

87 For some examples, see Peter Wolodarski, "Den allt dyrare 'Spöksonaten'," *Dagens Nyheter*, May 27, 2002; Mats Svegfors, "Låt välfärden variera i landet," *Dagens Nyheter*, July 6, 2003; Heidi Avellan, "Alla köar inte," *Sydsvenska Dagbladet*, November 4, 2003; "Jobb eller försörjning – alternativen är tydliga," *Dagens Industri*, July 6, 2006.

88 Assar Lindbeck, "Kvalitet eller rättvisa blir vårt val i vården," *Dagens Nyheter*, February 27, 2005.

on an economic model in which activities with highly different characteristics are lumped together as "the nonprogressive sector." Just because theatre, childcare and policing might all lag behind the average rate of productivity growth in industrial sectors, there are few who would seriously argue that there must be *one* singular solution to the cost disease that is applicable in all cases.

It may here be worth remembering that William Baumol already in 1967 discussed the severe consequences of the cost disease for the police. Nevertheless, I have not found a single explicit reference to policing in the Swedish reception of BCD. The application of this concept was in practice rather limited to, on the one hand, culture and the arts and, on the other, healthcare and other forms of care provided by the public sector. We have also seen examples of an almost existential reinterpretation, pioneered by Staffan Burenstam Linder, focusing on the lack of time in everyday life and why this problem cannot be solved by economic growth. All this should also be considered against the background of Gøsta Esping-Andersen's conclusion that in the period under consideration, the Swedish labor market became increasingly segregated by gender, as most new jobs went to women working in the public sector with precisely those services at the center of most discussions on BCD. Hence, it is truly remarkable that explicit references to gender were all but absent in the material studied here. This might obviously have to do with the fact that the circulation of economic knowledge, in this case as well as in many others, was mostly a male affair. It should be highlighted that BCD was not a discovery made individually by William Baumol – the intellectual contributors included several female US-American economists: Anne Scitovsky, Alice Vandermeulen and Mary I. Oates. But as BCD was established as a concept, named after William Baumol, its further circulation in Sweden was driven by men, many of whom were not economists themselves while often appealing to the authority of the famous US-American economist.

It is possible to distinguish between at least three kinds of policies proposed as a response to the cost disease. Furthermore, these correspond to the list of possible outcomes presented by William Baumol and Mary I. Oates in 1972. The first kind of policy is *redistribution*: the state takes on the responsibility for subsidizing certain services so that these can still be offered for the benefit of the public. This argument tends to be based on a relatively optimistic prognosis for long-term economic growth, assuming that there will always be enough money to redistribute by means of taxation. The reference to BCD as an argument for public subsidies has been particularly common in the context of cultural policy.

I propose the term *austerity* for the second kind of cost disease policy. It has mostly been articulated as a critique of the welfare state. Baumol's cost disease is here used to argue that in a near future, it may be necessary to cut down on the public provision of services such as healthcare, either by charging the individuals using the services or by allowing the quality of services to deteriorate. Thus, BCD could open the way for a moderate critique of the Swedish welfare state, which has differed considerably from the principled rejection of the welfare state as a whole associated with neoliberal thinkers such as Friedrich Hayek.

Degrowth is the third kind of policy which, mostly during the 1980s, was presented as a solution to the cost disease. This agenda included some utopian features and was defined by the affirmation of amateur activities as valuable to society, the reduction of working hours and the consolidation of a non-monetary "informal sector."

Advocates of each of these three programs have, as I have demonstrated, all expressed that the "cost disease" is a long-term process that should be more widely recognized. In each case, they have also been fond of reusing William Baumol's classical analogy of a string quartet that simply cannot play any faster. This indicates that as a rhetorical device, BCD is able to do something that perhaps could not be done without invoking the metaphor of "disease" or without the appeal to Baumol's authority as an economist. As we have seen, the long-term consequences of unbalanced productivity growth had been analyzed by other prominent economists prior to Baumol, including some Swedish economists whose observations circulated among a wide public in the 1950s – but without a rhetoric of social crisis. It seems like the *pathologization* of unbalanced growth was crucial for making BCD such an attractive (and flexible) rhetorical device ever since the late 1960s.

Possibly, it could even be fruitful to follow the theological intuition of Staffan Burenstam Linder and consider how BCD helped articulate a kind of secular "eschatology" otherwise excluded from the discipline of economics.

After all – as Susan Sontag analyzed in her essay *Illness as Metaphor* – there is a long tradition in political philosophy of talking about diseases, which are sometimes to be treated, sometimes to be violently attacked. "Disease equals death," according to Sontag.[89] This may or may not be the case with the political uses of Baumol's cost disease. However, the metaphor of disease has definitely been attractive for commentators wishing to direct people's attention away from short-term indicators and toward the more fundamental trajectory of long-term change in capitalist modernity.

---

[89] Susan Sontag, *Illness as Metaphor* (New York: Farrar, Straus and Giroux, 1978), 78, 81.

About the Contributor

Rasmus Fleischer is a researcher in economic history at Stockholm University focusing on cultural economy, media history and the critique of economic statistics. His current focus is on the measurement of inflation: the mostly implicit valuations made when statisticians decide to compare the prices of qualitatively different products in the Consumer Price Index. Together with Daniel Berg, he has recently published the monograph *Varors värde: Kvalitetsvärderingar i konsumentprisindex under 1900-talet* (2023). Previously, he has been involved in an interdisciplinary project examining the streaming service Spotify, co-authoring the book *Spotify Teardown* (MIT Press, 2019).

Katherine Arens
Memoirs as Postmemory: Adorno, Lazarsfeld, and the US Radio Project

Abstract: This essay focuses on two 1969 memoirs by Paul Lazarsfeld and Theodor Adorno, respectively, about the Rockefeller Foundation's Radio Research Project launched in 1933. These texts allow us to address the question of which kinds of data memoirs might actually provide. By contextualizing these two retrospective narratives, I argue that they need to be considered acts of postmemory, as narratives regarding a project imposing strategic gaps into historical truths and revealing deeply conflicting ideas about empirical research and in collective memories with regard to the tensions in and goals of the Radio Project, as well as to possible gaps between generations of work within the Frankfurt School itself. Both authors speak from within established professional identities as scholars of mass communication in the public sphere. However, the authors' works narrate for specific audiences whose collective memory may differ significantly from the facts of the authors' memories or postmemories of the same or parallel experiences – differences that can straightforwardly be recovered, if memoirs are to be considered reliable sources of historical data.

Keywords: Paul Lazarsfeld, radio listener research, Theodor Adorno, postmemory, memoir

Introduction

This essay focuses on two 1969 memoirs about the Radio Research Project, launched and sponsored by the Rockefeller Foundation as a two-year project grant starting in 1933, and which is today remembered as the site where two major twentieth-century intellectuals began their careers in the US as refugees from Nazi Germany. The first was written by Paul Lazarsfeld (1901–1976), a sociologist of Austrian-Jewish background who left projects in Vienna to become head of what became the Office of Radio Research, first at Princeton (1937–39), then at Columbia University (as founder of its Bureau of Applied Social Research).[1] The second essay was written by the

---

[1] Paul Lazarsfeld, "An Episode in the History of Social Research: A Memoir," in *The Intellectual Migration: Europe and America, 1930–1960*, eds. Donald Fleming and Bernard Bailyn (Cambridge, MA: Harvard University Press, 1969), 270–337. Another important text in this context is Paul

scholar he hired as a project assistant, thereby securing him an exit visa out of Nazi-controlled Germany: Theodor Adorno (1903–1969) known for his key role in the Frankfurt School.[2]

As we explore here, autobiographical texts such as these from the Radio Project bear witness not just to historical experiences but also how narratives tend to be revised as they are retold. This process of revision is currently mostly referred to as an effect of *postmemory*. As used in the context of Holocaust studies, scholars such as Marianne Hirsch define postmemory studies as illuminating how narratives regarding historical experiences may be passed on between generations: "Postmemory describes the relationship of the second generation [children of survivors] to powerful, often traumatic, experiences that preceded their births but that were nevertheless transmitted to them so deeply as to seem to constitute memories in their own right."[3]

However, the field of memory studies as originally mapped out by Maurice Halbwachs (1877–1945)[4] suggests that a broader interpretation of postmemory might be appropriate when dealing with memoir texts such as those from the Radio Projects in the context of historical interpretation. In studying memory, Halbwachs combined historical and sociological studies with both group and individual psychology to then make a distinction between autobiographical memories and historical memories on the basis of their source and impact on individuals. Two of his precepts are key when it comes to memoirs: (1) that direct experiences create memories of deeper impact (as do experiences made at earlier ages), and (2) that memories of the group (such as a nation or society) actually rewrite or reconstruct the past by using the mental images they employ in their present to re-imagine the past and the mental images inculcated, thus producing postmemories reinforced by their present society and reflecting its values.

Halbwachs specifies that each "past" is its own frame of reference, using the story of a little girl found in the forest in 1731. She could not explain where she

---

F. Lazarsfeld, *Radio and the Printed Page: An Introduction to the Study of Radio and Its Role in the Communication of Ideas* (New York: Duell, Sloan, and Pearce, 1940).

2 Theodor Adorno, "Scientific Experiences of a European Scholar in America," in *The Intellectual Migration: Europe and America, 1930–1960*, 338–370.

3 For an overview of this theory, see Marianne Hirsch, "The Generation of Postmemory," *Poetics Today* 29, no. 1 (Spring 2008): 103–128, quote on p. 103.

4 Cultural memory studies received scholarly attention in the work of Maurice Halbwachs, known in English particularly from the edited collection *On Collective Memory*, edited and translated by Lewis Coser (Chicago: University of Chicago Press, 1992); the more recent generation of theorists include Jan Assmann, *Das kulturelle Gedächtnis: Schrift, Erinnerung und politische Identität in früheren Hochkulturen* (Munich: Beck, 1992), and Aleida Assmann, *Der lange Schatten der Vergangenheit: Erinnerungskultur und Geschichtspolitik* (Munich: Beck, 1992).

came from and was thus brought to a new home: "The child has left one society in order to pass into another. It seems that at the same time the child will have lost the ability to remember in the second society all that he did and all that impressed him, which he used to recall without difficulty, in the first."[5] That "ability to remember," in turn, is based in society and aimed at the present:

> It is also in society that [people] recall, recognize, and localize their memories. [. . .] we place ourselves in their perspective [other people's] and we consider ourselves as being part of the same group or groups as they. It is in this sense that there exists a collective memory and social frameworks for memory; it is to the degree that our individual thought places itself in these frameworks and participates in this memory that it is capable of the act of recollection.[6]

Moreover, such acts of recollection work in two directions: individuals "use social frameworks when they remember" but also "the memory of the group realizes and manifests itself in individual memories."[7] And most relevant to the problem of memoirs or autobiographies:

> Society from time to time obligates people not just to reproduce in thought previous events of their lives, but also to touch them up, to shorten them, or to complete them so that, however convinced we are that our memories are exact, we give them a prestige that reality did not possess.[8]

And in doing so, "we adopt the attitude common to members of this group, that we pay attention to the memories which are always in the foreground of its way of thought."[9]

To use Halbwachs to expand on Hirsch: this is the narrative problem conditioning the value of memoirs as historical data. Memoirs not only reflect two historical frames of reference (past and present), they may also serve as acts of *both* group *and* individual postmemory. In other words, memoirs and similar autobiographical texts are not only products of tectonic shifts in the group's foundation of memory between the time of the narrated experience and the narrative, but such texts also attest to how their *authors* resituate and redesign their identities within their context of narration – and, in this case, across what might well be seen as a traumatic break, given that the professional and/or political collectives supporting them had disappeared in the tragedies of the Holocaust. Autobiogra-

---

5 Halbwachs, *On Collective Memory*, 37–38.
6 Halbwachs, *On Collective Memory*, 38.
7 Halbwachs, *On Collective Memory*, 40.
8 Halbwachs, *On Collective Memory*, 51.
9 Halbwachs, *On Collective Memory*, 52.

phies can thus also attest to how traumatic psycho-social experiences may be refracted in many ways, especially as breaks in identity or through shifts in the valuation of the narrative elements inherited from either of the two historical social frames comprising that identity.

Such breaks, I believe, are signaled in the difference between the two Radio Project memoirs. Lazarsfeld's and Adorno's autobiographical texts each recount how the Project facilitated their escapes from growing Nazi threats in Germany and brought them into new work contexts under conditions recoverable as uncontested facts. Lazarsfeld was hired due to his expertise in statistical methods and social science fieldwork in Vienna. His charge in the project was to uncover what listeners thought of radio and how they interacted with it. Adorno was taken onboard the project by Lazarsfeld in 1937–38 to work on radio music on the basis of his previous work on surveys and because he was identified as a significant scholar in need of a visa to enter the US. Lazarsfeld leveraged this project to assume a position as a significant voice in US debates on empirical social science methods. Adorno left the project in 1941 as a result of his growing antipathy to how the project framed the ways in which listeners and the mass media interact, as well as, probably, because he rejected the whole idea of contract work in its US framework.[10]

Behind these "facts," however, one can find highly different negotiations between the presents and pasts of each scholar – not just different identities as professionals but also two different approaches to overcoming the experience of geopolitical dislocation. Not only were these two scholars negotiating two different memory cultures (germanophone Europe and the US, each with different expectations of the story to be told), but they were also narrating their personal identities within two different time frames. How the two of them do this differs greatly, as we shall see. In consequence, we see different acts of postmemory represented in the affordances of this text type – evidence not only of what they claim to be and have been, but also of issues they elide as they renegotiate their identities between time and national frames. Such evidence points to how historians might be tempted to overestimate such accounts: what memoirs *leave out* provides an entirely different picture of the author's estimation of group memory

---

[10] For an overview, see Thomas Y. Levin and Michael von der Linn, "Elements of a Radio Theory: Adorno and the Princeton Radio Research Project," *The Musical Quarterly* 78, no. 2 (Summer 1994): 316–324. An exemplary brief summary of the conflicts involved, explained as different research paradigms, is Elihu Katz and Ruth Katz, "Revisiting the Origin of the Administrative versus Critical Research Debate," *Journal of Information Policy* 6 (2016): 4–12. Details on the project are found in Hynek Jeřábek, *Paul Lazarsfeld and the Origins of Communication Research* (London: Routledge, 2017).

and how he or she wishes to edit it (source experience and target audience alike). This should force readers to consciously evaluate the space between the *Wahrheitswert* of each text (which "truth" the authors are telling) and their *Wirklichkeitswert* to those memoirists (what they consider "real" issues and forces in each framework – information on which *kind* of postmemory they are enacting, consciously or subconsciously).

In some cases, geopolitical dislocations disrupt straight-line connections between history and memory so that collective memory as held in the mind of even a single historical generation or disrupted individual experience may be subject to postmemory revisions. As we shall see, this is the case when comparing these two contemporaneous memoirs regarding a shared project where the postmemory revisions differ greatly, not only due to national history narratives that have been frozen or broken off but also due to more specialized disciplinary or institutional conventions. The relationships between the two "cultures" – European social sciences and a US-based project in the same field – end up being strategized so that *each text* comes from a *different* cultural site in the same national culture and appeals to a different audience in the US (or perhaps beyond). The *Wirklichkeitswert* of each varies drastically, even as they rely on similar factual "truths."

The present essay thus explores these two memoirs with this caveat in mind, asking which kind of data they might actually provide as *negotiations* within the mode of postmemory as well as "factual" narratives. I found my impetus for questioning memoirs as data in Wulf Kansteiner's discussion on "Postmemory als wissenschaftliche Standarderzählung: Über den Nutzen und die Nebenwirkungen generationeller Erinnerungsgeschichten."[11] Kansteiner offers a cautionary tale regarding historical memory and the practices of historians while also problematizing, for example, how "standard accounts" of historical events are created around essentializing categories such as "generations," which reify temporal location, generational tropes, and the identities of age cohorts. Concepts such as postmemory reify the existence of generations, thereby legitimizing studying these in new ways. In particular, by creating a kind of ideal type for what a generation experiences or remembers, it becomes easier for individuals to identify with or reject this ideal type, which causes very specific kinds of historical blindness regarding the "connection between science and politics" "since hiding political goals facilitates the construction of scientific legitimacy" ("denn das Ausblenden

---

[11] Included in *Unsere Väter, unsere Mütter: Deutsche Generationen im 20. Jahrhundert*, ed. Volker Benkert (Frankfurt/M: Campus Verlag, 2020), 85–104. Kansteiner uses as an example the concept of "Wendekinder" as the essentialization of a generation's experience in recent German history.

politischer Zielsetzungen erleichtert die Konstruktion wissenschaftlicher Legitimität"[12]). Placing two memoirs next to each other, as I do here, makes them part of a single generation. However, I would like to establish some critical distance between the "memories" and the politics of the writers in these works, rather than following the generational convention, the "ideological privilege" for such inherited assumptions (*ideologische Aufwertung*[13]). As we shall see, these two retrospective narratives are based on experiences from scholars with deeply conflicting ideas concerning empirical research. In doing so, their memoirs point to shared (but varying) gaps in the collective memories in terms of the tensions in and the goals of the Radio Project. Lazarsfeld's and Adorno's texts look back at how they restructured their professional identities as scholars interested in theories of mass communication in the public sphere. They narrate versions of their own stories for the next generation from within the collective memory of those who survived and how they did so. In other words, they revise their memories for two different present audiences that do not share the same expectations regarding theory.

Adorno is very clear about his earlier objections with regard to both the project and to working within the institutional confines of sociology in the United States. In these statements, he speaks to the collective memory of the Federal Republic of Germany that by the late 1960s claimed to have broken with Nazism but also with "American occupation" in its intellectual life. Lazarsfeld details how the Radio Project evolved its models for empirical survey research, as he also situates Adorno's role in the project at a crossroads between the rapidly evolving contexts of theory and praxis in the social sciences in both the Federal Republic of Germany (FRG) and the US. The gaps between these two autobiographical memoirs, however, indicate the need to pay greater attention to their intended readers as evidence of ruptures in epistemic cultures and the "ideological privilege" that each of them asserts – and hence of how their work might need to be revalued by correlating the gaps in their narratives with the facts of their experiences.

In the following sections, I discuss these two Radio Project memoirs, first Lazarsfeld's, and then followed by Adorno's. I first situate each of them in its historical origin to then move on to consider each as a negotiation with a particular audience and personal-professional identity. My conclusion turns back to memoirs and other autobiographical texts as epistemic objects that require a different hermeneutics to recover the archive of data embedded in them.

---

12 Kansteiner, "Postmemory," 58.
13 Kansteiner, "Postmemory," 103.

Postmemory Project Narratives, 1: Lazarsfeld

Both Lazarsfeld and Adorno explain at length the "empirical social research" that the Radio Project was engaged in. Lazarsfeld describes the origins of the Radio Project, his role in it, and his grounds for hiring Adorno, followed by reasons for not renewing Adorno's contract. Adorno, on the other hand, devotes much of his text to comparing "his" empirical research to that of Lazarsfeld in an attempt to set off his own *Authoritarian Personality* (1950) off against it and to claim a different definition of what "survey work" needs to do.[14] The differences in their accounts, however, point to a deeper theoretical divide than just two different approaches to surveys, how they were to be constructed and administered, and what they were actually capable of showing.

Lazarsfeld came to the Radio Project from a Vienna that was heavily invested in social psychology and the practical consequences of social identity formation, both negative and positive.[15] He had first worked with Karl and Charlotte Bühler in the new experimental psychology laboratory at the Institute for Psychology (now the Charlotte Bühler Institute, where Karl was hired in 1922 and Charlotte in 1923). Lazarsfeld's wife (married 1926 and later divorced) was Marie Jahoda (1907–2001) who was remembered as an important British social psychologist and who, after receiving a teaching certificate in 1928 and a psychology PhD in 1933, was active in Vienna's Social Democratic Party and the social welfare projects associated with Red Vienna.

Karl was part of the Würzburg School of psychology and was interested in cognitive processing and Gestalt psychology as producing understandings aiding individuals in terms of self-realization and social position (Karl Popper was his advisee), while Charlotte worked on developmental psychology. Both were heavily involved in Vienna's reforms of the school and social welfare systems, initiated by and engaging in research on all aspects of social psychology, especially on the role of trauma with regard to individual identity and development.

---

14 For a broader picture of the Frankfurt School's survey research, see Emily Steinhauer, "Empirical Research as a Form of Participatory Knowledge? The Sociological Projects of the Frankfurt School as Democratic Practice," in *History of Intellectual Culture*, vol. 1: *Participatory Knowledge*, eds. Charlotte A. Lerg, Johan Östling, and Jana Weiß (Berlin: De Gruyter, 2022), 97–122.

15 Marx echoes this tradition in his insistence on raising "consciousness" of the working classes in his *Communist Manifesto*, as did reformers as far back as at least Ferdinand Tönnies (1855–1936) and forward to the Vienna Circle. This was done in dialogue with the idea of ideal types put forward by Max Weber (1864–1920) and the work of Wilhelm Wundt (1832–1920) in psychology/social anthropology. All considered human mind to be plastic and responsive to education, and mind to be formed within group contexts, in response to society yet also able to move freely within a range of choices in its networks.

The Bühlers' shared approach to social psychology rested on a commitment to study embodied mind (not just logical cognition or individual identity) and thus to focus on practical projects based on the psycho-social development of individuals through education and social welfare projects that could aid consciousness raising that could transform society. In consequence, their research paradigm combined empirical observation with critical praxis to critique the reification of scientific concepts and social norms and did not admit of hard boundaries between social, physical, and the human sciences. This work is today most familiar from Ernst Mach's *Analysis of the Sensations* (*Die Analyse der Empfindungen und das Verhältnis des Physischen zum Psychischen* [1886]), which described how science operated within a dual frame of reference – both cultural and as inductive-materialist science.

Scientific terminology, Mach notes, reifies observed data into categories that not only combine sets of data but also cultural values. The knowledge preserved in such terminology actually amalgamates two different kinds of truth value: a *Wahrheitswert* (value as producing truths of observation through which individuals and groups build possible identities as individuals, and groups are built), which need not necessarily be a *Wirklichkeitswert* (value as referring to a purported ontology beyond or behind an individual science's heuristic values about in how it deals with material evidence in all modes, including volitional, concrete, conscious, and unconscious). Due to potential gaps between the two, Mach posits that all sciences, regardless of discipline, require situated epistemological critiques of their materialities, especially of their signifiers used and the practices they establish or to which they habituate their users (including affect, social behaviors, conventions of all sorts, and community-based identities).[16]

The Radio Project was based on this more data-driven approach to theories of social knowledge. It was planned as a critical intervention into understanding how groups and individuals processed what they heard on the radio as a particular kind of material input or education and how investigators might *integrate* the new media into definitions of social identity by viewing it as a form of education. The project combined research in social psychology (how groups and individuals identifying with these groups function) with critical investigations into how a group's sign systems/signifiers and identifiers are used by individuals to create

---

[16] This model runs much closer to what Deleuze and Guattari term a *persona*, in *What Is Philosophy?*, trans. Hugh Tomlinson and Graham Burchell (New York: Columbia UP, 1994 [1991 in French]). They critique the concept of a "subject" as a reification from the bourgeois era. To correct this problem, they see the subject as *product* of an entity's engagement with a culture's epistemological practice and signification – as a subject visible/audible to that group by participating in its signifying practices. "Subjectivity" is thus for them a normative abstraction overlooking correlations between subject, self, and individuality – a notion that Adorno resisted.

identities. Survey research became a central tool for correlating words, behaviors, and identities, similar to what Lazarsfeld and Jahoda had already used in a now classic study on unemployment: *Die Arbeitslosen von Marienthal* (1932; English eds. 1971). Marienthal was an industrial community where high unemployment led to psychological and psycho-social consequences in the community that the study hoped to capture. The study's conclusions would not have endeared them to the Frankfurt School: they argued that individuals identifying with groups had positive impacts and found that, in industrial societies, work had potential social benefits that contributed to an individual's sense of self, society, and structure of life, meaning that work was more than a way for false consciousness to be imposed by capitalism on society. Hence, this project called into question several assumptions in traditional Marxism that devalued labor as inculcating *false* consciousness under capitalist structures.

This project, with its approach to identity formation, along with Lazarsfeld's textbook on education statistics and his experience of working on a survey of radio listeners (1930–31), qualified him for a two-year fellowship sponsored by the Rockefeller Foundation (1933–35), working with two US-based sociological projects: C. Luther Fry's work at the University of Rochester and Robert S. Lynd and Helen Merrell Lynd's Middletown Studies on cultural norms and response to social change in middle America (two volumes, 1929 and 1937). When Austria's fascist government in 1934 outlawed Socialists, Lazarsfeld decided to stay in the US, and the Rockefeller Foundation helped by extending his fellowship.

The title of Lazarsfeld's memoir is meant to highlight disciplinary methods in social research: "An Episode in the History of Social Research: A Memoir." His essay situates his work as part of an evolution in the European social sciences "dominated by philosophical and speculative minds" (p. 270) rather than empirical data. Yet Lazarsfeld's Europe was closer to that of the Bühlers: it was developing a new social science under figures such as Ferdinand Tönnies (1855–1936). Tönnies' 1887 work *Gemeinschaft und Gesellschaft: Abhandlung des Communismus und des Socialismus als empirischer Culturformen*[17] (Community and Society: An Essay on Communism and Socialism as Empirical Patterns of Culture) has long been considered foundational for modern sociology, influencing important theorists such as Georg Simmel, Émile Durkheim, and Max Weber.

Such models stressed multimodal investigations from both cultural history and science – from historical practice as well as from theory. Tönnies, for in-

---

17 Ferdinand Tönnies, *Gemeinschaft und Gesellschaft* (Leipzig: Fues's Verlag, 1887).

stance, combined philology (the discipline of his PhD) with biology and psychology. In *Kritik der öffentliche Meinung* (1922),[18] Tönnies also stressed that the social fields of words and practices need to be considered empirical evidence and that the reifications implicit in scientific terminology may be dangerous (as did Mach, and Kansteiner a century later). A new terminological construct such as "public opinion" figures as part of a word field that establishes a particular theoretical view connecting bodies with social practices, which together constitute the field of empirical evidence documenting the functionality of the self and the community. These newly defined data sets became the norm for innovators such as Lazarsfeld, who clearly followed Tönnies in observing that sociology was developing subdisciplines.[19]

Lazarsfeld summarizes what he considers his work's central premises in terms that encompass a sociology working beyond theoretical arguments, including what would today be called multimodal data, but which by no means could be termen un- or anti-theoretical. He identified how complementary fields of empirical data should be collected:

a) "Objective observations" should be added to "introspective reports."
b) Specific case studies should nuance statistical information.
c) A study object needs to be considered not only in its contemporary form but also in its previous states.
d) "Natural and experimental data" should be combined ("mainly questionnaires and solicited reports") and supplemented with "unobtrusive measures" collected without interference from the investigator.[20]

Lazarsfeld was thus from the first committed to a critical and engaged sociology combining qualitative and quantitative analyses, induction from evidence, as well as deduction from theoretical frameworks. Moreover, his explanations of statistical methods and data collection resonate strongly on the earlier European work on social signification to which I have alluded (Wundt, Mach) and on assumptions originating in socialist traditions emphasizing group contributions to identity and knowledge production (e.g. Tönnies and the "Red Vienna" of the Bühlers).

---

18 Ferdinand Tönnies, *Kritik der öffentlichen Meinung* (Berlin: Springer, 1922).
19 Tönnies described four distinct subdisciplines in sociology: pure sociology (theoretical sociology applying normative categories to understanding the social world), applied sociology (analyses of specific groups or situations), empirical sociology (which compares theory with practice), and practical sociology (used to create direct interventions into various scenarios).
20 Lazarsfeld, "Episode," 282–283.

His "innovation" in the US was integrating his statistical expertise into the US context of market and mass media research, thereby creating a paradigm for multimodal data analyses and survey design that called for definitions of how classes are formed by means of interpellation into existing structures. He wanted instead to chart how the public sphere works as a dynamic and evolving field of choices, rather than defining individuals as reified victims of mass media, as well as to nuance how data was to be collected and understood in new forms of social organization, such as those precipitated by the mass media.[21]

In his memoir, Lazarsfeld has thus begun to redact his own narrative to help make his project part of the US scene and to explain how the social-psychological research carried out in Vienna was adapted to a new context, yet without specifying potential conflicts between the two research environments. Nor does he adhere to the determinist views about mass media that would become central to the work of the Frankfurt School. Instead, he investigates how the products of culture and individuals are mutually predicating, and how words, practices, and acts of understanding are based in communication communities sharing knowledge, their "life space."[22] He thus excludes personality tests from his research model because "the social structure has dominance over individual variations"[23] and as he was looking to redefine "life space" rather than working to understand the public as class-bound in traditional terms.

Lazarsfeld makes one additional critical move, almost as an aside, noting that Leopold von Wiese, editor of a sociology journal in Cologne, "disapproved of using the term sociological for work which he considered essentially psychological."[24] Today, scholars all too often ignore that this "psychology" is not an individual one like that of Freud but rather a cognitive psychology, most familiar from the work of J. G. Herbart, which also existed in US educational theory, positing that mind develops within culture.[25] As minds develop, they come to store a "mass of representations" (*Vorstellungsmasse*) that have a certain intentional force as products of and influences on group and individual experience, a mass that *enables* but does not *require* how individuals function as speaking subjects within the group. This is what Lazarsfeld refers to as the "latent strategies" inher-

---

21 This work is also reflected in his *Radio and the Printed Page* (New York: Duell, Sloan and Pearce, 1940).
22 Lazarsfeld, "Episode," 277.
23 Lazarsfeld, "Episode," 278.
24 Lazarsfeld, "Episode," 286–287.
25 For information on this link, see Katherine Arens, "Pedagogy as Epistemology: Building the Subject of Knowledge," in *Meinong-Studien/Studies*, vol 11. *Herbartism in Austrian Philosophy*, ed. Carole Maigné (Berlin: De Gruyter, 2021), 85–108.

ent in social organizations and the material propensities of formalized networks within them (terminologies, practices, values, etc.).

In *Radio and the Printed Page*, Lazarsfeld provides an example of how social relations have shifted: "radio has broken the monopoly that print once held on the communication of ideas."[26] That expanded "communication of ideas" is also a social function reorienting psycho-social spaces and altering the mass of representations out of which groups and individuals build and change identities: "the effect of radio on reading is great, especially for certain strata of the population educated enough to have reading habits, but not so high on the upper cultural level, where people do not listen much to the radio and are so sophisticated that they are not likely to take rather unspecific advice on what they should read."[27] Lazarsfeld thus takes up radio as a mass medium, not only in terms of the ideology embedded materially into the medium, but also as a matter of personal positioning – here, calling into question the differentiation between high/popular culture. Radio does help in forming identities, but his phrasing suggests that it provides "advice" that the *unsophisticated* may otherwise not have had access to – thus a positive impact.

What is particularly interesting in these passages is how Lazarsfeld creates a narrative that embeds individuals into both collective and theoretical frameworks, thereby prioritizing the social constructivism of identity. In a United States becoming increasingly paranoid about collectivism (in various forms of the "Red Scare" and anti-communist propaganda), he creates a framework of research practice that both supports and undermines US market research – it is both empirical (in the form of questionnaire research) and social-psychological in a developmental sense, not just deterministic, given that classes are defined by larger networks of identity producing determiners, which automatically implicate individual choice and values.

Lazarsfeld has thus added a dimension to US market research speaking of identities that evolve within collectives, without mentioning the social justice issues built into educational and social-psychological research such as the Marienbad Studies. His personal story has been recast to render his science palatable to a US-based audience in an act of postmemory that augments US research norms without challenging them. Wittingly or unwittingly, Lazarsfeld has suppressed possible arguments as to whether or not the "big data" of questionnaire research only sketches the social-psychological networks reductively. He also tacitly redefines "class," neither in Marxist-economic terms nor as based on education, but in

---

26 Lazarsfeld, *Radio*, xiii.
27 Lazarsfeld, *Radio*, 324–325.

terms of media access and engagement, differentiating. He thereby differentiates between informed and uninformed readers and listeners in terms of their access to options or different truths of narrative, but they are not simply victims of class inscription once the conditions of their media access change.

Such elisions constitute acts of postmemory with respect to professional identity and competence, in that Lazarsfeld neither asks nor answers questions about *why* survey research needs to address both group opinions and the possibility of individual transformation through media exposure. By doing so, he focuses his readers' attention on research methods and not on social construction or class determinism. Hence, Lazarsfeld helps his transition into a professional role recognizable in the US – part of mass market research – without summoning up the demons of socialism or class determinism that run counter to US myths about the sovereignty of subjects. His act of postmemory preserves theory from Vienna, while effacing important theorists. He addresses a distinctly US audience and tacitly reinforces his own theoretical and methodological approaches.

Postmemory Project Narratives, 2: From Lazarsfeld to Adorno

Adorno's Radio Project memoir takes on a very different tone. Its very title openly signals Adorno's indictment of North American social sciences while situating his own experience as fragmented across two different identities: "Scientific Experiences of a European Scholar in America." Lazarsfeld's essay does confirm that gap in his own intake memo on Adorno from March 7, 1938, which situates both Adorno and himself as negotiating a radical break between their European identities and their possible US-American ones:

> [Adorno] looks exactly as you would imagine a very absent-minded German professor and he behaves so foreign that I feel like a member of the Mayflower Society. When you start to talk with him, however, he has an enormous amount of interesting ideas. As every newcomer, he tries to reform everything but if you listen to him, most of what he says makes sense.[28]

Adorno's essay thus becomes particularly interesting in how he carefully distances himself from the methodology of the Radio Project.

---

28 Lazarsfeld, "Episode," 301.

Part of Adorno's agenda is overt: he admits that he, as a European scholar, was utterly resistant to "assimilation" to the US-based sociology upon which the Radio Project was based:

> Not only was it natural for me to preserve the intellectual continuity of my personal life, but I quickly became fully aware of It in America. [. . .] By nature and personal history, I was unsuited for "adjustment" in intellectual matters. Fully as I recognize that intellectual individuality can only develop through processes of adjustment and socialization, I still consider it the obligation and at the same time the proof of mature individuality to transcend mere adjustment.[29]

Gauged by such statements, Adorno was demonstrating his "maturity" in working outside the "adjustment and socialization" of a group project (and tacitly denouncing colleagues such as Lazarsfeld).

But a second comparison comes to the fore: his difficulties within the Radio Project, which "did not arise entirely out of my own limitations," presumably as a "mature" European scholar. He states that colleagues at the Radio Project resented him as "a kind of usurper,"[30] which is at least partially refuted by Lazarsfeld's memoir, which points to Adorno's inability to work in a group, as well as his own support for this team member:

> I had known about the work of T. W. Adorno on the sociology of music. He is now a major figure in German sociology, and represents one side in a continuing debate between two positions, often distinguished as critical and positivistic sociology. I was aware of these controversial features of Adorno's work, but was intrigued by his writing on the "contradictory" role of music in our society. I considered it a challenge to see whether I could induce Adorno to try to link his ideas with empirical research.[31]

That challenge was not met. It seems that Adorno was unable or unwilling to connect theory with more practical contexts.

Lazarsfeld tried, in early 1938, to explain to his directors why Adorno needed to be taken seriously as having ideas important to their case:

> This seemed to be necessary since his interviews with people in the radio industry had led to complaints of biased questions and distorted replies. This was the result, I explained, of misunderstandings common in encounters of this sort [i.e., European scholars working in the US]. To straighten out the situation, I asked Adorno to summarize his ideas in a memorandum which I planned to circulate among various experts to secure a broader basis of support for his work. In June 1918 he delivered a memorandum of 160 single-spaced pages, entitled "Music in Radio." But it seemed to me that the distribution of this text would only

---

29 Adorno, "Scientific Experiences," 338–339.
30 Adorno, "Scientific Experiences," 349.
31 Lazarsfeld, "Episode," 322.

have made the situation more difficult, for in English his writing had the same tantalizing attraction and elusiveness that it had in German. The notion of "fetish" played – as could be expected from a neo-marxist – a central role.[32]

Where Lazarsfeld himself had stressed Adorno's ability to adapt his work to the US situation, then, Adorno elided what in practice distanced him from the Radio Project – and not (just) because he was a "usurper."

Adorno's theoretical claims were equally intransigent: he never moved from the position that music broadcast over the radio was anything but a commodity (no longer "art" but a way for the mass media to commodify taste and control culture). Radio music of any form, Adorno notes elsewhere, interpolates individuals into social structures with largely negative impacts.[33] He does confess that certain of his judgments were based on inadequate information and his need for a piece that was "American" to secure his employment. He had portrayed jazz as a genuine art form, but he

> had not realized how far "rationalization" and standardization had permeated the so-called mass media and thereby jazz, in whose production they had such a great role. I actually still considered jazz to be a spontaneous form of expression, as it so gladly represented itself, and did not perceive the problem of a calculated and manipulated pseudo-spontaneity, a second-hand kind [. . .][34]

As a "spontaneous form of expression," he had hoped jazz could still be genuine music – just not in the commodified form presented on the radio that was his early exposure to jazz.

For Adorno, the current social system was now entrenched through radio in new ways, by a mass medium aligned with capitalism that influenced individuals to support purposes running counter to their true interests as human beings and producers of value. The result, as he describes it, is the "atomization" of social relations among the workers, who no longer exhibit mutual solidarity as human beings but turn into competitors abstracted into social identities as workers.[35] Such individuals accept the inauthentic representations of their experience as real. Instead, they are taught what "important music" is supposed to be.

Adorno exemplifies how radio perpetuates inauthenticity in a story about his (German) maid's experience with music. Back in Germany, she used to attend concerts, but in the US, she is satisfied with listening to music on the radio, which

---

32 Lazarsfeld, "Episode," 323.
33 A position more explicit, for example, in Adorno's *Philosophical Elements of a Theory of Society* (Cambridge, UK: Polity, 2019), 38.
34 Adorno, "Scientific Experiences," 340–341.
35 Adorno, *Philosophical Elements*, 36–37.

for Adorno constitutes a sell-out of what music is supposed to be worth and a sign of its commodification and fetishization in creating false consciousness.[36] "The thesis [of Adorno's "Radio Symphony" essay] was that serious symphonic music, as transmitted by radio is not what it appears and that consequently the claim of the radio industry to be bringing serious music to the people is spurious. This essay immediately met with strong resistance."[37]

Yet again, Adorno attacks the medium of radio on theoretical grounds, assuming bad outcomes for everything on radio. He explicitly attacks the NBC Symphony Orchestra under the baton of the here unnamed Arturo Toscanini (who brought classical music to parts of the US that had never heard symphonic music played to world standards), as well as other programming aimed at public education and outreach, including the "Music Appreciation Hour." Such programs, he notes, although "highly regarded and widely listened to as a non-commercial contribution promoting musical culture, [were] propagating false information about music as well as a deceptive and untrue conception of it."[38]

His antipathies also extend to the "standardization" in pop music,[39] equating it with the "pseudo-individualism" or false consciousness that would be central to *The Authoritarian Personality* – a manufacturing of tastes that solidify a commercialized group identity at the expense of individuals. Commodified art reifies listeners (a *Verdinglichung*), as the music industry manufactures hits as normative "good" art, making listeners unconscious of how "their" choices rest on false consciousness, inculcated by the mass media:[40] "Less and less depends upon their own conscious and unconscious being, their inner life. [. . .] they are intentionally and unintentionally led to believe that everything depends on them. 'Man is the ideology of dehumanization.'"[41] The result is a "discrepancy between what society promises its members and what it actually gives them" since the "machinery" "remakes the people inwardly to conform to itself"[42] in a surrender of human agency to the top-down mechanical producers of false consciousness.

---

36 For additional examples of such degeneration, see Theodor Adorno, "Über den Fetischcharakter in der Musik und die Regression des Hörens," *Zeitschrift für Sozialforschung*, vol. VII (1938), 321–356. A translation is found in Theodor Adorno, *The Culture Industry: Selected Essays on Mass Culture*, ed. J. M. Bernstein (London & New York: Routledge, 1991), 29–60.
37 Adorno, "Scientific Experiences," 352.
38 Adorno, "Scientific Experiences," 340–341.
39 Echoed in Theodor Adorno, "On Popular Music," in *A Critical and Cultural Theory Reader*, eds. Anthony Easthope and Kate McGowan (London: Open University Press, 1992), 301–314.
40 He and Horkheimer later changed their terminology to "consciousness industry" instead of "mass media" to emphasize this point.
41 Adorno, "Scientific Experiences," 356.
42 Adorno, "Scientific Experiences," 357.

Adorno remains at the level of theorizing necessary effects, where Lazarsfeld had sought to uncover data pointing to *why* individuals made the choices they made (and whether these choices were indeed manufactured). Adorno, in contrast, claims that, by (his) definition, the Radio Project could not capture what he considers most important, the "objective content" of the music it studied – an objection that clearly points at Adorno's own reification of the work of art as "true" rather than any interest in what happens in encounters with various forms of art:

> I am still persuaded today, that in the cultural sphere what is regarded by the psychology of perception as a mere "stimulus" is in fact, qualitatively determined, a matter of "objective spirit" and knowable in its objectivity. I oppose stating and measuring effects without relating them to these "stimuli," i.e., the objective content to which the consumers in the cultural industry, the radio listeners, react. What was axiomatic according to the prevalent rules of social research, namely, to proceed from the subjects' reactions as if they were a primary and final source of sociological knowledge, seemed to me thoroughly superficial and misguided. [. . .] And finally, it had still to be determined how far comprehensive social structures, and even society as a whole came into play.[43]

In consequence, studying after-market situations in mass media such as radio becomes by Adorno's definition an inferior undertaking. All that may be uncovered, he posits, is that reactions to radio music "were themselves conditioned" by those same market forces that commodified the art[44] – an appeal to the traditional Marxist model regarding how individual consciousness is determined by the economic-material basis of existence.

When juxtaposed with Lazarsfeld's remarks, Adorno's remarks confirm his incompatibility with the Radio Project and expose rifts that Lazarsfeld's text papers over. Lazarsfeld aligns himself with US social science research but never overtly states what is at stake when his research paradigm confronts US market research, while Adorno claims his "mature" position as a European thinker. In these essays, however, they both elide facts/assumptions regarding their work that are straightforwardly recoverable from other texts in order to establish themselves in very different positions on the sociological research map. Lazarsfeld presents himself as a project manager trying to meditate between "European'" and US scholarship, while Adorno presents himself as a theoretician evoking German traditions of aesthetics that essentialize the artwork as purveying truth. In both narratives, there is no attempt to define social networks and the public sphere – contemporaneous arguments that would undercut the two theorists' self-justifications.

---

[43] Adorno, "Scientific Experiences," 343–344.
[44] Adorno, "Scientific Experiences," 345.

On a more practical level, such institutional incompatibility and Adorno's theoretical inflexibility had consequences: Lazarsfeld did not include Adorno in his grant renewal, a decision that freed Adorno to go to Berkeley and work there with the *Authoritarian Personality* project. That project did not diagnose the mechanisms of mass media and their impacts on individuals (for good or bad, as Lazarsfeld sought to chart) but rather the personalities or characters of individuals liable to accept conventionalism, authoritarianism, aggression, and stereotyping. Adorno's "F-Scale" thus essentially blames the victims of mass media.

If Lazarsfeld's postmemory rewriting of his discipline's shift focused on methodology, Adorno's postmemory rewriting implicates the definition of sociology itself – his rejection of the nuances of the subfields that Tönnies had suggested and his willingness to establish pure theory as his master discipline and professional identity. His account of *The Authoritarian Personality* not only claims it as theoretically more sophisticated than Lazarsfeld's Radio Project but also conflates theoretical design parameters with practical assessments of the ethics of the task at hand as he defines it. In doing so, the boundaries between *theory* as grounding scientific practice and *critical theory* as a social-political practice are irremediably broken down. The direction of Adorno's narrative thus suggests that, in reading his theory, current scholars need to assess his sense of self-authorization and essentializing of a certain intellectual class as a determining factor in the Frankfurt School's project. He posits in the work of art something "true" that will affect its consumers in positive ways (if it occurs in the concert hall and not over technically limited radio broadcasts) – an assumption that reifies a distinction between "high" and "popular" art, itself reified as part of the identity of "the sophisticated."

If Lazarsfeld helped to efface social constructivism as a viable theoretical model – to elide significant elements of the paradigms and projects in which he was trained –, then Adorno not only aligns theoretical sociology with politics but also elides any reference to the social psychology and social constructivism championed by his European colleagues such as Erich Fromm. Like Lazarsfeld, Adorno was clearly concerned with establishing himself in an intellectual leadership role, but in so doing, his acts of postmemory storytelling not only elided but also erased significant elements in the history of the Frankfurt School and in our understanding of its status as a social science project.

Adorno's Postmemory: Theory-Driven Praxis

The claims made for *The Authoritarian Personality* in Adorno's memoir deserve special attention not only as a clarification of his preference for theory (thus undercutting US social science) but also of his willingness to recast the history and reputation of the Frankfurt School for new audiences – how he erases the European history of social psychology for his US audience, while conforming to class-based expectations familiar to both Europeans and US readers.

The origin of the first such erasure is well-known: the term "authoritarian personality" used in Wilhelm Reich's *Massensychologie des Faschismus* (1933) to posit correlations between authoritarianism and individual repression and to combine psychoanalytic and social critical approaches to individual psyches. This explanation was taken over by Erich Fromm in his 1941 book *Fear of Freedom*,[45] which popularized the term as "authoritarianism" (and created the assumption that the term was Fromm's alone). They shared an approach to social psychology that was not unlike that of Lazarsfeld, tracking interplays between psychological and social forces as determining individual character.

Fromm devoted a long section to the authoritarian personality, explaining it as "based on concepts which deal with unconscious forces and the ways in which they find expression in rationalizations and character traits" (p. 117) and as "escape mechanisms" used by individuals to avoid confronting unpalatable situations such as Fascism. Fromm defines a "healthy" individual as someone who is "able to fulfill the social role he is to take in that given society" (p. 119) to "work in the fashion which Is required in that particular society [. . .] and participate in the reproduction of society" (p. 20). However, that "normalcy" does not necessarily correspond with what individuals desire for themselves. "Often he is well adapted only at the expense of having given up his self in order to become more or less the person he believes he is expected to be. All genuine individuality and spontaneity may have been lost" (p. 120), and he may be considered a cripple or stigmatized, which leads to that individual wanting to escape from the world and recapture what he was as an "individual" (p. 121), a state of isolation and fear that Fromm refers to as a "negative freedom." In Nazi Germany, such a flight out of the group into isolation often took the form of sado-masochistic, or even perverted, behaviors as the person surrenders individuality to authorities (p. 141).

---

45 Wilhelm Reich, *Die Massenpsychologie des Faschismus* (Copenhagen: Verlag für Sexualpolitik, 1933); Erich Fromm, *The Fear of Freedom* (London: Routledge & Kegan Paul, 1941). The first German edition was published in 1953.

In one sense, Fromm's psycho-social model provided the armature for *The Authoritarian Personality* but not necessarily a basis for a psychometric research program on mass culture. Adorno's report on his project typically presents survey questions and how they are interpreted as indications of individual character. Yet the kind of context provided by both Reich and Fromm – the sociopolitical contexts grounding particular personality structures, but which do not necessitate their taking any single form – is often missing in Adorno's report. Instead, Adorno reverts to a more classic argument structure about the reification and fetishization of false consciousness produced by the economic base, which is then mediated into subsequent generations as "needs" to be filled by ideal types with "good" work habits or a taste for "good art." In other words, he focuses on valuative dimensions of the character types (and flaws) involved, but attributes them to capitalism virtually without question.

Adorno's act of postmemory is signaled most clearly when he accuses Lazarsfeld of using a research paradigm based on data tracking what Adorno defined as commodified products based on the "bourgeois era" as a norm for his contemporary era – a value-driven analysis. In contrast, Lazarsfeld was trying to map the social-psychological effects of a new mass medium, one that realigned many individuals' exposure to and acceptance of information that had previously been defined by a particular class position – the bourgeoisie and its "fine" art. Adorno decided that Lazarsfeld was guilty of "invoking the supremacy of the system [which] becomes a substitute for insights into the concrete relationship between the system and its components"[46] and decries "the subjectively oriented analyses" in US-based sociological projects.[47] He neglects to mention that both Reich and Fromm (as well as the majority of the Berlin School of Freudianism) believed that the subjects were produced by these objective conditions, as opposed to Adorno's more classical model of the individual character as something outside these social models. Moreover, he rejects appeals to psychology as if it were all Freudian, rather than also potentially structural elements of a group, as the psychologists of the Berlin School would have assumed.

Adorno draws another line between US empirical sociology and that of the Frankfurt School project that misdirects his readers from a broader vision of sociology in Europe: he champions "free" research, meaning research that is not beholden to its financial backers (in Lazarsfeld's case, radio networks). However, Adorno's own subsequent project on the authoritarian personality was also subsidized, albeit without the kinds of deliverables and conditions written into Lazars-

---

46 Adorno, "Scientific Experiences," 357.
47 Adorno, "Scientific Experiences," 357.

feld's contracted opinion research. The Radio Project was thus judged by Adorno as serving its own instrument of fetishization: "Less and less depends upon [individuals'] own conscious and unconscious being, their inner life. In the meantime, the psychological as well as the sociological explanation of social phenomena has become in many ways an ideological camouflage [. . .]."[48] Thus Adorno claims that the Berkeley project "focusses upon subjective impulses" rather than ones stemming from a reified norm – from data collected from within the contexts being studied.[49]

There is an equivalent irony in Adorno's championing of the F-Scale as a corrective to this bad approach to data collection. Adorno himself contrasted what he did at Berkeley with what Brunswick had done in Vienna: she wanted "quantitative data,"[50] while he demanded qualitative data (in which he included individual personality data). Yet Lazarsfeld actually rejected classic personality surveys in his work due to the danger of such reification – qualitative data was viewed as having a different evidential status than quantitative data, but Lazarsfeld did include interviews that were more open-ended than the ones used by Adorno. However, Adorno conveyed his impression that, since the Berkeley project included both personality surveys and other quantitative data (often demographics), this was a sign that it was somehow "better" than the Radio Project in organizational terms: "The cooperation in Berkeley knew no friction, no resistance, no rivalry among scholars."[51]

Adorno worked hard to establish what was "critical" instead of "reified" about the Berkeley project and to tacitly erase the tradition in which the "authoritarian personality" was defined. For instance, he stressed that his questionnaires were not developed in an "inflexible" reliance on Freud: "Thus we simply had to abandon the dimension of the hostility of authoritarian types toward modern art, because this hostility presupposed a certain level of culture, namely that of actually having encountered such art, which the vast majority of our subjects had been denied."[52] This statement becomes even more interesting when we realize that the work was done in what was itself a fraught environment for Freudianism in the US, in the process causing friction between social constructivists such as Karen Horney,

---

48 Adorno, "Scientific Experiences," 356.
49 Adorno, "Scientific Experiences," 356.
50 Adorno, "Scientific Experiences," 359.
51 Adorno, "Scientific Experiences," 358. The use in psychoanalysis of sociological evidence from context was long established in Europe by voices such as Karen Horney, the Berlin "children's seminar" that included Annie Reich, and the Marxist analysts who were networked in the US through Otto Fenichel's *Rundbriefe* – as well as Erich Fromm and others whose reputations in the US preceded those of Horkheimer and Adorno by at least a decade.
52 Adorno, "Scientific Experiences," 360–361.

Annie Reich, or Otto Fenichel and the large number of dogmatically Freudian émigré analysts of the American Psychoanalytic Association. (Horney was expelled from the New York Psychoanalytic Institute in 1941 for questioning Freudian concepts like penis envy.)

Adorno's next statement reaffirms his tendency to favor theory over praxis, bolstered by his willingness to reify certain inherited philosophical concepts:

> It was not our main intention to determine present opinions and inclinations, and their distribution. We were interested in the fascistic potential. On this account, and to counteract it, we included in the investigation, as far as possible, the *genetic* dimension, the development of the authoritarian character. [. . .] more an exploration of possibilities than a collection of irrefutable findings.[53]

In such statements, Adorno is reifying individual consciousness under the rubric of "character" and its evolution rather than exploring it in relation to a socially constructed identity – he is arguing more on the level of Freud's Id than the Ego (the latter of which *is* actually socially constructed in Freud's theory).

That these choices need to be considered as part of postmemory can be attested in other ways, which is beyond the scope of this essay. But it is particularly noteworthy that Max Horkheimer's *Zeitschrift für Sozialforschung* in its 1938 volume (vol. 7) contained not only Adorno's own "Über den Fetischcharakter in der Musik und die Regression des Hörens," but also Maurice Halbwachs' "La psychologie collective du raisonnement," and "Bemerkungen zur Rundfunkmusik," an essay by Ernst Krenek (as Křenek), composer of the landmark modern opera *Jonny spielt auf* (1927). The latter is particularly important as it details quite precisely how radio music in various ways creates false consciousness for its listeners at a level of detail that could straightforwardly have been operationalized into a questionnaire asking how individuals "consumed" radio and evaluated what they heard.[54]

Nonetheless, Adorno considers his emphasis on character not to be a reflection of a norm but empirically grounded – he reifies personal identity or character as something that is not (just) empirically observable:

> In America I truly experienced for the first time the importance of what is called empiricism, though I was guided from youth on by the conviction that fruitful theoretical knowledge is impossible except in the closest contact with its materials. Conversely, I had to recognize with respect to the form of empiricism applied in scientific practice in America, that full scope of experience is fettered by empirical rules excluding anything that is inherent in the concept of direct life experience. By no means the worst characterization of what I

---

53 Adorno, "Scientific Experiences," 362.
54 As Pierre Bourdieu had done in *Distinction: A Social Critique of the Judgement of Taste* (Cambridge, MA: Harvard University Press, 1987).

had in mind would be a kind of vindication of experience against its translation into empirical terms. That was not the least important factor that led me to return to Germany [. . .][55]

The concept of "direct life experience" supports a theory greatly at odds with the social-constructivist model inherent in many pre-war publications from the original Frankfurt School. Adorno also confirms this directly in noting that he was "liberated from a certain naïve belief in culture and attained the capacity to see culture from the outside" in America, "where no reverential silence on the presence of everything intellectual prevailed, as it did in Central and Western Europe far beyond the confines of the so-called educated classes; and the absence of this respect inclined the intellect toward critical self-scrutiny."[56] Most significantly, he highlights his own *Metakritik der Erkenntnistheorie* (1956) as "the philosophical criticism of the scientific concept of the absolutely Primary that I employed in my books on the theory of knowledge" and rejects induction in the sciences ("the model hypothesis-proof-conclusion").[57] This last point is used once again to differentiate the Radio Project from the *Authoritarian Personality*:

> Only this much may be said: we never regarded the theory simply as a set of hypotheses but as in some sense standing on its own feet, and therefore did not intend to prove or disprove the theory through our findings but only to derive from it concrete questions for investigation, which must then be judged on their own merit and demonstrate certain socio-psychological structures.[58]

In other words, he once again accepts the reification of first principles regarding character and identity, as long as these terms remain on the level of philosophical theory rather than empirical evidence of psycho-social adaption.

Some Conclusions: Disciplinary Silos and Postmemory

These two first-person accounts of the Radio Project share with classical models of postmemory the fiat of recounting history within the affordance of palatability to their audiences in their two different understandings of the US frame of reference.

---

55 Adorno, "Scientific Experiences," 370.
56 Adorno, "Scientific Experiences," 367.
57 Adorno, "Scientific Experiences," 363. Theodor W. Adorno, *Zur Metakritik der Erkenntnistheorie*, in *Gesammelte Schriften*, vol. 5, ed. Rolf Tiedemann with Gretel Adorno, Susan Buck-Morss, and Klaus Schultz (Frankfurt/M: Suhrkamp, 1970).
58 Adorno, "Scientific Experiences," 363.

Each tries to establish the autobiographer as a credible intellectual persona with a significant voice in a particular intellectual context in ways that accommodate historical facts in patterns acceptable to their readers.[59] They are both first-person testimonies, even though they come from two different, almost incompossible frameworks of experience and practice in the framework of their production that are not bridged without effort and revisions of points of view. While both part of the experience of a single generation, the authors speak out of that generation's shared experience and to another, thus reframing pre-war experiences for two postwar intellectual cultures massively dislocated from their origins. Lazarsfeld speaks to the US as someone having salvaged some of Europe's scholarly program of social identity research into the postwar era, while Adorno is speaking to Europe in an era of rising anti-Americanism – a Europe that has had enough of what has been termed coca-colonization (after the soft drink) and especially a Germany eager to reclaim its intellectual hegemony over and against the America that Lazarsfeld works in and for.

What is presented in each autobiographical memoir does not necessarily imply the veracity or mendacity of their writers, but both texts do "leak" – each one contains clear nods or oblique references to a past history that they obscure in the texts, and both clearly report, if sometimes indirectly, on their authors' ethics and point of view. Yet taken as historical acts of witnessing, they present epistemological difficulties: erasures and elisions serving as willful or unintentional misdirection for their readers, supporting "standard accounts" with very particular contemporaneous goals and national references – the two cultures of Halbwachs' girl in the forest negotiated by adults with skills and agendas.

The most important takeaway from this comparison may be the context-boundedness of theory and perhaps within the refraction of several contexts. What seems to be a straightforward discussion of the Radio Project (pros and cons) actually rests on two extremely different models of the human mind, each contested in several dimensions from their pre-war starting points in Vienna or Frankfurt. They are narrated in the present from two highly different justificatory frameworks about professional authority and authorization, using terminology that seems par-

---

59 Also note that this approach to memoir as identity politics differs vastly from the approach in current work on autobiography or life writing, which study textual representations of self as an author's identity construction, rather than viewing identity construction as part of a public sphere negotiation, as I am doing here. The modern study of autobiography is often said to have begun with James Olney, *Metaphors of Self* (Princeton, NJ: Princeton University Press, 1972), while its most visible theoretical phase occurred in the 1980s with texts such as Sidonie Smith, *A Poetics of Women's Autobiography* (Bloomington: Indiana University Press, 1987) and Philippe Lejeune, *Le Pacte autobiographique* (Paris: Seuil, 1975), a term he coined which was popularized in English by the 1989 translation of his 1986 *Moi aussi* (Paris: Seuil, 1986) as *On Autobiography*, translated by Katherine Leary (Minneapolis: University of Minnesota Press, 1989).

allel, yet which stems from disparate logical frames (one affirming the relationship between individuals and groups, and the other denying its validity).

What these apparent incompossibilities suggest is that even technical philosophical treatises need to be read in light of the historical materialities that condition them, including distribution, praxis, professional training of the interlocutors, and the audiences for which they were intended. This is not a question of merely a professional debate or personal taste, but rather part and parcel of the documentality of autobiographical narratives – their status as social objects, which differs from the status of straight expository prose. These two texts share a generational context but reify *different* theoretical biases; where they differ and what they elide point to these differences without engaging them as cultural shifts or theoretical debates. Later scholars working with these texts as historical data need to consider them as interventions, as sallies into public reputations rather than as facts about the theories involved. By definition, a memoir is written by an unreliable narrator – not by a biographer, who can pretend to reliability.

In this case, questions of displacement and exile necessarily come to the fore – external motivations about how accounts of institutional history are staged, and theories edited. If such clusters of essays are viewed in isolation from each other and from their sources and target audiences, the scholars using them as historical evidence need to decide their status as conscious disinformation campaigns or unconscious mis-assessments of theories and terminology across divides of language and scientific cultures. In turn, such elisions often cause long-lasting "problems" for scholars trying to understand a body of work from within a disciplinary orthodoxy or a different national tradition – not all essays are written according to the same standards of truth value and identity value, and each needs to be assessed with regard to both. Moreover, standard narratives within disciplinary history about the "early" and "late" work of particular theoreticians may themselves be occluding the difference between evolutions in theoretical positions and transformations in the social and intellectual positioning of writers and speakers. Finally, any assumption that essays in any scholarly genre are somehow removed from considerations of self-marketing needs examining.

Katherine Arens is a professor of Germanic Studies at the University of Texas at Austin. Her work focuses on the history and epistemology of the humanities since 1750 and particularly on intellectual migration and the need to disambiguate regional germanophone cultures. Her most recent books are a volume (edited with Robert Dassanowsky) on *Interwar Salzburg* (2024) and *Vienna's Dreams of Europe: Thinking Beyond the Nation State* (2015), alongside essays on the foundation of art history as a human science, on anglophone historiography on Habsburg Austria, and on J. F. Herbart, J. G. Herder, and Robert Zimmerman as creating an inductive approach to the human sciences, especially the modern social sciences, that need to be set apart from traditional accounts of German Idealism as a coherent body of thought.

Section II: **Experimental Spaces**

Anne Kwaschik and Claudia Roesch

Experimental Spaces: Knowledge Production and its Environments in the Long Nineteenth Century

Abstract: This introduction conceptualizes man-made social environments as experimental spaces and arenas for scientific observation. First, it offers a broad definition of the term environment following Etienne Benson's conceptualization of environments as relational, mental and physical realms that exerted influence on various entities. It then discusses the investigative framework of experimental spaces including both a physical and discursive dimensions as well as the embedding of this special section in the history of knowledge. The central part of this introduction refers to the historiography on experiments in Science and Technology Studies (STS) and highlights how our approach is distinct linking conceptualizations of experiments with recent scholarship on intentional settlements as sites of knowledge production. We relate Bruno Latur's concept of the laboratory to practices of knowledge production in intentional settlements and agricultural communities. The third part addresses the entanglements between experimental spaces and settler colonialism, discussing a) how knowledge production could support imperial expansion, even for regions that were not (yet) imperial powers, b) how colonial infrastructures and a colonial mindset of settlers aided knowledge production in intentional settlements and c) how historiographical research about colonies as laboratories of modernity emphasizes that colonies became enabling spaces for utopian settlement projects in itself.

Keywords: Experiments, observation, knowledge production, colonialism, environments, laboratories

Introduction

In the aftermath of the French Revolution and the onset of industrialization, reformer and social scientist Charles Fourier conceptualized cooperative settlement colonies intended to serve as a testing ground for the new social order.[1] Fourier

---

[1] This special section emerged from discussions held during the retreat of the Konstanz Working Group on the History of Knowledge, focusing on "Utopias and Colonialism" in the summer of

Open Access. © 2024 the author(s), published by De Gruyter. This work is licensed under the Creative Commons Attribution-NonCommercial-NoDerivatives 4.0 International License.
https://doi.org/10.1515/9783111291383-006

clearly conceived of these "trial cantons" as experimental spaces while viewing the social realm as a subject of investigation and drawing upon epistemologies from the natural sciences to guide these experiments.[2] Approximately a century later, in 1911, Wolf Dohrn, a co-founder of the German garden city of Hellerau, characterized the settlement and its theater as a "Versuchsfeld" – a field for trials where reformers sought solutions to social issues through artistic practices.[3] Dohrn's use of the term "experimental space" to describe the community resonates with Fourier's approach in terms of outlining the *phalanx* a century earlier. They both viewed these spaces as arenas for observing, studying, and scrutinizing human interactions within their environments while employing methodologies and epistemologies akin to those used by natural scientists when studying bacteria in laboratories.

These two conceptualizations, designing man-made social environments as experimental spaces and as arenas for scientific observation, serve as the framework of this special section. This section endeavors to explore experimental spaces and the discourses surrounding them, analyzing how the concept of experimentation influenced knowledge production practices during the era of imperialism. In essence, the articles in this section investigate the role of experimental environments as sites for knowledge production extending beyond the confines of traditional academic institutions, such as academies, laboratories, and universities. They seek to understand how notions of experimentation shaped knowledge production across various contexts during the long nineteenth century, thereby positioning experimental environments as alternative settings for knowledge production beyond the natural sciences.

Experimental Spaces and Its Environments

This approach necessitates a broad understanding of the term "environment." In our delineation in this section, we adhere to Etienne Benson's recent exploration

---

2023. We extend our gratitude to all participants for the lively initial debate, to the reviewers of the articles and the section for their valuable comments and criticism, and to the editorial team of the journal for their meticulous work. The University of Konstanz supported this special section through its publication fund as part of the Excellence Strategy.

2 Charles Fourier, *The Theory of the Four Movements* (Cambridge: Cambridge University Press, 1996 [1808]), 318; see also Anne Kwaschik's contribution to this special section.

3 Wolf Dohrn, *Die Bildungsanstalt für Musik und Rhythmus Jaques-Dalcroze in Dresden-Hellerau. Ein Bericht mit 8 Abbildungen* (Jena: Eugen Diederichs, 1910), 9–10. Music Department, Staatsbibliothek Berlin, cited from Anne-Sophie Reichert's article in this special section.

of the environment as a subject of knowledge and concern over an extended historical period. Benson defines environments in a relational manner and conceptualizes them as mental and physical realms that not only exert influence but also produce decisive effects on entities.[4] According to Benson, such a "notion of environment calls our attention to the material conditions that are essential for any entity, including a concept, to emerge and persist."[5] Our objective in choosing the case studies in this special section was to investigate the intertwined social, natural, and aesthetic aspects of environments. These include considerations of climate (Roesch), geology and flora (Marktanner, Mazzoli), and social environments (Kwaschik, Reichert).

In these five case studies, intentional communities, colonial gardens, agricultural colonies, and artistic colonies are examined as experimental spaces. Consistent with Hans-Jörg Rheinberger's observation regarding the influence of space on an experimental system, we recognize the significance of incorporating environments into the exploration of experimental practices and discourses, particularly when analyzing the emergence of experimental settlements. Writing in German, Rheinberger distinguishes between "Orte" (physical spaces) and "Räume," which encompass discursive spaces and cultural techniques such as note-taking, laboratory journals, labeling, etc. He suggests utilizing these written remnants of experiments as a foundational element when investigating laboratory cultures.[6]

Following Rheinberger, this special section adopts a comprehensive conception of "experimental spaces" encompassing both physical and discursive dimensions. Rather than adhering to a rigid definition of experiment, we embrace a heuristic and actor-centered approach. Rather than applying established definitions of experiments, we begin our inquiry from the contextual frameworks and the actors involved, exploring their own accounts regarding the development of knowledge discourses and practices. This methodology places significant emphasis on the assertions and perspectives of historical actors, who perceived experiments as processes involving descriptions and adhering to specific protocols of setup and documentation, rather than mere attempts with contingent outcomes. They viewed experiments as rational techniques for generating new insights in relation to the social and natural world.

---

4 Etienne Benson, *Surroundings: A History of Environments and Environmentalisms* (Chicago: University of Chicago Press, 2020), 9, 12.
5 Ibid., 10.
6 Hans-Jörg Rheinberger, "Wissensräume und experimentelle Praxis," in *Bühnen des Wissens. Interferenz zwischen Wissenschaft und Kunst*, ed. Helmar Schramm (Berlin: Dahlem University Press, 2003), 367.

To give an example, engineer and settlement founder John A. Etzler explained this process when describing how a rational observer (whom he envisions as a male) came to recognize the use of steam power: "he mistrusts his judgment, suspects errors, goes back again to the most simple elements of conceptions, pursues again and again the course of his reasoning with the minutest attention to discover errors, compares his theory with experiments, and sees finally compelled his reason to admit the discovered truth."[7] In his pamphlet *The Paradise within the Reach of Men* (1833), Etzler suggests applying this process to finding new sources of energy and building intentional settlements on the North American continent. Addressing the US government, he promised that the "first and simplest experiments in their application will powerfully excite the minds and facilitate emigration and settling in wildernesses in a degree unexperienced yet."[8] Here, Etzler clearly described settlements on the US-American frontier as experiments in the use of technology, their economic setup, and their experimentation with new social orders in general.

To summarize, our section thus aims to develop a distinct perspective rooted in the history of knowledge, wherein experiments are conceptualized both as a category employed by actors and as a methodological concept. Our analysis begins with the recognition that experiments inherently establish spatial and organizational parameters within a defined setting, thereby shaping relationships with the surrounding environment, which we seek to explore. While we investigate the significance of contemporary experimental discourses – encompassing understandings of and attitudes toward experiments – the core emphasis of our articles lies in examining the implementation and configuration of experimental spaces in diverse environments.

Histories of Experiments in Science and Technology Studies and Beyond

This approach builds on prior research concerning various aspects of the extensive history of experiments, which has traditionally focused heavily on the natural sciences. Although our special section does not position itself in the history of science, it uses the definitions of experiment from this scholarship, which extends

---

[7] John Adolphus Etzler, *The Paradise within the Reach of All Men, without Labor, by Powers of Nature and Machinery. First Part* (Pittsburgh: Etzler and Reinhold, 1833), 17–18. See also Claudia Roesch's contribution in this special section.
[8] Ibid., *Second Part*, 4.

to its exploratory functions. The history of science has intensively researched the use and notion of experiments.[9] In this historiography, Francis Bacon's paradigmatic formulations became crucial. Bacon had abandoned the Aristotelian separation of artifacts and natural things in the *New Organon* (1620) and theorized, demonstrated, and justified the rational explanation of nature through experiments. In line with ideas of the Scientific Revolution, scholars in the history of science placed the "experiment" at the center of European science and thus turned it into a major component of their own disciplinary history.[10] In his analysis of early research on electrodynamics, Friedrich Steinle enhances the reflection on experimentation in the field and moves away from the traditional idea of hypothesis-based experiments.[11] He uses the term "exploratory experiments" to stress the importance of experiments in terms of generating new theories and concepts in contrast to its traditional role of subsequent justification and review. Literature on the history of the social sciences has pointed to the significance of the experiment for the establishment of their field as well.[12]

In contrast to these specific references, we engage with research perspectives in relevant literature on social experiments, such as in reform projects in Victorian England or in modernization projects in colonial settings.[13] Recent research, such as the study by Bartek Błesznowski, offers a deeper examination of the concept of social laboratories, thereby expanding our understanding of experimentation

---

[9] See, for instance, Steve Shapin and Simon Schaffer, *Leviathan and the Air Pump: Hobbes, Boyle, and the Experimental Life* (New Jersey: Princeton University Press, 1985).
[10] Hans-Jörg Rheinberger, "History of Science and the Practices of Experiment," *History and Philosophy of the Life Sciences* 23, no. 1, (2001): 51–63. For a critique of the development of this discipline from a global perspective, see Kapil Raj, "Thinking without the Scientific Revolution: Global Interactions and the Construction of Knowledge," *Journal of Early Modern History* 21, no. 5 (2017): 445–458.
[11] See, for instance, Friedrich Steinle, *Exploratory Experiments: Ampère, Faraday, and the Origins of Electrodynamics* (Pittsburgh: University of Pittsburgh Press, 2006).
[12] Anne Kwaschik, "Zwischen Wissenschaft und Utopie. Zur Plausibilisierung von Gesellschaftswissen im frühen 19. Jahrhundert," in *Vorläufige Gewissheiten. Plausibilität als soziokulturelle Praxis*, eds. Thomas Kirsch and Christina Wald (Bielefeld: Transcript Publishing, 2024), 97–114; Robert Brown, "Artificial Experiments on Society: Comte, G.C. Lewis and Mill," *Sociology Lens* 10, no. 1 (1997): 74–97.
[13] Fierce debates raged about sociopolitical reform measures with welfare state elements, which affected areas as diverse as the Poor Law experiments of Thomas Chalmers (1780–1847). Between 1813 and 1837 he launched a new system of poor relief to combat pauperism, and the model prison in Pentonville (1842), which was intended to establish a new penal policy. For a brief overview of literature on "colonial laboratories," see Guillaume Lachenal, "Le médecin qui voulut être roi," *Annales HSS* 65 (2010): 121–156.

within the realms of social psychology and cooperativism in Poland.[14] Błesznowski investigates how experimentation in conjunction with observation emerged as primary methodologies borrowed from the natural sciences, which contributed to establishing a distinct research field in the early nineteenth century.

Our selection of case studies is informed by recent sociological scholarship on intentional settlements as collaborative endeavors. These settlements bring together individuals with shared intentions – be they religious, ethnic, or socialist – to explore communal living arrangements. Scholars such as sociologist Michel Lallement have analyzed these settlements as tangible experiments ("expérimentations réelles") whose physical manifestations allow for empirical studies.[15]

Even though this section adopts a historical approach distinct from the perspectives found in Science and Technology Studies (STS), it is imperative to acknowledge the significant contributions made by these scholars in the realms of sociology and cultural anthropology with regard to research on the laboratory as a locus of knowledge production. This line of inquiry seeks to delineate the intricate mechanisms underlying knowledge production and the manner in which laboratory sciences attain legitimacy and influence societal transformations.[16] A prominent example is Bruno Latour, who illustrates how microbiologist Louis Pasteur's laboratory, alongside his discoveries regarding microbes, profoundly impacted agricultural practices, the social hygiene movement, and French society at large.[17]

While the articles in this section do not align with an STS framework, which we perceive as less conducive to a nuanced description of historical developments compared to our heuristic and actor-based approach, they are nonetheless influenced by Latour's suggestion that there are no clear boundaries between the scientific and social dimensions of laboratory practices.[18] Latour posits that laboratory scholars such as Pasteur exerted their transformative power not solely within the confines of a secluded laboratory but also through a dynamic interplay

---

14 Bartłomiej Adam Błesznowski, "Experimental Utopia: Edward Abramowski's 'Applied Social Science'," *Utopian Studies* 34, no. 1 (2023): 80–99.
15 He describes intentional communities as "expérimentations rélles qui se cristallisent dans des pratiques empiriquement observables." See Michel Lallement, *Un Désir d'Égalité. Vivre et travailler dans des communautés utopiques* (Paris: Éditions du Seuil, 2019), 20–21.
16 Karin D. Knorr-Cetina, "The Couch, the Cathedral, and the Laboratory: On the Relationship Between Experiment and Laboratory in Science," in *Science as Practice and Culture*, ed. Andrew Pickering (Chicago and London: University of Chicago Press, 1992), 113–138.
17 Bruno Latour, "Give Me a Laboratory and I Will Raise the World," in *Science Observed: Perspectives on the Social Study of Science*, eds. Karin D. Knorr-Cetina and Michael Mulkay (London and Beverly Hills: Sage, 1983), 141–170.
18 Ibid.

between the internal and external realms of the laboratory, spanning from the micro-level of the Petri dish to the macro-level of agricultural settings. This involved scaling shifts from the grand to the minute but also using inscriptions and statistics to visualize and simplify their successes for broader audiences.[19]

In order to grasp the relationship between theory and practice at play here, we define "experiments" in line with Latour's concept of the "laboratory," while we relate his concept of knowledge production to practices in intentional settlements and agricultural colonies. We do this (a) by conceptualizing the establishment of experimental spaces as a cultural technique and technology of knowledge production, (b) by investigating the discursive and material spaces in which these experiments occur, and (c) by investigating the movement between the inside and the outside, the micro- and the macro-level, and the scaling of scientific experiments while using the documentation of these as a source for our analysis.

The Impact of Colonialism

The circulation between the interior and exterior of experimental spaces is particularly significant in our research contexts. Historians of knowledge have consistently underscored that circulation represents one of the most crucial attributes of knowledge.[20] Knowledge not only circulates within national borders but also transcends various imperial boundaries, albeit with constraints. This raises questions regarding the impact of colonialism. Recent historiography has frequently examined the interplay between colonial spaces and knowledge circulation, thereby highlighting colonial constraints in the utilization and neglect of indigenous knowledge. The knowledge traversing between the periphery and the metropole often corresponds to the perspectives of the informed European bourgeois gaze and carries substantial cultural, political, and economic significance.[21]

---

19 Latour, "Give Me a Laboratory," 163.
20 Daniel Speich-Chassé and David Gugerli, "Wissensgeschichte. Eine Standortbestimmung," *Traverse: Zeitschrift für Geschichte* 19 (2012): 85–100, 90; see also Johan Östling, David Larsson Heidenblad, and Anna Nilsson Hammar, "Developing the History of Knowledge," in *Forms of Knowledge: Developing the History of Knowledge*, eds. Johan Östling, David Larsson Heidenblad, and Anna Nilsson (Nordic Academic Press: Falun, 2020), 9–26, 15.
21 David Arnold, *The Tropics and the Traveling Gaze: India, Landscape, and Science, 1800–1856* (Delhi: Permanent Black, 2005), 6; Harald Fischer-Tiné, *Pidgin Knowledge. Wissen und Kolonialismus* (Diaphanes: Zurich, 2013).

Different strands of research have developed in order to explain these processes of knowledge production and exclusion.[22] Three findings in previous research are particularly relevant for this thematic section. First, we have research offering the insight that colonial knowledge production and support of imperial projects were not the result of a formal national colonial structure. With regard to the German case, Sebastian Conrad has shown that German-speaking scholars, merchants, and settlers supported imperialism long before the German Empire, mainly through colonial knowledge production and by participating in large-scale population schemes.[23] Once formal German and Italian empires had been established, as shown in the articles by Marktanner and Mazzoli in this volume, colonial scientists often followed British examples of establishing research stations or colonial gardens as centers of knowledge production.

Second, analyzing imperial infrastructures provides us with research on how the practical desires of the colonial powers to build technical infrastructures and the interests of social activists, scientists, and other colonial actors intersected on the ground.[24] However, as wide-ranging and specific as this research is, it has rarely addressed the relationship between colonialism, utopianism, and intentional communities.[25] One exception is Stephen Stoll's *The Great Delusion*, which at great length discusses the colonial mindset of German American engineers trying and failing to set up a colony in Venezuela.[26] Intentional communities and research gardens are especially linked to settler colonialism, as many nineteenth century social reformers set out to establish these in the colonies of the French and British empires. They viewed colonial landscapes as empty spaces where they could easily obtain land, often for free, and conduct experiments in the service of colonial powers and their own grander visions.

---

22 For a brief overview, see Anne Kwaschik, "Scientific Colonialism: Zum konstitutiven Zusammenhang von Wissen und 'colonial governance'," in *Herrschaft und Wissen*, eds. Peter Weingart, Gunnar Folke Schuppert, and Roland Römhildt (Baden-Baden: Nomos-Verlag, 2022), 115–142.

23 Sebastian Conrad, "Rethinking German Colonialism in a Global Age," *The Journal of Imperial and Commonwealth History* 41, no. 4 (2013): 543–566; see also H. Glenn Penny, *German History Unbound: From 1750 to the Present* (Cambridge: Cambridge University Press, 2022), 50.

24 Dirk van Laak, *Imperiale Infrastrukturen. Deutsche Planung für die Erschließung Afrikas 1880 bis 1960* (Paderborn: Ferdinand Schöningh, 2004), 53–54.

25 For Fourierist settlements, see, for instance, Jean-Louis Marçot, "Les premiers socialistes français, la question coloniale et l'Algérie," *Revue d'histoire critique* 124 (2014): 79–95; Laurent Vidal, *Ils ont rêvé d'un autre monde. 1841* (Paris: Flammarion, 2014); Pamela M. Pilbeam, "The Colonization of Algeria: The Role of Saint-Simonians," *French History and Civilization: Papers from the 19th George Rudé Seminar, July 10–12, 2014*, ed. Julie Kalman 6 (2015): 189–196, available online: https://h-france.net/rude/wp-content/uploads/2017/08/Title-PageVol6.pdf.

26 Steven Stoll, *The Great Delusion: A Mad Inventor, Death in the Tropics and the Utopian Origins of Economic Growth* (New York: Hill and Wang, 2008), 108–116.

Third, this thematic section follows the critical readings of the influential and widespread language of colonies as "laboratories of modernity." As lucidly demonstrated by Guillaume Lachenal when discussing primarily research in the field of colonial medicine, the majority of studies use the concept in a simplified and metaphorical fashion: they equate the rationalizing intentions ("gouvernementalité expérimentale") with the final implementation in a way that is problematic.[27] In light of the fact that this discourse was used by the colonial authorities themselves, it should be all the more analytically delimited. Nevertheless, there is no question regarding the epistemological value of the concept of "laboratories of modernity." It points to the function of the colonies as an enabling space ("espace d'opportunité") for ambitious and utopian projects (as well as for the colonists' racism and brutality). Moreover, the "colonial laboratory" calls for a closer examination of the failure of these experiments ("analytique d'échec"), which is rarely taken into account.

Structure of the Section and Summary of the Articles

Building on this research, we study the materiality and performativity of the "experiment" by employing the notion of "experimental spaces." With a dual focus on experimental spaces in both spatial and discursive dimensions, the articles in this special section examine an array of environments ranging from colonial gardens to intentional communities and internal colonies, their objectives, and the perspectives of the various historical actors involved. The selection of five case studies aims to explore the social, natural, and artistic dimensions of knowledge production within experimental environments, thereby facilitating an investigation of spaces in which social order was constructed, contemporary societal ailments were identified, and new applications of natural resources were explored.

In **Claudia Roesch's article "Talking about the Weather: Climate Knowledge as a Colonial Practice in Intentional Settlements,"** she views climate knowledge production as a precondition for social and botanical experiments in the Americas. The article examines the meteorological knowledge produced by the settlers in the context of intentional community projects in the Americas between the 1820s and the 1840s. Furthermore, it also investigates how religious, ethnic, and early socialist settlers collected meteorological data and climate infor-

---

27 Lachenal, "Le médecin qui voulut être roi."

mation and how they turned this into useful climate knowledge in order to make important decisions regarding colonialization and the cultivation of staple foods. The article shows how ethnic networks of German American settlers facilitated the exchange of climate knowledge and how they contributed to creating a discourse of the tropics as an experimental environment. Finally, it suggests that the settlers' preference for book knowledge and observations in ethnic networks over indigenous knowledge offers an explanation for the failure of many of their settlement plans.

Anne Kwaschik's article "Experimental Discourse and Fourierist Settlements" examines the Fourierist doctrine and movement as a socio-epistemic program, specifically focusing on its experimental discourse encapsulated in Fourier's concept of the *phalanstère*. The article emphasizes the dynamic interplay between conceptual frameworks and practical endeavors by investigating reflections on these *phalanstères* as social test units. In its exploration of experimental practices, the article highlights a frequently overlooked aspect of Fourierism and elucidates the infrastructural impact of colonialism. With a specific focus on the Union agricole du Sig in Algeria as a case study, the article demonstrates the intersection between Fourier's experimental model and the complexities of colonial realities. The experimental discourse is highlighted as a central aspect of Fourierism, emphasizing its role and legacy in shaping and redefining social norms and structures.

Alina Marktanner's "Experimenting for Empire" moves away from intentional settlements to imperial settler colonies as an experimental space for agriculture. Using phytopathology – the study of plant diseases – as a case study, this article places field study collaborations between scientists and planters within discourses on colonial economy, hygiene, and a "civilizing" mission of colonialism. It contends that plant pathology knowledge was a hybridized construct blending multiple disciplines as well as lay knowledge. The experimental sites were agricultural research stations in the West African colonies of the German Empire that were intended to make practical information available to planters and improve local farming practices, while providing a civilizing mission to indigenous populations. Researchers in these experimental gardens often adopted trial-and-error methods instead of relying on some kind of elaborate methodology. They also had to collaborate with local planters and indigenous farmers, even though they viewed the latter as in need of education and oversight by white men.

Gilberto Mazzoli in his article "Climates of Migration" approaches colonial agricultural knowledge through the lens of Italian American immigration, agricultural diplomacy, and its relationship to Italian colonialism in the early twentieth century. The article analyses discourses and practices surrounding migrants' gardening knowledge used to establish colonies for Italian immigrants in the American South. Italian actors envisioned these as part of an informal Italian empire, while US-American commentators saw them as an opportunity to relocate Southern European agricultural laborers from the overcrowded East Coast cities to the South. The article highlights the role of these projects for the Italian Colonial Agricultural Institute in Florence and argues that both Italian and US-American scientists and government representatives viewed agricultural colonies as an experiment in managing population flows through transatlantic migration and gardening.

Anne-Sophie Reichert's article "Knowledge in Motion: Research and Experimentation at Hellerau's School for Rhythmik," contrary to the first four articles addressing the question of colonialism and experimental spaces in overseas colonies of Western European empires, approaches the garden city of Hellerau as a colony within imperial Germany. This case study shows how the environment of the garden city enabled experiments in Émile Jaques-Dalcroze's rhythm school, a place where dance choreographies were turned into new means of studying bodily movement and human physiology. The article examines the development of *Rhythmik* – a new method for rhythmical body movement – as a transdisciplinary effort uniting dancers, artists, social reformers, physiologists, and scientists. In a methodological reflection, the article argues that a process-oriented history of knowledge is useful for documenting a research community circulating its information through experimental research, teaching, and building networks.

In conclusion, the articles elucidate how the studied experimental spaces facilitated knowledge production and dissemination beyond the confines of traditional academic institutions, while fostering dialogues among various stakeholders, including activists, social reformers, practitioners, and scientists. Based on the results of the case studies, this special section underscores that settlements were not isolated entities but rather interconnected components within global networks of knowledge exchange spanning agriculture, botany, climatology, and the social sciences. Actors engaged in these networks and infrastructures both contributed to and drew upon knowledge, in addition to employing methodologies established by laboratory sciences in the preceding century, such as absorbing written knowledge, publishing in scientific journals, observational practices, and systematically recording and collecting experimental data. These interactions sometimes resulted in significant contributions to various fields. For example, the cultivation of bodily and sensory knowledge within the German *Lebensreform* movement illustrates how rhythmic movement emerged as a research practice that complemented and challenged mechanistic and rationalist approaches to understanding and transforming modern society. Internal colonies and imperial settlements in the long nineteenth century thus played a pivotal role in the transition of experimental methodologies from academic laboratories to broader societal contexts, thereby signifying a notable evolution in the dissemination and application of such methodologies.

Claudia Roesch is a post-doctoral researcher at the University of Konstanz affiliated with the history of knowledge working group. Her research interests include the history of knowledge and technology, North American history, gender and the family, and migration history. Her current research project "Utopian Engineering" investigates the role of science and engineering knowledge in social reform projects in the nineteenth-century Atlantic world. Her most recent publication is "Owen and the Engineers: Cross-Fertilization between Engineering and Early Socialism in the Owenite Tradition," *Global Intellectual History* (2023): 1–16.

Anne Kwaschik is a professor of contemporary history at Konstanz University with a special focus on the history of knowledge. Her research focuses on knowledge cultures and scientization processes such as the scientization of colonialism, the epistemology of health feminism, and the history of social experiments. Recent publications include "Reconstructing Colonial Sociology," *Social Science History* 48, no. 1 (2024), DOI: https://doi.org/10.1017/ssh.2023.23; "'We Witches': Knowledge Wars, Experience and Spirituality in the Women's Movement in the 1970s," *NTM* 31 (2023), DOI: https://doi.org/10.1007/s00048-023-00359-w

Claudia Roesch
Talking about the Weather: Producing Climate Knowledge as Colonial Practice in Intentional Communities in the Americas, 1820s–1840s

Abstract: This article explores the production and dissemination of climate knowledge in intentional communities in the Americas between the 1820s and the 1840s. It views climate knowledge as a prerequisite for social and scientific experiments within settlement spaces. Through three case studies, I investigate how settlements collected climate data, utilized it to select locations, determined which crops were suitable for cultivation, and attracted prospective settlers: the religious and cooperative settlement of New Harmony, Indiana, the German ethnic colony of Saxonburg, Pennsylvania, and the unsuccessful scheme by German American engineers John Adolphus Etzler and Conrad Friedrich Stollmeyer to run a machine-based cooperative settlement in Venezuela. I view all these settlement schemes as experiments in pursuing a new order of society. In these experimental spaces, practices of observing and experimenting with regard to social and natural phenomena converged. Settlers created refined climate knowledge by collecting raw data on weather phenomena, seeking information through their own ethnic networks, and relying on book knowledge and travel accounts by previous colonizers. Through their newspapers, they disseminated ideas regarding the tropics as a favorable space for agricultural and mechanical experiments. They generalized with regard to regional climates, marginalized local knowledge, and contributed to discourses of tropicality. However, these communities ultimately failed as the settlers arrived unprepared for the heat and humidity. This article demonstrates that talking about the weather, collecting climate data, and writing about these events proliferated a colonial mindset and contributed to settler colonialism, even when practiced by groups standing outside of formal empires.

Keywords: intentional communities, global Germans, climate knowledge, settler colonialism, Owenism, agriculture

Introduction

On September 1, 1827, at 7 am, the temperature in New Harmony, Indiana was 66 degrees Fahrenheit (18.8 degrees Celsius).[1] There was no wind and only a few clouds in the sky. By 2 pm, the temperature had risen to 82 degrees Fahrenheit (27.8 degrees Celsius) and there was still no wind and only a few clouds. At 9 pm at night, it was 68 degrees Fahrenheit (20 degrees Celsius), again no wind and clear skies. Throughout the entire day, the temperatures ranged from 62 degrees F (16.7 degrees C) to 82 degrees F. Based on nine readings throughout the day, the average temperature on September 1 was 71.5 degrees F (21.9 degrees C).[2]

Historians know these precise dates because the residents of the New Harmony community diligently collected climate data, including temperature, wind, cloud formations, and precipitation, three times a day. They recorded it in a meteorological journal and, once a month, published the journal entries in the settlement newspaper, the *New-Harmony Gazette*.

Unfortunately, there is no such careful documentation of climate data available for the Paria Peninsula in Venezuela. However, German engineer John Adolphus Etzler, who wanted to establish an intentional community based on wind-powered machinery and a cooperative model for the economy, presumed that in northeastern Venezuela, much like the tropics as a whole, the wind would be sufficiently strong to provide ample power for his machines. Etzler also assumed that the climatic conditions were sufficiently warm and dry to cultivate staple foods for the undernourished and impoverished masses in the industrial centers of Europe.[3]

Nevertheless, when Etzler started to plan the community, he lacked exact knowledge of the climatic conditions on the Paria Peninsula. The settlement project failed after numerous settlers succumbed to yellow fever, sun exposure, and dehydration. The surviving settlers abandoned the endeavor when they realized that they did not have enough supplies and that clearing the land would take several years. Economic historian Steven Stoll argues that the settlers' ignorance of

---

[1] I would like to express my gratitude to my fellow authors in this special section and the participants of 2023 Bodensee Retreat on the history of knowledge for their valuable feedback on various stages of this article, to the editors of this journal and the two anonymous reviewers for their enthusiastic and helpful comments, to the German Historical Institute Washington for generously sponsoring the archival research for this article and to Stephen Stoll and Reinaldo Funes Manzote for sharing their material will me.

[2] "Meteorological Journal Kept at New Harmony," *New-Harmony Gazette* 2, no. 52 (October 3, 1827): 416, access with courtesy of the Vassar College Special Collections Library.

[3] John A. Etzler, *The Paradise within the Reach of All Men, without Labor, by Powers of Nature and Machinery*, vol. 1 (Pittsburgh: Etzler and Reinhold, 1833), 11.

the local conditions in Venezuela was the primary reason why this colonization project failed.[4]

These two examples illustrate just how essential knowledge concerning climate, geology, flora, and fauna was for the success of settler colonialism in general, and experimental communities in particular. They also show that through their planning and data collection, nineteenth-century socialists became an integral part of the Western European colonization project in the Americas, even though these settlers were not representatives of a formal empire and often originated from regions without any colonies of their own.

In this article, I use the climate as the lens through which I investigate the entanglements between knowledge, intentional communities, and settler colonialism. I adopt sociologist Michel Lallement's definition of intentional communities as an umbrella term for communities founded by people with a common goal to experiment with new forms of social cohabitation.[5] Hence, I consider these settlements experimental spaces where a cross-fertilization between social science and engineering was intended to bring about a new order of society. In this article, I argue that observing and documenting the local climate served as prerequisites for experimental settlement projects.

Social reformers specifically needed climate knowledge as a resource for selecting a settlement site and for determining which agricultural practices to utilize. I understand climate knowledge as a refined product actively created by settlers through the practices of observing, collecting raw climate data, and gathering information from their networks, scientific books, or travel accounts. In their writings, they interpreted these types of data and generated a coherent understanding of the climate in the Americas, which they then circulated within their networks in the Americas and back in Europe.[6] To explore these practices of knowledge circulation and production, I use correspondence between the settlement founders and the newspapers they published to disseminate their knowledge in the settlement community and to future settlers. I specifically investigate

---

[4] Steven Stoll, *The Great Delusion: A Mad Inventor, Death in the Tropics and the Utopian Origins of Economic Growth* (New York: Hill and Wang, 2008), 127.

[5] This includes both religious and early socialist settlements. See Michel Lallement, *Un Désir d'Égalité. Vivre et travailler dans des communautés utopiques* (Paris: Éditions du Seuil, 2019), 16.

[6] In the distinction between data, information, and knowledge, I adhere to Ghanesh D. Bhatt's definition of data as raw, information as conveyed through conversation, and knowledge as the product of the interpretation of data and information based on previous knowledge. See Ghanesh D. Bhatt, "Knowledge Management in Organizations: Examining the Interaction between Technologies, Techniques, and People," *Journal of Knowledge Management* 5, no. 1 (2001): 68–75, 69.

the sources of knowledge cited in their articles and how these reflected on their own observation practices, experiments, and networks.

I interpret the terms "experiment" and "observation" as actual practices conducted by settlers, not as metaphorical terms. As demonstrated by historian Anne Kwaschik, transporting the concept of the experiment from the laboratory to the social realm was a guiding principle for social reformer Charles Fourier.[7] Similar to the Fourierists, the Owenites frequently used the terms "experiment" and "observation" while viewing the practice of founding settlements as a form of applied social science. This extended beyond experimenting with new social orders and included applied knowledge regarding technology and botany.[8] The climate impacted all three realms – the socio-economic, the mechanical, and the agricultural – which is why producing climate knowledge was a crucial practice in intentional communities, regardless of whether settlers represented socialist, religious, or ethnic types of settlements.[9]

In an actor-centered approach, I investigate the reformers in three different types of settlements: the Harmonist/Owenite settlement in New Harmony, John Roebling's attempt to establish a German ethnic colony in Saxonburg, Pennsylvania, and Etzler's scheme to run a machine-based colony in Venezuela. While the Venezuelan colony was intended to serve as an experiment in mechanization already from the outset, and while New Harmony served as an experimental space for a new social order as well as botanical trials, Saxonburg can be considered a socio-economic experiment. Here, Roebling aimed to test the best way to organize the economy of an ethnic enclave. All case studies are connected through a network of settlers and locations, with pietist dissenter and New Harmony founder George Rapp at the core of this network. Etzler and Robeling had lived with Rapp in Economy, Pennsylvania in 1831.[10] Rapp, furthermore, sold his previous settlement, New Harmony, to Robert Owen in 1826, who used it as a site for his social

---

7 Anne Kwaschik, "Zwischen Wissenschaft und Utopie. Zur Plausibilisierung von Gesellschaftswissen im frühen 19. Jahrhundert," in *Vorläufige Gewissheiten. Plausibilität als soziokulturelle Praxis*, eds. Thomas Kirsch and Christina Wald (Bielefeld: Transcript Publishing, 2023), 119. See also Anne Kwaschik's article in this volume.
8 For botany experiments, see also the articles by Alina Marktanner and Gilberto Mazzoli in this volume.
9 In this paper, I distinguish between (1) religious settlements, which were founded based on a spiritual motive, even if they practiced a cooperative form of labor; (2) socialist settlements, which were set up to put Robert Owen's or Charles Fourier's theories into practice; and (3) ethnic settlements, which were created with the intention to find an alternative space for a national group feeling suppressed in their homeland.
10 Joel Nydahl, ed., *The Collected Works of John Adolphus Etzler* (New York: Delmar, 1977), xv.

experiments. After Owen gave up New Harmony and returned to Britain, he promoted Etzler's ideas of a machine-driven paradise in his British newspapers.

In the first part of this article, I present some theoretical-methodological considerations on the biases of using observation as a knowledge production practice and the link between socialist settlement experiments and settler colonialism. Second, I explore the collection and circulation of climate data in the Rappite/Owenite settlement of New Harmony as an example of knowledge production practices in intentional communities. Third, I examine the use of climate knowledge for the choice of location for German emigree engineer John A. Roebling's ethnic colony in Saxonburg. Finally, I discuss how climatic imaginations led to the utopian colonial project created by Etzler and his business partner Conrad Friedrich Stollmeyer in Venezuela. I reevaluate the failure of this experiment through the lens of climate knowledge,[11] arguing that their generalizations of climate knowledge with regard to the tropics and their preference for book knowledge over local expertise resulted in the expedition's failure.

Intentional Communities, Settler Colonialism, and Knowledge Production

Colonization projects had since the beginning of European settler colonialism in the Americas struggled as a result of the settlers' ignorance of climatic conditions. The most notable example is Jamestown, the first permanent English settlement in Virginia, where two-thirds of the settlers died in the first year as the colonizers had underestimated the climatic challenges of the Chesapeake Bay.[12] In the early stages of European expansion, according to climate historian Sam White, settler colonialists assumed that the climate in North America would resemble that of Mediterranean Europe.[13] However, they soon realized that the summers were hotter and more humid, the winters were colder and harder, and the transition periods in the spring and fall were much shorter. Until the early nineteenth century, they had limited secure knowledge of the local climatic conditions beyond

---

[11] See, for instance, Robert N. Proctor, "Agnotology: A Missing Term to Describe the Cultural Production of Ignorance (and Its Study)," in *Agnotology. The Making and Unmaking of Ignorance*, eds. Robert N. Proctor and Londa Schiebinger (Stanford: Stanford University Press, 2008), 1–33.
[12] Sam White, *A Cold Welcome: The Little Ide Age and Europe's Encounter with North America* (Cambridge, MA: Oxford University Press, 2017), 111.
[13] White, *Welcome*, 30.

the Appalachian Mountains, and these conditions varied significantly from region to region.

The production of knowledge, including climate knowledge, plays a key role in early nineteenth-century intentional communities in the Americas, whether they were religious, ethnic, or socialist. Settlement founders John Arthur Roebling, Robert Owen, and John A. Etzler consistently emphasized that their utopian visions of society were grounded in rationalism, observations, and laws of science.[14] Observations, data collection, and teaching scientific laws and practices (such as the laws of thermodynamics) turned into central knowledge production practices in intentional communities, frequently presented as methods for establishing a more rational society in Owen's writings, starting with his "New View of Society" published serially from 1813 to 1816.

Most activists came from an educated background and considered themselves the vanguard of modern society. The term "rational observation" was frequently used to denote their refined skills. Here, engineer John A. Etzler offered the example of a kitchen maid who was familiar with steam power upon seeing boiling water raising the lid of a pot. But it took a rational observer to apply this observation to experiments and harness it for powering machinery.[15] Etzler in his text assumed that observations were generally objective and rational, and to illustrate his point, he presented a woman from the lowest social and educational class as capable of making that observation. However, his concept of observations is inherently problematic. Whoever made this observation needed to have the privilege of time to watch the boiling water, reflect on it, and report it – something that a busy kitchen maid likely did not have. For observations to transform into refined knowledge, they needed to circulate through conversations, letters, or print media. This, naturally, favored an observer who was literate, had access to networks, and possessed a certain authority based on age, gender, class, race, and educational status. The intersectional categories of gender, race, and class served as exclusionary barriers, determining whose observations were circulated and transformed into refined knowledge. Literacy, language, and ethnicity represented additional factors

---

14 See, for instance, Robert Owen's review of Etzler's monograph *The Paradise*, Robert Owen, "The 'Paradise'," *New Moral World*, November 21, 1835, accessed through the Vassar University Library, Special Collections.
15 Etzler, *Paradise*, vol. 1, 17. For an overview of the debate regarding observation as an evidence-based practice among nineteenth-century social reformers, see Kwaschik, "Zwischen Wissenschaft," 112–114.

marginalizing observations made by women or indigenous populations, typically ignored in the conceptualizations of colonial climates.[16]

Despite its biases, the term "observation" alludes to the idea that reformers aimed at transferring scientific practices from the laboratory into the field – quite literally: a field near Oxford, a peninsula in Venezuela, or the backwoods of Indiana could become the site of social and technological experimentation.[17] Recent historiography has shown that the experimental spirit of socialist settlers was not just a matter of terminology but a lived practice.[18] However, historian Hannah Ahlheim has argued that when closely investigating the process of social reform development in Robert Owen's writings, he imitated the practice of engineers rather than those of laboratory scientists. Engineers constantly observed, maintained, and readjusted their machines in a factory.[19] Yet, both laboratory chemistry and engineering were applied sciences that also relied on applying previous academic knowledge and coming up with creative ideas to produce new knowledge concerning the natural world.

Reformers who practiced a form of cooperative economy are often referred to as "utopian socialists," even though some scholars now reject this term as it solidifies Marxism as a scientific version of socialism.[20] But settlers were only utopian in a temporal sense of the word, signifying their ability to imagine a future that was radically different from their past and present.[21] Their visions were

---

16 See David Arnold, *The Tropics and the Traveling Gaze: India, Landscape, and Science, 1800–1856* (Delhi: Permanent Black, 2005), 8–9.
17 For breaking down conceptual barriers between the inside of the lab and the outside of the political realm, see Bruno Latour, "From Multiculturalism to Multinaturalism: What Rules of Method for the New Socio-Scientific Experiments?," *Nature and Culture* 6, no. 1 (2011): 1–17, here 12–13.
18 See Anne Kwaschik, "Gesellschaftswissen als Zukunftshandeln: Soziale Epistemologie, genossenschaftliche Lebensformen und kommunale Praxis im frühen 19. Jahrhundert," *Francia: Forschungen zur westeuropäischen Geschichte* 44 (2017): 192.
19 Hannah Ahlheim, "Ex Machina. Die Gestaltung der Utopie in der Arbeitswelt des britischen Frühsozialisten Robert Owen," *Historische Zeitschrift* 311 (2020): 61.
20 In fact, one of Robert Owen's followers had invented the term socialism as shorthand for the term social science to denote his experimental village schemes. See Gregory Claeys, "'Individualism', 'Socialism' and 'Social Science': Further Notes on a Process of Conceptual Formation, 1800–1850," *Journal of the History of Ideas* 47, no. 1 (1986): 81–93, 88.
21 After praising Owen, Fourier, and Saint Simon for their experimental spirit in their early writings, Engels and Marx go on to reject them as Utopians in *Socialism: Utopian and Scientific*. Their followers then denounced Owenites and Fourierists as counterrevolutionary. Yet, the term utopian socialism stuck in academic writing. Recent sociological scholarship has tried to rehabilitate the term Utopianism by shifting the focus from the fictional character of reform schemes to its orientation toward the future. For the definition of Utopianism as the ability to imagine a rad-

rooted in their own observations, witnessing the unfolding of the Industrial Revolution in Britain and the political changes after the Napoleonic wars in both Britain and the southern German states. The reformers believed that traditional societies were inhibited by religion and old elites, and they aspired to construct a new society based entirely on rationality.

Reformers themselves often rejected the term Utopianism.[22] Nevertheless, US-American historiography has frequently studied their various projects under the umbrella term American Utopianism.[23] Determining factors for categorizing settlers as such, according to historian Chris Jennings, included founding separate communities, networks between members of different groups, and the convergence of a religious belief in paradise and the perfectibility of men with a post-Enlightenment belief in the triumph of science, mechanics, and rationality.[24] Jennings, like most individuals in the US-American historiographical tradition, focuses on the failures of these communities. While he emphasizes that many communities failed because they expected that "paradise was just around the corner,"[25] the main argument in this perspective is that secular intentional communities failed because their notion of cooperative economy contradicted the US-American ideals of individualism and entrepreneurship.[26] However, the fact that communities practiced a shared economy on the inside did not mean that they lacked entrepreneurial skills when dealing with trading partners outside their communities. In fact, the Harmonist society ran a successful textile manufacturing operation and the Roebling and Stollmeyer families became business magnates in New Jersey and Trinidad respectively.

The intricate settlement plans and economic activities automatically linked them to settler colonialism. Settlers utilized the infrastructures of empire when traveling on the routes of British colonialism: they frequented shipping routes to North America and the Caribbean and relied on colonial communication networks

---

ically different future, see Ruth Levitas, *The Concept of Utopia* (Oxford: Peter Lang, 2010 [1990]), 62–63. Ruth Levitas, *Utopia as Method: The Imaginary Reconstruction of Society* (Basingstoke: Palgrave Macmillan, 2013), 17.

22 See Levitas, *Concept of Utopia*, 44.
23 Most recently, Chris Jennings, *Paradise Now: The Story of American Utopianism* (New York: Random House, 2016); Donald E. Pitzer, ed., *America's Communal Utopias* (Chapel Hill & London: University of North Carolina Press, 1997).
24 Jennings, *Paradise Now*, 4.
25 Jennings, *Paradise Now*, 14.
26 The first to make this argument is Frank Podmore, *Robert Owen: A Biography* (New York: D. Appleton and Company, 1924), 336. For a more complex interpretation of this, see Arthur Bestor, *Backwoods Utopias: The Sectarian Origins and the Owenite Phase of Communitarian Socialism in America, 1663–1829* (Philadelphia: University of Pennsylvania Press, 1950).

for correspondence, food, and consumer goods. Intentional communities were built based on settler colonialism, and community founders accepted invitations from new colonial nation-states for land grants, tax exemptions, and exemptions from military service.[27] In the case of ethnic Germans, recent historiography has demonstrated that Germans of various trades and backgrounds participated in colonialism long before Germany became a united nation-state and empire.[28] In particular the British Empire and its metropole of London came to serve as a base for German-speaking colonial agents.[29] In this regard, according to Sebastian Conrad, German emigrants became actors not only in global population politics but also circulators of imperial knowledge long before the German Empire itself acquired colonies.[30]

My main argument is that the emigrants' engagement with climate knowledge reveals that their intentional communities were linked to experimental discourses, as well as to imperialism, ethnic networks, and book knowledge on their respective regions. Through their letters and newspaper publications, they circulated this knowledge among potential emigrants in Britain and the German lands. Climate knowledge constitutes an important aspect of colonial knowledge, and studying such knowledge demonstrates how settlements engaged with their networks and contemporary colonial science.[31] The case of climate knowledge in intentional communities illustrates the entanglements between knowledge, colonialism and experimental social reform, the dissemination of science beyond the laboratory, and the use of natural science practices such as observations even in secluded communities. This reveals the proliferation of scientific practices, beyond the lab and colonialism, deep into social reform circles in the mid-nineteenth century.

---

27 For a general observation, see H. Glenn Penny, *German History Unbound: From 1750 to the Present* (Cambridge: Cambridge University Press, 2022), 27. For Etzler's specific consideration regarding Venezuela, see Stoll, *Delusion*, 108.

28 See, for instance, Penny, *German History*; David Blackbourn, "Germans Abroad and 'Auslandsdeutsche': Places, Networks and Experiences from the Sixteenth to the Twentieth Century," *Geschichte und Gesellschaft* 41, no. 2 (2015): 321–346, here 334; Sebastian Conrad, "Rethinking German Colonialism in a Global Age," *The Journal of Imperial and Commonwealth History* 41, no. 4 (2013): 543–566, here 552.

29 Penny, *German History*, 50.

30 Conrad, "Rethinking," 553.

31 For a thorough reflection on how meteorological observations contributed to internal colonialism in nineteenth-century United States, see Sara J. Grossman, *Immeasurable Weather: Meteorological Data and Settler Colonialism from 1820 to Hurricane Sandy* (Durham: Duke University Press, 2023), 42, 48.

New Harmony: Climate Observations for the Cultivation of Strange Fruits

As mentioned earlier, Robert Owen purchased New Harmony from George Rapp in 1826. This settlement was situated in the backwoods of Indiana, and the Harmonists abandoned it due to a combination of financial, medical, and religious reasons.[32] Owen's plan was to establish a community in which members would rotate between agricultural, industrial, and intellectual labor, and where children would be taught in a communal fashion. In early 1826, Owen left his sons in charge of the settlement while traveling across the United States to promote his communitarian scheme. Most followers who decided to move to New Harmony were teachers, scientists, and intellectuals, earning them the nickname "a boatload of knowledge."[33]

Since the Rappite period, New Harmony had been configured as an experiment in communal living and scientific knowledge production. The Harmonists installed the first steam engine west of Cincinnati, while Harmonist women conducted experiments in scientific botany in the settlement gardens.[34] There had been no contacts made with indigenous people in the region, as they had been displaced before the German Pietists arrived.

The meticulous documentation of climate data described at the beginning of this article was a habitual practice that the Owenites took over from the Harmonists. According to climate historian Linda Richter, collecting data and creating tables on weather phenomena was a common practice among meteorologists in the

---

[32] Historians argue whether George Rapp decided to abandon the settlement for religious reasons, whether community members were plagued by fevers, or whether they lacked access to the markets on the East Coast. In 1831, Roebling alludes to the economic argument, while historian Karl Arndt finds the medical argument to be the most plausible. Jennings, finally, suggests a mix between religious and mercantile arguments. See Karl J.R. Arndt and Patrick R. Brostowin, "Pragmatists and Prophets: George Rapp and J.A. Roebling versus J.A. Etzler and Count Leon, Part 2," *Western Pennsylvania Historical Magazine* 52, no. 2 (1969): 173; Jennings, *Paradise Now*, 104–105.

[33] See Donald E. Pitzer, "The Original Boatload of Knowledge Down the Ohio River: William Maclure and Robert Owen's Transfer of Science and Education to the Midwest, 1825–1826," *Ohio Journal of Science* 89, no. 5 (1989): 128–142.

[34] According to Emmanuel D. Rudolph, botany was one of the few fields for women to practice science in the early nineteenth century, as they were excluded from academies and laboratories. See Emanuel D. Rudolph, "Women in Nineteenth Century American Botany: A Generally Unrecognized Constituency," *American Journal of Botany* 69, no. 2 (1982): 1346–1355. Letters by Gertrude Rapp to her adoptive uncle Frederic Rapp reveal that women in the settlement were the main caretakers of the orchards. See transcript of Gertrude Rapp, letter to Frederic Rapp (March 31, 1824), in Harmonist Society Collection Folder 7, New Harmony Working Men's Institute.

German-speaking lands in the late eighteenth century.³⁵ Sara J. Grossmann has recently shown that standardized climate sheets for meteorological observers started to spread in the eastern United States in the 1820s.³⁶ While Grossman relates the practice of weather data to the US-American nation-building process and settler colonialism, Richter adopts a transnational perspective, arguing that the aim was to observe regularities and predictable annual patterns of weather occurrences. Richter relates the collection of median temperatures, calculated daily by the Owenites, back to Alexander von Humboldt and his contribution in terms of mapping out different climate zones across the globe.³⁷ Through their collection, both the Harmonists and Owenites contributed to this global meteorological endeavor.

The collection of climate data and its monthly publication also served to inform their own community members on how to practice agriculture. This was not a weather forecast in the contemporary sense of the word; however, thanks to the precise recordings of weather phenomena, new settlers could make predictions regarding temperatures, sun exposure, and precipitation for each month. Most settlers had only arrived in New Harmony along with Owen in 1826. They did not know when a new season began in southwest Indiana, when the first frost would arrive, and how much precipitation they could expect in a given month. In fact, in 1827, the temperature dropped below freezing for the first time on September 28.³⁸

In addition to meteorological charts, the Owenite weekly newspaper *New-Harmony Gazette* regularly published articles on cultivating plants and processing agricultural products, many of which had not been cultivated in New Harmony during the Rappite period.³⁹ A few articles introduced readers to new mechanical methods of processing fruit, while others explained the cultivation of exotic plants in the global south. A third group of articles presented advice on how to cultivate non-native plants on the Indiana frontier, often reprinting articles from other US-American newspapers. The article on the "Cultivation of the Almond" was a reprint from the *Delaware Gazette*. It reported on some unnamed author's experiment to grow almond trees in Philadelphia, which normally thrive in a "temperate

---

35 See Linda Richter, *Semiotik, Physik, Organik: Eine Geschichte des Wissens vom Wetter, 1750–1850* (Frankfurt am Main: Campus, 2019), 204–206.
36 Grossmann, *Immeasurable*, 32–36.
37 Richter, *Semiotik*, 246–248.
38 "Meteorological Journal Kept at New Harmony," *New-Harmony Gazette*, October 3, 1827, 416.
39 According to order forms for plants and seeds from 1822, out of the plants featured in the *New-Harmony Gazette*, the Rappites had only attempted to grow apples, grapes, cucumbers, and poppies. See the transcript of a letter by George W. Dewey to George Rapp (March 11, 1822), in Harmonist Society Collection Folder 7, New Harmony Working Men's Institute.

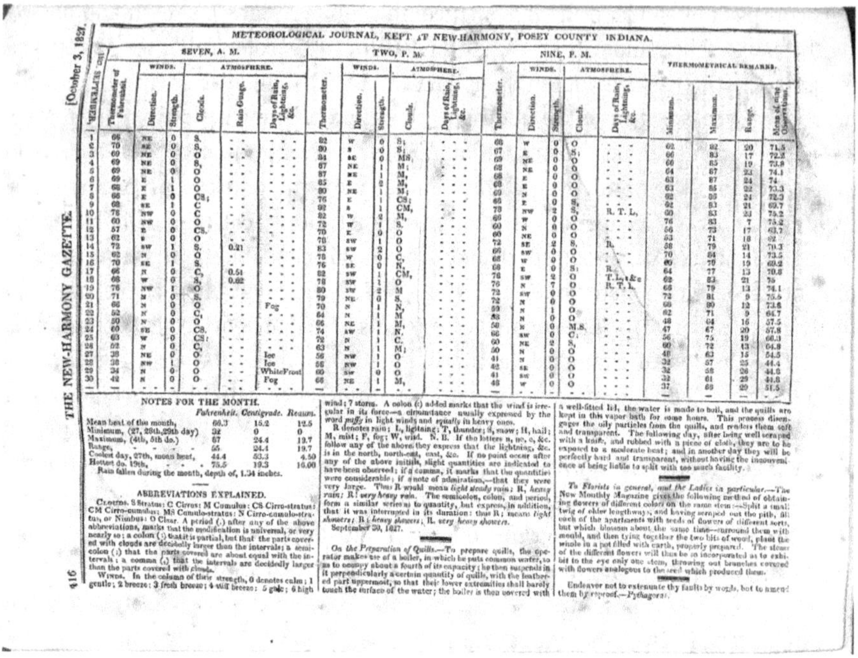
THE NEW-HARMONY GAZETTE.

[October 3, 1827.

METEOROLOGICAL JOURNAL, KEPT AT NEW-HARMONY, POSEY COUNTY INDIANA.

NOTES FOR THE MONTH.

ABBREVIATIONS EXPLAINED.

416

Figure 1: Aggregated climate chart for September 1827, in: "Meteorological Journal Kept at New Harmony," New Harmony Gazette, October 3, 1827, 416, reprint with courtesy of the Vasser College Special Collections Library.

and warm climate."[40] The author knew that almond trees needed lots of sunshine, and due to "the warm days of March and April," all of his almonds budded. To the author's surprise, the trees even survived most winters, and he was able to harvest between twenty and seventy almonds per tree per year. Only "the cold and cutting winter of 1820 and the late frost of April 1821" destroyed the harvest, but as he knew that "such frost happened rarely," he recommended "farmers, gardeners, and others" to cultivate almonds as a nourishing and tasty fruit.

An article on the benne plant, which produces sesame seeds, in length quoted a Dr. Smith from Baltimore on the uses and cultivation of the plant. Interestingly, it advocated using a liquid paste from the leaves to treat children's ailments rather than adding the seeds to one's diet. According to the article, the plant required "a warm climate" and was "easily injured by the frost," which meant that

40 "Cultivation of the Almond," *New-Harmony Gazette,* December 20, 1826, 95.

it should not be planted until the middle of May or early June.[41] The reason why the *New-Harmony Gazette* published an instruction on how to plant benne was that the leadership of the settlement had procured some sesame seeds. The editors of the *New-Harmony Gazette* acknowledged that they had conducted experiments related to growing sesame over the summer and that their expectations "as to the value of the plant had been fully realized."[42] The experiment had been a success and as the authors were convinced of the usefulness of sesame, they urged other settlers to cultivate it as well. This illustrates that botany experiments in New Harmony continued to occur once Owen and his sons took over.

While the almond tree originates in the Mediterranean, the benne plant is originally found in Sub-Saharan Africa and southern Asia. Some of the plants presented in the *Gazette* could be found in northern Europe, but the climate of the American Midwest offered new opportunities to grow non-native plants. The meticulous collection of climate data helped adjust the planting seasons of these "exotic" plants to the local climate in an exact and rational fashion. Considering that most of the New Harmony residents were educated elites, who had no prior knowledge of agriculture, the *New-Harmony Gazette* became the hub for circulating information concerning farming methods, climatic conditions, and the results of experiments. Climate data, combined with information on the cultivation of "exotic" plants reprinted from other news outlets, formed the basis for the agricultural experiments in New Harmony. It represented one variable when deciding which plants to cultivate in the cooperative settlement. In addition, data collection constituted an important knowledge production practice not only for the settlement as such but also for the entire state of Indiana. Whether or not they wanted to, socialist settlers became supporters of colonialism through their data collection practices.

Ethnic Networks to Find the Perfect Location for a Settlement

Climate knowledge was crucial not only for deciding which plants to grow, but also for choosing the site for a new settlement, as evidenced by the letters written by engineer John Augustus Roebling. Roebling immigrated to the United States in

---

41 The authors misspell the English name of the plant, but give the Latin name "Sesamum Indicum," which indicates that they refer to the benne (sesame) plant and not the bene plant, see "The Bene Plant," *New-Harmony Gazette*, May 30, 1827, 277.
42 "The Bene Plant," 277.

1831 with a group of engineers from Thuringia. His plan was to establish a "new Germany" that was free from the oppression of the Prussian military state.[43] Initially, he had intended to establish a colony to grow tobacco, as his parents were tobacco traders, and to experiment with the best form of internal social organization for this community.

Before he could start his experiment to create a communal tobacco farm, he gathered all the information he could get regarding possible locations by traveling through the Midwest and talking to other German immigrants. In November 1831, he wrote two lengthy letters about his insights to his friend Ferdinand Baehr, who was waiting back in Thuringia to cross the Atlantic along with Roebling's family.[44] At the beginning of his first letter, Roebling admitted that he had not known all that much about the geological and climatic conditions of the American Midwest before he arrived there. He claimed that most travel accounts he had read turned out to be false, whereas his childhood friend John A. Etzler's reports were the "most correct, most thorough, most objective," except for his business considerations.[45] Roebling admitted that he had initially considered building his settlement in the American South due to the favorable meteorological climate, but abolished this idea due to the unstable political climate regarding slavery.[46] He considered Indiana, Ohio, and Illinois, where most German immigrants settled, unsuitable due to the high humidity and swampiness of the region. He assumed that most German settlers did not know any better when choosing to settle in these states.

According to his understanding of medicine, "warm sun miasmas" – toxic particles arising from swamps – caused fevers and made most of the inhabitants

---

[43] As Glenn Penny recently argued, many global German emigrees in the 1830s and 1840s sought to recreate the lifestyles they were used to at home but could not keep up due to the revolutionary upheavals in central Europe, see Penny, *German History*, 29.

[44] The original German letters by John A. Roebling to Frederic Baehr are held at Rutgers University Archives and Special Collections. Xerox copies of the German originals and transcripts produced by Karl J.R. Arndt and his secretaries are found in the Harmonist Collection at the Communal Studies Archive at the University of Southern Indiana. Arndt and Patrick R. Brostowin published translations of two letters in the following journal articles: Karl J.R. Arndt and Patrick R. Brostowin, "Pragmatists and Prophets: George Rapp and J.A. Roebling versus J.A. Etzler and Count Leon, Part 1," *Western Pennsylvania Historical Magazine* 52, no. 1 (1969): 1–27; Arndt and Brostowin, "Pragmatists Part 2," 171–198. Quotations originate from the English translation.

[45] John. A. Roebling, Letter to F. Baehr, November 2, 1831, in Arndt and Brostowin, "Pragmatists Part 1," 8.

[46] Roebling, "Letter to F. Baehr, November 2, 1831," in Arndt and Brostowin, "Pragmatists Part 1," 8.

of the southern Midwest look pale and ill.[47] He also found the proliferation of mosquitos to be a nuisance. It was only in the area around Pittsburgh that people seemed healthy to Roebling and, in contrast to Missouri, where German settlers had recently started to move, there was transportation available to access the markets in the Eastern cities. He described Pittsburgh as the most industrial city in the United States but rejected the mountainous valleys south of the city, as they would not produce enough wind to blow away the miasmas. He also rejected locations in the woods due to the lack of air circulation and his fear that the frequent thunderstorms might make trees fall onto the settlement. In the end, he settled for the flat meadowland of Butler County, north of Pittsburgh, which he described as "paradise."[48]

In his second letter, he admitted that he had chosen this region primarily for its healthy weather, though the fact that the waterways provided transportation and a site for a water mill also came in handy.[49] As for the cultivation of his settlement, Roebling sought advice from George Rapp, with his twenty-five years of experience of running a religious cooperative settlement in three different locations. Even though he disagreed with Rapp's religious teachings, Roebling considered him one of the best-informed farmers in the German American settler community.[50] Based on Rapp's advice, Roebling decided that his settlement should manage the land in a communal fashion since a common investment meant more gains and lower risks. He then switched to sheep farming rather than tobacco farming, even though sheep and cattle had a hard time thriving in the cold Pennsylvania winter. In addition, he asked his friend Ferdinand Baehr to bring seeds when he came over from Germany, including rape seeds and poppy seeds to produce vegetable oil. He also asked Baehr to bring over books on science, chemistry, and specifically technology.[51] The letters indicate the importance of climate knowledge to the ambitious settlement leader: first in order to pick a location for his settlement, and second to decide which commodities to produce. As travel accounts turned out to be unreliable, Roebling used the information and experiences of previous settlement experiment leaders such as John A. Etzler or George Rapp to make his own decisions. By interpreting his obser-

---

[47] Roebling, "Letter to F. Baehr, November 2, 1831," in Arndt and Brostowin, "Pragmatists Part 1," 9–10.
[48] Roebling, "Letter to F. Baehr, November 2, 1831," in Arndt and Brostowin, "Pragmatists Part 1," 7–24, 26.
[49] Roebling, "Letter to F. Baehr, November 2, 1831," in: Arndt and Brostowin, "Pragmatists Part 1," 171.
[50] Roebling, "Letter to F. Baehr, November 2, 1831," in Arndt and Brostowin, "Pragmatists Part 1," 172–174.
[51] Roebling, "Letter to F. Baehr, November 2, 1831," in Arndt and Brostowin, "Pragmatists Part 1," 190.

vations with regard to geography and climate and the information he received from others, he created a lengthy survey of climate knowledge on the American Midwest for further settlers from Thuringia.

However, it is noticeable that all sources of information in Roebling's letters were other German immigrants. This was in part due to his poor language skills; in the early part of his letter, he admitted that he had to rely on Etzler's fluency in English. But it is also very likely that he viewed those who inhabited a similar habitus and outlook as himself as the most reliable. However, this also meant that he unintendedly excluded local knowledge not conveyed through his own ethnic networks. In the end, he located his colony Saxonburg some 27 miles northeast of Pittsburgh, within a day's ride from Rapp's Economy.[52]

Book Knowledge and Ignorance in Venezuela

However, Roebling's travel companion Etzler did not follow his friend's example by interviewing other settlers about the local micro-climate, health conditions, and economy when planning an experimental settlement in Venezuela. Here, he intended to combine Fourierist economic principles with trials of modern machinery: the Satellite, a mechanical plow attached to a windmill, and the Naval Automaton, a wind-powered speedboat. These were meant to use wind- and waterpower as sources of energy and promised to reduce human labor to a minimum. Both had failed in trial runs in England when the Satellite broke down in a field near Oxford and the Naval Automaton sank in the River Thames.[53] Subsequently, Etzler and his business partner Conrad Friedrich Stollmeyer planned to run trials of the machinery in more favorable climate conditions in the tropics.

Before drafting the Venezuela scheme, Etzler had parted ways with his childhood friend Roebling in August of 1831. According to Roebling, they had a disagreement as Etzler planned to move on to Missouri despite Rapp's warning that this would make it difficult to access the markets on the East Coast. Roebling described Etzler's knowledge regarding the US as typically very thorough, but he was "too easy" in some of his considerations due to his stubbornness and lack of business sense.[54] According to the Harmonist correspondence, Etzler did not venture out West right away but stayed in Economy throughout 1833, where he trans-

---

52 Arndt and Brostowin, "Pragmatists Part 1," 185.
53 Stoll, *Delusion*, 15.
54 Roebling, "Letter to F. Baehr, November 2, 1831," in Arndt and Brostowin, "Pragmatists Part 1," 1, 8.

lated newspaper articles and wrote his own settlement scheme *The Paradise within the Reach of Men*, which he published in Pittsburgh that same year.[55] By 1840, Etzler had acquired a new partner in Conrad Friedrich Stollmeyer, an immigrant from Ulm who published a German language newspaper in Philadelphia and was active in the abolitionist movement and Fourierist Society of Philadelphia.[56] Stollmeyer and Etzler traveled to Britain in 1841 and 1843 respectively after realizing that US-American audiences and the US government were not particularly interested in their scheme. In Britain, however, they had found an ardent supporter in Robert Owen, who had returned there after his New Harmony experiment had failed. As a trade union leader and newspaper editor in the 1830s, Owen wrote a flamboyant review of Etzler's *Paradise* in his paper *New Moral World*.[57]

In his newspapers, Owen offered Stollmeyer and Etzler a platform where they could promote their own colonial settlement plans. Stollmeyer also put articles about Etzler's inventions and schemes in Fourierist and Chartist newspapers in London.[58] By 1845, the two immigrants founded the Tropical Emigration Society, a joint-stock company raising funds from its 1,500 members to finance a settlement in the tropics.[59] Etzler chose the Paria Peninsula in Venezuela mainly for political reasons: Venezuela was a republic where Europeans could obtain land for free and were exempt from military service.[60] He was also convinced, as he laid out in his 1833 publication, that any tropical region between the 30th latitude north and south (roughly in-between the Florida panhandle and the northern tip of Brazil) was ideal for his settlement scheme as the whole region provided winds to run his Satellite and to cultivate tropical fruits.[61] As pointed out by climate historian Linda

---

55 See Christian von Bonnhorst, Letter to Romeli L. Baker (May 29, 1833) and Romeli L. Baker, Letter to Jacob Heinrici (June 3, 1832), File 35A, Folder 129/179, Harmonist Papers CS053, University of Southern Indiana Archives & Special Collections.
56 See Nydahl, *Collected Works*, xvii; Ulrike Kirchberger, *Aspekte deutsch-britischer Expansion: Die Überseeinteressen der deutschen Migranten in Großbritannien in der Mitte des 19. Jahrhunderts* (Stuttgart: Steiner Verlag, 1999), 92.
57 Robert Owen, "The 'Paradise'," *New Moral World*, November 21, 1835, 32, accessed through the Vassar University Library, Special Collections.
58 See, for instance, "Miscellaneous: Mr Etzler's Invention," *The London Phalanx*, September 4, 1841; "Review of: Paradise Within the Reach of All Men without Labor by Power of Nature and Machinery. By J.A. Etzler – Cleave, Shoe Lane, Fleet Street," *The London Phalanx*, August 1842, 80–82.
59 See Kirchberger, *Expansion*, 116.
60 Stoll, *Delusion*, 108.
61 John Adolphus Etzler, *The Paradise within the Reach of All Men, without Labor, by Powers of Nature and Machinery. Second Part* (Pittsburgh: Etzler and Reinhold 1833), 11.

Richter, the 1830s and 1840s represented the period when climatologists were trying to describe different global climate regions based on Alexander von Humboldt's calculations of median temperatures.[62]

Etzler and Stollmeyer contributed to the discourse on tropicality with their publications. According to historian David Arnold, tropicalization means "the conceptualization and representation of the tropics in European imaginations and experiences," thus producing a notion of the tropical regions as fundamentally different from Europe but intrinsically linked with each other.[63] These representations included scientific measurements as well as sensuous experiences by European travelers and artistic expressions found in literature and visual art. European commentators conceptualized the tropics as both a place of abundance as well as of danger due to its sun exposure, humidity, vegetation, and wildlife.[64] Tropicality, in essence, describes a cultural process of inventing the tropics as a homogenous space that became a geographical fact with far-reaching political, economic, and cultural implications, thus tying the production of knowledge on the tropics to colonial exploitation and the marginalization of indigenous groups and their experiences.[65]

Neither Etzler nor Stollmeyer had ever been to Venezuela, although Etzler had traveled to Haiti in 1839 – that is, after he had first written about a common tropical climate.[66] Nevertheless, in the Tropical Emigration Society's own newspaper *The Morning Star*, the engineers tried to dispel possible doubts among their investors by focusing on the advantages of the tropical climate in general. In the spring of 1845, *The Morning Star* ran a three-part series "On Climate; Particularly of Venezuela and the Tropics" written by society member Charles Stillwell. It also published a four-part travel report of "A Voyage up the Orinoco and Ramble through Venezuela."[67] With regard to the climate and location, the travel report referred to Humboldt, as well as to Charles Darwin and Francis Hall's 1825 report

---

[62] Richter, *Semiotik*, 248–249.
[63] For a definition of the concept of tropicality, see Arnold, *Tropics*, 110, 231.
[64] Reinaldo Funes Manzote argues that tropicality underwent a shift in meaning from commodities production in the nineteenth century to tourism in the twentieth century. See Reinaldo Funes Monzote, "The Greater Caribbean and the Transformation of Tropicality," in *A Living Past. Environmental Histories of Modern Latin America*, eds. John Soluri, Claudia Leal, and José Augusto Pádua (New York and Oxford: Berghahn, 2018), 45–66.
[65] Arnold, *Tropics*, 5, 110–115.
[66] See Nydahl, *Collected Works*, xvi.
[67] Charles Stillwell, "On Climate; Particularly of Venezuela and the Tropics Part 1," *The Morning Star*, May 31, 1845, 164–165; "A Voyage up the Orinoco and Ramble through Venezuela Part 4," *The Morning Star*, May 31, 1845, 161–164.

on emigration to Colombia.[68] In the first part of the article, the unknown author cited Humboldt's travel reports, stating that in the city of Cumaná, some 250 km west of the intended settlement, there was "a warm sunny climate, the sky being for ten months of the year cloudless, and for two months only variable by rains and sunshine. [. . .] The thermometer averages 81 to 82 degrees."[69] On the southern part of the Orinoco River, which is about 500 km south of Etzler's intended settlement, there would be "almost a continual rain for ten months of the year, and for two months only rain and sunshine alternative. The soil is there of the most exuberant fertile and covered with dense forest." The average temperature would be 80 degrees F or 26 degrees C. In the area in-between those two points, the author assumed that there would be "a medium between the two extremes of moist and dry weather."[70] Accordingly, he concluded that the best place to establish a settlement was at the northern edge of the Orinoco Delta due to its "delightful temperatures and healthful places for settlements."[71] Etzler obtained land on the Paria Peninsula from the Venezuelan government that was some 400 km off from this path.

Charles Stillwell's article "On Climate; Particularly of Venezuela and the Tropics" provided advice on how Europeans could survive the tropical climate in order to facilitate colonial exploitation. He recommended abstaining from alcohol and to adopt a vegetarian diet,[72] which was not a surprise as Stollmeyer was a lifelong supporter of the temperance movement, while Etzler advocated vegetarianism.[73] To be self-sufficient vegetarians, the society was to cultivate "the most valuable plants" based on their nutritional value, including bananas, plantains, maize, sugar cane, potatoes, sweet potatoes, several European and South American fruits and nuts, and seeds for oil.[74]

With regard to both diet and dress, the article recommended that settlers follow the examples of Hindus in India. Also, the author recommended regular exer-

---

68 In the same issue, the *Morning Star* also featured a review of Colonel Francis Hall, *Colombia – Its Present State in respect of Climate, Soil, Production, Population, Government, Commerce, Revenue, Manufacture, Arts, Literature, Manners, Education, and Inducements to Emigration* (Philadelphia: Small, Parker, Littell, Marot & Walter 1825). There is no evidence that the members of the TES were personally acquainted with any of the authors.
69 *Voyage*, 163.
70 *Voyage*, 163.
71 *Voyage*, 163.
72 Stillwell, "Climate Part 1," 164.
73 Gregory Claeys, "John Adolphus Etzler, Technological Utopianism, and British socialism: The Tropical Emigration Society's Venezuela Mission and its social context 1833–1848," *English Historical Review* 101 (1986): 360.
74 *Voyage*, 162.

cise to prevent what British doctor Benjamin Moseley described as "a promptitude and bias to Pleasure, and an alienation from serious thought and deep reflection" found in the inhabitants of the tropics. According to Moseley's 1803 work *A Treatise on Tropical Diseases* (based on his practice in Jamaica), a tropical climate caused laziness in thought and work ethics among its inhabitants.[75] Instead of the climate, Stillwell argued that what caused laziness among people in the tropics was "moral restraint, temptations to vice, the facility of the mind" and a lack of positive role models – all things that the society tried to amend. Nevertheless, it was the responsibility of the individual member to acquire "knowledge of the artificial aids to the preservation of health" in the tropical climate, as the whole society was dependent on the health of the individual.[76]

At the end of the article, the author provided a list of nine sanitary rules and nine guidelines when picking a location. The location should be on grasslands, with fresh air and fresh water. It should not be damp, marshy, or "saturated with moisture"[77] to avoid miasmas and mosquitos. Contrary to the claim of economic historian Steven Stoll that the founders of the Tropical Emigration Society did not care about tropical diseases, they were indeed concerned, even though they downplayed this risk in most of their publications.[78]

Instead, their ignorance materialized in the local specificities of the location they chose. None of the leaders of the society had ever been to Venezuela or the Paria Peninsula specifically. Within the concept of tropicality, they assumed that texts written about one tropical region could easily be applied to another. Examining the authors and works that the newspaper articles cited, they were all published in English or German, including Hall's travel account in Colombia, Moseley's experiences in Jamaica, Humboldt's voyage along the Orinoco River, or Darwin's travels along the southern coast of South America. The paper viewed all of the tropics as having the same conditions in terms of humidity, flora, and fauna. This was a striking generalization, especially considering that Roebling described even the microclimate north and south of Pittsburgh as different.

Unlike the Owenites at New Harmony, the Tropical Emigrations Society did not collect meteorological data, and unlike Roebling, they did not ask locals for their input. Instead, they relied on book knowledge on tropicality that provided general information on the continent but not on the specific location they had

---

75 Charles Stillwell, "On Climate; Particularly of Venezuela and the Tropics Part 4," *The Morning Star* 23 (June 14, 1845), 181. They refer to Benjamin Moseley, *A Treatise of Tropical Diseases; On Military Operations; and on the Climate of the West Indies* (London: T. Cadell, 1787).
76 Stillwell, "Climate Part 1," 165.
77 Stillwell, "Climate Part 4," 181.
78 Stoll, *Delusion*, 127.

chosen. Etzler selected the settlement site based on political considerations and the availability of cheap land. As Stoll has shown, the settlement failed when settlers were surprised by the uncleared land, the rocky ground, the heat, and the prevalence of yellow fever. While Stoll argues that what led to the settlement failing was the community leaders' ignorance of the tropics, I would specify that their ignorance of local differences, their preference for book knowledge published in German and English, and their lack of interactions with local communities were what brought the colonial project to a premature end.

Conclusion

Climate knowledge played a key role in intentional communities, influencing the choice of location, the health of community members, and the choices of which crops to plant. However, settlers often lacked prior knowledge regarding the local climate conditions of the regions they aimed to colonize. Collecting climate knowledge became a prerequisite for settlers embarking on experiments in agriculture, mechanization, or social organization. Hence, settlers emphasized observing and collecting climate data as an initial step in community-building. In New Harmony, settlers initiated their own data collection while the Tropical Emigration Society relied on book knowledge. Roebling, on the other hand, traveled extensively, made observations, and sought advice from experienced farmers.

Climate knowledge was intrinsically linked to agriculture. Settlers turned their colonies into experimental laboratories, not only testing social and technological innovations but also various agricultural practices. Whether experimenting with sesame and almonds in Indiana or testing the hardiness of tobacco during winter in Pennsylvania, intentional communities contributed to broadening colonial projects through their agricultural experiments.

However, none of these observations were conducted in a void. They occurred within discourses of tropicality and experimental spaces. Settlers engaged with scientific knowledge by reprinting articles on scientific experiments or citing renowned scholars' concepts of the tropics. Their preconceived notions concerning health and nutrition involved an interaction with scientific knowledge from academia, which was often unquestioningly accepted as evidence or guidelines for decision-making. Scientific knowledge was generally trusted and served as a supplement to the experimental knowledge gained in the colonies. If that knowledge contradicted the settlers' own assumptions, they presented counterevidence based on their own observations. These observations, however, were biased toward educated men of the same ethnic group and social class. The activists did not interact with indigenous observations whatsoever and cited few texts produced in languages other than German or English.[79]

The intentional communities were not isolated; they were interconnected with each other and the broader world. Settlers relied on information shared by fellow countrymen, and leaders like George Rapp played a crucial role in disseminating information and promoting colonial schemes. Correspondence and publications circulated knowledge among communities of potential emigrants in Europe.

Cooperative settlers and utopian engineers in various ways engaged with settler colonialism and processes of tropicalization. Their boats traveled on the routes of empire, they consumed colonially produced knowledge, and when collecting climate data and conducting experiments, they produced applied knowledge that helped further the settler colonial project in the Americas. Intentional communities and settler colonialism were strongly entangled not just through the settlers' colonial mindset but also in the very down-to-earth practices of chatting about the weather. Talking about the weather was not merely chit-chat; it was a form of knowledge production aiding future settlers in decisions regarding crop cultivation, choosing location, and social experiments, thereby supporting the settler colonial project as a whole.

Claudia Roesch is a post-doctoral researcher at the University of Konstanz affiliated with the history of knowledge working group. Her research interests include the history of knowledge and technology, North American history, gender and the family, and migration history. Her current research project "Utopian Engineering" investigates the role of science and engineering knowledge in social reform projects in the nineteenth-century Atlantic world. Her most recent publication is "Owen and the Engineers: Cross-Fertilization between Engineering and Early Socialism in the Owenite Tradition," *Global Intellectual History* (2023), 1–16.

---

[79] Stollmeyer's 1845 pamphlet *The Sugar Question Made Easy* mentions only one Spanish-language publication in its bibliography: Italian-Venezuelan military adviser Agostin Codazzi's *Resúmen de la geografía de Venezuela* (1841). See Conrad Friedrich Stollmeyer, *The Sugar Question Made Easy* (London: John Wortham 1845), 6.

Anne Kwaschik
Experimental Discourse and Fourierist Settlements in the 1840s and 1850s

Abstract: This article examines Fourierism as a socio-epistemic program, specifically focusing on its experimental discourse encapsulated in Fourier's concept of the *phalanstère*. The study is systematically divided into three main sections, where the initial section introduces Fourier's social philosophy, elucidating its theoretical foundations and characterizing Fourierism as an experimental initiative merging theory and practice. The subsequent section delves into the establishment and evolution of the experimental discourse among Fourier's followers between the 1830s and the 1870s. The emphasis here is on the dynamic interplay between conceptual frameworks and practical applications. The third section, finally, explores the colonial dimension of Fourierism by using a case study of the Union agricole du Sig in Algeria to demonstrate the intersection of Fourier's experimental model with the complexities of colonial realities. The article concludes by underscoring the enduring legacy of Fourier's experimental practices and their significant impact on social organization and theory, particularly within the cooperative movement. The experimental discourse in Fourier's model is highlighted as a pivotal aspect, thereby emphasizing its role and legacy in shaping and redefining social norms and structures.

Keywords: Fourierism, Algeria, 1840s, Colonialism, Settlements, Intellectual Socialism, Early Social Science Ideas

Introduction

Since the 1960s, industrialized nations have deliberated on an experimental approach to social reform instigated by social scientists. This approach involves testing solutions to major societal problems in smaller, controlled environments and refining them based on the results.[1] Interestingly, this experimental approach does not exclusively exist in modern knowledge-based societies; it also resonates

---

[1] For example, see D. T. Campbell, "Reforms as Experiments," *American Psychologist* 24, no. 4 (1969): 409–429; Noortje Marres, "The Experiment in Living," in *Inventive Methods: The Happening of the Social*, eds. Celia Lury and Nina Wakeford (London and New York: Routledge, 2012), 76–95.

∂ Open Access. © 2024 the author(s), published by De Gruyter. This work is licensed under the Creative Commons Attribution-NonCommercial-NoDerivatives 4.0 International License.
https://doi.org/10.1515/9783111291383-008

with historical social reform endeavors in the early nineteenth century. Emerging as a response to the social question and the dual revolution, these movements, termed "early socialism," combined reform initiatives, political activism, social theory, and the creation of alternative communal and work structures, known as "associations." Although varied in form, these associations aimed to build prototypes of future societal models on a small scale.[2]

This article investigates Fourierist associations as experimental spaces encompassing physical, material, and discursive aspects. Originating in France in the 1830s, Fourierism gained prominence through mobilization campaigns, disputes, and highly mediatized debates in relation to the theory and practice of Charles Fourier's (1772–1837) socio-scientific project to establish an alternative social order. Fourier designed his associations as alternative communities to test and evaluate the principles of an emerging social order on a micro-scale, thus emphasizing the integration of theory and practice. Initial isolated realizations in these communities in the 1830s paved the way for a serial phenomenon in subsequent decades, particularly during the 1840s and 1850s, with over 40 communities established globally by adherents and former affiliates of the movement. Following Fourier's death in 1837, these community experiments were primarily carried out outside Europe, particularly in recently conquered territories or during colonial wars. Fourierists or ex-Fourierists founded more than 40 settlements around the world, including in Latin America, North Africa, New Caledonia, and approximately 30 settlements in the United States.[3] Flourishing during the July Monarchy, Fourierism gained political relevance during the 1848 revolution and persisted in various forms during the Second Empire.[4]

This process of establishing a new social order involved a thorough evaluation and reflection of the implementations in order to enhance and refine future model associations, examining both unachieved objectives and interim successes while considering environmental, human, and societal factors as explanatory variables.[5] It entailed an evolving discourse that transitioned toward the integration of practi-

---

[2] *S'unir, travailler, résister. Les associations ouvrières au XIXe siècle*, eds. Carole Christen, Caroline Fayolle, and Samuel Hayat (Villeneuve d'Ascq: Presses universitaires du Septentrion, 2021); Pamela Pilbeam, *French Socialists before Marx: Workers, Women and the Social Question in France* (Montreal: McGill-Queen's University Press, 2000).

[3] Otohiko Okugawa, "Annotated List of Communal and Utopian Societies, 1787–1919," in *Dictionary of American Communal and Utopian History*, ed. Robert S. Fogarty (Westport, Greenwood Press, 1980), 173–233.

[4] Bernard Desmars, *Militants de l'utopie? Les fouriéristes dans la seconde moitié du XIXe siècle* (Dijon: Les presses du réel, 2010).

[5] On the processual character of experiments, see Anne-Sophie Reichert's article on Émile Jaques-Dalcroze's rhythm school in the garden city of Hellerau in this special section.

cal experiences and insights into the essential conditions to achieve a successful comprehensive or partial application of Fourierist principles. This iterative and reflective approach imbued Fourierist pursuits with a distinct "experimental" quality and positioned them as central topics for historical investigations into the generation and development of social knowledge in the early nineteenth century.[6]

The primary objective of this article is to demonstrate how this discourse of experimentation shaped the identity of the Fourierist movement. Hence, the article invokes the concept of the "laboratory" as conceptualized by Bruno Latour to examine the erasure of traditional boundaries between theory and practice in the experimental context represented by Fourierist settlements. Latour's interpretation of the "laboratory" deconstructs the traditional boundary between scientific and societal realms by conceiving it as a domain in which scientists actively reconfigure both scientific and social environments through experimental procedures.[7] Crucially, the laboratory transcends its function as a mere site of scientific inquiry. It emerges as a means through which science exerts influence upon the external world, including the social sphere. This influence is exerted by transposing actors (understood as acting entities creating associations) into the laboratory setting, regardless of whether these actors are microscopic organisms or social collectives.[8] This conceptualization implies that the laboratory not only serves as a space for scientific investigation but also as a nexus wherein scientific pursuits and social dynamics converge and interact, mutually shaping and being shaped by the broader societal context.

Based on these observations, this article systematically examines the experimental discourse within Fourierism, thus departing from metaphorical references to "experiments" and "laboratories" commonly found in existing research.[9] More importantly, the article challenges the prevalent classification of these initiatives as "utopias." Using the term "utopia" to describe these early social projects is fraught with complexities. First, it emphasizes the primacy of ideas and obscures the notable distinction that these "utopias" were, in fact, executed in practice, meaning that they diverged from the conventional utopian designs. Second, the historical deployment of "utopia" as a polemical and political epithet, something that Fourierists and other social thinkers actively defended themselves against in their writings,

---

6 Anne Kwaschik, "Gesellschaftswissen als Zukunftshandeln," *Francia* 44 (2017): 189–211.
7 Bruno Latour and Steve Woolgar, *Laboratory Life: The Construction of Scientific Facts* (Princeton: Princeton University Press, 1986), 23–27.
8 Bruno Latour, "Give Me a Laboratory and I Will Raise the World," in *Science Observed*, eds. Karin D. Knorr-Cetina and Michael Mulkay (London and Beverly Hills: Sage, 1983), 141–170, 158.
9 For example, see Annick Osmont, "L'exportation des modèles utopiques Outre-Mer au XIXe siècle. La foi expérimentale des disciples," *Les Annales de la recherche urbaine* 42 (1989): 19–26.

adds further intricacy.¹⁰ Third, the persistent use of "utopia" perpetuates Marx and Engels' dichotomy between utopian and scientific socialism,¹¹ which thereby obscures the scientific claims embedded within Fourierism. Paradoxically, however, Marx and Engels, while delegitimizing the Fourierist communal projects as the mere "experimental realization of [their social] Utopias," inadvertently acknowledged the experimental nature of these initiatives.¹²

This article builds on established research fields by basing its analysis on scholarly studies of Fourierist communal practices.¹³ To gain a comprehensive understanding of all aspects of this discourse, it also delves into the extensive historiography of ideas encompassing both scientific and "utopian" domains.¹⁴ In its exploration of experimental practices, the article draws attention to a commonly neglected facet of Fourierism to highlight the infrastructural impact of colonialism.¹⁵ It underscores that a significant number of the Fourierist experiments were not merely facilitated by colonial conditions but were intricately shaped by them, often unfolding in territories having recently been colonized or undergoing colonial warfare. This perspective elucidates the complex interplay between colonial dynamics and the practical realization of Fourierist ideas, thereby adding a key dimension when it comes to understanding this social movement.

To summarize, this article offers a critical reevaluation of Fourierist associations by positing them as experiments. It is structured into three distinct sections:

---

10 Ruth Levitas, *The Concept of Utopia* (Syracuse: Syracuse University Press, 1991), 38. For a conceptual-historical classification, see Lucian Hölscher, "Utopie," in *Geschichtliche Grundbegriffe. Historisches Lexikon zur politisch-sozialen Sprache in Deutschland*, vol. 6, eds. Otto Brunner, Werner Conze, and Reinhart Koselleck (Stuttgart: Klett Cotta, 1990), 733–788.
11 Gregory Claeys, "Early Socialism as Intellectual History," *History of European Ideas* 40, no. 7 (2014): 893–904, 893–894; Roger Paden, "Marx's Critique of the Utopian Socialists," *Utopian Studies* 13, no. 2 (2002): 67–91.
12 Karl Marx and Friedrich Engels, "The Manifesto of the Communist Party," in *The Marx-Engels Reader*, ed. Robert C. Tucker (New York and London: Norton, 1980 [1848]), 469–500, 499.
13 Michel Lallement, "Living in Utopia in the 19th Century: A Comparison of France and the United States," *Comparative Sociology* 20 (2021): 45–69; Carl J. Guarneri, *The Utopian Alternative: Fourierism in Nineteenth-Century America* (Ithaca: Cornell University Press, 1991); Henri Desroche, *La société-festive. Du fouriérisme écrit aux fouriérismes pratiqués* (Paris: Éd. du Seuil, 1975).
14 Piotr Kuligowski and Quentin Schwanck, "Between Science and Utopia: Physical and Astronomical Notions within French and Polish Fourierism," *Historical Reflections/Réflexions Historiques* 48, no. 2 (2022): 1–17, accessed February 15, 2024, doi: 10.3167/hrrh.2022.480201; John Tresch, *The Romantic Machine: Utopian Science and Technology After Napoleon* (Chicago and London: University of Chicago Press, 2014).
15 Michèle Madonna-Desbazeille, "L'Union agricole d'Afrique: Une communauté fouriériste à Saint-Denis du Sig, Algérie," *Cahiers Charles Fourier* 16 (2005): 51–63, accessed February 15, 2024, https://www.charlesfourier.fr/spip.php?article284.

(1) an introduction to Fourier's social philosophy; (2) an analysis of the development and progression of the experimental discourse among his adherents between the 1830s and the 1870s; and (3) a discussion on the influence of colonialism in this context with a specific focus on the case study of Union agricole du Sig in Algeria. Each section contributes to a nuanced understanding of Fourierism as a social movement distinguished by its experimental discourse. This comprehensive examination of the Fourierist project not only illustrates the dynamics of social experimentation but also contributes significantly to our understanding of how early social theories were tested, adapted, and understood in their contemporary contexts.

Fourier's Experimental Approach

Fourier's social reform initiative, conceptualized as a novel social science program, was underpinned by a theoretical approach applying Cartesian doubt to the concept of civilization. Fourier challenged both the prevailing social order and the state of social philosophy, contending that the political and modern sciences of his era had not only lost their credibility but also made social issues even worse.[16] He argued for a radical rethinking of society:

> Doubt must therefore be applied to Civilisation: we must doubt its necessity, its excellence and its permanence. These are problems which the philosophers do not dare to consider because if they started being suspicious of Civilisation, they would risk invalidating their theories, which are all linked to Civilisation and which will all fall with it as soon as a better social order is found to replace it.[17]

Fourier's vision advocated integrating society and science while asserting that "social well-being" ("le bien social") could only be achieved by establishing a yet-to-be-developed science of society.[18] This understanding assigned a specific role to this science of society, which would enable examining current societal circumstances and developing future directions. By mediating between temporal horizons, this science merges lived realities and future aspirations, thereby clarifying, interpreting, and actively influencing transformative developments. Embracing this perspective marked a post-revolutionary rationality that fostered the devel-

---

16 Charles Fourier, *The Theory of the Four Movements* (Cambridge: Cambridge University Press 1996 [1808]), 7.
17 Ibid., 8.
18 Ibid.

opment of social science ideas and foresight in social planning. Fourier's model was in stark contrast to the concept of "revolution" as a sharp turn, instead favoring a gradual, evolutionary approach over abrupt, revolutionary change. Disillusioned by the violence of revolutionary politics, notably the Lyon insurrection and the siege of the Convention in 1793, Fourier embarked on a more harmonious and stable path in his social reform project.

In his words, Fourier "discovered" the laws of attraction and associated them with experimental practices. He designed a plan centered on the concept of "natural association" where individual desires harmonize with the common good. Thus, his concept of passionate attraction, aligned with Saint-Simon's law of universal gravitation, posited human society under the governance of "social physics."[19] Fourier's design involved individuals voluntarily associating, organizing communities according to their own laws, needs, and desires, and uniting resources for the benefit of all. Members of the association would be "driven to work by competition, self-esteem and other stimuli compatible with self-interest."[20] He envisioned autonomous social units as the nucleus of his broader theory of social reorganization and social science. The "trial cantons," representing small profit-sharing social units, served as experimental models embodying the associative principle.

The cantons were themselves produced by a *phalange*, which was Fourier's term for an "association"[21] or communal group, and arranged around a social palace called *phalanstère* (phalanstery). While Fourier never produced a finalized design, his drawings of a three-winged Versailles-like building with courtyards became the accepted version of the social palace. Fourier's luxurious edifice constituted the local and experimental center of the envisioned community, while the "trial cantons" served as a model for any form of social (re)organization.[22]

In this setting, Fourierist experiments involved an intense analysis of a specific, limited segment of the community. Fourierists viewed this approach as a

---

19 John F. Beecher, *Charles Fourier: The Visionary and His World* (Berkeley, Los Angeles, and London: University of California Press, 1987), 172–173. Claude Henri de Rouvroy, Comte de Saint-Simon (1760–1825), known as Henri de Saint-Simon, was a French sociopolitical theorist and is regarded as one of the three "founding figures of utopian socialism," alongside Charles Fourier and Robert Owen. For an overview of differences and similarities, see Antoine Picon, "Utopian Socialism and Social Science," in *The Cambridge History of Science*, vol. 7, The Modern Social Sciences, eds. Theodore M. Porter and Dorothy Ross (Cambridge: Cambridge University Press, 2003), 71–82.
20 Fourier, *Theory of the Four Movements*, 11.
21 Ibid., 318.
22 Victor Considérant, *Destinée sociale* (Paris: Libraires du Palais-Royal, 1834), vol. 1, 482; see Laurent Baridon, "The Fourierist Phalanstère: Building a New Society through Architecture?" in *The Companions to the History of Architecture*, vol. 3, Nineteenth-Century Architecture, eds. Martin Bressani and Christina Contandriopoulos (Hoboken, NJ: John Wiley & Sons, 2017), 1–20.

method used to investigate and ultimately address social issues. However, contemporary critics of social experiments made a metaphorical comparison to Jonathan Swift's *Gulliver's Travels*. They likened social experiments in general to the manner in which the king of Brobdingnag manipulated Gulliver, meticulously scrutinized him, and altered his position to observe different perspectives. They rejected the practicality of experiments in the social sphere and opposed the concept of manipulating a segment of the community, comparing it to "taking a portion of the community in our hand, as the king of Brobdingnag took Gulliver, viewing it from different aspects, and placing it in various positions, to solve social problems."[23]

Fourier developed his social theory within the naturalist framework of his time. In this context, the semantics of "discovery" and "invention" were part of empirical legitimization patterns. Using an empiricist language, he based his social science on established natural science laws: "I soon saw that the laws of passionate attraction agreed in all respects with the laws of material attraction as explained by Newton and Leibniz, and that there was *a unified system of movement for the spiritual and the material world*."[24] Fourier expanded Newton's idea that every object in the universe attracts any other to the social sphere with a varying force,[25] thereby centering on the very ties and relationships between individuals that make something like society visible and explorable. By introducing his social theory as a succession and extension of Newton, he pursued a twofold goal. First, he intended to distinguish himself from other social projects by claiming a scientific understanding of association (against the "frauds" of his time, including the manufacturer and socialist Robert Owen (1771–1858) whose "associations" in some sense competed with those of Fourier).[26] Second, he sought to lay the foundations of a new science rooted in experimental practice, one that proved "useful to the social body."[27]

---

[23] George Cornwall Lewis, *A Treatise on the Methods of Observation and Reasoning in Politics*, 2 vols. (London: Parker, 1852), vol. 1, 165. See Robert Brown, "Artificial Experiments on Society: Comte, G.C. Lewis and Mill," *Journal of Historical Sociology* 10, no. 1 (1997): 74–97.
[24] Fourier, *Theory of the Four Movements*, 16 (emphasis is original).
[25] Charles Fourier, *Le nouveau monde industriel et sociétaire, ou invention du procédé d'industrie attrayante et naturelle distribuée en séries passionnées* (Dijon: Les Presses du réel (2001 [1829]), 31; Kuligowski and Schwanck, "Between Science and Utopia."
[26] On Owenite settlements, see Claudia Roesch's article in this special section.
[27] Fourier, *Theory of the Four Movements*, 8.

Fourier in *La théorie des quatre movements* (*The Theory of the Four Movements*) outlined the idea of the universe as a "pan-social" set of dependencies including nature and society within a quasi-cosmological system:[28]

> The animal, organic and material movements are co-ordinated with the social movement, which is primary. This means that the properties of an animal, a vegetable, a mineral, or even a vortex of stars represent an effect of the human passions in the social order, and that everything, from atoms to stars, is an image of the properties of the human passions.[29]

Fourier claimed that the social was not a specific domain of reality but a principle of connections and thus not to be separated from other forms of connections and attraction. Similar to Saint-Simon, his concept of society is thus more akin to a "sociology of association" as developed by Bruno Latour[30] than to August Comte (1798–1857) or Émile Durkheim (1858-1917), who conceived of the subject of social research as a structured whole of social relations, a "methodological entity."[31]

The use of "experiments" to establish a social science field also stemmed from the naturalist framework and was prevalent in numerous social science theories in the early nineteenth century.[32] Dating back to Bacon, experiments have played a pivotal role in advancing scientific knowledge and served as a recognized method for acquiring and validating insights in the natural sciences.[33] In the eighteenth century, "experiment" and "observation" became focal points in broader intellectual discourse catalyzed by the prize question posed by the Dutch Société des Sciences in Haarlem in 1769: "En quoi consiste l'art d'observer?" ("What does the art of

---

28 Volny Fages, "Ordonner le monde, changer la société. Les systèmes cosmologiques des socialistes du premier XIXe siècle," *Romantisme* 159, no. 1 (2013): 123–134, accessed February 15, 2024, https://www.cairn.info/revue-romantisme-2013-1-page-123.htm.
29 Fourier, *Theory of the Four Movements*, 38.
30 Bruno Latour, *Reassembling the Social: An Introduction to Actor-Network-Theory* (Oxford and New York: Oxford University Press, 2005), 9.
31 Bruno Latour and Vincent A. Lépinay, *The Science of Passionate Interests: An Introduction to Gabriel Tarde's Economic Anthropology* (Chicago: Prickly Paradigm Press, 2009), 84.
32 Anne Kwaschik, "Zwischen Wissenschaft und Utopie. Zur Plausibilisierung von Gesellschaftswissen im frühen 19. Jahrhundert," in *Vorläufige Gewissheiten. Plausibilität als soziokulturelle Praxis*, eds. Thomas Kirsch and Christina Wald (Bielefeld: Transcript Publishing, 2024), 97–114; Brown, "Artificial Experiments."
33 A relevant aspect in this context is the research field on the history and epistemology of experimentation established by Rheinberger and his research group at the Max Planck Institute for the History of Science. See, for instance, Hans Jörg Rheinberger, "History of Science and the Practices of Experiment," *History and Philosophy of the Life Sciences* 23, no. 1 (2001): 51–63.

observation consist of?").[34] Fourier's challenge to conventional knowledge paradigms—applying Cartesian doubt to societal structures—aimed to gain credibility for his theories through established scientific methodologies. He leveraged the epistemic authority of the natural sciences by invoking "observation" and "experiment" to legitimize and validate the social knowledge he proposed, akin to other social thinkers in their respective thinking. Unlike other social theorists such as John Stuart Mill (1806–1873) or Comte, who remained at the theoretical level, Fourier and his followers pursued actual experiments with social relations, thereby reconfiguring them into new arrangements. By conceptualizing the "social movement" as a research subject grounded in Newtonian principles, Fourierists placed social practice at the forefront of reflection.

Transformation and Reflection: Fourierist Implementations

Beginning in the early 1830s, the Fourierist movement focused on conceptualizing and establishing a model associative community. Victor Considérant (1808–1893), an engineer and army captain, played a pivotal role in propagating and reinterpreting Fourier's ideas, particularly after his affiliation with the École Polytechnique at Paris in 1826. Over the years, he increasingly adopted the "self-appointed role as a guardian of Fourierist orthodoxy."[35] The Saint-Simonians assimilating Fourier's social theory in the aftermath of the July Revolution facilitated the formation of a Fourierist "school." Considérant strategically presented the experimental *phalange* as a practical, achievable, and scientifically grounded objective, thereby broadening the movement's appeal. This led to increased engagement in the form of organizing conferences, creating groups in numerous cities, and extending the movement's influence on an international scale.[36]

Fourierist activists engaged in practical tests of the associative model by establishing small, self-governed communities. These communities resided in specifically designated experimental spaces, deliberately and to a significant degree insulated from external influences (with arrangements for guests typically at the

---

[34] Lorraine Daston and Elizabeth Lundbeck, eds., *Histories of Scientific Observation* (Chicago and London: University of Chicago Press, 2011). All translations from French are mine unless otherwise stated.
[35] Jonathan Beecher, *Victor Considérant and the Rise and Fall of French Romantic Socialism* (Berkeley: University of California Press, 2001), 124.
[36] Pilbeam, *French Socialists*; Desmars, *Militants de l'utopie*.

periphery or in specifically designated accommodations).[37] While the overarching ambition of constructing a phalanstery provided a unifying and defining purpose for the movement, the challenges encountered during early implementations precipitated divergent views on the path forward. The initial trials, notably at Condé-sur-Vesgre (1832–1833) and Scăeni (1835–1836), located in the Wallachia region of the Habsburg Empire, which is now part of Romania, served as both prototypes and subjects of analytical study.[38]

The brief existence of Condé-sur-Vesgre significantly influenced the subsequent implementation process and led to a recalibration and resizing of later trials. The group's following venture, the Colonie sociétaire de Citeaux (1841–1844), notably did not adopt the term *phalange*. In this phase, Scottish writer Arthur Young (1810–1897) and Belgian feminist Zoé Gatti de Gamond (1806–1854) emerged as key figures.[39] However, their initiatives met with resistance from Considérant, who, as the head of the Ecole sociétaire, was committed to preserving the purity of Fourierist doctrine. Considérant believed that the premature and potentially unsuccessful realization of these social ideas could damage their reputation. Therefore, following Condé-sur-Vesgre, he argued for first securing widespread public support for Fourierist principles prior to their practical application, as he was concerned that hasty and incomplete implementations might compromise the credibility of this social theory.

This divergence regarding the timing of realizing projects spawned a significant conflict. Networks around the Polish revolutionary Jean Czynski and Gatti di Gamond opposed the orthodox stance and argued for the immediate establishment of colonies as a step toward globally spreading and evaluating Fourier's social science. They believed in initiating phalanxes, albeit incomplete, to demonstrate the viability of the concept, thereby effectively validating the theory through its practical application. Their perspectives were propagated through various publications and guidebooks, with their journals bearing significant names such as *Le premier phalanstère* (The First Phalanstery, 1841) and *Le nouveau monde* (The New World, 1839–1844).

As a result, there was a comprehensive reevaluation of the implementation strategy. The scope of the "essais" was reconsidered, focusing on "essais partiels" (partial trials). During the 1840s, the merits and drawbacks of these partial trials, in

---

[37] Charles Fourier, *Théorie de l'unité universelle*, vol. 2 (Dijon: Les Presses du réel, 2001 [1822]), 346–351.

[38] Beecher, *Considérant*, 118–121; Dan Berindei, "Le Phalanstère de Scaieni en Valachie," *Cahier Charles Fourier* 2 (1991): 69–80.

[39] Thomas Voet, *La Colonie phalanstérienne de Cîteaux, 1841–1846: Les Fouriéristes aux champs* (Dijon: Editions de l'Université de Dijon, 2001).

terms of their role in paving the way for the ultimate realization, were vigorously debated in the Fourierist journal *La démocratie pacifique* (Peaceful Democracy, 1843–1851) under Considérant's editorship. The key concept revolved around conducting a partial experiment of the theory—initially applying it to a specific location—and making the subsequent phase of the implementation contingent on the outcomes of this partial trial: "If the theory were condemned by practice, we would move on to other trials."[40]

The political developments in France in 1848 raised expectations that Fourierism could become a cornerstone of the republic. Considérant, elected to the Constituent Assembly after 1848, leveraged his role as the head of the Ecole sociétaire to endorse the experimental approach as a political strategy. In his parliamentary speech in 1849, he asserted the necessity of numerous partial experiments and continuous modifications to achieve the establishment of a single *phalange*. Employing a common and mechanistic imagery of progress, he aimed to clarify the "novel social mechanism":

> The creation of the first locomotive, in terms of the relationship between its components and the railway, was first an invention and then a series of studies, trials, and experiments. Once this had been achieved, the railroad enterprise was a simple business [affaire]. The organization of a first phalanx is necessarily itself a relatively costly and difficult experiment. Those that follow, as soon as we can study a model that works in the right proportions, will be nothing but business (affaires). [...] It is a great experiment, the experiment of a novel social mechanism.[41]

This quotation exemplifies the experimental discourse inherent in Fourierism, where Fourier's conception of a novel social mechanism undergoes a series of evaluations, adaptations, and adjustments in response to local conditions, thereby prompting further reflection on the mechanism itself. This iterative process, symbolically initiated by the inaugural *phalange* or "first locomotive," is driven by its momentum and was envisioned to cultivate a modern, global infrastructure. The railway metaphor underscores the significance of small social units as an innovative infrastructure for progress. However, this trajectory was disrupted by the political upheavals of the time, leading Considérant to leave France in 1849.

This turn of events led him to favor what he termed "new societies" as ideal settings for social experimentation. In his writings, Considérant emphasized the central role of the environment, construed broadly to encompass climatic condi-

---

40 *La démocratie pacifique*, August 1, 1844 ("si la théorie était condamnée par la pratique, on passerait à d'autres essais").
41 "Discours de Victor Considérant à l'Assemblée constituante," *La démocratie pacifique*, April 4, 1849.

tions, vegetation, natural resources, and local attitudes toward social innovation, along with the inherent traits of the population. Notably, he singled out the US-American context as particularly conducive to social experiments, justifying the establishment of a new colony there despite his prior reluctance in terms of further experimental initiatives.[42] Following an enlightening visit to the North American Phalanx (NAP) outside Freehold, New Jersey (1843–1855), which he deemed a "zoophyte sociétaire"[43] rather than a "realization," he established the short-lived colony of La Réunion (1855–1857) near Dallas, Texas.

La Réunion was part of a foundational wave that peaked in the 1840s and 1850s with settlements predominantly established in the Americas. Experimental communities tended to be smaller and more limited in scope. By the mid-1840s, the discourse had evolved from questioning the feasibility of experiments to exploring the conditions and lessons learned from case studies. Activists engaged in discussions on implementing an alternative world while considering global scales. In essence, the Fourierists' experimental discourse revolved around the value of practice over theory, thus highlighting a shift in focus from theoretical considerations to the practical implementation of their social ideas.

In accordance with the utopian tradition, the experimental space was delimited, defined, and organized. The "trial cantons" were arranged based on sociopetal architecture, which is meant to foster human interactions, ranging from brief and chance encounters at intersections to emotional engagements in the peristyles of the social palace's arcades. It is notable that only a few settlements actually constructed the central social palace, the *phalanstère*. It was only in 1853, with the secession of the Raritan Bay Union from the NAP, that a more substantial four-story *phalanstère* was actually built.[44] In most instances, the community functions of the edifice were fulfilled by modest structures, such as the Hive community house at Brook Farm in West Roxbury, Massachusetts (1841–1847)—a two-story farmhouse that served as the organizational hub of community life. According to personal accounts, members would gather at their "hive" coming from all directions for meals or evening dances, following the rhythm of the day.[45]

---

[42] Victor Considérant, *Au Texas* (Paris: Librairie Phalanstérienne, 1854). For the English version, see Victor Considérant, *The Great West: A New Social and Industrial Life in Its Fertile Regions* (New York, 1854). The text is abridged and modified for public relations purposes in the United States.

[43] Considérant, *Au Texas*, 12.

[44] Carl J. Guarneri, *The Utopian Alternative: Fourierism in Nineteenth-Century America* (Ithaca: Cornell University Press, 1991), 322–326.

[45] John T. Codman, *Brook Farm: Historic and Personal Memoirs* (Boston: Arena Publishing Company, 1894), e.g. 61, 92, 97. The transcendentalist community Brook Farm (1841–1847) adopted Fourierist ideas starting in 1844. Brook Farm is one of the best-known communities due to the

The case of the United States illustrates that constructing the edifice was contingent upon local regulations, adaptation, and communal negotiations. Plans for expanding existing structures were devised, and transitional modes were implemented; for instance, the NAP enhanced its 1851 phalanstery with a covered piazza, verandas, and galleries, where interconnected buildings were accessible through covered passageways. However, community members specifically argued against opting for a lavish architectural style. Nationally, the decision to forgo a *phalanstère* was rationalized as an US-American manifestation of communal practice, showcasing a juxtaposition between scientific Fourierism and pragmatic Fourierism at the grassroots level. This decision was not perceived as a critique of social reorganization but rather as its partial realization and a transitional form labeled as "practical partial reform."[46]

Communal life in Fourierist communities adhered to serial laws, where Fourier aimed to determine the optimal number and combination of individuals based on intricate calculations of series of attractions and passions, predominantly outlined in *Le nouveau monde industriel et sociétaire* (The New Industrial and Societary World).[47] These series governed the composition of various collective working groups and the daily rotation of group members between different activities. This approach was partially applied in communities such as the NAP, which established six series, covering aspects from agriculture to recreation (agricultural, stock, manufacturing, domestic, educational, and festal series).[48]

Beyond organizing experimental community life, serial laws were also envisioned as a means to generate the new social science. This programmatic perspective is explicitly articulated in the inaugural editorial of Considérant's theoretical journal *La Phalange. Journal de la science sociale* (The Phalanx. Journal of Social Science):

> The SERIES is the graded, regular, and natural mode of classification of all the inequalities which constitute a system of varieties; it combines *variety* in *unity*. The SERIES is the mode of combinations and *harmonic* relations. TO ORGANIZE, TO PUT IN ORDER, is to form SERIES. Outside the SERIES there is no order.[49]

---

fact that Nathaniel Hawthorne, one of its founding members, fictionalized his experience in his novel *The Blithedale Romance* (Boston: Ticknor and Fields, 1852).

46 Guarneri, *Utopian Alternative*, 242.

47 He calculated the number of 1,620 members, which, however, was never considered in the implementations. Fourier, *Le nouveau monde industriel*, 85–133.

48 Charles Sears, *The North American Phalanx: An Historical and Descriptive Sketch* (Prescott: John M. Pryse, Publisher, 1886), 5–6. Considérant did not consider the principle implemented when he visited the NAP before establishing his own colony in Texas, Considérant, *Au Texas*, 12.

49 *La Phalange* 1 (1836): 1 (emphasis in original). See John Tresch, "The Order of the Prophets: Series in Early French Social Science and Socialism," *History of Science* 48 (2010): 315–342.

While Fourierists viewed serial laws as a dynamic foundation for community experiments based on social science,[50] contemporary skeptics and later critics found nothing but a flawed implementation of Fourier's concepts. They often mocked the organization of labor[51] and cited the short-lived nature and limited spread of these experiments as proof of the practical failure of this theoretical framework. However, these implementations were integral to an experimental series for social change, as outlined in the communities' writings. Fourier himself regarded the initial communal groups as preliminary "drafts, sketches," acknowledging that "the distributive theory will need to be informed by local practice" in such novel foundations.[52] He envisioned the first communities as "compasses" guiding future societal transformation through an extensive, long-term process.

Although the evolution of these settlements after the 1850s did not align with the initial plans, the experimental series arguably persisted beyond La Réunion. Subsequent undertakings, regardless of their distinct presentations, continued to enrich the collective experience. A notable example is Jean-Baptiste André Godin (1817–1888), a French industrialist involved in the La Réunion attempt and manager of the Société de colonisation européo-américaine du Texas. Starting in 1859, Godin initiated a new associative form with the Familistère de Guise in Picardie, Northern France.[53] This community housed industrial workers in family units within a Fourier-inspired, profit-sharing work environment. Despite Godin's increasing tendency, common among many, to distance his project from Fourier,[54] the Familistère's central pavilion, featuring a vast glass courtyard completed in 1865, unmistakably drew inspiration from Fourier's experiments.

---

50 See, for instance, the NAP experience. Community members described the effects of the serial work organization as the beginning of the new society, Sears, *NAP*.
51 Wilhelm Roscher, "Betrachtungen über den Sozialismus und Kommunismus," *Zeitschrift für Geschichtswissenschaft* 3 (1845): 418–461, 540–564, 456–457.
52 Fourier, *Théorie de l'unité universelle*, vol. 2, 337.
53 He had also enquired about the serial organization of the NAP, where the members could assign themselves freely. Charles Sears to Jean Baptiste Godin April 22, 1853. Bibliothèque centrale du Conservatoire national des Arts et Métiers, Papiers de Jean-Baptiste André Godin FG 17/2.
54 Jean Baptiste Godin to Joseph Pouliquen (Condé-sur-Vesgre), December 7, 1865: "Le Familistère ne réalise ni l'harmonie des passions, ni l'association des forces et des facultés humaines, ni l'éducation rationnelle, ni le travail attrayant. Ce n'est donc pas la découverte de Fourier que j'ai mise en pratique, aussi n'ai-je pas voulu que l'on s'y méprenne. Le Familistère n'est pas le Phalanstère." Bibliothèque centrale du Conservatoire national des Arts et Métiers, Papiers de Jean-Baptiste André Godin FG 15/8.

Algeria as Experimental Space

When Fourierists concurred regarding the imperative of initiating the new social program, they envisioned their experimental space as unoccupied, untouched land, presupposing that the "specimen of the new world" would be established "upon these soils, today a wilderness."[55] However, this "wilderness" pertained to a foreign culture and constituted part of a distinct spatial configuration and imagination.[56] In most instances, the land was inhabited by indigenous populations, and the Fourierist implementation program in reality hinged on acquiring land and organizing the social unit as a "contact zone" structured by the colonial situation. These issues were pivotal given the global dissemination of these experiments, and they coalesced into a more cohesive discourse when the Fourierists identified Algeria as an experimental space.

Since the landing of the Armée d'Afrique in the coastal town of Sidi-Fredj in 1830, Fourierist circles campaigned to establish communities in Algeria in accordance with Fourier's social theory. In 1838, Gatti de Gamond was among the first to outline Fourier's theories as the basis for a systematic colonization of Algeria, proposing an extension of this plan to encompass the entirety of Africa. Following the modular and mechanical logic of social change, the "nucleus of the new society" was manifested as a cooperative farm of 300–400 families: "Starting from the foundation of a first societal farm in this region, the imagination sees no limits to the conquest and propaganda. The whole of Africa covered with phalanxes subject to a unitary regime."[57] She was supported by Czynski, who dedicated himself to popularizing a "natural association" and advocated for "scientific exploration" in *Le nouveau monde*. He integrated this concept into a phased model for the colonization of Algeria, proposing that capitalists should only proceed with implementation once scientists had thoroughly explored the country and developed a plan.[58] Fourier's concept was construed as a tangible and conducive guide for colonizing Algeria. Consequently, questions of "native politics" and colonialism were

---

55 Considérant, *The Great West*, 58.
56 Norbert Finzsch, "The Smooth Space of the Nomads: Indigenous Outopia, Indigenous Heterotopia and the Example of Australia," in *Ecocritical Concerns and the Australian Continent*, eds. Beate Neumeier and Helen Tiffin (Lanham, Boulder, New York and London: Lexington Books, 2020), 27–41.
57 Zoé Gatti de Gamond, *Fourier et son système* (Paris: Librairie sociale, 1838), 322.
58 He published the articles collected in a book: Jean Czynski, *La Colonisation d'Alger d'après la théorie de Charles Fourier* (Paris: Librairie sociale, 1839). See Piotr Kuligowski, "Un fouriériste dans la vie politique polonaise: polémiques de Jan Czyński (1801–1867)," *Cahiers Charles Fourier* 30 (2019): 125–142.

intricately linked to the experimental discourse, an aspect often underestimated in research due to its focus on Saint-Simonian Orientalism.[59]

In the context of community implementation,[60] the Union agricole d'Afrique, situated southeast of Oran in Saint-Denis-du-Sig, emerged as an exemplar of a "natural association." Granted the status of a "civil colonization company" by a royal order in November 1846, it spanned an expanse of approximately 2,000–2,500 hectares in the Oran region, adjacent to the Sig River and near a dam. The original blueprint aimed to accommodate roughly 300 families, totaling some 1,500 individuals. However, only five families had settled by February 1847. The Union saw a gradual influx of 150–200 people between 1849 and 1851, and despite challenges such as diseases and fatalities, it slowly stabilized. The early settlers more resembled a metropolitan missionary elite than a fraternal collective, with backgrounds primarily found in bourgeois and military circles: twelve were professionals such as doctors, surgeons, lawyers, or merchants, sixteen were army officers from Lyon and Besançon, Fourier's birthplace, and only one hailed from Paris.[61] Internal strife persisted, leading to the 1847 establishment of a supervisory committee by the general assembly of shareholders, which comprised officers, civil servants, and notables from Oran. After five years, the community nearly dissolved but underwent several revivals until Fourierist influences were completely erased from its statutes in the early 1890s.[62]

Despite later transformations, the agricultural union in its formative years prided itself on presenting an alternative model of colonization rooted in the associative approach. This model aimed to foster a synergy of interests between capitalists and workers as an antidote to the social "fragmentation" ("morcellement")—a central Fourierist concept symbolizing the *malaise* of modern capitalist society.[63] This fragmentation referred to various tangible aspects, such as private property, or more abstract notions of social isolation and individualism. A cornerstone principle of the Union was the indivisibility of ownership, organized through shares, with land, buildings, and equipment collectively belonging to the shareholders. This approach was in stark contrast to the prevalent colonial model based on the

---

59 For example, Osama Abi-Mershed, *Apostles of Modernity: Saint-Simonians and the Civilizing Mission in Algeria* (Stanford: Stanford University Press, 2010); Magali Morsy, *Les Saint-Simoniens et l'Orient: Vers la modernité* (Aix-en-Provence: Édisud, 1990).
60 Almi mentions a previous attempt to establish a *phalanstère* in Sidi Ferruch by Adrien Berbrugger in 1833, Said Almi, *Urbanisme et colonisation. Présence française en Algérie* (Liège: Mardaga, 2002), 41.
61 Bernard Desmars, "Liste des actionnaires de l'Union Agricole d'Afrique (1847)," *Cahiers Charles Fourier*, accessed February 15, 2024, https://www.charlesfourier.fr/spip.php?article1312.
62 Ibid., 146.
63 Beecher, *Considérant*, 127.

individual ownership of land parcels and houses, a common practice in other parts of Algeria.[64]

From the perspective of the activists, the associative model was deemed crucial for what they believed to be optimal colonial practice, particularly in terms of fostering connections between "diverse elements."[65] These connections were envisioned to be forged through shared interests and habitual interactions, rather than through force and suppression.[66] As indicated in the administrative reports, "Human ambition could not conceive of a more splendid stage or drama than to organize, in accordance with unified plans, both production and population across an expanse of two square leagues."[67] This vision included the creation of an intercultural social palace, which blended Moorish and "civilized" architectural styles, thus diverging from the ideal type proposed by Considérant.[68]

The Fourierists' approach to civil colonization differed greatly from other colonial methods, particularly in its vehement opposition to military strategies. They contended that in a civil colony, where individuals are free, excessive pressure would lead to resistance and withdrawal. Hence, it was essential for them to govern and motivate without exerting too much pressure ("squeezing too much").[69] They further asserted that military action was antithetical to the associative model, arguing that "while repression of the natives might be a regrettable necessity in fragmented cultures, the grand associated culture, which harmonizes the most diverse elements, does not have these harsh imperatives."[70]

In line with this philosophy, the French settlers chose not to displace the indigenous population. Instead, they transformed their supposed right of conquest into a "favorable rental contract."[71] Consequently, the indigenous population remained on their ancestral lands while maintaining their agricultural practices; however, they were obliged to pay for the right to stay on this land. They established their tents, forming two douars of the Gharabas and "about a dozen douars of the Thallaïtes," and were granted access to all facilities in an effort to demon-

---

64 Union agricole d'Afrique, société civile de colonisation. Compte rendu par le Conseil d'administration et le rapport de l'administration de la colonie pour l'exercice de 1847–1848 (Besançon: Imprimerie de Sainte-Agatha Ainé, 1849), 49.
65 This is a dominant conceptual figure, see the following argument in this section. For a direct quote, see, for example, ibid., 21.
66 Ibid., 20.
67 Ibid., 58.
68 Ibid., 49.
69 Ibid., 42.
70 Ibid., 21.
71 Ibid., 20.

strate the benefits of French governance.⁷² This strategy of "integration by rent" proved successful, as evidenced by the annual renewal of contracts by the Arab leaders.

It is imperative to acknowledge that the Union's daily operations were marked by hierarchical structures and an assumed superiority of French culture. The envisioned fraternal society fell short of achieving a state of equality among its members. Notably, the Arab populations were not fully integrated. The settler community only constituted a minority, whereas the majority consisted of salaried workers, some residing in the nearby town of Saint-Denis. Segregation was evident in communal life and manifested in practices such as separate dining arrangements.⁷³

Moreover, the settlers' actions demonstrate a clear orientation toward colonial concepts of civilization. Although they acknowledged and valued indigenous traditions, similar to the Saint-Simonian circles, they endorsed particular civilizational ideals. These included advocating for nomadic populations transitioning to sedentary lifestyles and for advancing integrated educational initiatives for Arab and French children within the Union's institutions.⁷⁴ Furthermore, they supported more unconventional ideas, such as "a more significant improvement" of women's "destiny" in Algeria.⁷⁵ This position aligned with Fourierists advocating for the emancipation of women in Europe.

Just like in the European and transatlantic contexts, the associative model in Algeria was not fully realized. A significant example illustrating the limitations in community building is the failure to implement the practice of collective property, despite the nomadic traditions in the region. Barthélemy-Prosper Enfantin, known as "Father Enfantin" (1796–1854), the leader of the dissolved Saint-Simonian circles, in his seminal work on Algerian colonization elucidated how the absence of private property in nomadic cultures favored a communal approach to colonization.⁷⁶ He drew on the arguments of Amédée Marion (1800–1868), who since the early 1840s had been devising plans for the Bône region in western Algeria.⁷⁷ Discussions en-

---

72 Union 1849, 41. The colony followed the governor's colonization project for the province of Oran. Lieutenant General Lamoricière, himself a former Saint-Simonian and acting governor in 1845 (when Marshal Bugeaud requested a leave of absence), specifically asked for colonies not to "entail the displacement of a considerable portion of the Gharrabas tribe," Projets de colonisation pour les provinces d'Oran et de Constantine (Paris: Imprimérie royale 1847), 10, 12.
73 Ibid., 45.
74 Ibid., 42.
75 Ibid., 15.
76 Madonna-Desbazeille, "L'Union agricole d'Afrique."
77 Adrien Berbrugger, "M. Marion," *Revue africaine. Journal des travaux de la Société historique algérienne* 12 (1868): 139–143.

sued concerning the parallels between Algeria's tradition of collective property and the *système sociétaire*, especially during the establishment of the farming group in Sig.[78] However, these ideas failed to materialize in both the Oran and the Bône regions. Nonetheless, the subscription of some Arab dignitaries as shareholders was seen as an initial step toward achieving the agricultural union's envisioned "mixed Franco-African character":

> The very inclusion of Arab chiefs within the Union will endow it with a blended Franco-African character. Given that the Union's association will not be exclusively capitalist, it is hoped that the colony will eventually showcase a number of Arab workers integrated with European families. Such an alliance example, and the Union's success, could be critically influential in terms of colonization and the African question.[79]

The community project evidently did not meet the criteria of a *phalange*, which prompted reflections and discussions regarding the practical implications of the associative principle. During a commemorative banquet in Algiers in April 1848, 72 colonists and Fourierists gathered to reaffirm and assess the status of the communal initiative in Algeria. The majority recognized the disheartening results; however, there was no fundamental questioning of either the specific project or the broader social experiment. The challenges were ascribed to local conditions, thus necessitating adaptations and pragmatic, partial solutions:

> We have adopted aspects from Phalansterian theories that seemed suitable for the specific context [. . .] What we have accomplished possesses a lesser degree of perfection; however, these very imperfections might appeal to those numerous individuals who seek a guiding principle rather than a rigid system in associative ventures, as well as to those who are apprehensive that their ideal may not be realized in the near future.[80]

Examining the reflections of Fourierists in Algiers on the community's character as a half-realized phalanx reveals the significance of the process in which these experiments were embedded. This perspective suggests that experiments cannot inherently "fail." Recent research has shifted the focus away from viewing the dissolution of a community as a historical failure toward exploring different legacies.[81] In the experimental discourse, self-reflexivity was vital for revising theoreti-

---

[78] *L'Union agricole d'Afrique. Nouveau système de colonisation de l'Algérie* (Lyon: Imprimerie de Léon Boitel, 1846).
[79] Ibid., 126.
[80] *Phalanstère en Algérie* (Algiers: A. Bourget, 1848), 40.
[81] Michel Antony, "Les communautés utopiques sont-elles toujours condamnées à disparaître?" *Cahiers d'histoire. Revue d'histoire critique* 133 (2016): 19–42; Michel Cordillot, "Rethinking the failure of the French Fourierist colony in Dallas," *Praktyka Teoretyczna* 3, no. 29 (2018): 118–133.

cal reasoning through exposure to various practical settings and external conditions. Establishing a small core community under unfavorable conditions affirmed the viability and validity of the social reform program for activists. It also allowed for future changes and extensions, as seen in the enduring Sig community. The ongoing crises and revivals until the 1890s fueled and sustained the experimental discourse.

During one of the last crises, Considérant joined the board of directors of Sig in 1873. Opposing the impending sale of Sig in 1879, he emphasized the unique comprehensive character of the community compared to the locally and thematically limited endeavors of the Familistère in Guise and Leclaire's profit-sharing house painting company in Paris.[82] While these two were the most developed social experiments, he explained, they had reached the limits of their development due to their overly narrow base, which, at the same time, was the reason for their success and exemplary character. Bound to one specialty—producing enameled cast iron and painting buildings, respectively—they now experienced an end to their development ("arrêt de développement"), and they no longer had the potential to represent a cell ("alvéole") of the new society. Even if these attempts seemed more advanced, Considérant concluded, only Sig would have the potential to further develop the system into a full community by adding other elements.[83]

Considérant developed this idea in the face of a political situation having undergone considerable changes compared to the 1840s. In the 1870s, his suggestion to extend the experiment in Sig included a critique of other established forms of social reform and socialism from which Considérant explicitly distanced his program. As a non-revolutionary and peaceful response to the social question, he was convinced that the associative model was more likely to be implemented in the coming decades, whereas the brutal and revolutionary forms of socialism would only lead to a violent apocalypse of capitalism.[84]

---

[82] The house painting enterprise Maison Leclaire was founded in Paris in 1826 as a profit-sharing business. On the positive reception of Leclaire, see Helen McCabe, "John Stuart Mill and Fourierism: 'Association', 'friendly rivalry' and distributive justice," *Global Intellectual History* 4, no. 1 (2019): 35–61.

[83] Lettre de M. Considérant à M. le commandant Gautier, secrétaire de l'Union du Sig, *Bulletin de l'Union agricole de l'Afrique* (1879): 93–124; 110, 111.

[84] Ibid, 111.

Conclusion

This article posits Fourierism as a socio-epistemic program integrating theory and practice. It utilizes the concept of the laboratory to explore the *phalanstère* as a space in which social organizational forms undergo reconfiguration, thus challenging divisions between the history of science and the history of politics. The distinction between theory and practice dissolves in the "social laboratories" of Fourier, which blur the scientific and non-scientific boundaries. This reconfiguration is central, especially in the context of the early nineteenth century, a time when the social sciences were not yet formally established and social reform was intertwined with developing social epistemology. It allows for sidestepping inquiries into the "scientificity" of early nineteenth-century social thought.

The historical significance of Fourierism transcends its theoretical contributions. It played an active role in shaping a realm of social knowledge existing beyond the bounds of academic legitimacy while interconnecting its various facets. This understanding of society facilitated analyzing contemporary societal conditions and formulating future trajectories. Aligned with concepts such as "horizons of expectation" and "spaces of experience,"[85] this knowledge served as a mediator between lived experiences and future aspirations, thereby elucidating, interpreting, and actively impacting transformative processes.

Its significance becomes apparent when examining its practical implementations, particularly in the colonial context of Algeria. The Union agricole du Sig serves as a key example of Fourierist principles meeting the complexities of indigenous cultures and populations. The Algerian experience, with its blend of idealism and practical challenges, showcases the dynamic interaction between Fourierist ideals and the realities of colonial administration. Despite hierarchical structures and cultural disparities, the experiment in Algeria reflected Fourier's commitment to a cooperative, non-military approach while envisioning a mixed Franco-African character. The enduring lessons from this colonial experiment contributed to a nuanced understanding of Fourierism's viability and adaptability, thereby showcasing its relevance as a non-revolutionary response to the evolving social question in the 1870s.

By drawing parallels with Latour's concept of the laboratory, it emphasizes the transformative potential of small-scale experiments in relation to reconfiguring societal patterns. The relatively closed structure of Fourier's sites can be lik-

---

[85] Reinhart Koselleck, "Space of Experience and Horizon of Expectation: Two Historical Categories," in Reinhart Koselleck, *Futures Past: On the Semantics of Historical Time*, trans. Keith Tribe (Cambridge: MIT Press, 1985).

ened to Latour's description of the strength of laboratory sites in Pasteur's universal vaccination project. Latour argues that the essence of the laboratory is not found in its scale but in testing possible modes of operation and the "modifying of scale."[86] Ultimately, this involves the dissemination of new patterns in society. Similarly, Fourier utilized elements from the social reality of industrial capitalism to forge a new social framework, emphasizing social cohesion in associations by unifying passions and affects. Fourier aimed to "invent" a model of social life applicable on a broader scale with the *phalanstère* serving as a cooperative form of life.

To summarize, Fourier's experimental practice in his associative model was key to its legacy. His vision of social units, as part of a social science, anticipated a new form of society and shared an interest in theorizing the transition toward societal transformation. This approach contrasted with Marxism's state-centered concept and offered a unique perspective on social change. Fourier's model, which was focused on harmonizing individual passions and affections within cooperative associations, sought to "invent" a new social framework applicable on a broader scale. This legacy significantly influenced the cooperative movement at the end of the nineteenth century, as recognized by cooperative activists and Marxist critics alike.[87] Fourierism thus emerges not as one of the undeveloped precursors to socialism but as an independent social epistemology combining social theory with small-scale practical experiments. In this context, Fourier's "expériences sociétaires"[88] targeted societal reform on a grand scale, thus positioning his work as a serious alternative in the realm of social organization and theory.

Anne Kwaschik is a professor of contemporary history with a special focus on the history of knowledge at Konstanz University. Her research focuses on knowledge cultures and scientization processes such as the scientization of colonialism, the epistemology of health feminism, and the history of social experiments. Recent publications include "Reconstructing Colonial Sociology," *Social Science History* 48, no. 1 (2024), DOI: https://doi.org/10.1017/ssh.2023.23; "'We Witches': Knowledge Wars, Experience and Spirituality in the Women's Movement in the 1970s," *NTM* 31 (2023), DOI: https://doi.org/10.1007/s00048-023-00359-w

---

86 Latour, "Give Me a Laboratory," 67.
87 Pierre Dardot and Christian Laval, *Common: On Revolution in the 21st Century* (London and New York: Bloomsbury, 2019), 250; Charles Gide, *Fourier, précurseur de la coopération* (Paris: Association pour l'enseignement de la Coopération, 1924), 13–20; Minsun Ji, "With or Without Class? Resolving Marx's Janus-Faced Interpretation of Worker owned Cooperatives," *Capital and Class* 13 (2019): 1–25.
88 Lettre de M. Considérant, 111.

Alina Marktanner
Experimenting for Empire: Plant Health as an Agricultural Problem in German East Africa, Togo and Cameroon, 1905–1914

Abstract: Plant health was a primary concern for German colonial agriculturalists around 1900. On the one hand, plant health and diseases determined the profitability of cash crops and the plantation economy. On the other hand, colonists associated plant diseases with a lack of "hygiene" and allegedly inferior agricultural practices. The article demonstrates the transdisciplinary, applied and experimental nature of phytopathological knowledge production in tropical agriculture. Plant pathologists blended multiple forms of disciplinary and layman knowledge to tinker with plants in the field and assess possible causes for and remedies against plant diseases. However, they also tried to apply experimental methods to control and discipline the indigenous populations. This article scrutinizes agricultural research stations and plantations as sites for phytopathological studies, scientists of various disciplinary backgrounds as their primary drivers and field trials as their primary method. Based on the travel reports and articles of Walter Busse and Julius Vosseler, two phytopathologists working in German Cameroon, German Togoland and German East Africa, the article shows that scientists collaborated with planters in terms of fending off plant diseases while also aiming to impart European agricultural techniques to indigenous farmers. Agricultural knowledge production did not only feed into plantation practices but also became a playfield for the ambivalent "cultural mission."

Keywords: agricultural research stations, plantation, colonialism, field sciences, applied science

Introduction

High imperialism went hand in glove with scientific knowledge production.[1] A characteristic of this period, starting in the mid-nineteenth century, was the "scien-

---

[1] In revising this article, I benefited from the lively discussions held at the Bodensee-Retreat "Wissensgeschichte" organized by Anne Kwaschik in Konstanz in June 2023. I thank the section editors and the reviewers for insightful comments and suggestions.

tization of colonialism."² Numerous research institutes and education tracks in the various imperializing European nation-states and international scientific conferences were aimed at understanding and controlling the colonial project. However, the role of medical discourses with regard to plant diseases has rarely been examined.³ This article studies colonial discourses on phytopathology and forms of phytopathological expertise in the German colonies in Africa in the early twentieth century. Phytopathology, the study of plant diseases, their origins, their prevention and their cures, serves as an emblematic example of a scientific endeavor connecting different areas of knowledge in various functional domains during the colonial era. In the colonial context, research on plant health and diseases blended approaches from botany, zoology, mycology, entomology, meteorology and agricultural sciences. Furthermore, phytopathological research was not limited to academic knowledge; it also relied heavily on practical insights gained in tropical agriculture. In turn, it offered research findings that could be applied to benefit colonial policy and the colonial economy.

This article follows scientists and laypeople who, in the German colonies around 1900, produced knowledge concerning plant health. The main argument is that phytopathological research in tropical agriculture was a transdisciplinary and applied form of knowledge production pursued by scientists in agricultural

---

2 On the nexus between science and empire, see Alves Duarte da Silva, Matheus, Thomas A. S. Haddad and Kapil Raj, "Science and Empire: Past and Present Questions," in *Beyond Science and Empire: Circulation of Knowledge in an Age of Global Empires, 1750–1945*, eds. Alves Duarte da Silva, Matheus, Thomas A. S. Haddad and Kapil Raj (London and New York: Routledge, 2024); Andrew Goss, ed., *The Routledge Handbook of Science and Empire* (London: Routledge Taylor & Francis Group, 2021); Anne Kwaschik, "Die Verwissenschaftlichung des Kolonialen als kultureller Code und internationale Praxis um 1900," *Historische Anthropologie* 28, no. 3 (2020); Daniel R. Headrick, *The Tools of Empire: Technology and European Imperialism in the Nineteenth Century* (New York: Oxford University Press, 1981). Out of many elucidating case studies, see Jens Ruppenthal, *Kolonialismus als "Wissenschaft und Technik": Das Hamburgische Kolonialinstitut 1908 bis 1919* (Stuttgart: Steiner, 2007); Carsten Gräbel, *Die Erforschung der Kolonien: Expeditionen und koloniale Wissenskultur deutscher Geographen, 1884–1919* (Bielefeld: Transcript Publishing, 2015); Sebastian Beese, *Experten der Erschließung: Akteure der deutschen Kolonialtechnik in Afrika und Europa 1890–1943* (Paderborn: Brill Schöningh, 2018); Moritz von Brescius, *German Science in the Age of Empire: Enterprise, Opportunity and the Schlagintweit Brothers* (Cambridge: Cambridge University Press, 2019).
3 On German and Italian entomological research in colonial spaces, see Tomás Bartoletti, "The Transimperial Emergence of Pest Control Research: Economic Entomology Between Europe and the Tropical World, c. 1890–1930," *Comparativ* 32, no. 6 (2022). On the challenges of establishing transatlantic regulations to prevent the spread of pests around 1900, see Stéphane Castonguay, "Creating an Agricultural World Order: Regional Plant Protection Problems and International Phytopathology, 1878–1939," *Agricultural History* 84, no. 1 (2010).

research stations and planters in the field attained by an experimental approach of trial and error. Its modes of application were aimed at the colonial regime's combined economic and cultural objectives. While agricultural science always oscillated between basic and applied research, phytopathology in the colonies primarily sought to preserve and advance the plantation economy and intervene in indigenous agricultural practices to implement European norms and control the colonized population. Hence, phytopathological studies did not exclusively serve to support the German colonial plantation economy, as argued by Samuel Eleazar Wendt.[4] Rather, the application of phytopathological knowledge was used both to make the colonial plantation economy profitable *and* to introduce European concepts of tropical hygiene, thereby dismissing the long-lasting wealth of the native population's agricultural knowledge.[5] However, control over the native population's environment and human surroundings proved fragile as colonists had imperfect knowledge of local conditions while their disciplinary measures did not avert resistance.

Hitherto, studies in the German history of agriculture and the agricultural sciences seem to have neglected the colonial period. While several works examine the agricultural sphere in the German Empire, the Weimar Republic and the Third Reich, they do not broaden the geographical focus to include the colonized areas, nor do they consider the prevalent imperial mindset at the time.[6] The most comprehensive overviews of phytopathology as a field were authored by practitioners. The narratives presented usually center on heroic figures and include educational ele-

---

[4] Samuel E. Wendt, "Securing Resources for the Industries of Wilhelmine Germany: Tropical Agriculture and Phytopathology in Cameroon and Togo, 1884–1914," in *Environments of Empire*, eds. Ulrike Kirchberger and Brett M. Bennett (Chapel Hill: The University of North Carolina Press, 2020).

[5] In this regard, phytopathologists in West and East Africa shared similarities with German coffee planters in Guatemala. At the turn of the twentieth century, German plantation owners and geographers promoted the perception of Guatemalan tropical nature as untamed and "uncivilized," viewing the establishment of plantations as a means to transform it into organized and productive landscapes. Christiane Berth, "Between 'Wild Tropics' and 'Civilization': Guatemalan Coffee Plantations as Seen by German Immigrants," in *Comparing Apples, Oranges, and Cotton: Environmental Histories of the Global Plantation*, ed. Frank Uekötter (Frankfurt a. M.: Campus, 2014).

[6] Thomas Wieland, *"Wir beherrschen den pflanzlichen Organismus besser,. . .": Wissenschaftliche Pflanzenzüchtung in Deutschland, 1889–1945* (Munich: Deutsches Museum, 2004); Volker Klemm, *Agrarwissenschaften in Deutschland: Geschichte – Tradition; von den Anfängen bis 1945* (St. Katharinen: Scripta Mercaturae Verl., 1992); Ulrich Kluge, *Agrarwirtschaft und ländliche Gesellschaft im 20. Jahrhundert* (Munich: Oldenbourg Wissenschaftsverlag, 2005).

ments addressed to an audience aspiring to the practice of phytopathologists.[7] Thus, the colonial setting as a playfield and driving force for agricultural innovation both in the "metropole" and in the "peripheries" has barely been considered. At the same time, while colonial historiography has produced groundbreaking works on medicalized discourse,[8] comprehensive narratives on the study of plant diseases during high imperialism have been few and far in-between.[9] Scrutinizing historical discourses on plant diseases addresses this gap. The attempts of colonists to stabilize hierarchical regimes and the utter instability of these regimes become visible in the discourses related to identifying and taming specific plant diseases.

In terms of method, this article aims to both scrutinize colonial medical discourses and to embed them in their materiality, following recent contributions elucidating the intricate nature of "colonial knowledge."[10] The materiality of phytopathological knowledge included both the research station and the field. The hybrid mode of knowledge production – in the laboratory and in the field – may be grasped thanks to critical laboratory studies. Karin Knorr-Cetina, Bruno Latour and Steve Woolgar have shown that laboratory research methods and their societal contexts were not separate but deeply intertwined.[11] More recently, historical studies of the life sciences have joined in the task of tearing down the alleged wall between laboratory and field sciences.[12] Just like other field sciences around 1900, the study of plant health can only be understood when acknowledging the experimental mindset of its actors. Phytopathologists did not need full-fledged laboratories to conduct experiments. The method to which they ascribed epistemological validity was the field trial, which was based on trial and error and frequent repetition. This article, however, shows that the experimental mind-

---

[7] Herbert Hice Whetzel, *An Outline of the History of Phytopathology* (Philadelphia: W. B. Saunders Company, 1918); Geoffrey Clough Ainsworth, *Introduction to the History of Plant Pathology* (New York: Cambridge University Press, 1981).

[8] For instance, Megan Vaughan, *Curing Their Ills: Colonial Power and African Illness* (Stanford: Stanford University Press, 1991); Wolfang Eckart, *Medizin und Kolonialimperialismus: Deutschland 1884–1945* (Paderborn: Schöningh, 1997).

[9] A notable exception is Wendt, who adopts an economic history approach, Wendt, "Securing Resources."

[10] Ricardo Roque and Kim A. Wagner, "Introduction: Engaging Colonial Knowledge," in *Engaging Colonial Knowledge: Reading European Archives in World History*, eds. Ricardo Roque and Kim A. Wagner (London: Palgrave Macmillan, 2014).

[11] Bruno Latour and Steve Woolgar, *Laboratory Life: The Construction of Scientific Facts* (Princeton: Princeton University Press, 1979); Karin Knorr-Cetina, *The Manufacture of Knowledge: An Essay on the Constructivist and Contextual Nature of Science* (Oxford: Pergamon Press, 1981).

[12] Robert E. Kohler, *Landscapes and Labscapes: Exploring the Lab-Field Border in Biology* (Chicago: University of Chicago Press, 2010); Raf de Bont, *Stations in the Field: A History of Place-Based Animal Research, 1870–1930* (Chicago: University of Chicago Press, 2015).

set went beyond mere agricultural questions. The attempt to control one's surroundings by inducing stimuli and testing for their effects shaped both the scientific approach of phytopathologists and their attempts to interject in traditional knowledge and practices. Hence, both the laboratory and the field constituted central experimental spaces in which colonial hierarchies were performed.[13]

The sources used mostly originate from the written professional records left by the actors in focus: Walter Busse and Julius Vosseler. Busse and Vosseler produced travel reports, periodical articles and personal notes stored in the Prussian Secret State Archives, the Senckenberg German Entomological Institute and the Berlin State Library. The two perspectives discernible from the records allow for a multi-sited and longer-term view on the development of phytopathological discourse and practices in tropical agriculture. The two men exhibited differences but also shared commonalities. While Busse conducted two expeditions to German Togoland and German Cameroon, Vosseler was permanently based at the Biological Agricultural Research Station Amani in German East Africa. Busse mostly generated his knowledge by interacting with planters and conducting trials on the ground, while Vosseler consulted international academic journals and engaged in academic exchanges with scientists based at research stations run by different empires. In both cases, the marriage between theoretical and experiential knowledge characterizing agricultural sciences was prominent. Already in the German Reich and its African colonies, phytopathology thus appeared as a remarkably versatile endeavor: not exclusively laboratory nor exclusively a field science, not just pure science nor just applied science.[14] The study, reception and use depended on the actors and the materiality of usage involved.

I begin by portraying the actors, sites and methods related to the study of plant health in the German colonies around 1900. Next, I discuss the phytopathologists' economic motives for making the colonial plantation economy thrive and their way of identifying ways to combat plant diseases together with European planters on the ground. Finally, I show that phytopathological trials extended

---

13 On the notion of experimental spaces, see the introduction to this thematic section.

14 Science studies have confirmed the blurred lines between fundamental and applied research in the nineteenth century. See Graeme Gooday, "'Vague and Artificial': The Historically Elusive Distinction Between Pure and Applied Science," *ISIS* 103, no. 3 (2012), https://doi.org/10.1086/667978; Robert Bud, "'Applied Science': A Phrase in Search of a Meaning," *ISIS* 103, no. 3 (2012), https://doi.org/10.1086/667977. See also Shapin's account on dietetics in seventeenth century England, which argues that no scientific activity can indeed be understood without taking its concrete circumstances of origin and practical implications into consideration. See Steven Shapin, *Never Pure: Historical Studies of Science as If It Was Produced by People with Bodies, Situated in Time, Space, Culture, and Society, and Struggling for Credibility and Authority* (Baltimore: Johns Hopkins University Press, 2010).

way beyond purely economic considerations. They were also aimed at altering the agricultural practices of indigenous farmers in order to control the conduct of the colonized population.

Doing Phytopathology: Agricultural Research Stations and Field Trials

As a field of research, phytopathology around 1900 served as a convergence point for individuals from academia, agriculture and the foodstuff industry. It was carried out both in academic institutions and in practice-oriented field stations, utilizing a diverse range of methods from controlled experiments in enclosed laboratories to hands-on trial-and-error approaches in agricultural settings on the ground. This section presents the main *actors*, *sites* and *methods* involved in the study of plant diseases in the German colonies.

The main *actors* fueling phytopathological knowledge production were pharmacists, zoologists or botanists turned phytopathologists. Around 1900, there was no scientist exclusively trained in phytopathology. Instead, plant diseases became an area of interest for individuals coming from other academic areas. This was even more true in the colonies: More often than not, practical considerations and a shortage of academic staff led colonists to move into and adopt different areas of expertise. For colonial science, this meant a trend toward generalization rather than specialization.[15]

Walter Busse and Julius Vosseler were chiefly involved in phytopathological studies in the German African colonies, primarily German East Africa, German Togoland and German Cameroon. Busse obtained his habilitation in botany in 1900 after having studied pharmacology. Following this, he carried out botanical expeditions to German East Africa, to the botanical gardens 's Lands Plantentuin in Buitenzorg (Dutch East Indies), to German Cameroon and to German Togoland. These expeditions were funded by the Kolonialwirtschaftliches Komitee, a private body of financiers enthused by the colonial idea aimed at promoting economic activities in the German colonies.[16] In 1905, Busse joined the civil service by accepting a position at the Kaiserlich Biologische Anstalt für Land- und Forstwirtschaft, the administrative body tasked with identifying means to protect plant

---

15 Jürgen G. Nagel, *Die Kolonie als wissenschaftliches Projekt: Forschungsorganisation und Forschungspraxis im deutschen Kolonialreich* (Hagen: FernUni Hagen, 2013), 409–411.
16 On the Kolonialwirtschaftliches Komitee, cf. the forthcoming dissertation by Andreas N. Donay.

health and issuing laws concerning plant protection. In 1906, he became head of the Department of Agriculture and Forestry at the Reichskolonialamt where he remained until 1911.[17] More of a civil servant than a scientist, Busse represented the colonial government with regard to the Amani station and deducted measures for colonial policy from his botanical-agricultural travels. As Busse visited Amani and his findings were received by the researchers based there,[18] his observations on the Togolese and Cameroonian situation entered phytopathological thinking concerning German East Africa, a vastly different geographical and climatic region.

While the Kolonialwirtschaftliches Komitee funded its last phytopathological expedition in 1907,[19] this by no means marked the end of phytopathological research in the colonies. On the contrary, the researchers based at the Amani station continued to consolidate and expand on Busse's previous findings, while trying to introduce their results into existing agricultural practices. Chief among them was Julius Vosseler. Vosseler, born in 1841 in Besigheim, obtained his doctorate in 1885 and his habilitation in zoology in 1893 in Stuttgart, where he worked at the Königliche Naturalienkabinett for about a decade. In 1903, he joined Amani as its zoologist and specialized, in the broadest sense of the word, in the study of vermin and pests. Although Vosseler lived in Amani together with his wife, there are no records preserved revealing much about his private life, such as diaries, travelogues or personal correspondence. His unpublished records held at the Senckenberg German Entomological Institute exclusively concern his research: excerpts summarizing the academic papers he read and notes for manuscripts he wrote based on his readings. The way in which he structured his notes indicates Vosseler's keen interest in pests, as he organized his excerpts according to the taxonomy of threats to plant health.[20] Vosseler left German East Africa in 1909 to accept a position as the director of the Hamburg Zoo, which he headed for the following 18 years.[21] While employed in the colonial service, both Busse and Vosseler approached their research in a hands-on manner, seeking to put phytopathological insights into practice.

---

17 "Busse, Walter Carl Otto (1865–1933)," https://plants.jstor.org/stable/10.5555/al.ap.person.bm000051684.
18 Walter Busse is frequently mentioned in the extensive correspondence maintained by Karl Braun, head botanist at Amani 1904–1920: Geheimes Staatsarchiv Preußischer Kulturbesitz Berlin, Nachlass Karl Braun, 1902–1934.
19 Wendt, "Securing Resources," 54.
20 See Vosseler's records at the Deutsche Entomologisches Institut in Müncheberg: DEI, Nachlaß Julius Vosseler, Inventarium 75, 1904–1906.
21 Georg Grimpe, "Julius Vosseler zum 70. Geburtstag," *Der zoologische Garten* 4, no. 10/12 (1931).

The main *sites* for phytopathological research to thrive were agricultural research stations and plantations. Raf de Bont refers to "stations in the field" as "every institution for instruction or research in the life sciences [. . .] located in (or next to) the field." Following his definition, such stations are here understood as "true hybrids, mixed in their institutional origins, financial resources, scientific goals, research practices, and composition of visitors."[22] In the German-speaking countries, agricultural research stations had existed since the 1830s and fueled studies in agronomy, which became a vibrant field in Germany in the 1860s. With the onset of formal German colonialism after the Berlin Conference 1884–1885, the Reich also began to establish agricultural research stations in the colonies. Thus, the German Empire followed an approach similar to that of the British across the British Empire,[23] the Dutch in the East Indies[24] and the French in Algeria.[25] The flora was essential for commodifying and 'elevating' the colonized land. Founded around 1889, Victoria in Cameroon was the first German colonial experimental garden. As a state-financed institution, the Research Institute for Land Improvement (Victoria) was intended to increase the yields of surrounding privately run plantations through novel methods in crop science. In 1902, thus a little more than a decade after the Research Institute for Land Improvement, the Amani Biological Agricultural Institute was established in the Usambara Mountains in German East Africa.[26] Originally, the institution was launched as a forestry and agricultural research station with the cooperation of the Botanische Zentralstelle

---

[22] Bont, *Stations in the Field*, 4.
[23] Richard Drayton, *Nature's Government: Science, Imperial Britain, and the 'Improvement' of the World* (New Haven: Yale University Press, 2000).
[24] On 's Lands Plantentuin in Buitenzorg, Dutch East Indies, see Andrew Goss, *The Floracrats: State-Sponsored Science and the Failure of the Enlightenment in Indonesia* (Madison: University of Wisconsin Press, 2011); Robert-Jan Wille, *De stationisten: Laboratoriumbiologie, imperialisme en de lobby voor nationale wetenschapspolitiek, 1871–1909* (Nijmegen: Radboud University, 2015); Andreas Weber and Robert-Jan Wille, "Laborious Transformations: Plants and Politics at the Bogor Botanical Gardens," *studium* 11, no. 3 (2018) and the contributions in this special issue: Florian Wagner, "From the Western to the Eastern Model of Cash Crop Production: Colonial Agronomy and the Global Influence of Dutch Java's Buitenzorg Laboratories, 1880s–1930s," in *Agrarian Reform and Resistance in an Age of Globalisation: The Euro-American World and Beyond, 1780–1914*, eds. Joe Regan and Cathal Smith (London and New York: Routledge, 2019). See Mazzoli's contribution in this thematic section on the role of the Italian Agricultural Colonial Institute of Florence in terms of establishing Italian agricultural colonies in the United States.
[25] Christophe Bonneuil and Mina Kleiche, *Du jardin d'essais colonial a la station expérimentale, 1880–1930: Eléments pour une histoire du CIRAD* (Paris: CIRAD, 1993).
[26] Christoper A. Conte, *Highland Sanctuary: Environmental History in Tanzania's Usambara Mountains* (Athens: Ohio University Press, 2004).

in Berlin.[27] By the time the British administration took over the Institute in 1919–1920, Amani had become well-known to visiting scientists and travelers to Africa from various European countries. The directors Franz Stuhlmann (in office 1903–1908) and Albrecht Zimmermann (in office 1911–1920) and the few scientific staff members, such as Karl Braun, were engaged in lively correspondence with experimental gardens in other colonial states and exchanged duplicate journals as well as seeds and seedlings with them.[28] This flow of personnel, artifacts and knowledge through a wide network of gardens across the empires made stations like Victoria and Amani "remarkably international," as stressed by von Brescius and Dejung.[29]

Contemporary descriptions portray research environments such as Buitenzorg and Amani in an idealized manner. References to 's Lands Plantentuin emphasize its rejuvenating ambience for scholarly endeavors, while extolling the diverse flora and fauna in the gardens as well as the favorable climatic conditions.[30] Nevertheless, agricultural research stations were not isolated entities; instead, institutions such as the Amani Institute were intricately linked to other colonial establishments, including the colonial administration, economy and, notably during World War I, even warfare when Amani played a role in supplying food to German settlers.[31] In examining plant diseases, this study expands the focus to the plantation as a central site for experimentation and a necessary companion of the research station. Phytopathological observations primarily occurred in the field, with research inquiries by plant pathologists aimed at addressing practical challenges faced by planters on

---

27 Katja Kaiser, *Wirtschaft, Wissenschaft und Weltgeltung: Die botanische Zentralstelle für die deutschen Kolonien am Botanischen Garten und Museum berlin* (Lausanne: Peter Lang, 2021).
28 On Stuhlmann, see Benjamin Gollasch, *Franz Ludwig Stuhlmann und die kolonialen Reformbestrebungen in Deutsch-Ostafrika vor 1906: Vom Forschungsreisenden zum politischen Entscheidungstrager* (Munich: Allitera Verlag, 2021). Despite the fact that Albrecht Zimmermann was an acclaimed botanist who held high-ranking positions in both Buitenzorg and Amani, no historical account on his life and scientific activities has as of yet been presented. The obituary written by Karl Braun, Zimmermann's assistant, provides some biographical insights: Karl Braun, "Albrecht Zimmermann. Nachruf," *Phytopathologische Zeitschrift* 3 (1931). Karl Braun himself left an extraordinarily expansive body of work, private records and a collection of artifacts stemming from his 16 years in Amani. The "Karl Braun Collection" is currently researched by a German-Tanzanian team funded by the German Lost Art Foundation. See Sebastian Möllers and Lea Steinkampf, "Stade Museums: A Colonial Era Collection Is Being Researched Together with Partner Institutions in Tanzania," *Expotime* no. 2 (2023).
29 Moritz von Brescius and Christof Dejung, "The Plantation Gaze: Imperial Careering and Agronomic Knowledge Between Europe and the Tropics," *Comparativ* 31, no. 5/6 (2021): 580.
30 Goss, *Floracrats*, 61.
31 Albrecht Zimmermann, Mitteilungen aus dem Biologisch-Landwirtschaftlichen Institut Amani, Niedersächsisches Landesarchiv, Dep. 10, Nr. 02285, 118.

the ground and controlling the work of colonized individuals. In this sense, as succinctly emphasized by Peano, Macedo and Le Petitcorps, "plantations are perfect laboratories to bring together environmental and labour dimensions."[32] Stations such as Victoria and Amani, which were embedded in the surrounding plantation ecology, enabled scientists and practitioners to produce phytopathological knowledge and intervene with traditional practices. However, even if the layout of a plantation seemed to follow "technical expertise and hierarchical control," practice in the field entailed numerous unforeseen and unintended challenges.[33]

In terms of *method*, phytopathological research most closely followed the trends shaping the agricultural sciences. The introduction of chemical methods in the agricultural sciences, a turn associated with the name of Julius Kühn (1825–1910),[34] was paramount in developing externally applied remedies against plant diseases. Copper, mercury and sulfur constituted the main materials for insecticides and fungicides that planters and farmers could use as sprays or dusts. The Bordeaux mixture was developed as the first fungicide in 1882 and became a standard appliance against downy mildew, as was the case for lime-sulfur against the peach leaf curl.[35] As the disciplines of zoology and veterinary medicine grew, so did the field of phytopathological zoology. Thus, in the fifth volume of the *Handbook of Plant Diseases* from 1932, the potentially harmful impact of vertebrates, birds and mammals on plant growth was considered on equal footing with fungi and insects.[36]

Just like in the agricultural sciences, the preferred method of phytopathologists in tropical agriculture was the field trial (German: *Feldversuch*). Historian Frank Uekötter has shown which epistemological stance was attributed to the field trial around 1900.[37] While agricultural scientists did conduct chemical experiments in the laboratory to assess soil quality or determine formulas for plant nutrients, they never dismissed the field trial as a valuable source of insight – regardless of reported mistakes, inexact measures or the irreproducibility inherent in the practical approach. Agricultural scientists even encouraged farmers to con-

---

[32] Irene Peano, Marta Macedo and Colette Le Petitcorps, "Introduction: Viewing Plantations at the Intersection of Policital Ecologies and Multiple Space-Times," in *Global Plantations in the Modern World: Sovereignties, Ecologies, Afterlives*, eds. Colette Le Petitcorps, Marta Macedo and Irene Peano (Cham: Palgrave Macmillan, 2023), 5.
[33] Peano, Macedo and Le Petitcorps, "Viewing Plantations," 7.
[34] Klemm, *Agrarwissenschaften*, 200–201.
[35] George M. Reed, "Phytopathology 1867–1942," 166.
[36] Otto Appel and Ludwig Reh, *Handbuch der Pflanzenkrankheiten* (Berlin: Paul Parey, 1932).
[37] Frank Uekötter, *Die Wahrheit ist auf dem Feld: Eine Wissensgeschichte der deutschen Landwirtschaft* (Göttingen: Vandenhoeck & Ruprecht, 2012), 81–89.

duct trials in the field themselves. While numbers could be neglected, the field trial was indispensable.

This is in contrast to what Sarah Jansen observes with regard to applied entomology in the late nineteenth century. In her view, the mathematization of biological experiments was a sign of validity and scientificity that applied entomologists had to exhibit for their results to be accepted.[38] Here, Jansen uses an a priori definition of what constitutes an experiment as her point of departure: "First, the isolation of an event; second, the identifiability of the event's elements; third, the stability and homogeneity of the constraints of the technical things enabling the observation of isolated and identifiable elements."[39] In colonial settings, phytopathologists adopted a practical approach akin to agricultural sciences by conducting field trials. They did not engage in complex theoretical frameworks or rely on sophisticated equipment. Instead, their experiments were grounded in problem-driven approaches characterized by iterative trial-and-error processes.

This approach also influenced research at the Amani station. In 1902, the Amani station's chemist, Victor Lommel, conducted a study near Mkamba, a rural location south of Dar es Salaam, to determine if a recent locust infestation could be controlled by infecting the insects with fungi. Armed with 20 vials of fungal cultures, he enlisted the help of local villagers to collect the insects for him. He then treated the insects with the fungal cultures to induce infection. After infecting them, Lommel released them back into the environment to initiate an epidemic among the locust population.[40] Jansen's criteria for defining an experiment were hardly met in the case of Lommel's study. Lommel attempted to isolate the specific event, which was the infestation of locusts with the fungus, by separating the infected animals and observing them for some days following the infection. One night, however, due to a lack of necessary storage materials, all the selected insects perished before Lommel could even infect them. Moreover, the physical conditions for observation were often chaotic. The locust swarms frequently changed location unpredictably, and Lommel could not always personally witness these shifts, instead relying on hearsay to track their movements. Notably, Lommel's account does not suggest that mathematical analysis was required to lend scientific credibility to his findings. His report was published in the *Berichte über*

---

38 Sarah Jansen, *"Schädlinge": Geschichte eines wissenschaftlichen und politischen Konstrukts 1840–1920* (Frankfurt a. M.: Campus, 2003), 142–190.
39 Jansen, *Schädlinge*, 144. This and all the following quotations from German materials are translated into English by the author.
40 Victor Lommel, "Bericht über eine Reise nach der Gegen von Mkamba zwecks Infizierung von Heuschreckenschwärmen mittelst des Heuschreckenpilzes," *Berichte über Land- und Forstwirtschaft in Deutsch-Ostafrika* 1 (1903).

Land- und Forstwirtschaft in Deutsch-Ostafrika, a publication by the German East African Government aimed at providing information to colonial planters and financiers in the German Reich. In the realm of phytopathology in tropical agriculture, the emphasis was on practical, hands-on experiments directly addressing the challenges faced daily by plantation owners, rather than relying on mathematical formalization. This resulted in a dual objective of phytopathological research: increasing the yield of cash crops and imparting what they considered superior, "hygienic" agricultural techniques.

Phytopathologists for Cash Crop Production

Using the experimental method of the field trial, scientists at agricultural research stations tied their knowledge to concerns of planters on the ground. To a large extent, this concerned the economic prospects of cash crop production, thus leaving the study of medicinal plants on the back burner. The literature has shed light on the potentially drastic impacts of plant diseases on the colonial plantation economy and, consequently, on the complex interplay of actors from the colonial administration, planters and scientists. Wenzlhuemer shows how disastrous plant diseases could play out in colonial settings. In Ceylon, "King Coffee" had dominated the British plantation economy since the early 1850s. When the first signs of *Hemileia vastatrix*, or coffee leave disease, showed up in the 1870s, the planters were startled and frustrated by the seemingly arbitrary appearance of symptoms. Not only was the colonial plantation economy severely affected but indigenous farmers also suffered a drastic decline in crops. Wenzlhuemer emphasizes what botanists already proclaimed at the time: Monocrop cultivation was a risky affair and threatened the objective of valorization.[41]

Building on Wenzlhuemer, Offermann retraces how the outbreak of an epidemic suddenly led to heightened levels of attention with regard to scientific expertise in the form of Ceylon's botanic garden Peradeniya. Examining the complex relationship between colonial administration, scientists and planters, he argues that planters for the longest time maintained a skeptical attitude toward scientists. Upon its founding in 1843, Peradeniya did not significantly influence the plantation economy. Planters were supported by the colonial administration and counted on practical skills that they disseminated through the Planters' Association. It was only at the onset of the coffee leaf disease that the scientists at Peradeniya were put in a

---

[41] Roland Wenzlhuemer, *From Coffee to Tea Cultivation in Ceylon, 1880–1900: An Economic and Social History* (Leiden: Brill, 2008), 62–69.

special position. When all experiential knowledge was exhausted, scientific knowledge seemed like a beacon of hope.[42] Accordingly, as Wendt states, understanding plant health and how to preserve it was of "paramount concern" for a broad array of colonial actors, including the colonial administration, private financiers such as the Kolonialwirtschaftliches Komitee, individual scientists and, importantly, practitioners in the field.[43]

The economic lens guiding phytopathological inquiries is shown in the problem definitions presented in the sources. In a report on his 1905 expedition to German Cameroon and German Togoland, Walter Busse elaborated on what he considered the two main plagues in the regions: the cacao blight and the bark bug. The blight was caused by various fungi nesting in the cacao fruit, at first rendering the fruits light brown and, at a later stage, yellow-whitish.[44] The bark bug attacked young cacao tree branches and extracted their juice.[45] As they both affected cacao trees, these pests weakened one of the central cash crops in the region.

In Busse's efforts to combat blight and the bark bug, experiments at various points played a crucial role. Field trials were carried out to identify possible causes and solutions, as planters could only report specific symptoms exhibited by the plants. In many cases, the exact cause of the issues was not immediately clear. To pinpoint the causes of diseases, plant pathologists employed various methods, one of the primary approaches being inoculations. During inoculations, potential disease triggers were introduced into healthy plants to observe any resulting symptoms. In Busse's investigation of blight, he injected the fungus *Phytophthora* into 20 cacao fruits and the fungus *Colletotrichum incarnatum* into three additional cacao fruits. In the first group, nine fruits quickly exhibited the typical symptoms of blight. In the second group, only one fruit showed signs of infection, still demonstrating that *Colletotrichum* also constituted a potential threat to the cacao tree.[46]

---

42 Michael Offermann, *Peradeniya, Pflanzer und die Presse: Die Zusammenarbeit der botanischen Gärten und der Pflanzer bei der Bekämpfung des Kaffeerosts auf Ceylon Ende des 19. Jahrhunderts* (Heidelberg: Ruprecht-Karls-Universität, 2013). Cf. Barbara Hahn's provocative question regarding the determining character of a cash crop for its social, political and economic surroundings, Barbara Hahn et al., "Does Crop Determine Culture?" *Agricultural History* 88, no. 3 (2014), https://doi.org/10.3098/ah.2014.088.3.407.
43 Wendt, "Securing Resources," 45.
44 Walter Busse, "Reisebericht der pflanzenpathologischen Expedition des Kolonial-Wirtschaftlichen Komitees nach Westafrika," *Der Tropenpflanzer* 9 (1905): 28.
45 Busse, "Reisebericht," 33.
46 Busse, "Reisebericht," 31.

In addition to identifying causes for plant diseases, experiments were also aimed at finding possible solutions. In the course of fighting the bark bug, planters tried various measures with different levels of success. At the Victoria plantation in Cameroon, planters had coated the trees "with a suspension of ordinary lime." In his report for the periodical *Der Tropenpflanzer*, Busse weighed in on the attempt: "This remedy is not recommended, because only the trunk and the stronger branches can be treated, but the younger shoots remain free, because the delicate flowering plants suffer and finally, because the procedure requires too much time." Upon inspection, Busse still found the coated trees lined with bark bugs, thereby concluding that the measure was not even effective. A remedy tried at a different farm – a "decoction of Quassia, pure or in combination with soap or petroleum soap emulsion" – exhibited "such uneven results" that Busse advised to "abandon this method, too."[47] At the Plantation Oechelhausen, the planter Köthe had variously tried a "pure petroleum soap mixture," "sulfur liver" and "sulfur calcium" – all to no avail. Only "a solution of 2.5 kg yellow soap in 100 liters water" proved effective to some extent. Yet, Busse warned of the remedy's "disadvantage of being too easy to wash off: a single heavy rain could impair the effect in an unexpected way." When it came to the trials conducted during his stay in German Cameroon, Busse turned toward a remedy developed at the Moliwe plantation: a mixture of Schweinfurter Grün, petroleum, soap, soda and water. On top of that, he also recommended using "a pure suspension Schweinfurter Grün in water [. . .] with an addition of carpenter's glue to reduce wash-off."[48] Thus, the experiential knowledge of planters was not without benefit to the phytopathological inquiry but, on the contrary, constituted practical trials in the field that the plant pathologist could build on.

Besides coming across chemical means through trial and error, colonial planters and indigenous farmers actively participated in plant pathological experiments as these required long-term observation. Traveling on a Buitenzorg stipend for a limited period,[49] Busse appreciated that individual planters played an active role in phytopathological research on site. During his expedition through German Togoland, Busse encountered the German planter Robinson "whom I

---

47 Walter Busse, "Reisebericht III der pflanzenpathologischen Expedition des Kolonial-Wirtschaftlichen Komitees nach Westafrika," *Der Tropenpflanzer* 9 (1905): 251.
48 Busse, "Reisebericht III," 252.
49 On the Buitenzorg stipends, see Florian Wagner, "Inventing Colonial Agronomy: Buitenzorg and the Transition from the Western to the Eastern Model of Colonial Agriculture, 1880s–1930s," in *Environments of Empire*, eds. Ulrike Kirchberger and Brett M. Bennett (Chapel Hill: The University of North Carolina Press, 2020), 111. Issued by the German government between 1898 and 1914, these travel stipends were used to fund expeditions to the Buitenzorg botanical garden in the Dutch East Indies but also to other German colonies.

have come to appreciate as an excellent observer." Together, both men went to great lengths to identify the harmful insect that "had pitted or curled [the cotton roots] to sometimes an astonishing extent."[50] Busse recommended conducting further trials with antifungals to restore the health of the cotton plants. Robinson's plantation at Nuatyä would be "the suitable place" and Robinson himself was "without a doubt the suitable personality" for such trials.[51]

Similarly to Busse, Julius Vosseler from the Amani station reached out to the German planters and invited them to share their knowledge and experiences to determine the origins of specific plant diseases. To be sure, the exchange with planters on-site did not constitute the only source of knowledge for Vosseler. He took extensive notes based on his readings in journals such as *Tropical Agriculture* or the *Agricultural Bulletin*.[52] Thus, he took the planters' knowledge or routines with a grain of salt and at times skeptically questioned their approaches. For instance, Vosseler dismissed a method tried by African and Indian farmers in the Usambara region and adopted by German planters to prevent coconut trees from losing their fruits before they had matured (plucking a nail into the trunk).[53]

Still, various accounts reveal a collective approach toward conducting field trials and pinpointing the exact reasons and remedies for any given plague. Depending on his ongoing research interests or current threats to plant health in the region, Vosseler called on the colonial planters to send in specimens of particular insects or report how the disease in question unfolded on site. After several planters had already shared their observations of the leaf curl having afflicted cotton plants, Vosseler stated that the question of the origins of the disease seemed to be more or less settled. Still, he invited planters to send in more experience reports tying his request to the practical concern of battling the disease: "The more versatilely the question is dealt with, the faster and more thoroughly it is clarified."[54] Vosseler's motivation was partly found in pure science, partly in making the resulting knowledge useful in the field: The faster a threat to plant health could be addressed, the smaller the hurdle for establishing a functioning plantation economy.

---

50 Walter Busse, "Reisebericht II der pflanzenpathologischen Expedition des Kolonial-Wirtschaftlichen Komitees nach Westafrika," *Der Tropenpflanzer* 9 (1905): 180.
51 Busse, "Reisebericht II," 181.
52 DEI, Nachlaß Julius Vosseler.
53 Julius Vosseler, "Altes und Neues über Kokosschädlinge," *Der Pflanzer* 3, no. 17/18 (1907): 276–277.
54 Julius Vosseler, "Noch einmal die Kräuselkrankheit," *Der Pflanzer* 1, no. 18 (1905): 282.

Pest Control for Empire: Tropical Hygiene and the Civilizing Mission

While the economic interest in phytopathological forms of knowledge is apparent in travelogues and periodicals, it should be noted that the context of tropical agriculture offered another subtext to the ways in which plant diseases were studied and remedied: the objective of "educating" and "elevating" the colonized population, related to fears of the prospect that the "natives" could not be controlled.[55] Even though there was no German term directly corresponding to the British "civilising mission" or the French *"mission civilisatrice,"* similar tendencies were seen in parts of the German colonial activities. Referred to as *"Kulturarbeit"* (cultural work) or *"Kulturmission"* (cultural mission), German colonists negotiated ways to intervene in local routines and impart their norms upon the colonized population.[56] This motif of the civilizing mission not only figured in religiously driven missionary activities.[57] The agricultural sphere seemed to be another area where the indigenous population could be "educated" and their lives "improved." This perspective overlooked the centuries-old knowledge of indigenous farmers with regard to soil cultivation, crop rotation and fertilization, something that Sebald has highlighted for Togo and Koponen for Tanzania and Zanzibar.[58] Duala and Bamileke entrepreneurs had steered agricultural development in the Cameroonian littoral from the 1880s and onwards.[59] Hence, the educational attempts largely defeated their purpose, which did not deter the colonists from trying.

---

[55] The civilizing missions of various empires have been discussed extensively, such as by Boris Barth and Rolf Hobson, eds., *Civilizing Missions in the Twentieth Century* (Boston: Brill, 2021). On colonial anxieties, see the contributions in Harald Fischer-Tiné, ed., *Anxieties, Fear and Panic in Colonial Settings: Empires on the Verge of a Nervous Breakdown* (Cham: Palgrave Macmillan, 2016); Maurus Reinkowski and Gregor Thum, eds., *Helpless Imperialists: Imperial Failure, Fear and Radicalization* (Göttingen: Vandenhoeck & Ruprecht, 2012); Ann Laura Stoler, *Along the Archival Grain: Epistemic Anxieties and Colonial Common Sense* (Princeton: Princeton Univ. Press, 2009).

[56] Jürgen Osterhammel, "Epilogue: From Civilizing Missions to the Defence of Civility," in *Civilizing Missions in the Twentieth Century*, eds. Boris Barth and Rolf Hobson (Boston: Brill, 2021), 209.

[57] Richard Hölzl and Karolin Wetjen, "Negotiating the Fundamentals? German Missions and the Experience of the Contact Zone, 1850–1918," in *Negotiating the Secular and the Religious in the German Empire: Transnational Approaches*, ed. Rebekka Habermas (New York and Oxford: Berghahn, 2019).

[58] Peter Sebald, *Togo 1884–1914: Eine Geschichte der deutschen „Musterkolonie" auf der Grundlage amtlicher Quellen* (Berlin: Akademie-Verlag, 1988), 119–128.

[59] Andreas Eckert, "African Rural Entrepreneurs and Labor in the Cameroon Littoral," *The Journal of African History* 40, no. 1 (1999).

Busse's expedition reports exemplified the 'developmental' attempts of the phytopathologists. His texts contained lengthy remarks on the local population at the beginning and the end, thus framing his arguments through a cultural narrative. German planters were vocal regarding their violent attitude toward the indigenous population and advocated for the use of force in disciplining the indigenous workforce. Busse, deviating from the openly dehumanizing discourse, called for "educating" natives in the agricultural techniques of the white man. In his view, the colonized needed to be introduced to proper agricultural methods for hygienic reasons. Since he identified air circulation as a driver for spreading fungi, plantations not tended according to the "proper" way seemed like a potential source of further infections and thus a threat to the plantation economy.[60] This echoed the contemporary discourse of "tropical hygiene" prominent in tropical medicine.[61] Although Busse highlighted that numerous European plantations were in an equally regrettable state as their owners did not fight the sources of disease, no lengthy calls for action were aimed at the Europeans.

However, while arguing for the generally flawed disposition of farmers in the Victoria district in Cameroon, he conceded that "not all of these farms deserve a derogatory judgment."[62] According to him, a farm run by an African man named Beecroft in close vicinity to the plantations of the Westafrikanische Pflanzungsgesellschaft Victoria exhibited exceptional results, which he attributed to Beecroft's level of knowledge and the fact that he had adopted European phytopathological practices:

> This farm testifies to the extraordinary intelligence and agricultural talent of its owner. It is quite a valuable property, and, as far as the infestation by the bark bug is concerned, it does not differ in any way from the equally infested plots of some European plantations, where control attempts have not been made or have been insufficient. Incidentally, it should be noted that Beecroft has taken action against the bark bug in the same way as the West African planting company Victoria, by pruning and liming.[63]

Believing in the indigenous potential to "develop" with the right kind of guidance, Busse suggested that any measures taken on indigenous farms in the Victoria district should meet three criteria: they should be "simple to carry out," "cheap" and "controllable." For this reason, Busse did not endorse the mandatory implementa-

---

60 Busse, "Reisebericht III," 254–255.
61 Sarah Ehlers, "Disease Control and Human Experimentation: Networks, Practices, and Biographical Pathways from Colonial Medicine to Nazi Germany," in *Colonial Paradigms of Violence*, eds. Michelle Gordon and Rachel O'Sullivan (Göttingen: Wallstein Verlag, 2022).
62 Busse, "Reisebericht III," 254–255.
63 Busse, "Reisebericht III," 254.

tion of the method of removing bark bugs from trees, which he considered "still indispensable for European plantations for the time being" as an obligatory measure implemented by the local population "because it is quite uncontrollable."[64] In addition to outlining potential measures, Busse took steps to instruct the indigenous population on-site. He had planned to conduct a practical course for a group of Cameroonian farmers, teaching them how to administer a serum using a syringe. He complained that he was unable to proceed with the course due to the absence of the required materials, which had not been delivered from the German Reich in time.[65] Still, he viewed his role as extending beyond diagnosing diseases and making specific recommendations for remedies. He saw himself as a facilitator of practical knowledge and transferring skills with a dual objective: protecting the plantation economy and influencing the behavior of the local population to impart European agricultural practices.

Julius Vosseler's writings reveal the flipside of Busse's belief in "developing" indigenous agriculture: the lack of knowledge on flora and growth techniques that the colonists brought to the table and the fears of failing to control a population that far outnumbered the small number of German settlers and planters. As a zoologist at the Amani station in German East Africa, Vosseler published extensively in the bi-weekly periodical issued by the institution: *Der Pflanzer*, a "guidebook for tropical agriculture" as the subtitle indicated aimed at German planters in the East African region. From 1905 to 1914, the scientists at the Amani station condensed their findings in *Der Pflanzer* to derive practical forms of application from their studies that could elevate the German plantation economy. Just like Busse's travels enabled encounters between science, colonial policy and economic practice, *Der Pflanzer* could have served as an arena for shared knowledge. Yet, in contrast to the interpersonal knowledge transfer effectuated by the traveling consultant Busse, the impact of written advice seemed limited. Söldenwagner notes that few German planters were eager to gain agricultural knowledge and skills, thus largely ignoring *Der Pflanzer*.[66] Hence, while officially aimed at the planter community, the periodical mainly strengthened the self-affirmation of Amani researchers like Vosseler.

Vosseler's writings show that phytopathological experts viewed indigenous knowledge from a distance and appropriated traditional agricultural techniques where they exhibited superior results. A case in point was the unsuccessful attempt to pursue monoculture in Amani. Unfamiliar with the quality of the soil,

---

64 Busse, "Reisebericht III," 254–256.
65 Busse, "Reisebericht III," 255.
66 Philippa Söldenwagner, *Spaces of Negotiation: European Settlement and Settlers in German East Africa, 1900–1914* (Munich: Martin Meidenbauer, 2006), 142–143.

the weather conditions and the various vermin and pests, the Amani staff had weeded out any plants they considered a disturbance to the eye to instead plant single crops. Vosseler was perplexed by the contrast between the unhindered growth of cucumbers in the fields of indigenous farmers and the severe fungal impact on crops at the research station. Acknowledging the disappointing outcomes, he conceded that adopting the local farmers' practice of crop variation might be beneficial: "[F]ield and root crops also suffer from the same pests as the cucumber when planted in isolation, but remain unaffected when associated with other plants. Should the habit of the blacks to grow their crops in mixed cultivation perhaps be due to this experience?"[67] While conflating the various ethnic groups of Arabs and Swahilis who looked back on a substantial farming tradition in East Usambara,[68] Vosseler also revealed an epistemic insecurity: After all, not only could indigenous planters learn from Europeans, the opposite was also true.

However, colonial insecurities were not only epistemic. Through Vosseler's account, we can also observe the colonists' anxious attempts to control the indigenous populations. Not only weather conditions, fungi and insects seemed to threaten the crops: Through the eyes of the colonists, the colonized subjects revolting also appeared like pests. Since 1905, Vosseler regularly published texts about threats to the coconut tree in *Der Pflanzer*. In an article from 1907, he deviated from his usual focus on fungi and insects and stated "quite an increase in enemies to the coconut tree," including mammals.[69] In his view, one mammal stood out among the hostile elements: "In the series of creatures, the human being stands above all in this regard, naturally as the anima nigra, as the black variant."[70] Planters had reported an increased number of coconut thefts that allegedly cut the copra yields in half. Referring to rumors that half of the population on the island Mafia on the east coast was engaging in coconut theft, Vosseler made projections regarding the dire potential impact of large-scale stealing on the plantation economy: "robberies" would have "an inhibiting effect on the operation of existing plantations by Europeans and paralyze the entrepreneurial spirit for new plantations." In addition, thieves did not differentiate between "ripe and half-ripe nuts," thereby contaminating the copra yield: "This reduces the value of

---

67 Julius Vosseler, "Gurkenschädlinge in Ostusambara," *Der Pflanzer* 1, no. 18 (1905): 287.
68 Juhani Koponen, *Development for Exploitation: German Colonial Policies in Mainland Tanzania, 1884–1914* (Helsinki: Lit Verlag, 1995), 197–212.
69 Vosseler, "Kokosschädlinge," 288.
70 Vosseler, "Kokosschädlinge," 288.

the product and the reputation of the producing country on the world market. So another indirect disadvantage!"⁷¹ Just as Busse extensively laid out possibilities to combat pests through chemical means, Vosseler went to great lengths to elaborate on means to prevent theft – conceptualizing the colonized themselves as a pest that had to be combatted:

> Perhaps the mentioned method of setting traps may be enough of a deterrent. However, it should not be forgotten that the thieves soon learned to use long sticks to close the traps in front of them and render them harmless. Moreover, the suggested idea of covering tree trunks with sharp metal spikes and thorns would not provide absolute defence, would cost a lot of money, and make harvesting more difficult. Nighttime guards are also of little help. They often perform their duties inadequately without proper control. [. . .] Fences made of barbed wire or living thorn hedges may perhaps serve their purpose best, despite significant initial costs, especially for smaller plantations, if they are consistently maintained.⁷²

While seemingly demonstrating the colonists' range of ways to exert control, Vosseler's account revealed the insecurities and fears that the colonists frequently grappled with. As Reinkowski and Thum point out, many such colonial fears were not grounded in reality.⁷³ At the time of Vosseler's writing, virtually no German planter was based on Mafia. Sunseri speaks of only one German planter on the island by 1910 and states that five more followed within four years, resulting in a total number of six German planters on Mafia by 1914.⁷⁴ The copra production on Mafia was dominated by Arab and Swahili plantations running on slave labor, and Indian traders exported copra from the island to the mainland markets. Rather than impoverishing the copra plantations, the slaves were responsible for protecting the coconut trees from pests such as "monkeys, wild pigs, and birds," as well as climbing the trees, the latter being a "particularly strenuous job."⁷⁵ When German planters settled on Mafia, the pre-existing plantation infrastructure and available labor force quickly turned Mafia into "German East Africa's

---

71 Julius Vosseler, "Altes und Neues über Kokosschädlinge (Schluss)," *Der Pflanzer* 3, no. 19/20 (1907): 290.
72 Vosseler, "Kokosschädlinge (Schluss)," 290.
73 Maurus Reinkowski and Gregor Thum, "Helpless Imperialists: Introduction," in *Helpless Imperialists: Imperial Failure, Fear and Radicalization*, eds. Maurus Reinkowski and Gregor Thum (Göttingen: Vandenhoeck & Ruprecht, 2012), 11.
74 Thaddeus Sunseri, "Slave Ransoming in German East Africa, 1885–1922," *The International Journal of African Historical Studies* 26, no. 3 (1993): 498.
75 Sunseri, "Slave Ransoming," 497.

chief source of copra."[76] Vosseler's projected fear had not materialized. Still, in his writing, he showed that the colonial mind could seamlessly transfer the epistemic category of a pest to subjugated human beings.[77]

Concluding Remarks

Considered in conjunction, the accounts of Busse and Vosseler exemplify the same "complicated mix of developmental fantasies, colonial insecurities, and racism" discerned by Sarah Ehlers among colonial physicians.[78] Pest control in the German colonies was meant to fulfill various objectives: on the one hand, the valorization of lands and plants and, on the other, pursuing the cultural mission of "elevating" the indigenous population. Thus, the agricultural research station as an experimental setting drew its raison d'être directly from impacting its immediate surroundings: the plantation economy in its racialized environments. In addition, a few individuals funded by the Kolonialwirtschaftliche Komitee traveled to various colonies in different climatic zones and visited plantations to conduct field trials on site. Here, phytopathology followed an experimental logic. Phytopathologists such as Walter Busse created controlled settings for trials and provoked reactions to be studied in order to identify plagues and ways to fight them. To a significant extent, phytopathological field trials were based on the experiential knowledge gained by the planters on site, and planters and scientists worked alongside to build the plantation economy.

The study of two actors rooted in different institutional settings and with different interpretations of the colonial agenda shows that both the economic objectives and the cultural mission could be pursued differently. Travel reports, articles in periodicals and archival material give an in-depth picture, albeit leaving the perspective of the indigenous population obscured. Busse advocated for "educating" and "helping" indigenous farmers in the face of planters' calls for disciplining the local labor force in a harsh and possibly violent manner. In contrast to Busse, Vosseler defined black individuals as "pests" themselves, likening them to the fungi, insects and other animals that the plants needed protection from. Hence, a paternalistic position met with a racialized view.

---

76 Sunseri, "Slave Ransoming," 498.
77 Jansen shows how the German notion of *Schädling* (pest) came into being between 1840 and 1920, blending entomological knowledge and motifs of social hygiene, see Jansen, *Schädlinge*.
78 Ehlers, "Disease Control," 112.

In 1909, when he was already employed as a civil servant at the Reichskolonialamt, Busse was critical that the Amani station had not done enough in terms of "elevating" indigenous agriculture but had primarily focused on biological research.[79] In this regard, he echoed the credo of "scientific colonialism" that had become the official agenda of the Reichskolonialamt under Bernhard Dernburg.[80] Following the approach of the civilizing mission, Dernburg had since 1907 sought to preserve the colonies by "improving" them through scientific means and more labor-friendly policies.[81] In 1910, one year after Busse's intervention, Amani scientists started to offer structured courses to German planters and focused more on "indigenous crops" in their research, following the direction of the Reichskolonialamt.[82] Curiously, 1909 was the year that Vosseler left Amani to return to the Reich. He was replaced as Amani's zoologist by Hermann Morstatt, who quickly became an expert on plant pathological trials.[83] Even after returning to the Weimar Republic after 1919–1920, Morstatt published several manuals on plant protection.[84] Thus, knowledge production began in the colonies and circulated back to the metropole.

This article has shown that an experimental mindset guided the pursuit of the phytopathologists involved in tropical agriculture. The study of plant diseases was significantly shaped by an approach of trial and error, while being aimed at solving concrete issues at hand in the tending of cash crops. At the same time, the sources reveal that the experimental approach extended beyond tinkering with plants and their health. In the same way, Vosseler scrutinized how to combat plant diseases and mused on ways to keep the insurgent indigenous population at bay, thereby demonstrating the colonists' epistemic and material insecurities. This is relevant to the study of science and empire overall: A medicalized mindset was characteristic of the time of high imperialism and shaped the colonists' attitude toward people, places and things. Comparing and contrasting the colonial medicalized view of humans, plants and animals alike is beyond the scope of this

---

79 Nagel, *Kolonie*, 333.
80 Andrew Zimmerman, "Ruling Africa: Science as Sovereignty in the German Colonial Empire and Its Aftermath," in *German Colonialism in a Global Age*, eds. Bradley Naranch and Geoff Eley (Durham: Duke University Press, 2014), 100.
81 Katharina Abermeth, *Heinrich Schnee: Karrierewege und Erfahrungswelten eines deutschen Kolonialbeamten* (Kiel: Solivagus Praeteritum, 2017), 263–267.
82 Nagel, *Kolonie*, 333.
83 "Personalien," *Der Pflanzer* 5, no. 10/11 (1909); Hans Sachtleben, "Entomologische Chronik," *Beiträge zur Entomologie* 9, no. 5/6 (1959): 710–12, https://doi.org/10.21248/contrib.entomol.9.5-6. 708-712.
84 Hermann Morstatt, "Zur Ausbildung für den Pflanzenschutzdienst," *Zeitschrift für Pflanzenkrankheiten* 31, no. 3/4 (1921).

article. However, how a medicalized lens guided the inquiry of a range of pre-disciplinary endeavors in the colonies, be it in botany, entomology, mycology or zoology, constitutes an intriguing object for further inquiry.

Alina Marktanner is a postdoctoral researcher at the Chair for Modern History (C19–21) with its Knowledge and Technology Cultures, RWTH Aachen University. In her dissertation titled "Behördenconsulting," she investigated the emergence of management consulting in the German public sector after the 1970s. Her second book project focuses on the history of pest control in German East Africa and British India around 1900. Her research interests include the history of science, knowledge and technology, political and administrative history and global and colonial history.

Gilberto Mazzoli
Climates of Migration: Science, Race, and Agricultural Diplomacy between Italy and the United States, 1895–1916

Abstract: At the turn of the twentieth century, the Italian and US governments sought to create agricultural development projects as a way to direct new Italian migrants toward allegedly underpopulated areas of North America and relocate urban migrants to so-called rural colonies. In order to tailor migrants and national interests, diplomats, politicians, agrarian experts, and social reformers developed a new basis for international collaboration labeled *agricultural diplomacy*. Scientific studies emerged to prove the potential of the southern US states as colonies. This paper focuses on exploring this transnational entanglement of science, race, economy, and politics with Italian migrants in the United States and their ecologies. These agricultural colonies turned out to be spaces of experimentation for both scientific and political purposes: Italian agronomists tested crops and collected data on climates, while Italian diplomats viewed such spaces as useful for experimenting with their ideas of informal expansionism. At the same time, US-American actors – USDA scientists, Southern landowners, and governmental officials – also looked at these agricultural colonies as experimental spaces: testing new forms of agricultural production that could improve urban food provisioning while changing the racial geography of both the city and the countryside.

By highlighting the contribution of the Italian Agricultural Colonial Institute of Florence and its agronomists in the transnational relationship labeled *agricultural diplomacy*, this paper emphasizes its role in the scientization of colonial practice.

Keywords: environmental history, Italian migration, experimental agriculture, climate politics, migrant and colonial transnational knowledge

Introduction

At the turn of the twentieth century, the Italian and US governments sought to create agricultural development projects as a way of directing new Italian migrants toward allegedly underpopulated areas in North America and relocate urban migrants to so-called rural colonies.[1] On the Italian side, these strategies should be understood as a form of "emigrant colonialism," as labeled by historian Mark Choate.[2] He uses this term to describe a particular trend in Italian foreign policy in which the Italian élites looked at their emigrant communities scattered around the globe as tools to "safeguard *Italianness*" abroad and fulfill imperialist purposes.[3] In the decades spanning 1880 to 1920, the notion of "colonial policy" embraced ideas of economic expansion in connection with migrants.[4] Furthermore, as recently highlighted by Lucy Riall, such transnational ties dated back to the early nineteenth century and are representative of Italian ambitions to have global influence before – and better than – formal colonialism. Following the successful assimilation of ordinary migrants reveals "hidden spaces of empire" and the global making of Italy as an "offshore nation."[5]

On the US-American side, the establishment of agricultural colonies with Italian migrants should be understood under the policy of "Americanizing" immigrants. Such a policy served two main purposes. First, finding a solution to the "urban question": the millions of immigrants arriving from Southern and Eastern Europe were stuck in the cities on the US-American East Coast and their presence was portrayed as an obstacle to a desired urban modernity. Second, the creation of agricultural colonies was seen as an opportunity to replace African Americans in the rural South after the abolition of slavery in 1865 and the subsequent Great Migration to the industrial North. For the US-American government and landowners, Italian immigrants combined the skills necessary for strong agricultural

---

[1] I wish to thank all the colleagues with whom I discussed the matter of this article over conferences and workshops, and in particular: Marco Armiero, Roberta Biasillo, Rosetta Giuliani Caponetto, Colin Fisher, Bernhard Gißibl, Alice Gorton, Anne Kwaschik, Riley Linebaugh, Alina Marktanner, Sara Müller, Anne-Sophie Reichert, Lucy Riall, Claudia Roesch, Daniele Valisena, and Stéphane Van Damme. Furthermore, I am grateful to the editors of this journal and, lastly, to the anonymous peer reviewers for their precious remarks and comments.

[2] Mark Choate, *Emigrant Nation: The Making of Italy Abroad* (Cambridge: Harvard UP, 2008), 2.

[3] Mark Choate, *Emigrant Nation*, 57–58. Furthermore, the word *Italianità* frequently reoccurs in the sources produced by the Italian government at the time, such as in the Bollettino Emigrazione Italiana (BEI).

[4] Alberto Acquarone, *Dopo Adua: Politica e Amministrazione Coloniale* (Roma: Ministero per i beni culturali e ambientali, 1989), 261.

[5] Lucy Riall, "Hidden Spaces of Empire: Italian colonists in Nineteenth Century Peru," *Past and Present* 25 (2022): 193–233; Lucy Riall, "Offshore Nation: Italians 'Overseas' in the Nineteenth-Century World," *Storica*, 28, no. 83/84 (2022): 9–51.

labor while also being white, which many landowners looked favorably upon.[6] As recently shown by Lauren Braun-Strumfels, a partnership between Italy and the United States in the last decade of the nineteenth century with regard to managing Italian migrants played a substantial role in shaping the restrictive immigration policy of the United States in the early twentieth century.[7] This dialogue included the possibilities of creating agricultural colonies and resettling migrants from the East Coast cities to the South.[8]

Nevertheless, environmental history has recently proved to be a fruitful field of inquiry unveiling new links between the Italian global migratory experience and its relationship with the environment.[9] This means that if we put the environment at the center of the analysis – focusing on agriculture and more deeply analyzing the role of Italian scientific institutions – new details emerge to expand the view on such a transnational dialogue. All institutional actors involved – social and urban reformers, government officials, Italian diplomats, journalists, agronomists, landowners – shared the common goal of managing migrants by exploiting their gardening skills. For some, gardening represented a way to educate immigrants and thus open up a path toward their possible Americanization. For others, gardening was the best means to clear modern cities of *undesirable* elements, while replacing other *undesirables*, the African American farmworkers, in Southern states. Hence, gardening emerged as the connecting element between all parties involved in a transnational network. I have labeled this entanglement between foreign policy, international science, imagined environments, private firms, and the agricultural knowledge of migrant communities as *agricultural diplomacy*.[10]

---

[6] For an overview of how Italians in the US navigated race hierarchies and *whiteness*, see: Stefano Luconi, "Italian Immigrants, Whiteness, and Race: A Regional Perspective," *Italian American Review* 11, no. 1 (2021): 4–26.

[7] Lauren Braun-Strumfels, *Partners in Gatekeeping: How Italy Shaped U.S. Immigration Policy over Ten Pivotal Years, 1891–1901* (Athens: Georgia UP, 2023).

[8] Lauren Braun-Strumfels, "'A Desirable Class of Homeseekers': Colonization, Race, and Italian Migration in the Progressive Era US South," *Journal of American Ethnic History* 43, no. 2 (2024): 34–69.

[9] Marco Armiero and Richard Tucker, eds., *Environmental History of Modern Migrations* (New York: Routledge, 2017); Roberta Biasillo, Claudio De Majo, and Daniele Valisena, "Environments of Italianness: For an Environmental History of Italian Migrations," *Modern Italy* 26, no. 2 (2021): 119–124.

[10] For a deeper analysis of this entanglement of urban politics, Italian diplomacy, and migrants' gardening skills and the environment, see Gilberto Mazzoli, "Italianness in the United States between migrants' informal gardening practices and agricultural diplomacy (1880–1912)," *Modern Italy* 26, no. 2 (2021): 199–215.

Furthermore, adopting the perspective of environmental history allows us to conceptualize these agricultural colonies as experimental spaces. Such a conceptualization is relevant for the following reasons. First, approached as experimental spaces, agricultural colonies reveal how, and which, scientific knowledge was produced to support their establishment, as well as which actors and institutions contributed to these knowledge discourses: perceptions regarding climates, soil surveys, and gardening experimentation were intertwined with migratory and colonial policies in terms of affecting the cultural construction of a place as suitable for establishing a settlement with a specific population group. In addition, rethinking the role of such experimental spaces in colonial practice underlines the complex entanglement between science and colonialism characterizing the beginning of the twentieth century.[11]

Second, such a conceptualization sheds new light on the historical relationship between US-American agriculture and immigration, while revealing just how experimental agriculture was in the United States at the turn of the twentieth century. One example is truck farming, which could be considered an experiment in terms of a more sustainable form of agriculture, which is why it caught the interest of the US government and the US Department of Agriculture (USDA).[12] At the time, truck farming became more and more common among US-American farmers for an array of reasons: changes in the dietary habits of city-dwellers following the increase of urban populations due to migration influxes, the diffusion of railroad networks, and refrigeration systems allowing for better transit and commerce of otherwise perishable vegetables. Added to this was the establishment of agricultural experiment stations and the end of slavery in the South, all of which concurred with the rise of the practice of truck farming.[13] Hence, the extent of the diffusion of truck farming as a mature industry was supported by many US-American actors at the same time as immigrants – like the Italians – became available as suitable farm laborers.

Finally, analyzing the actual agricultural practices and experiments, rather than exploring the Progressive Era debates concerning these colonies as a gateway for studying US race relations and the desirability of immigrants, reveals a

---

[11] Anne Kwaschik, "Die Verwissenschaftlichung des Kolonialen als kultureller Code und internationale Praxis um 1900," *Historische Anthropologie* 28 (2020): 399–423.

[12] Scott J. Peters and Paul A. Morgan, "The Country Life Commission Reconsidering a Milestone in American Agricultural History," *Agricultural History* 78, no. 3 (2004): 289–316.

[13] James L. Jr. McCorkle, "Moving Perishables to Market: Southern Railroads and the Nineteenth-Century Origins of Southern Truck Farming," *Agricultural History* 66, no. 1 (1992): 42–62; James L. Jr. McCorkle, "Agricultural Experiment Stations and Southern Truck Farming," *Agricultural History* 62, no. 2 (1988): 234–243.

much more complex picture of Italian immigration to the US. It highlights the role of migrants and their gardening skills as well as their willingness to experiment with crops that were native to their homeland but not to the US-American soil even though they were considered adaptable to the American climate. Furthermore, it highlights the active role of the Italian state in this transnational relationship: surely Italian governmental actors contributed to solving a pressing US-American question. At the same time, however, their participation in the dialogue was shaped by the opportunity of an economic and political – albeit informal – expansionism.

There were several actors who also contributed to imagining these experiments of agricultural colonization. Among them, we find Edmondo Mayor des Planches, who served as the Italian ambassador to the United States during 1901–1910, Prof. Antonio Ravaioli, the commercial delegate at the Italian embassy in Washington, Carl Bernhard Schmidt, a German recruiting agent for US railroad companies and senator in Colorado, and Louis Magid, the president of the Silk Association of America. Within this transoceanic network, science and scientists stood out with the specific task of proving the potential of the southern US states as prosperous rural colonies.

A pivotal institution between Italian and US parties was the Istituto Agricolo Coloniale Italiano (IACI)[14] founded in Florence in 1907 and which was tasked with providing colonial agents with the necessary scientific knowledge on agriculture and other sciences. Italy's foreign policy in these decades viewed its emigrant population as a colonial opportunity, and the founding of an institution such as the IACI should be understood as part of this policy. In the early documentation produced by the IACI and its scientific director, Gino Bartolommei Gioli, the presence of an emigrant population to be supported in the acclimatization phase was considered a major driver behind the creation of the institute. In its foundational charter, the IACI states that its foremost objectives were "to prepare agents who are specialists in colonial agriculture, for service to our migrant population" and "to act as an information center for the diffusion of reports on colonial culture, and on the economic and agrarian conditions of non-European countries subject to agricultural immigration."[15] In this context, the institute was tasked with scientifically backing the interests of Italian communities, the state, and the Americanization attempts of US officials. Italian agronomists such as Tito Tabet and Gino Coppini were tasked with exploring the conditions of the environments in which a colonization project was planned. Through experimental cultivation, soil sur-

---

14 Italian Colonial Agricultural Institute, hereinafter IACI.
15 Istituto Agricolo Coloniale Italiano, *Statuto* (1909): 5–6.

veys, and by studying the climate, they contributed to creating a body of information on US-American environments that would serve Italian colonial efforts. By uncovering underexplored avenues of the global history of Italy and its expansionist ambitions, this paper aims to investigate the interplay between science, race, and transnational politics with the environment that occurred between Italy and the US during the early decades of the twentieth century.

The paper is structured in two main parts driven by two research questions. First, what was the role of climate, agricultural knowledge, and the environment in the transnational relationship between Italy and the United States aimed at regulating migratory flows? Second, how did professional agronomists contribute to creating scientific knowledge in support of these experimental agricultural colonization projects proposed by the Italian government? Hence, the first part explores the settings of this entanglement of the Italian and US foreign policies regarding the possible creation of agricultural settlements. This phase saw the emergence of the idea of a necessary *acclimatization* of Italian migrants to the areas in which an agricultural colonization project was planned. These ideas of *acclimatization* needed scientific support, which is why the second part of the paper focuses on the work of the IACI and its agronomists to explore the role of a scientific institution in Italian foreign policy toward the United States at this time. Using the documentation it produced, it is possible to unveil perceptions and understandings of the new climates and environments but also ideas on how to exploit new US-American regions through agricultural experimentation.

This paper relies on multiple primary sources: US-American newspapers, correspondence between Italian diplomats and US-American landowners held at the Historical Diplomatic Archives of the Italian Foreign Ministry in Rome, and archival briefs and research papers produced by the agronomists of the IACI.

1 Contextualizing Climates: Gardening, Race, and the Politics toward *Acclimatizing* Italian Emigrants at the Turn of the Twentieth Century

Between 1880 and 1924, more than four million Italians reached the United States, the majority settling in the large cities on the East Coast.[16] Many Italian migrants

---

[16] Humbert Nelli, *From Immigrants to Ethnics: The Italian Americans* (Oxford: University Press, 1983), 62.

practiced agriculture on the outskirts of major US cities as a part-time activity, while their main occupations were in the city, in factories or construction.[17] At the time, Italians alongside immigrants from Eastern and Southern Europe were depicted as unhealthy subjects, living in US-American cities that were, in turn, described as unhealthy places for them. Immigrant neighborhoods were known for being overcrowded and for their poor hygienic conditions. Furthermore, US authorities feared the political activism of these migrants. These narratives contributed to creating an "urban problem" that needed a solution.[18]

A possible solution started to emerge with the new century as the Italian government pursued relocation plans involving various actors at different times. One of their main advocates was Edmondo Mayor des Planches. During his term as ambassador in Washington (1901–1910), he welcomed a few inspectors and scientific experts sent by the Italian government to evaluate the environmental and economic conditions of the land designated for establishing agricultural colonies. In 1904, Mayor des Planches suggested to the Italian government that it should send Adolfo Rossi, inspector of the Royal Immigration Department of Italy, to the United States. During his journey across Italian settlements in the United States in 1904, Rossi visited several Italian vegetable gardens on the outskirts of San Antonio and came to view Texas as a suitable destination for Italians, where there were promising opportunities for agriculture. At the same time, he admitted to being skeptical of a possible relocation of Italians to California due to the seasonal (and thus unstable) need for agricultural laborers in the wine industry.[19]

In 1904, Prof. Antonio Ravaioli, commercial delegate at the Italian embassy in Washington, released a report on the possibilities of agricultural colonization in the United States using Italian migrants. First, Ravaioli looked at agricultural colonization as a remedy to the heavy inflow of Italian migrants to urban areas. His report examined every region of the United States, describing the preexisting Italian agricultural colonies and reflecting on which states might have offered better conditions for establishing new settlements, such as Georgia, North and South Carolina, Virginia, Louisiana, Arkansas, and Texas. Second, Ravaioli stated that climatic similarities between these areas and Italy would lead to cultural familiarity through crop cultivation and thus make Italian migrants feel at home. Ravaioli also suggested ways to improve the agricultural and economic conditions of the South after the abolition of slavery. In his view, these lands found their soil impoverished by extensive cultivation. A substitution, or juxtaposition, of a new

---

17 Luigi Villari, *Gli Stati Uniti d'America e l'Emigrazione Italiana* (Milano: Fratelli Treves, 1912), 256–257.
18 Mazzoli, *"Italianness* in the United States."
19 Bollettino dell'emigrazione italiana (BEI) no. 16 (1904): 104–108.

form of intensive cultivation, such as truck crops for vegetable markets, would allow the soil to regain its fertility. Furthermore, continued Ravaioli, the introduction of a European workforce – seen as already familiar with this type of intensive cultivation – was seen as favorable: "among them, the Italians are the most suited, particularly due to the warm climates."[20]

On January 5, 1905, Lous B. Magid, president of the Silk Association of America, wrote a letter to Mayor des Planches with the aim of building a colony of silkworm farmers in Georgia consisting of a few Italian families. Magid opened the letter – written in Italian – by stating that despite his German heritage, he was very much acquainted with Italy and its culture as he had graduated from the Istituto Bacologico in Padua in northern Italy. Since then, Magid had entered the silk industry and spent the previous three years planning the introduction of silkworm cultivation and a spinning mill in Tallulah Falls, a mountain village in Georgia. Across an area of 3,000 acres, he had already planted 200,000 mulberry trees. Magid went on to compare the US climate to the Italian climate, stating that "the weather conditions in Georgia, and hence in Tallulah Falls, are precisely the same as they are in Northern Italy" and, furthermore, "Georgia is currently anxious to attract migrants from Italy."[21]

Magid more than once emphasized his strong preference for families coming from the north of Italy consisting of at least four workers each. He would then provide each family with an area of 25 acres to cultivate legumes and vegetables next to the mulberry trees. "I believe that this could be very attractive to an Italian family," added Magid, "this area already hosts 10,000 American families interested in silk cultivation, but there is no doubt that Italian families would profit from their greater agricultural expertise."[22] Louis Magid invited Dr. L. H. Mandowsky, a physician on the *Prinzessin Irene* of the North German Lloyd steamship company, to be the scientific advisor for this colonization project. Dr. Mandowsky's first role was to inspect the climate conditions of Tallulah Falls. Later on, he would become the physician of the colony. When interviewed about his task by the *Atlanta Journal* on January 4, 1904, Mandowsky emphasized his expertise in such colonization projects, citing his previous collaboration with North German Lloyd. When asked why Tallulah Falls was a suitable place for setting up a silk colony with Italian migrants, he replied that "first, the climate here is ideal" since it is comparable with Italy, and second,

---

[20] "La colonizzazione agricola negli Stati Uniti in rapporto all'immigrazione italiana. Relazione del Prof. A. Ravaioli addetto commerciale a Washington," BEI no. 4 (1904): 18. This the following quotations from Italian sources have been translated into English by the author.
[21] ASDMAE, Fondo Ambasciata Italiana a Washington (1902–1912), b. 119, f. 2456.
[22] Ibid.

the Italian Colony that Mr. Magid will bring here will be one of the most thrifty and honest kind, as they come from Northern Italy. They understand the culture and manufacture of silk to perfection. They will not only raise silk, but they understand raising vegetables and making the finest wine and cheese in the world.[23]

The letter and the newspaper article highlight the assumptions made by authorities and scientific experts that the American South was a suitable destination for Italian migrants due to the climate being similar to that of the Italian peninsula. This is also one of the sources associating a migrant background (in this case northern Italy) with specific agricultural skills. Nevertheless, this last presumption – that northern Italians were associated with good agricultural skills – shows that a racist bias against Italians from southern Italy existed on an institutional level. Also, the possibility of growing vegetables for their own consumption was here used to attract migrants to move to Georgia for this colonization project.

The "urban problem" was still an urgent topic in March 1907. *The Sun*, a New York City newspaper, published an article titled "For Italian Farm Colonies," discussing the possibility of dispersing Italians from East Coast cities to rural settlements as part of a "plan to lessen congestion and crime in big cities." The article mentioned the proposal of a scheme for agricultural colonization "to relieve the congested districts in large cities, particularly in New York, Boston, Washington, New Orleans, and Chicago, and to reduce the percentage of criminality." According to the journalist at *The Sun*, such criminality was "the direct result of factory life and the unnatural conditions which surround the immigrants in a large city." This association with urban life and crime was reiterated with the purpose of supporting the relocation of urban Italians, as they were living in "unnatural conditions."[24] Relocating urban migrants meant putting them in an environment considered more "natural" and healthier for them.

In 1907, the Italian government sent another inspector from Rome, Dr. Brunialti. *The Sun* wrote that Dr. Brunialti would start a "tour of inspection through the states of the central West and the Northwest" in order to explore possibilities to relocate urban Italians to Wisconsin and Minnesota. On this tour, Dr. Brunialti was accompanied by Carl Bernhard Schmidt, a German recruiting agent for railroad companies and a senator in Colorado, Guido Servadio, Italian vice-consul in Denver, and Arminio Conte, Italian consul in Milwaukee. When interviewed, Consul Conte claimed that "Italians are naturally farmers. They are accustomed to

---

23 Ibid. The interview comes from a clipping of the newspaper *Atlanta Journal* found in the archival folder 119.
24 "For Italian Farm Colonies," *The Sun* (New York), March 3, 1907, 12.

living in the open air and they are not adapted to factory work."[25] This statement, imbued with a deterministic misconception of Darwin's ideas, was instrumental in communicating to the US government that the countryside was the ideal setting for Italians.

Relocating Italian immigrants from the crowded urban East, as stated by Consul Conte, had the aim "to preserve the virtues of our people and the good name of our race in America" but also to relieve US-American cities from crime.[26] In order to do so, the Italian government knew that financial aid to immigrants was needed and that "this large sum of money must be raised in some way," possibly with the cooperation of US-American landowners. In addition, the article concluded by reflecting on whether the climate of the north or the south of the United States would better suit Italians. Consul Conte stated that "the climate in the northwest is too cold and the winters too severe for our people [. . .] states further south are favored because of their warmer climate."[27] Interestingly, this article published in *The Sun* is one of the rare sources to mention the possibility of relocating Italians to the north of the US. In fact, in working together, the US and Italian governments had the common aim of relocating Italian immigrants from East Coast cities to the rural South.

In these sources, we see a difference emerging in how immigrants were portrayed in the American Northeast and in the South. As we have seen, in the urban North immigrants from Eastern and Southern Europe were depicted as an (urban) problem. In the rural South, on the other hand, immigrants were portrayed as a solution. After the end of slavery, many African Americans started the Great Migration to the industrial North, leading to Southern landowners and politicians being interested in finding immigrant labor to replace them. For landowners at the time, there was neither an immigration problem nor an urban question (which, in fact, became more relevant in the first decade of the twentieth century, with the massive influx of immigrants from Europe) but more – as pointed out by Katherine Benton-Cohen – of a "race problem."[28] Attracting immigrants from Europe not only meant available cheap labor but also a significant increase in the *whiteness* of the American South. During this period, race was one of the main reasons driving

---

25 Ibid.
26 Ibid.
27 Ibid.
28 Katherine Benton-Cohen, *Inventing the Immigration Problem: The Dillingham Commission and its Legacy* (Cambridge: Harvard UP, 2018), 200–205.

US-American landowners and politicians to maintain relationships with Italian diplomats and promote the creation of agricultural colonies with Italian migrants.[29]

Alongside the perceived "race problem," the environment also entered the scene as an important factor in framing the foreign policies of these decades. The reference to Italians as being suited to the climate of the South is a recurring argument in sources produced by US-American and Italian authorities. The idea to put migrants to work in these areas was strongly linked to their easy *acclimatization* to a new environment. Debates concerning acclimatization had characterized the scientific community in many European countries since the end of the eighteenth century and throughout the nineteenth: scientists and academics in disciplines such as geography, botany, medicine, biology, and anthropology fiercely discussed "how plants and animals may be introduced – either artificially or naturally – into climatic regions different from their domestic habitat so that they may survive and propagate in the new environment."[30] Soon, questions regarding the acclimatization of humans in new territories also entered the debates, along with the rise of many acclimatization societies in Germany, France, Great Britain, and the United States.[31] In European empires such as the French and the British, discourses related to the acclimatization of plants, animals, and humans played a major role in influencing politics and settlement projects. This interest resulted in the production of a large body of scientific literature filled with statistical data on many areas of the world.[32] Collecting climate data was a common daily practice in the US in the nineteenth century, also in a few intentional communities such as the religious and cooperative settlement of New Harmony, Indiana, and the German ethnic colony of Saxonburg, Pennsylvania. This practice played a key role in

---

[29] For a deeper analysis of how Italian immigrants to the American South navigated racial hierarchies, see Jessica Barbata Jackson, *Dixie's Italians: Sicilians, Race, and Citizenship in the Jim Crow Gulf South* (Baton Rouge: Louisiana State University Press, 2020), 15–31.

[30] David N. Livingstone, "Human Acclimatization: Perspectives on a contested field of inquiry in science, medicine, and geography," *History of science* 25 (1987): 359–394, 359. For a deeper analysis of the debates regarding *acclimatization*, see also Warwick Anderson, "Climates of Opinion: Acclimatization in Nineteenth Century France and England," *Victorian Studies* 35, no. 2 (1992): 135–157; Costanza Bonelli, "Clima, razza, colonizzazione. Nascita e sviluppo della medicina tropicale in Italia (fine XIX sec. – metà XX sec.)" (PhD diss., Sapienza Università di Roma 2019), 303–358.

[31] David N. Livingstone, "Human Acclimatization," 363.

[32] Michael A. Osborne, "Acclimatizing the World: A History of the Paradigmatic Colonial Science," *Osiris* 15 (2000): 135–151.

influencing the decision on whether and when agricultural experimentation should be attempted by the settlers.[33]

We also find references to this idea of *acclimatization* in Italian sources. In 1895, Vincenzo Grossi reflected on this topic on the pages of Italian journal *Nuova Antologia* in a long article on Italian emigration to the Americas. Here, the Italian physician pointed out that it was necessary for the Italian government to start to regulate emigration. A starting and fundamental point in terms of pursuing this aim, Grossi underlined, would be the *acclimatization* of the emigrants to new areas in order to avoid human losses.[34] Even if he in his research mainly referred to equatorial regions with less temperate climates, Grossi nonetheless brought the climate argument to the discussion concerning the selection of possible sites for Italian agricultural colonies in the US. Indeed, climate considerations were to become one of the fundamental questions for the Italian government to grapple with when managing the country's migratory flows. These tropes – race and climate – characterized the attempts to create agricultural colonies, as they were often repeated and discussed by Italian and US-American actors. Let us now explore how the necessary scientific support to these agricultural colonization plans was provided by an Italian institution.

2 Scientizing Climates: Professional Agronomists and the Italian Colonial Agricultural Institute

The Istituto Agricolo Coloniale Italiano (IACI) was founded in Florence in 1907 by Gino Bartolommei Gioli, a member of the renowned Accademia dei Georgofili, an institution devoted to the study of agriculture, forestry, and botany.[35] Gioli started reflecting on the necessity of an agricultural colonial institution in Italy in the first years of the twentieth century after he had spent a few months in Eritrea studying the possibility of agricultural colonization in that area.[36] The necessity to train ex-

---

[33] See Claudia Roesch, "Talking about the Weather: Producing Climate Knowledge as Colonial Practice in Intentional Communities in the Americas, 1820s–1840s" in this book.
[34] Vincenzo Grossi, "L'emigrazione Italiana in America," *Nuova Antologia* LV, no. III (1895): 19. In italics in the original text. Grossi uses the Italian word "acclimatazione."
[35] The Accademia dei Georgofili was founded in 1753 in Florence to promote and improve the study of agriculture, mostly in Tuscany. It gained the status of national institution in 1897.
[36] As noted by Franco Cardini and Isabella Gagliardi, the Italian Botanical Society also shared the same interests in creating an institution to address colonial agriculture in the early years of twentieth century. For a deeper analysis of the history of the foundation of the IACI and its relationship with the history of Italian colonialism, see Franco Cardini and Isabella Gagliardi, *Italy*

perts in colonial agriculture led to the creation of the IACI, with Gioli becoming its science director.[37] A year after its launch, the IACI introduced specific courses on colonial agriculture, both theoretical and practical. For the academic year 1908–1909, the IACI offered its young students courses such as: Colonial Agriculture, Colonial Botany, Economic Geography and History of the Colonies, Colonial Zootechnics and Livestock Hygiene, Chemistry, Colonial Engineering, Hygiene of the Colonist, and foreign languages such as English, French, and Spanish. When advertising these courses, Gioli emphasized the link between agricultural colonization and emigration, while claiming that the Italian population had a predisposition for agriculture and that most Italian emigrants work in agriculture.[38]

In 1907, right after its establishment, the IACI started publishing *L'Agricoltura Coloniale*, its official journal. The first issue featured the scientific agenda of the journal and once again presented Gioli's reflection on the link between emigration and the necessity to have specific technical training to pursue colonization aims. In fact, he stated that "in Italy we cannot address the migratory problem without considering our colonial unpreparedness." He then claimed that the role of the institute would be exactly to fill this lack of technical skills, writing that the IACI "will undoubtedly be one of the most suitable tools for the technical preparation of future agricultural colonizers, whether they want to use the resources of our colonies or whether they intend to establish themselves in foreign countries and colonies."[39] These words also confirm that at an institutional level, Italian élites looked at emigration with a colonial gaze. It is also interesting to note Gioli's opinion regarding Italian emigrants, whom he described as having "innate dispositions [. . .] to adapt to the most disparate climatic environments" and "truly admirable natural aptitudes in the exercise of agriculture."[40] Gioli also commented

---

and Lands, in *L'Istituto Agronomico per l'Oltremare. La sua storia*, AA.VV. (Firenze: Masso delle Fate, 2007), 12–37.

37 Mori Attilio, "L'istituto Agricolo Coloniale e la sua Origine, Atti dell'Istituto Agricolo Coloniale Italiano," *L'Agricultura Coloniale* 1 (1907): 74–79.

38 Gino Bartolommei Gioli, "ISTITUTO AGRICOLO COLONIALE ITALIANO: FIRENZE," *Bullettino della R. Società Toscana di Orticultura* 3.a serie, vol. 13, no. 7 (1908): 209–212.

For a deeper analysis of the scientific content of the agricultural colonial training offered by the IACI, see Riccardo De Robertis, "From colonialism to cooperation: The training of tropical agricultural experts in Florence (1908–1968)," *Journal of Agriculture and Environment for International Development (JAEID)* 113, no. 2 (2019): 253–271; Riccardo De Robertis, "Observe and imitate the work of the colonizer: Agricultural education for Africans in the Italian colonies," *Italia Contemporanea* 302 (2023): 34–55.

39 Gino Bartolommei Gioli, "Il Programma dell'Agricoltura Coloniale," *L'Agricultura Coloniale* 1 (1907): 2.

40 Ibid., 1.

on what he rephrased as the "Italian problem," namely the tendency of Italian emigrants to settle in the US-American cities on the East Coast instead of looking for agricultural jobs in rural areas. In this regard, Gioli agrees with the majority of Italian politicians and intellectuals supporting these projects – such as Mayor des Planches – reaffirming that agricultural jobs were more suitable for emigrants and would allow them to increase their wealth and social standing. Gioli concluded with a statement that summed up the importance of migratory flows for the political agenda of the IACI: "therefore it is precisely towards the land that we must direct our migratory current, without distinction of social class."[41]

The Institute's official publication included reports compiled by experts sent to the Americas with the purpose of evaluating colonization proposals submitted to the Italian government by US-American railway and mining companies looking for immigrant manpower. These agronomists were tasked with verifying soil conditions, fertility, and which types of crops were suitable for cultivation on certain land. The first issue of *L'Agricultura Coloniale* reported that on May 25, 1907, *La Tribuna Italiana Transatlantica*, an Italian American newspaper from Chicago, published a letter addressed to its director, Alessandro Mastro-Valerio, who besides his job as a journalist was also a social worker close to Jane Addams and a strong advocate of creating agricultural colonies with Italian migrants.[42] The author of this letter was C.B. Schmidt, the above-mentioned German recruiting agent who had helped create agricultural colonies with Mennonites in Kansas and with Germans and Italians in Pueblo, Colorado. Schmidt also worked as a recruiting agent for the company Rock Island-Frisco System. In his letter, Schmidt informed Mastro-Valerio that the US government had studied the environmental and economic condition of some areas in Texas and the Gulf of Mexico in order to host Italian migrants from

---

41 Ibid.

42 Alessandro Mastro-Valerio was born in Italy in 1855. After he emigrated to the United States in 1882, he started to work at Hull House together with Jane Addams and studied Italian settlements in Chicago. He was the editor of the US newspaper *La Tribuna Italiana* and contributed to the Industrial Commission, compiling surveys about Italian colonies in rural areas in the US, such as Vineland in New Jersey, Sunnyside and Tontitown in Arkansas, Asti in Sonoma County, California, and other settlements of truck farmers around Memphis, Tennessee and in Louisiana and Mississippi. He was personally involved in establishing an agricultural colony in Daphne, Alabama. In 1890 and 1893, he led a group of Italians from Chicago to Alabama, receiving assistance from the USDA to obtain seeds, shrubs, tools, and agricultural publications. From these reports, it emerges that Mastro-Valerio shared the opinion of the Italian diplomats that sending migrants to farm could resolve the overcrowding in some American cities. See JoAnne Ruvoli, "An Agricultural Colony in Alabama: Hull-House and the Chicago Italians," in *Small Towns, Big Cities: The Urban Experience of Italian Americans*, eds. Dennis Barone and Stefano Luconi (New York: AIHA, 2010), 146–164.

the East Coast cities and create agricultural colonies together with them. The "Italian problem," as a problem of the US-American urban East Coast, was also mentioned in this article, once again repeating the claim that agricultural colonization could be the solution to overcrowded cities. In cities, Italian emigrants could hardly find favorable living conditions as they competed with workers of other nationalities. US-American society was largely unwelcoming when it came to Italian immigrants as a result of their precarious situation. However, Schmidt viewed the narrative pushed by US-American institutions that the Italians were a menace as full of prejudices. He instead believed that Italian migrants were good workers, but just not well-acquainted with the economic possibilities that US-American agriculture could offer them.[43]

Schmidt also said a few remarkable words about the agricultural skills of Italian emigrants, highlighting their importance to the economic development of the US. The article went on to report on the experience of Schmidt in settling a colony with Italian migrants in Pueblo, Colorado, in the previous years. Some 200 Italian families were employed as fruit growers and truck farmers, and this group achieved great results both economically and in terms of respectability. They were praised for the luxuriant vegetable gardens they set up through hard work and for their frugality and reliability as workers. Schmidt also reflected on the possible motives why Italian migrants became uninterested in pursuing agricultural jobs after immigrating to the United States:

> I am convinced that the main reason for why so few Italian emigrants devote themselves to agriculture lies in the fact that they are completely unaware of the opportunities of acquiring inhabited land in our vast country on very advantageous terms. They come here with the preconception that they have to work only for wages, because wages are higher here than in Italy, and because some of their compatriots exploit this idea for their own profit.[44]

With these words, Schmidt confirmed his position as one of the strongest advocates of the relocation plans of Italian migrants from the cities on the East Coast to the American South. The article ended by mentioning a plan for agricultural colonization proposed by the Rock Island-Frisco System and already approved by the Italian government. According to this plan, families of Italian migrants who relocated to Texas could, in addition to being able to buy land for reasonable prices, still benefit from the Homestead Acts, which would allow them to get some 160 acres of land for free following a legal declaration of intention to become a

---

43 "Colonizzazione agraria italiana nel Sud-Ovest degli Stati Uniti," *L'Agricoltura Coloniale* 1 (Firenze: IACI, 1907), 65–67.
44 Ibid.

US citizen and some additional smaller bureaucratic procedures.[45] The Italian government showed interest in this project and activated its experts in agronomy – through the IACI – to visit the area and study its environmental conditions.

Hence, the IACI in 1907 sent the agronomist Tito Tabet to southwest Texas to report on soil conditions and fertility with regard to the creation of the abovementioned agricultural colony promoted by the Rock Island-Frisco System railway company. To pursue this objective, the company employed a professor of agriculture (named Dr. White) with close links to the recruiting agent C.B. Schmidt. The Rock Island Company put some effort into soliciting the cooperation of landowners and aimed to build a society to provide settler families with "soil, home, tools, livestock, and seeds."[46]

In his report, published in 1908, Tabet wrote several pages analyzing the current conditions for agriculture in the United States while also describing his journey from New York to Texas during which he also visited Kansas, Colorado, New Mexico, and Tontitown – the Italian colony in Arkansas managed by Father Bandini. Tabet also visited a private ranch, not far from Saint Gertrude, Texas, that was managed by Robert J. Kleberg II.[47] For Tabet, this farm served as an example of what could be achieved with agricultural colonization in the area of southwest Texas. Kleberg had set up his farm seven years earlier with the help of Dr. Gino Coppini, an Italian agronomist who had graduated from the Agrarian School in Pisa. In 1905, Coppini had founded an experimental agricultural farm in Raymondville, Texas, with the aim of creating "the model of the Italian Colony, to serve as a guide for all the agricultural Italian colonies in the United States." Coppini collaborated closely with the IACI, and reports of his agricultural experiments – on cotton, olive trees, and grapevine in particular – were published in the institute's journal.[48] Kleberg's farm was surrounded by thriving vegetable gardens full of cabbage, onions, tomatoes, celery, cucumbers, beans, lettuce, carrots, and more. These vegetables were then sold at markets in nearby towns such

---

[45] Ibid.

[46] Tito Tabet, *Per la Colonizzazione Agraria del Texas* (Firenze: Ramella, 1908), 3–4. Held at library of the Italian Agronomic Overseas Institute, Florence, this report was originally published in *L'Agricultural Coloniale* anno II, vol. 1 (February 1908).

[47] Kleberg II was the legal counselor of the landowner and livestock entrepreneur Richard King. After King's death, Kleberg ran his ranch. See: https://www.tshaonline.org/handbook/entries/king-richard.

[48] Coppini wrote these words to Edmondo Mayor des Planches on March 11, 1905. This letter also contains Coppini's ideas concerning agricultural colonization in the US. ASDMAE, Fondo Ambasciata Italiana a Washington (1902–1912), b.143, f. 3166. For a deeper analysis of the experience of Coppini and his role in connection to the IACI, see Gino Coppini, "La coltivazione del Cotone ne Sud-Ovest Texas," *L'Agricultura Coloniale* anno III, vol. 1 (1909): 1–24.

as Corpus Christi. Tabet was struck by the potential of these lands with regard to truck farming. In support of this view, he added to his survey a comparative list of the crops cultivated there along with a list of the average prices for each vegetable in the urban markets. Despite being a private ranch, it represented the ideal agricultural experiment, which interested a governmental institution such as the IACI. This example also highlights the complex layers of actors and knowledge involved in this agricultural diplomacy and how such an entanglement of actors and knowledge shaped these agricultural experiments.

After several weeks with Kleberg and Coppini, Dr. Tabet specified three evaluation criteria to adhere to when choosing locations to create agricultural colonies: salubrity, potable water, and a range of suitable weather temperatures. He also focused on setting the "fundamental parameters for agricultural exploitation": the potential fertility of the soil, the availability of water in relation to suitable crops for the chosen place, and the climate. In concluding the report, Tabet made a comparison of the climate of south Texas with the "northern shores" of Sicily, writing that these two regions shared a "salubrious climate and mild temperature, but with lower rates of rainfall."[49] By comparing these two climates, Dr. Tabet's objective was to make Texas appear familiar to those reading the report. In conclusion, Tabet wrote that if Texas was chosen as a destination for Italian emigration, it could become "the new California" and thus successful. Tabet's evaluation of the climate of Texas provided the scientific background to support the agricultural colonization projects with Italian migrants in Texas that the Italian government wished to pursue and for which it activated the experts from the IACI.[50]

This scientification of colonization projects provided by the IACI sought to support the argument for relocating Italians, thereby adding significant weight to it. Furthermore, in addition to the inquiries published in *L'Agricultura Coloniale* and the IACI's reports, there is a large amount of correspondence on specific agronomic matters held in the archives of the Italian Foreign Ministry. For instance, the Italian government asked the USDA for numerous scientific publications on various topics: the latest news in cultivation techniques and soil experiments, re-

---

[49] Tabet, *Per la Colonizzazione Agraria del Texas*, 31.
[50] Echoes of these colonization projects also reached the Italian Colonial Institute in Rome. Texas was among the few reconnaissance missions undertaken by the Italian Colonial Institute in the first years after it was founded. Furthermore, in 1908, *Rivista Coloniale*, the official journal of the institute, published an essay about Italian emigration and the colonization of Texas that mentioned the idea of creating the Italian Society for Texas to support such colonization. Gustavo Chiesi, "La nostra Emigrazione agli Stati Uniti e la Colonizzazione Italiana nel Texas," *Rivista Coloniale*, Fascicoli I, vol. 5 (Rome, 1908).

ports on crop diseases, innovations in farmers' tools and machinery. There were also some requests for particular varieties of crops and sample sets of chemical fertilizers to be used in Italy for experimentation.[51]

The correspondence between the IACI president Gioli and Ambassador Mayor des Planches is worth mentioning since it supports the argument that the IACI gave scientific backing to these experimental agricultural colonization projects with Italian migrants. On May 2, 1909, Gioli wrote a letter to Mayor des Planches, carefully describing the IACI's educational activities related to scientific and agricultural matters, such as courses on colonial agriculture and botanical experimentation with imported seeds and species. Gioli suggested that it was perhaps possible to introduce the crops uncovered in this research to Italy. Gioli also emphasized how IACI initiatives had already found support from Italians abroad who were interested in agricultural issues. The purpose of this letter was to promote the institute's expertise in colonial agriculture and to offer scientific support from the IACI for agricultural colonization projects in the United States. Moreover, Gioli asked Mayor des Planches to intercede with US institutions (such as the USDA) to send agricultural products and publications to the IACI.[52] This last request matched the intentions of the Italian Ministry of Agriculture, Industry, and Commerce, which in 1908 had started to collect data on educational and experimental institutions working with agriculture and forestry around the world. Accordingly, Mayor des Planches in January 1909 wrote a letter to the USDA General Secretary James Wilson to obtain such information.[53]

A few words must be added regarding the role of James Wilson as the general secretary of the USDA. Wilson started his mandate in 1897 and was determined to end the reputation of the USDA as a mere provider of free seed samples and an institution exclusively devoted to answering simple farming questions. It was Wilson's idea that the USDA should act more like a research center attached to a university. This policy shift led to a change in the wider scientific practice of the Progressive Era, in which the boundaries between scientific professions were not particularly defined. The USDA started to become more interested in bacteriology and soil fertility, and in 1897, the Bureau for Seed and Plant Introduction, known as the "plant explorers" team was founded as well. This bureau was imbued with the idea that improving agriculture meant improving society: many USDA scien-

---

51 ASDMAE, Fondo Ambasciata Italiana a Washington (1902–1912), b.119.
52 Ibid., b.119, f. 2471.
53 Ibid. For the correspondence, ASDMAE, Fondo Ambasciata Italiana a Washington (1902–1912), b.119, f. 2457. For further reading on the history of USDA and James Wilson, see Philip J. Pauly, *Fruits and Plains: The Horticultural Transformation of America* (Cambridge: Harvard UP, 2007), 99–130.

tists believed that living on a good soil would lead to a happier life (typical of the ethos of the Progressive Era).[54]

Interestingly, not all reports published by the IACI were in favor of agricultural colonization projects. As we have seen, along with soil fertility, the perception of climate played a major role when evaluating suitable locations for agricultural colonies. In a few cases, the presence of diseases, such as malaria, was also an important consideration – not to say the main consideration – that experts took into account in their reports and that could impact the evaluation.[55] During his reconnaissance of the lands to the southwest of Norfolk, Virginia, the agronomist Guido Rossati delivered a negative verdict with regard to settling a colony in this area. First, wrote Rossati, these areas were mostly swamplands, which, in order to become profitable for cultivation, required intensive drainage followed by the heavy use of fertilizers, both natural and chemical. Such drainage processes would be very expensive; however, they could make the soil suitable for garden crops (*ortaglie* in Italian) such as potatoes, peas, cabbage, tomatoes, spinach, eggplants, and strawberries, but not for fruit trees and crops with longer roots, which are unable to penetrate soil rich in clay. Second, in addition to such difficulties, Rossati noted the great presence of mosquitoes and the high danger of malarial fever that "our immigrants" would face. Finally, it is interesting to notice that in case the government attempted to set up a colony in that area, Rossati suggested employing migrants from areas of central and southern Italy with a similar climate and swampy soil, such as the Maremma area in Tuscany, the Pontine Marshes in Lazio, the plains in Basilicata, and the Simeto Valley in Sicilia. Once again, we have evidence of an IACI report specifying which migrants were suitable for possible agricultural colony sites based on their experience of certain climatic backgrounds. Rossati closed his report by saying that there were more suitable areas for colonization in the United States.[56]

---

54 Mark I. Finlay, "Science, Promotion, and Scandal: Soil Bacteriology, Legume Inoculation, and the American Campaign for Soil Improvement in the Progressive Era," in *New Perspectives on the History of Life Sciences and Agriculture*, eds. D. Phillips and S. Kingsland (2015): 205–229, Springer Verlag. See also Stuart Shulman, "The Business of Soil Fertility: A Convergence of Urban-Agrarian Concern in the Early 20th Century," *Organization & Environment* 12, no. 4 (1999): 401–424; Mark D. Hersey "What We Need Is a Crop Ecologist: Ecology as an Agricultural Science in Progressive Era America," *Agricultural History* 85 (2011): 297–321.
55 Malaria has been a variable in the choice for a new place to settle found in guides for emigrants. In fact, it often served as an actor itself with a large impact on the success – or failure – of a colony. See Marco Armiero, "Migrants and the Making of the American Landscape," Armiero and Tucker (2017), 53–70.
56 BEI no. 16 (1904): 35–41.

These institutional actors shared many beliefs regarding how and where Italian migrants should settle in the US. As the correspondence and reports show, scientists and politicians built a shared network in which they acted on and shared their ideas. An example of this is presented by Guido Rossati when he joined Adolfo Rossi, the inspector of the Royal Immigration Department of Italy, on his trip to the US at the beginning of 1904. They were sent to the country following the suggestion of the influential Ambassador Mayor des Planches. As scientific experts, they were asked to evaluate certain patches of land in the states of Mississippi, Louisiana, and Arkansas. In his report, Rossati took an additional aspect of the land into account. He claimed that the area of the Mississippi Delta, in addition to being suitable for the cultivation of cotton, was also extremely good for experimenting with the production of all kinds of vegetables due to its fertile soil and strategic location. The area in question was located between a few large railroad nodes, namely, the Yazoo and Mississippi Valley Railroad, the Illinois Central Railroad, and the Southern Railway, which would have allowed farmers to sell their produce as far away as the urban markets in Saint Louis and Chicago. However, Rossati added that despite these favorable conditions, the climate of the area was particularly unhealthy during the summer months. This was due to the heavy presence of mosquitoes and the custom of drinking rainwater collected in washbowls, which was a source of malaria for farmers. Nevertheless, Rossati concluded: "Italians, for climatic reasons, are considered suitable for the American South, and are also welcome there for their reputation as good, honest, and modest workers."[57] These experiments of agricultural colonization in the American South failed due to a lack of cooperation between Italy and the United States and due to the reluctance of Italian emigrants to accept the economic conditions of the proposed settlements.

Conclusion

In 1916, the IACI reprinted, as a separate pamphlet, a report written by O.G. Capra originally published in July that same year in *L'Agricoltura Coloniale*. This pamphlet titled *The Colonisation in the United States* reflected on the possibilities and attempts concerning agricultural colonization in the United States, emphasizing the role of railroad companies and landowners. It stated how these experiments were complicated and slowed down by bureaucracy but also stimulated by speculation and a hunger for profit. Capra confirmed the interests of Italian politicians

---

57 BEI no. 14 (1904): 13.

in the agricultural colonization of Africa when he wrote: "if we are real patriots, we must work with any means to limit emigration, the colonizing and agrarian forms [of emigration] in particular. In our time, we need cultivators for our countryside, for our colonies in Africa."[58] However, a few lines later, Capra expressed his support for agricultural colonization in the United States, claiming that Italian élites should look at such colonization as a way to solve the US-American emigration problem. He also added that "my impression is that for Italians in the United States, it would be convenient to leave the cities for the countryside, but they must be helped and directed to do this." Such convenience would increase – wrote Capra – as any produce could be cultivated in the US given that all climates were to be found in this country.[59] These words underline how the interest of the IACI with regard to the emigrant population in the United States continued even after the Italian government shifted its colonial policies toward the African continent.[60]

This paper focuses on exploring the transnational entanglement of science, race, economy, and politics with Italian migrants in the United States and their ecologies. It highlights the experimental aspect in a series of agricultural colonization projects carried out at the turn of the twentieth century and which saw the contribution of a wide array of political and institutional actors in both the US and Italy. All these actors had different aims but a common plan: create agricultural colonies to relocate Italian migrants from the East Coast cities to the rural South, where they could benefit from their gardening skills. These agricultural colonies turned out to be spaces of experimentation for both scientific and political purposes. Here, Italian agronomists tested crops and collected data on climates, while Italian diplomats viewed such spaces as useful for experimenting with their ideas of informal expansionism. At the same time, US-American actors – USDA scientists, Southern landowners, and governmental officials – also looked at these agricultural colonies as experimental spaces in terms of testing new forms of agricultural production that could improve urban food provisioning while changing the racial geography in both the city and the countryside. Never-

---

58 O.G. Capra, "La colonizzazione negli Stati Uniti" (Firenze: IACI, 1916), 6.
59 Ibid.
60 The interest of the IACI in North America with regard to informal agricultural colonization in the twentieth century is a research avenue that deserves more historical scrutiny and that could help unveil a longer trend in Italian agricultural diplomacy. On IACI and Africa, see Roberta Biasillo, "Socio-ecological colonial transfers: Trajectories of the Fascist agricultural enterprise in Libya (1922–43)," *Modern Italy* 26, no. 2 (2021): 181–198; Michele Sollai, "How to Feed an Empire? Agrarian Science, Indigenous Farming, and Wheat Autarky in Italian-Occupied Ethiopia, 1937–1941," *Agricultural History* 96, no. 3 (2022): 379–416.

theless, despite their failure, such political projects required scientific support, which led the Italian government to activate its experts.

Hence, this paper highlights the contribution of the Italian Agricultural Colonial Institute of Florence and its agronomists in the transnational relationship named *agricultural diplomacy*, while underlining its role in the scientization of colonial practice. The IACI experts, through a series of scientific surveys in the United States, provided the necessary knowledge in support of the plans of both the Italian and US-American governments. They observed climates, tested soils, and experimented with crops, keeping in mind which areas were suitable for a profitable *acclimatization* of the Italian migrants. Such *acclimatization* would have contributed to the success of the experimental colony, thus pleasing US authorities, which sought to clear the East Coast cities from the "problematic" Italian immigrants. Exploring these decades of Italian foreign policies through the lens of environmental history allows us to uncover untold aspects of the Italian migratory experience in the United States while at the same time also highlighting the role of experimental spaces and agricultural knowledge in the support of colonial endeavors.

Gilberto Mazzoli is a post-doctoral researcher in North American environmental history at the University of Konstanz tied to the ERC project "Off the Road: The Environmental Aesthetics of Early Automobility." His research focuses on the merging of environmental history with migration and urban histories in the nineteenth and twentieth centuries. His recent publications include "*Italianness* in the United States between migrants' informal gardening practices and agricultural diplomacy, 1880–1912," *Modern Italy* 26, no. 2 (2021).

Anne-Sophie Reichert
Knowledge in Motion: Research and Experimentation at Hellerau's School for Rhythmik

Abstract: In the early twentieth century, experimental dance emerged not only in the form of performance but also as a proto-scientific research practice in collaborations between dancers, social reformers, physiologists, and natural scientists. Analyzing the scientific presuppositions and methods of dance research in Emil Jaques-Dalcroze's rhythm school, I contextualize early experimental dance within the discourse on the "experimentalization of life" in the history of science. It is no coincidence that Dalcroze's *Rhythmik* occurred in an experimental environment, Germany's first garden city of Hellerau. Hellerau's founders emphasized bodily, sensory, aesthetic, and artistic practices as veritable forms of knowledge, complementing and contrasting mechanist, rationalist understandings of modern society. The willingness to supersede tradition, to explore and innovate, which characterizes experimental environments, allowed for dance to be taken seriously as a form of empirical research that would lead to new insights on the workings of body and mind, as well as to individual and social change. Dance as research results in dynamic forms of knowledge that may as such be historicized within emerging traditions of the history of knowledge. To account for experiential, somatic, and tactile forms of knowledge, I recuperate Farquhar's concept of "knowing practice"; in other words, thinking of knowledge as something that we do rather than have.

Keywords: experimental dance, artistic research, embodied knowledge, German Lebensreform, Émil Jaques-Dalcroze, Rudolf von Laban

Introduction

Scholars of experimental dance have suggested that dance emerged not only as a performance practice but also as a mode of proper scientific research that investigated human dynamic embodiments in close collaboration with natural and social scientists.[1] To probe and extend this proposition in the context of the history

---

1 See, for instance, Sabine Gehm, Pirkko Husemann, and Katharina von Wilcke, "Introduction," in *Wissen in Bewegung: Perspektiven der künstlerischen und wissenschaftlichen Forschung im Tanz,*

of knowledge, this article revolves around a concrete site of experimental dance research: Émile Jaques-Dalcroze's rhythm school in Germany's first garden city Hellerau.[2]

If experimental dance practice in the early twentieth century is to be taken seriously as a research practice, and I would argue that it should, it is a practice that results in epistemic processes, systems, and techniques and may as such be historicized within emerging traditions of the history of knowledge. After all, scholars in the history of knowledge have since its inception argued that knowledge of the sciences and arts practically overlaps and crosspollinates.[3] In this regard, I build on recent developments in the history of science, historical epistemology, the history of ideas, and the history of knowledge seeking to include people, practices, materials, and traditions of studying, learning, and knowing that exceed and subvert the primarily textual canon of classical Western science and knowledge.[4]

---

eds. Sabine Gehm et al. (Bielefeld: Transcript Verlag, 2007), 15–22; Anke Abraham "Künstlerisches Forschen in Wissenschaft und Bildung. Zur Anerkennung und Nutzung leiblich-sinnlicher Erkenntnispotenziale," in *Tanzpraxis in Der Forschung – Tanz als Forschungspraxis, Choreographie, Improvisation,Exploration*, eds. Susanne Quinten and Stephanie Schroedter (Bielefeld: Transcript Verlag, 2016), 19–36; Gabriele Klein, "Praktiken des Tanzens und des Forschens. Bruchstücke einer praxeologischen Tanzwissenschaft," in *Visionäre Bildungskonzepte im Tanz: kulturpolitisch handeln, tanzkulturell bilden, forschen und reflektieren*, eds. Margrit Bischof and Regula Nyffeler (Zurich: Chronos, 2009), 103–15; Claudia Fleischle-Braun, "Das Erbe Der Tanzmoderne Im Zeitgenössischen Kontext Ein Beispiel Kooperativer Praxisforschung," in *Tanzpraxis in der Forschung – Tanz als Forschungspraxis: Choreographie, Improvisation, Exploration*, eds. Susanne Quinten and Stephanie Schroedter (Bielefeld: Transcript Verlag, 2016), 49–60.

2 For this article, I rely on primary and secondary sources on experimental dance in Germany, Austria, and Switzerland. I do so based on the fact that the experimental dance movement of the 1910s–1930s, which provided the context for a "prototype of scientific-practical research about bodies, corporeality and movement in space and time" is distinct to the German-speaking world at the time. See Janet Adshead-Lansdale, "Tanzforschung," in *Tanz*, ed. Sibylle Dahms et al. (Stuttgart: Metzler Verlag, 2001), 28–36. However, experimental dance was already from the outset entangled with a variety of global influences and branched out internationally with the onset of the two world wars and dance research protagonists emigrating. The global circulation of practices and knowledge informing dance research is starting to be investigated. For example, the group Moving Margins hosts workshops and symposia to diversify the history of dance, slowly building an alternative archive to extend and question the Euro-American canon of dance history.

3 Philipp Sarrasin, "Was ist Wissensgeschichte," *Internationales Archiv für Sozialgeschichte der deutschen Literatur* (2011), 165.

4 Lorraine Daston, "The History of Science and the History of Knowledge," *KNOW: A Journal on the Formation of Knowledge* 1, no. 1 (2017): 131–154; Johan Östling, David Larsson Heidenblad, Erling Sandmo, Anna Nilsson Hammar, and Kari Nordberg, "The History of Knowledge and the Circulation of Knowledge: An Introduction," in *Circulation of Knowledge: Explorations in the History of Knowledge*, eds. Johan Östling, Erling Sandmo, David Larsson Heidenblad, Anna Nilsson Hammar, and Kari Nordberg (Lund: Nordic Academic Press, 2018).

The history of knowledge perspective is useful in this case as it enables me to synthesize arguments and ideas from different "knowledge provinces" and academic disciplines from an interdisciplinary angle and thereby disclose material, socio-cultural, and theoretical entanglements difficult to discern from a disciplinary perspective.[5] First and foremost, an entangled history of arts and science allows me to study and understand the dancers as researchers and empiricists, a perspective not possible to adopt if the history of science restricts its field of inquiry to the academic sciences.[6] In addition, I draw from dance studies which have extensively analyzed early twentieth-century experimental dance and somatic disciplines and which have recently started to theorize dance as a research practice.[7] However, in contrast to recent works in dance and cultural studies, which embed the respective dance practices in their complex political contexts, I contextualize experimental dance within the discourse on the "experimentalization of life" in the history of science.[8] To supplement archival research on Dalcroze's rhythm school in the music department at Staatsbibliothek Berlin and in the Staatsarchiv Dresden, I rely on political and cultural histories of early twentieth-century Germany, as well as architectural, art, and local histories of Hellerau. Finally, writing about a research practice based on motion and sensory experience, the aim of this article is to develop an approach to systematically account for bodily, process-based forms of knowing in the history of knowledge.

The article presents three connected arguments. First, I propose to understand Émile-Jaques Dalcroze's *Rhythmik* in the equally experimental context in which it emerged: Germany's first garden city Hellerau. In Hellerau, what conducting an experiment entailed was not defined in the scientific laboratory. Experiments were carried out in a newly designed factory, a communal housing cooperative, in architecture, stage design, and movement education and research

---

5 Sarrasin, "Was ist Wissensgeschichte," 167.
6 Rheinberger defines their innovative nature as key to the common ground of the arts and sciences. Hans-Jörg Rheinberger, "Experiment, Forschung, Kunst," lecture presented at the annual meeting of the German Dramaturgical Society, 2012. See also Daston, "History of Science," 142–143 and Henning Schmidgen, *Forschungsmaschinen: Experimente zwischen Wissenschaft und Kunst* (Berlin: Matthes & Seitz, 2017).
7 In addition to the texts mentioned in footnote 1, see also the section on artistic research in the edited volume *Dance and Theory*, eds. Gabriele Brandstetter and Gabriele Klein (Bielefeld: Transcript Verlag, 2013) and Katharina Kleinschmidt, *Artistic Research als Wissensgefüge. Eine Praxeologie des Probens im zeitgenössischen Tanz* (Munich: Epodium, 2018). These texts describe research practices in contemporary dance.
8 Peter McLaughlin, "Der neue Experimentalismus in der Wissenschaftstheorie," in *Die Experimentalisierung des Lebens: Experimentalsysteme in den biologischen Wissenschaften 1850/1950*, eds. Hans-Jörg Rheinberger and Michael Hagner (Berlin: Akademie-Verlag, 2018[1995]), 207–218.

at the Dalcroze school. Knowledge gleaned from experimentation emerged between everyday life and professional research, both influenced by the reformist zeitgeist of the early twentieth century.[9] In this sense, Dalcroze's *Rhythmik*, as part of the overall concept of the garden city Hellerau, can be understood as an experiment aimed at observing, understanding, experimenting with, and ultimately altering human nature and culture toward the end of transforming individuals and a society in crisis.[10]

Second, I show that dance research undertaken at the Dalcroze rhythm school constituted a concerted transdisciplinary effort involving a number of people, methods, and materials that appear to belong to distinct, sometimes antagonistically positioned traditions from a present-day perspective. This, in turn, separates the arts from the sciences and the academy from the artisans and laymen.[11] In this regard, I follow Rheinberger's invitation to "take into view the arts and sciences from a unified historical perspective," thus disclosing the peculiar proximities of the two in early twentieth-century Germany to better understand how experimental dance was developed and acknowledged as a scientific practice.[12] Akin to Smith's description of artisanal epistemologies of craftspeople, the experimental dancers surrounding Dalcroze and his school focused on experience, observation, experimentation, and manipulation to study themselves.[13]

Third, I argue that while the history of knowledge approach proves useful when it comes to accounting for the diverse research community surrounding Dalcroze and the Hellerau rhythm school, a discussion is nevertheless needed on how the history of knowledge theorizes knowledge that is experiential, somatic, and tactile, tied to communities, techniques, and teachings at least as much as to artifacts, books, articles, audio recordings, or film. This discussion has occurred

---

[9] Daniel Speich Chassé and David Gugerli, "Kulturgeschichte in der Schweiz: Eine historiographische Skizze," *Traverse – Zeitschrift für Geschichte* 19 (2012): 86.
[10] Current research methods in experimental and contemporary dance grew directly out of the research practices developed in dance schools, laboratories, and artist colonies in the early twentieth century. See Susanne Quinten, "Kinästhetische Kommunikation und Intermediäre Wissenstransformation als Forschungsmethoden in tanzkünstlerischen Kontexten," in *Tanzpraxis in der Forschung – Tanz als Forschungspraxis: Choreographie, Improvisation, Exploration*, eds. Susanne Quinten and Stephanie Schroedter (Bielefeld: Transcript Verlag, 2016). See also Claudia Fleischle-Braun, "Das Erbe Der Tanzmoderne Im Zeitgenössischen Kontext Ein Beispiel Kooperativer Praxisforschung," in *Tanzpraxis in der Forschung – Tanz als Forschungspraxis: Choreographie, Improvisation, Exploration*, eds. Susanne Quinten and Stephanie Schroedter (Bielefeld: Transcript Verlag, 2016).
[11] Smith, *Lived Experience*.
[12] Rheinberger, "Experiment, Forschung, Kunst."
[13] Smith, *Lived Experience*.

in dance studies, a discipline that has grappled with the dynamic nature of its knowledge practices and bodies since its inception, as well as in the interdisciplinary field of embodied knowledge and cognition, where sports scientists, learning scientists, phenomenologists, sociologists, and anthropologists of the body describe and analyze tactile and sensuous knowledge processes.[14] In a concluding outlook, I thus propose how such practice-oriented knowledge theories may enrich the history of knowledge.

Émile Jaques-Dalcroze and Experimental Culture in Hellerau

The year was 1905 and whenever he was not at work, Karl Camillo Schmidt, the founder of the Dresdner Werkstätten für Handwerkskunst went on bike rides in the hilly surroundings of Dresden.[15] Schmidt was on the hunt for a new location for his quickly expanding company. While in the UK, he had learned about Ho-

---

14 On dance studies, see, for example, Ben Spatz, *What a Body Can Do: Technique as Knowledge, Practice as Research* (London, New York: Routledge, 2015); Carrie Noland, *Agency and Embodiment: Performing Gestures/Producing Culture* (Cambridge, MA: Harvard University Press, 2009); Einav Katan Schmid, *Embodied Philosophy in Dance* (London: Palgrave MacMillan, 2016); Deirdre Sklar, "Remembering Kinesthesia: An Inquiry into Embodied Cultural Knowledge," in *Migrations in Gesture*, ed. Carrie Noland (Minneapolis: U. of Minnesota Press, 2008), 85–112; Sabine Huschka, *Wissenskultur Tanz: historische und zeitgenössische Vermittlungsakte zwischen Praktiken und Diskursen* (Bielefeld: Transcript Verlag, 2009), as well as the sections "Tanz als Wissenskultur," "Körperwissen und -Gedächtnis," and "Tanzgeschichte und Rekonstruktion" in Gehm, Husemann, von Wilcke, *Wissen in Bewegung*, 23–228, and the section on archives in the edited volume Gabriele Brandstetter and Gabriele Klein, eds., *Dance and Theory* (Bielefeld: Transcript Verlag: 2013). On embodied cognition, see, for example, Tim Ingold, "Culture on the Ground: The World Perceived Through the Feet," *Journal of Material Culture* 9, no. 3 (2004): 315–340; Josh Berson, *Computable Bodies: Instrumented Life and the Human Somatic Niche* (New York: Bloomsbury Academic, 2015); Anna I. Corwin and Cordelia Erickson-Davis, "Experiencing Presence: An Interactive Model of Perception," *HAU: Journal of Ethnographic Theory* 10, no.1 (2020): 166–182; Nick Crossley, "Researching Embodiment by Way of 'Body Techniques'," *The Sociological Review* 55, no.1 (2007): 80–94; Thomas Fuchs, "Intercorporeality and Interaffectivity," in *Intercorporeality: Emerging Socialities in Interaction*, eds. Christian Meyer, Jürgen Streeck, and J. Scott Jordan (New York and Oxford: Oxford University Press, 2017), 3–24; Greg Downey, "'Practice without theory': A neuroanthropological perspective on embodied learning," in *JRAI* 16, no.1 (2010): 22–40; Michael Kimmel, Dayana Hristova, and Kerstin Kussmaul, "Sources of Embodied Creativity: Interactivity and Ideation in Contact Improvisation," *Behavioral Sciences* 8, no. 6 (2018).
15 Klaus-Peter Arnold, *Vom Sofakissen zum Städtebau. Die Geschichte der Deutschen Werkstätten und der Gartenstadt Hellerau* (Dresden and Basel: Verlag der Kunst, 1993), 331.

ward's garden city movement and the first garden city of Letchworth, built thirty-five miles outside of London in 1903. Schmidt was keen to bring Howard's idea to Germany. He acquired 140 hectares of slightly hilly land with lush vegetation, overlooking Dresden and the Elbe valley and known as Aue am Heller, and he named his new village-to-be Hellerau. The foundation stone for the Deutsche Werkstätten Hellerau was laid down in April 1909. Only one year later, his company and its workers relocated from Dresden to Hellerau.

Hellerau was an innovation in suburban development and architectural design as Schmidt wanted to avoid a generic and functionalist company town.[16] Architect Richard Riemerschmid designed winding paths that fit the terrain, lined with quaint houses that linked together markets, workshops, and factories.[17] Schmidt was the first German businessman to build a factory aimed at being worker-friendly by design. The building itself was narrow with large windows so that every worker would have a workstation by a window (Figure 1).[18] In contrast

Figure 1: Drawing of the furniture factory in Hellerau. Personennachlass Klaus-Peter Arnold, Hauptstaatsarchiv Dresden.

---

16 Karl Lorenz. *Wege nach Hellerau. Auf den Spuren der Rhythmik* (Dresden: Hellerau-Verlag, 1994), 55.
17 Music Department, Staatsbibliothek Berlin, *Die Bildungsanstalt für Musik und Rhythmus Jaques-Dalcroze in Dresden-Hellerau. Ein Bericht mit 8 Abbildungen* (Jena: Eugen Diederichs, 1910).
18 Erich Haenel, "Die Gartenstadt als Waffe im Kampf um sozialen Frieden," in *Hellerau leuchtete. Zeitzeugenberichte und Erinnerungen*, eds. Ehrhardt Heinold and Günther Großer (Dresden: Verlag der Kunst, 2007), 98.

to the usual workers' housing built by Krupp and others, the workers' homes were owned independently by a housing cooperative. Air baths and a *Gesellschaftshaus* (social house) for the "restoration of the spirit and of art" were built in the center of Hellerau.[19]

Establishing a garden city, a worker-friendly factory, and communal housing and leisure opportunities may be contextualized as part of the *Lebensreform*, a diverse set of reform movements, communities, and policies originating from the mid- to late nineteenth century in the German Empire. Features included returning to a more natural state of human life in the face of industrialization and urbanization, a vegetarian diet, protocols for restricted alcohol and tobacco intake, dress reform, alternative medicine and naturopathy, air baths, nudist culture, hiking, and gymnastics movements, as well as the uptake of South and East Asian religious traditions and thought. Elements of these reform movements were already influenced by ethnic and racist beliefs.[20]

On an evening in October 1909, Schmidt and Wolf Dohrn, the newly hired secretary of the furniture factories and son of marine biologist Anton Dohrn, went to see a presentation of *Rhythmik*, a new method for rhythmic body movement devised by the Swiss composer and music pedagogue Émile Jaques-Dalcroze in Dresden. Dalcroze was in search of a residence and financier for his new method. Enthralled by the performance they had witnessed, Schmidt and Dohrn decided to win Dalcroze over for Hellerau. After visiting the factory and the garden city, where only a handful of houses were taking shape, Dalcroze agreed to come under the condition that a school would be built for him.

Just as Dohrn understood Dalcroze's method as a significant aesthetic practice to enrich the emerging community in Hellerau, Dalcroze realized the artistic license offered by a place like Hellerau for his research. In his first public lecture in Dresden, he reasoned that while one would only be able to open an ordinary music school in a metropolis, in Hellerau "one would succeed to develop rhythm to the height of a social institution, that is to a pedagogical principle for the general public, to a uniting, invigorating, and educational force."[21]

---

19 Marco De Michelis and Vicki Bilenker, "Modernity and Reform, Heinrich Tessenow and the Institut Dalcroze at Hellerau," *Perspecta* 26 (1990): 150.
20 For an overview, see Eva Barlösius, *Naturgemäße Lebensführung. Zur Geschichte der Lebensreform um die Jahrhundertwende.* (Frankfurt a.M.: Campus, 1997). For the body movement culture in *Lebensreform*, see Bernd Wedemeyer-Kolwe, *Der neue Mensch: Körperkultur im Kaiserreich und in der Weimarer Republik* (Würzburg: Königshausen und Neumann, 2004).
21 *Die Bildungsanstalt*, 9–10.

Dohrn commissioned the reform architect Heinrich Tessenow and the cornerstone for the Bildungsanstalt Jaques-Dalcroze was laid down on April 22, 1911 (Figure 2). Six months later, Dalcroze moved into the already finished left wing of his new school and began teaching some 130 students.[22]

Figure 2: Entrance to the Bildungsanstalt Jaques-Dalcroze. The structure was designed by Heinrich von Tessenow, while the Yin Yang Emblem was designed by Alexander von Salzmann (Fotoarchiv Deutsche Werkstätten Hellerau, Hauptstaatsarchiv Dresden).

The managing director of the school was Dohrn, while Dalcroze served as artistic director.[23] The Bildungsanstalt Jaques-Dalcroze was primarily envisioned as a

---

[22] Wolf Dohrn to Dr. Roscher. Hellerau, October 17, 1911. Page 11, Folder 1. Bildungsanstalt Jaques-Dalcroze, Sächsisches Staatsministerium, Hauptstaatsarchiv Dresden.
[23] Empfehlung der Bildungsanstalt durch die Amtshauptmannschaft, (September 20, 1911), Page 3, Folder 1. Bildungsanstalt Jaques-Dalcroze, Sächsisches Staatsministerium, Hauptstaatsarchiv Dresden.

school for vocational training for laymen, dancers, and dance teachers, with classes in *Rhythmik*, *solfège*, and improvisation. The students were housed and catered for in a dormitory next to the school, and housing and classes were separated by gender.[24] A key element in the school curriculum was a two- to three-year-long *Rhythmik* teacher training program. Laymen classes were offered as well, and Hellerau's residents benefitted from reduced fees (Figure 3).[25]

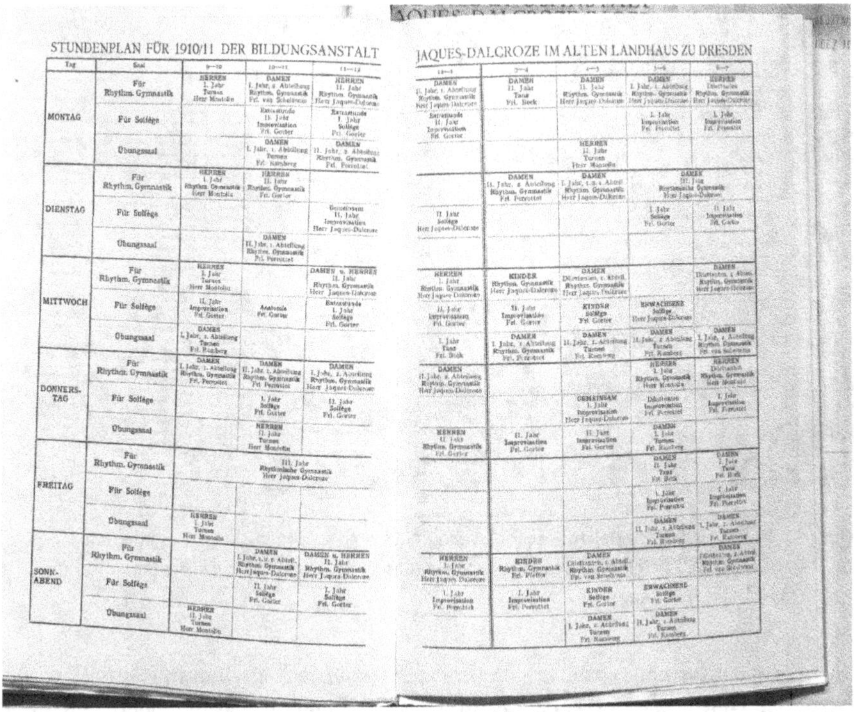
STUNDENPLAN FÜR 1910/11 DER BILDUNGSANSTALT JAQUES-DALCROZE IM ALTEN LANDHAUS ZU DRESDEN

MONTAG

DIENSTAG

MITTWOCH

DONNERSTAG

FREITAG

SONNABEND

Figure 3: Schedule for the Dalcroze school in its provisional home: "Altes Landhaus zu Dresden." Der Rhythmus: ein Jahrbuch (1911), 9. Bildungsanstalt Jaques-Dalcroze, Sächsisches Staatsministerium, Hauptstaatsarchiv Dresden.

Tessenow's building plan and the stage and light furnishings of Adolphe Appia and Alexander von Salzmann in the great hall of the *Rhythmik* school were designed to encourage a supportive environment for Dalcroze's rhythmics. It omit-

24 Schulordnung (August 15, 1911), Folder 1. Bildungsanstalt Jaques-Dalcroze, Sächsisches Staatsministerium, Hauptstaatsarchiv Dresden.

25 *Die Bildungsanstalt*, 14.

ted decorative elements superfluous to a movement conceptualized as research. Since adornments would distract from research, Appia and von Salzmann focused on creating an extremely simple and functional space with straight lines and rectangular angles. Other than the overall structure of the building, the design of the large hall was dynamic: it could be rearranged indefinitely to suit the *Rhythmik* studies (Figure 4).

Figure 4: Grand Hall of the Dalcroze school with Appia's practicals in the back. Der Rhythmus: Ein Jahrbuch, (1913), 22. Folder 1. Bildungsanstalt Jaques-Dalcroze, Sächsisches Staatsministerium, Hauptstaatsarchiv Dresden.

Surrounded by smaller rehearsal studios for *solfège* and rhythmic exercise, the grand hall constituted the school's central space, extending over two floors and often used for performances. Dalcroze was eager to publicly showcase his new method for rhythmic education; yet he never understood these presentations as plays.[26] On the contrary, he believed that the shows were moments in which an audience was invited to observe a process of exploration and experimentation.[27]

---

[26] Émile Jaques Dalcroze: "Tanz und Bühnenkunst sind nur Nutzanwendungen und Ergebnisse einer rhythmischen Ausbildung," *Die Bildungsanstalt*, 4.

[27] Dalcroze wrote: "I certainly have no intention of establishing a theater at Hellerau. I am no friend of the theater, this playing, which — usually with no conviction — is served up to blasé spectators." Quoted in Richard Beacham, "Appia, Jaques-Dalcroze, and Hellerau, Part One: 'Music Made Visible'," *New Theatre Quarterly* 1, no, 2 (1985): 160.

Theodor Heuss, a *realpolitiker* and ally of Dohrn, did not understand why the latter was interested in gymnastics.[28] However, Dohrn recognized the philosophical as much as educational potential of rhythm as a force to organize human social life:

> Rhythm, which was the teacher of all beginnings of social life, economic labor and artistic creation, continued as companion, patron and steward of work and life through thousands of years of human development and remained as such since human body movement has been the dominant element of labor. No trade without its respective songs to sing along, no individual who did not spend many hours a day in rhythmic pursuit. Unconscious, without wanting it or searching for it, the individual was animated and cared for by the rhythm of his [sic] occupation. And this outer order was the precondition for his inner balance. Humanity has lost this rhythm, it has been dislodged from the center of our life, the workshops. The ballrooms are not packed because of hedonism; it is here that the necessary utterance of a drive that has been robbed of its normal pursuit manifests itself.[29]

For Dohrn, Dalcroze's rhythmic education embodied the motiv that initially drew him to Schmidt's furniture factories and the overall project Hellerau. For him, the real social experiment concerned whether aesthetic practices could solve the social question, whether rhythm would hold true as a guiding principle to reform humanity. In the words of Heuss: "By returning to people the sense for the good rhythm of bodily movement, a fundamental contribution to the solution of the social tension should have been reached."[30] Different from the political, economic, and hygienic reform measures envisioned under the Wilhelmine regime, Dohrn believed that by honing the artistic and aesthetic sensibilities of people, it was possible to improve humanity. Hellerau was the perfect opportunity to test this belief: "through rhythm, the inhabitants of Hellerau could be transformed into men of the future."[31]

Dohrn's dedication to the Dalcroze school in Hellerau would prove fruitful: only one year later, leading artists, writers, and intellectuals such as Le Corbusier, Martin Buber, Gertrud Bäumer, Rainer Maria Rilke, Thomas Mann, Gerhard Hauptmann, Franz Kafka, Emil Nolde, Mary Wigman, Bernard Shaw, Paul Clau-

---

28 Theodore Heuss, "Werkbund-Beginn," in *Hellerau leuchtete. Zeitzeugenberichte und Erinnerungen*, eds. Ehrhardt Heinold and Günther Großer (Dresden: Verlag der Kunst, 2007), 32.
29 Wolf Dohrn's speech for the cornerstone ceremony, in *Der Rhythmus: ein Jahrbuch* (1911), 9. Bildungsanstalt Jaques-Dalcroze, Sächsisches Staatsministerium, Hauptstaatsarchiv Dresden. English translation by author.
30 Heuss, "Werkbund-Beginn," in *Hellerau leuchtete*, 32. English translation by author.
31 De Michelis and Bilenker, "Modernity," 153.

del, Upton Sinclair and many more came to the first summer festival of the Bildungsanstalt Jaques-Dalcroze.³²

Rhythmik: An Experimental Practice

With mixed feelings, Rainer Maria Rilke wrote a letter to Hugo von Hofmannsthal in late October 1913, reporting back on Paul Claudel's play *Verkündung* [*Proclamation*] at the Festspielhaus Hellerau, produced with Dalcroze's rhythmics students. Rilke was unsure regarding the improvised style of the work he had seen; in his view, it too prominently echoed Hellerau's overall *Versuchscharakter* [experimental character].³³ Von Hofmannsthal, on the other hand, approved of Dalcroze's work as a powerful technique to counter mechanization:

> The efforts of the Dalcroze school seem to be directed toward concentrating the mental faculties to me, leading to a necessary higher realm, positioned against the mechanizing zeitgeist and therefore worth promoting in every sense.³⁴

Rilke, however, remained suspicious. In a letter to novelist Helene von Nostitz a couple of days later, he articulated his ambivalence in more detail:

> Hellerau's people, like big children, are getting themselves into something that they do not understand. But God knows, maybe they learn it by doing. And do not even get into the murky waters that theater is today but get to the bottom of something clear and pure right away, and that would be to the benefit of all of us. [. . .] I believe one understands it in the sense Dohrn intended when one thinks of the Festspielhaus as a research station, as a sort of laboratory and as such, it is not fitting to come from far away in festive attire. One would have to arrive as unimposingly as possible, busying oneself with an apron and safety goggles, and observing the investigations that develop in this light-retort under blue-green radiation.³⁵

While Rilke's letter primarily expressed his bewilderment as to the incompatibility of a research environment and a performance with an audience, what should attract our attention is his explicit figuration of the Festspielhaus Hellerau as a

---

32 Lorenz, *Wege nach Hellerau*, 38.
33 Rainer Maria Rilke to Hugo von Hoffmansthal, "Dieses Spielhaus—eine Art Laboratorium" (October 22, 1913), in *Hellerau leuchtete*, 304.
34 Gutachten über die Schulfeste der Bildungsanstalt Jaques Dalcroze. Folder 1. Bildungsanstalt Jaques-Dalcroze, Sächsisches Staatsministerium, Hauptstaatsarchiv Dresden. English translation by author.
35 Rainer Maria Rilke to Helene von Nostitz (November 4, 1913), in *Hellerau leuchtete*, 305–307. English translation by author.

laboratory. Why would Rilke think of a *Rhythmik* stage performance as a *Versuchsstation* [trial or test station]?

Rilke was not the only one to summon this comparison. With Wolf Dohrn leading the way, Émile Jaques-Dalcroze, Adolphe Appia, Alexander von Salzmann, Paul Claudel, and contemporaries such as Karl Scheffler, Hans-Horst Kreisel, and Max Schillings described the Festspielhaus and the overall venture of Hellerau as a real-time experiment: as a *Versuch* [trial, or test], an *Entwicklungsexperiment* [development experiment], or a *Sozialexperiment* [social experiment].[36] When teaching piano and solfège at the music conservatory in Geneva, Dalcroze had noticed that his pupils had difficulty to fully grasp, that is, to understand *and* to feel music:

> I found that for nine-tenths of my pupils harmony was merely a question of mathematics, that they could not hear the chords they wrote down and therefore were unable to appreciate music to its full extent. Music is not purely intellectual; it works through the senses—it sets our whole organism in vibration. If this organism is incapable of responding in all its parts, the brain will register incomplete sensations.[37]

After watching a student rhythmically jumping across puddles while on a break, Dalcroze started to try out movement exercises in his lessons.

Pupils would move parts of their body according to a rhythm provided by Dalcroze, and different body parts could execute different rhythms (Figure 5). Dalcroze hoped that these exercises would establish a relationship between a mental and bodily understanding of music, thereby turning his pupils into better musicians.[38]

These early attempts are important to note as they show how Dalcroze's *Rhythmik* began as an exploratory investigation with the goal of enhancing musical ability. It was only much later that it would first be built into a system for movement education that could be taught and trained, and then into a style of stage performance. The public performance of *Rhythmik* was understood as a presentation of the latest research findings of the students and Dalcroze following a consistent empirical method.[39] Accordingly, and in line with the overall embrace of science in the arts, Dalcroze consciously fashioned himself and his students as

---

36 Wolf Dohrn, "Aber ein Experiment bleibt es," in *Hellerau leuchtete. Zeitzeugenberichte und Erinnerungen*, eds. Ehrhardt Heinold and Günther Großer (Dresden: Verlag der Kunst, 2007), 275–276.
37 Émile Jaques-Dalcroze, *The Jaques-Dalcroze Method of Eurhythmics: Rhythmic Movement*, vol. I (London: Novello & Co., 1920), iii.
38 Jaques-Dalcroze, *Method*, iii–v.
39 Dalcroze cited from Michael Faßhauer, *Persönlichkeiten in der Geschichte Helleraus* (Dresden: Rat des Stadtbezirkes Nord, Abteilung Kultur, 1988). Personennachlass Klaus-Peter Arnold, Hauptstaatsarchiv Dresden.

Figure 5: Embodiment of four-four time. Der Rhythmus: ein Jahrbuch (1911), 9. Bildungsanstalt Jaques-Dalcroze, Sächsisches Staatsministerium, Hauptstaatsarchiv Dresden.

researchers who were exploring, developing, and testing a new movement system. He wrote:

> Just three years ago, the sandy hills of Hellerau were untouched. Today, proud buildings rise, and avid scouts investigate unknown paths of psycho-physical borderlands, trying to give back the human to itself in their own way. Our searching is a striving, a pure, sincere striving which does not care for profit but serves the progress of humanity.[40]

Dalcroze did not refer to his dance and movement practice as research in a metaphorical sense. He was directly concerned with investigating patterns of body movement, sense perception—especially the kinesthetic sense—and emotion. Like his successor Rudolf von Laban, he published popular science books and sci-

---

[40] Émile Jaques-Dalcroze, "Dem Andenken an Wolf Dohrn," *Sonderheft der Dalcroze Schule*, March 1914. Folder 2, 169. Bildungsanstalt Jaques-Dalcroze, Sächsisches Staatsministerium, Hauptstaatsarchiv Dresden. English translation by author.

entific articles on body movement education and the health benefits of regular movement training. When Dalcroze spoke of rhythmics as an experiment, he meant that the development of this new movement system was open-ended. Dalcroze quickly found out that his new method generated the desired effects, yet he continually evolved the repertoire of movements.

Dalcroze was driven by empiricist ideals: only systematic practical studies would yield an ample understanding of the human body in movement and consequently help people understand the effects of bodily exploration and training on individual development and on German society. Notwithstanding this focus on exploratory body movement as a proper science, Dalcroze understood his movement practice as a means for artistic creation and expression and as a pedagogical tool for somatic education as well.[41] While change was to be effected on individuals, the research and teaching of rhythmics and expressive or experimental dance represented a collective endeavor between teachers and students, dancers, and scientists.[42] Dance concepts and techniques were developed in collective work processes, based on the lessons of the members of the research group involved.[43]

A short paragraph in an essay written for the annual publication of the Dalcroze school provides a glimpse into how Dalcroze personally might have adopted a scientific perspective:

> After Dalcroze's first developmental experiments concerning a systematic bodily expression of rhythm: "The artist suffered from the inability to precisely conceive and express in words and concepts what he saw intuitively and was supposed to realize with the full force of his soul. He needed a terminology, a scaffold for his meditation and striving. The professor of physiological psychology at the University of Geneva, Mister Eduard Claparède, who was very interested in rhythmic gymnastics because of what he had seen and heard, helped to provide this terminology, and Dalcroze complemented by reading and thought what he had learned from his conversations with Claparède. Like this, he was able to pit his pedagogical and artistic experiences against scientific facts and to connect the two."[44]

While Dalcroze's collaboration with Claparède ended when the former left Geneva, encounters with life scientists continued in Hellerau. At the Waldhaus Hellerau, neurologist Dr. Jolowicz and pediatrician Dr. Meischeider-Jolowicz hosted children who needed medical supervision but were nevertheless enrolled in the

---

41 Gabriele Brandstetter, *Tanz-Lektüren: Körperbilder Und Raumfiguren Der Avantgarde* (Freiburg: Rombach, 2013), 524.
42 Fleischle-Braun, "Das Erbe," in *Tanzpraxis*, 51.
43 Fleischle-Braun, "Das Erbe," in *Tanzpraxis*, 52.
44 Adolphe Appia, "Über Ursprung und Anfänge der rhythmischen Gymnastik," *Der Rhythmus: ein Jahrbuch*, (1911), 9. Folder 1, 13. Bildungsanstalt Jaques-Dalcroze, Sächsisches Staatsministerium, Hauptstaatsarchiv Dresden. English translation by author.

classes at the Dalcroze school, often with the goal of alleviating their illnesses. Dr. Jolowicz researched the medical benefits of the Dalcroze method and taught elementary anatomy classes at the Dalcroze school.[45] The salutary benefits of the Dalcroze method were advertised in medical journals and practiced in various European medical institutions. In Hellerau, showings of *Rhythmik* performances were organized for physicians from Berlin and for the Vereinigung für Natur- und Heilkunde, thus effectively transforming a movement lesson into a de-facto public laboratory. The performances for physicians at the Dalcroze school resembled the Pasteurian laboratory more than they did the Boylean: research was brought out of its initial incubation space and into the world, consequently gaining explanatory force in hitherto uncharted realms. Unlike Pasteur's bacteria, *Rhythmik* did not travel as effortlessly. Anybody interested in rhythmics had to and did make the trek to Hellerau. Here, the value and validity of *Rhythmik* as a life-enhancing practice were extended beyond the arts and into the life sciences.

Notwithstanding Dalcroze's personal scientific trajectory, his embrace of scientific method and experimentation can be viewed as part of a larger scientification of modern life. Dalcroze's school manager Wolf Dohrn, for example, saw Hellerau as a *Versuchsfeld* [trial or test field], one certainly informed by the oeuvre of his father Anton Dohrn. Dohrn the elder had opened the first public research station for marine biology in Naples in 1872. With the increasing industrialization at the end of the nineteenth century and the onset of the *Lebensreform*, sociopolitical measures aimed at curbing the rising poverty were deliberately referred to as social experiments. Philosopher of science Hans-Jörg Rheinberger describes this phase as the *Entgrenzung des Labors* [dissolution of laboratory boundaries]: research in the life sciences aimed at solving the social question and thus took its experiments out of the laboratory and into society to provide immediate relief.[46]

At least since 1848, natural scientists had advocated for progressive politics informed by scientific innovation with regard to seeking answers to the social, economic, and cultural tensions accompanying the transition to industrial capitalism.[47] Influenced by these practical developments in the life sciences, many social activists, critics, and scholars turned to *Wissenschaft* [experimental science] for

---

[45] "Berichte der Dalcroze-Schule" (January 1914). Folder 2, 169. Bildungsanstalt Jaques-Dalcroze, Sächsisches Staatsministerium, Hauptstaatsarchiv Dresden.

[46] Hans-Jörg Rheinberger and Michael Hagner, eds., *Die Experimentalisierung des Lebens: Experimentalsysteme in den biologischen Wissenschaften 1850/1950* (Berlin: Akademie Verlag, 1993), Introduction.

[47] Kevin Repp. "'More Corporeal, More Concrete': Liberal Humanism, Eugenics, and German Progressives at the Last Fin de Siècle," *The Journal of Modern History* 72, no. 3 (2000): 689.

solutions to the social question.[48] In her contribution in this special issue, historian Anne Kwaschik terms this an "experimental approach to social reform."[49] With regard to the example of housing cooperatives, she furthermore describes how social theorists and reformers in the nineteenth century already fashioned their social theories and experiments on rational principles based on the natural sciences. These reformers aimed to change society by employing rigorous scientific principles to the organization of society and daily life.[50] It seems likely that the language of the experiment and the laboratory made its way from the scientifically minded social reformers and the humanistically inclined life scientists in the metropolis to some of the sites in which dance research was pioneered: the rhythmics school of Émile Jaques-Dalcroze in Germany's first garden city of Hellerau, planned and frequented by exactly those scientifically inclined humanists gathering in the clubs of Berlin.

Scientists, although certainly not all of them, endorsing dance as a form of experiment that could lead the way to improve society may still seem farfetched. Yet as natural and social scientists took their experiments out of controlled environments to provide immediate relief, they were at the same time preoccupied with what historian of science Anne Harrington has referred to as a "re-enchanting of science."[51] There was the felt, urgent need for some kind of holistic organicism in the face of exclusively rational and mechanist understandings of body and mind, which were unable to sufficiently well explain how individual organisms develop and adapt. As much as artists and dancers sought to become experimental and scientific, scientists and scholars yearned for holistic and not merely mechanistic answers to their questions regarding human nature and development. The emphasis in dance research on the plasticity and adaptability of the human body and mind proved precisely that humans were organic rather than mechanistic.

---

48 Repp, "More Corporeal," 689–690.
49 Anne Kwaschik, "Experimental Discourse and Fourierist Settlements in the 1840s and 1850s."
50 Anne Kwaschik. "Gesellschaftswissen als Zukunftshandeln," *Francia. Forschungen zur westeuropäischen Geschichte* 44 (Ostfildern: Jan Thorbecke Verlag, 2017), 193.
51 Anne Harrington, *Reenchanted Science: Holism in German Culture from Wilhelm II to Hitler* (Princeton: Princeton University Press, 1996).

Social Change Begins in Training One's Will and Observing the Motion of One's Body

Dalcroze's research not only sought to develop *Rhythmik* as a new movement system. At the same time, it constituted an investigation into the self. Here, the individual body was the primary research instrument.[52] Dalcroze held that one should know oneself thoroughly and develop the ability to create original ideas before studying the ideas of others.[53] Only a schooled self with a trained perception and expression could engage in a productive exchange with others. Hence, there were specific exercises to train and develop the will.[54]

> Rhythmics is essentially a matter of personal experience. When asked what it is and to what it leads it is easy for me to explain how I conceived the idea, to quote the actual results, to demonstrate some of the exercises, but the real answer is only to be obtained by actual experience of the method. A scientist may describe to you the theoretical and practical application of electricity, or of radium, but that does not explain what these two great forces are. You may read all the histories of religion which have ever been written and yet not experience religious faith. [. . .] Rhythmics—on whatever lines it is taught—is more than a pedagogic method. It is indeed a force—analogous to electricity or to the great chemical and physical forces of Nature—which has the power of restoring us to a knowledge of ourselves, of making us aware not only of our own forces but also of those of others—the forces of humanity.[55]

Here, we may discern how Dalcroze hoped that his work would contribute to solving the social question. Only somebody schooled in moving and using her body while equipped with trained perception would be able to restore "man to knowledge of himself"; a form of knowing that valued one's bodily intelligence and that, according to Dalcroze, had been eradicated by modern, mind-centered understandings of human nature.[56] A return to a bodily, sensorial understanding of the human being and intelligence through regular movement training, Dalcroze argued, would alleviate the ills of mechanization and rationalization and consequently improve humanity.[57]

The emphasis on somatic and sensory rather than intellectual development mirrors the phenomenological and vitalist zeitgeist of the time. Intellectuals, so-

---

52 Émile Jaques-Dalcroze, "Was die Rhythmische Gymnastik ihnen gibt und was sie von ihnen fordert," *Der Rhythmus: ein Jahrbuch* (1911), 41. Folder 1, 13. Bildungsanstalt Jaques-Dalcroze, Sächsisches Staatsministerium, Hauptstaatsarchiv Dresden.
53 Jaques-Dalcroze, "Rhythmische Gymnastik," 33.
54 Jaques-Dalcroze, "Rhythmische Gymnastik," 33–34.
55 Jaques-Dalcroze, *Method*, iii–vi.
56 Jaques-Dalcroze, *Method*, iii.
57 Jaques-Dalcroze, "Rhythmische Gymnastik," 41.

cial reformers, and even scientists believed that reason and intellect alone were not enough to solve the crisis of modernity in German society.[58] Through a phenomenological and empiricist lens, however, scientific modernism and an overall scientification of life could be embraced while the body was trusted as an intuitive sensor and research instrument.[59] In this milieu, dance research such as that of Dalcroze emerged to complement purely rationalist scientific research in addressing pressing social issues concerning economic precarity, physical wellbeing, and modern alienation. Collaborating with a range of scholars and scientists, Dalcroze and his disciples hoped to offer a holistic rather than disciplinary approach to research and experimentation.

In this sense, Dalcroze's practice serves as a paradigmatic example of agentive self-observation and self-formation, a modern dispositive of power in itself.[60] Coupled with a new understanding of human physiology in which the body is directed from the inside, the *Lebensreform* body culture conceived of physical training as a self-induced and self-regulated practice cultivating embodied individual personality and free will.[61] In line with this, Dalcroze's *Rhythmik* aimed for the cultivation of individuality through observation in movement. People were encouraged to enhance and strengthen their own will by experiencing themselves in rhythmic movement.

This kind of forming of the self was not self-serving. Rather, individual cultivation of body and mind was considered a necessary condition toward a greater social good.[62] In this regard, Dalcroze's project was motivated by what Alina Marktanner has referred to as "developmental fantasies" in her contribution to this special issue.[63] By training their perception and motion, dance students would not only be educated but would also become better moral citizens.[64]

---

[58] Wolf Dohrn's speech for the cornerstone ceremony, in *Der Rhythmus: ein Jahrbuch* (1911), 13. Folder 1. Bildungsanstalt Jaques-Dalcroze, Sächsisches Staatsministerium, Hauptstaatsarchiv Dresden.
[59] For empirical and theoretical contributions on dance as research as this developed in the field of dance studies, see Susanne Quinten and Stephanie Schroedter, eds., *Tanzpraxis in der Forschung – Tanz als Forschungspraxis: Choreographie, Improvisation, Exploration* (Bielefeld: Transcript Verlag, 2016).
[60] Hillel Schwartz, "Torque: The New Kinaesthetic of the 20th Century," in *Zone 6: Incorporations*, eds. Jonathan Crary and Sanford Kwinter (New York: Zone Books, 1992), 71–127. See also Harold B. Segel, *Body Ascendant: Modernism and the Physical Imperative* (Baltimore: Johns Hopkins University Press, 1998).
[61] Maren Möhring, *Marmorleiber. Körperbildung in der deutschen Nacktkultur 1890–1930* (Cologne: Böhlau Verlag, 2004), 77–87.
[62] Möhring, *Marmorleiber*, 86.
[63] Alina Marktanner, "Experimenting for Empire: Plant Health as an Agricultural Problem in German East Africa, Togo and Cameroon, 1905–1914."
[64] In this regard, not only the nationalist and racist undertones of modern dance but also the colonial and imperial entanglements of experimental communities in Germany are relevant. See,

The return to a "natural body" flowing in the right rhythm would engender moral as well as political change.[65] Thus, movement training was intentionally used as a site for moral inculcation. More generally, the idea that successful social change begins with change at the level of the embodied individual was a greater motif of *Lebensreform* culture, supported by gymnasts, dancers, artists, craftspeople, natural scientists, physicians, and social reformers. The notion that work on and through the somatic self would not only transform individuals but aid humanity at large—from knowing oneself to becoming efficient on the assembly line—is a theme described by historians as the "physical imperative of modernity,"[66] a "new kinaesthetic of the twentieth century,"[67] or "kinaesthetic knowing."[68]

What becomes apparent for the Dalcroze school in Hellerau, if sources are scrutinized from an interdisciplinary perspective, is the prevalence of experimentalism and the explicit entanglement of artistic, social, and scientific practices and theories.[69] What conducting an experiment actually meant was not solely defined in the scientific laboratory at the time. Experimental language and practice cross-fertilized and developed amid aesthetic, scientific, and socio-political realms.

The *Rhythmik* school of Dalcroze provides the first instances of dance as scientific research practice. However, Dalcroze did not operate in a vacuum. After he had to leave Germany due to the onset of the First World War, the school in Hellerau remained an educational site with a focus on experimental work with dance researchers and teachers such as Elsa Gindler, Dora Menzler, and Marianne Pontan. In addition to Dalcroze, more research-oriented dance teachers

---

for example, Saskia Köbschall, "Deutsch, Natürlich und Nackt. Die Lebensreform und ihre kolonialen Verflechtungen," *E-journal Institute for Art Education* 15 (2019), https://blog.zhdk.ch/iaejournal/files/2019/03/AER15_K%C3%B6bschall_D_20190315.pdf.

65 The scientific neutrality of research-oriented dance practice, which dance teachers used to advertise and advocate for their practice, has rightly been put into question. Invocations of naturalness, scientific or evolutionary facts, and abstraction have and continue to exclude and denigrate non-Western traditions and diversity in society at large and in dance communities more specifically. For a historical critique of the politics underpinning early *Lebensreform* dance, see Bernd Wedemeyer-Kolwe, *Der neue Mensch*; Ana Isabel Keilson, "The Embodied Conservatism of Rudolf Laban, 1919-1926," *Dance Research Journal* 51, no. 2 (2019): 18–34; Arabella Stanger, *Dancing on Violent Ground: Utopia as Disposession Euro-American Theater Dance* (Chicago: Northwestern U. Press, 2021). For a recent critique of the moral presuppositions of somatics, see Doran George, *The Natural Body in Somatics Training* (New York: Oxford University Press, 2020).
66 Segel, *Body Ascendant*.
67 Schwartz, "Torque."
68 Zeynep Çelik Alexander, *Kinaesthetic Knowing: Aesthetics, Epistemology, Modern Design* (Chicago: The University of Chicago Press, 2017).
69 Trudy Dehue, "Die Entstehung der Experimentiergesellschaft," in *Kultur im Experiment*, eds. H. Schmidgen, Peter Geimer, and Sven Dierig (Berlin: Kulturverlag Kadmos, 2004), 86–89.

such as Rudolf von Laban and Oscar Schlemmer entered the stage of the German dance and movement scene. Although often portrayed as solitary geniuses, Dalcroze, Laban, and Schlemmer had many aides and collaborators. Primarily, they trained the first generations of predominantly female experimental and expressive dancers, dance teachers, and somatics, as well as dance researchers such as Nina Gorter, Rosalia Chladek, Dore Hoyer, Kurt Jooss, Irmgard Bartenieff, Mary Wigman, Marie Adama von Scheltema, Suzanne Perrottet, and Katja Wulff.[70] Some of these, such as Rudolf von Laban and Mary Wigman, actively collaborated with the German Nazi regime, performing at government-initiated events and leading and teaching state-funded dance institutions.[71] Others fled Nazi Germany and founded dance and movement education programs in Switzerland, Italy, the United Kingdom, and the United States. Often directly influenced by European dance research, somatic programs such as the Alexander technique, the Feldenkrais method, and Mabel Elsworth Todd's ideokinesis, developed at her movement research laboratory at Columbia University, took shape across the Atlantic.[72]

Knowledge in Motion

Dance researchers in the early twentieth century understood very well that it was crucial to produce knowledge objects in order to be taken seriously as scientists. Findings could only be compared, ordered, and analyzed if they were based on written research, while a disciplinary canon could only be founded if it was based on a collection and tradition of such objects of knowledge. Without written proof, the ephemerality of dance would turn out to represent a large obstacle to public and scholarly recognition.[73] Early dance researchers such as Dalcroze and Laban thus published popular science books and scientific journal articles while taking photographs of their research spaces and set-ups simultaneously. Most importantly, movement notation was envisioned as an integral element of not only

---

70 For a historical overview of the German dance scene in the first half of the twentieth century, see Susan Manning and Lucia Ruprecht, eds., *New German Dance Studies* (Urbana, IL: University of Illinois Press, 2012).
71 Susan Manning, *Ecstasy and the Demon: Feminism and Nationalism in the Dances of Mary Wigman* (Berkeley: University of California Press, 1993).
72 For outlines of the history of somatics as a field, see Doran George, *The Natural Body*; Don Hanlon Johnson, ed., *Bone, Breath & Gesture: Practices of Embodiment* (Berkeley: North Atlantic Books, 1995); Martha Eddy, "Somatic Practices and Dance: Global Influences," *Dance Research Journal* 34 (2002): 46.
73 Adshead-Lansdale, "Tanzforschung," 28.

practical dance research but a scholarly *Tanzwissenschaft* to come. Laban, for example, developed a notation system for movement, first referred to as Kinetographie and today called Labanotation. Furthermore, Laban commissioned a dedicated "Tanzschreibstube" at the Deutsche Tanzbühne Berlin in 1935.[74] Dance practice is based on and includes systems of notation, and these notation systems have had an impact on dance studies and beyond.[75] Nevertheless, of the more than fifty existing systems for dance notation, no one has been universally accepted, meaning that dance still lacks a unified system of documentation.[76] A definitive canon that can be compiled, referenced, and studied remains elusive. Yet, a comprehensive compilation of research notation and other forms of post-hoc documentation would not capture the phenomenon of dance research as an experiential and epistemic practice. In experimentation, understanding is not only gained cognitively but in perceptive and somatic experience as well. If we concede that such dynamic ways of knowing constitute a key element of human culture and knowledge, how can we get a grip on them?

As mentioned in the introduction, scholars from a wide range of disciplines continue to unpack the nature of what they call tacit, practical, embodied, experiential, or kinesthetic knowledge. This research suggests that neither cognitive nor somatic findings take the form of propositional content in human memory. However, a comparative overview of the existing approaches exceeds the scope of this article. Nevertheless, something that we can learn from this literature for the history of knowledge is that in experiential and experimental settings that focus on human motion and somatic experience, knowledge is sometimes best described as something processual, bound to the practices in which it is enacted. To account for movement practices such as dance research in the history of knowledge, I thus suggest moving beyond an object-focused history toward a history of what Farquhar has described as "knowing practice."[77] From here, we can outline which role somatic, tactile, and other experiential processes of knowing and learning play in the history of knowledge.

---

[74] Frank-Manuel Peter, "The German Dance Archive, Cologne (Deutsches Tanzarchiv Köln)," *Dance Chronicle* 32, no. 3 (2009): 476–489.

[75] Whitney Laemmli, "How to capture movement," *Historical Studies in the Natural Sciences* 52, no. 1 (2022): 132–135.

[76] Yvonne Hardt, "Communicating with dance: A historiography of aesthetic and anthropological reflections on the relation between dance, language, and representation," in *Body–Language–Communication I*, eds. Cornelia Müller, Alan Cienki, Ellen Fricke, Silva Ladewig, David McNeill, and Sedinha Tessendorf (Berlin: De Gruyter, 2013), 433.

[77] Judith Farquhar, *Knowing Practice: The Clinical Encounter of Chinese Medicine* (New York: Routledge, 2019 [1994]). See also Jaida Kim Samudra, "Memory in Our Body: Thick Participation and the Translation of Kinesthetic Experience," *American Ethnologist* 35, no. 4 (2008): 665–681.

The early twentieth-century experimental dancers were a community of researchers who understood phenomena such as perception, cognition, motion, and sometimes emotion in experimental and reflective movement practice. Describing the extensive yet often implicit networks of the early twentieth-century experimental dancers, Rothe has thus characterized the knowledge of the dance researchers not only as practical and experimental but as topological as well.[78] The dance researchers were furthermore teachers and as such, they were arbiters of the skills, techniques, and observations they made. This is how they knew—in movement experience and in reflection on this experience, as humans drawing on their tactile, perceptive, cognitive, and social capacities in experience.

A knowing practice such as dance research can be observed and described empirically, as it is enacted and passed on, as it is trained, habituated, and creatively altered in experimentation. It can be reconstructed through oral histories, books, articles, research diaries, photographs, and video footage. Retracing the legacies and networks of practitioners, we can study how a knowing practice—in this case Dalcroze's dance research registers—differs, adapts, and travels across individuals and communities of practice. A knowing practice interweaves with and draws on textual and theoretical materials of knowledge: a notation system, manual, or book. Yet akin to sociologists and anthropologists of science, we may ask what kind of knowing practice enabled these writings in the first place. Processual definitions of knowledge such as "knowing practice" are not only well-suited to account for dance research. They can prove useful to account exactly for the kind of non-canonical, "non-modern," manual, aesthetic, and non-theoretical forms of knowledge that the history of knowledge aims to include, thereby theorizing skilled practices as culturally specific sites of knowledge making.

Anne-Sophie Reichert is a cultural anthropologist interested in somatic and affective forms of knowledge, bodily learning, habits, and skills. She studied political science, political theory, and anthropology in Berlin, Chicago, Davis and Berkeley and received her PhD from the University of Chicago with a dissertation on motion and perception skills in dance practice. She is a co-founder of ALASKA-Studio for Feelings, an arts education initiative creating immersive environments, interactive sculptures, and hosting workshops on bodily and emotional literacy. She teaches anthropology of body and mind, anthropological theory, and feminist science studies and collaborates with artists and scientists.

---

78 Katja Rothe, "The Gymnastics of Thought: Elsa Gindler's Networks of Knowledge," in *Encounters in Performance Philosophy*, eds. Laura Cull and Alice Lagaay (London: Palgrave MacMillan, 2014), 199.

Section III: **Engaging the Field**

Aleksandra Kaye, Raphael Schlattmann, Malte Vogl,
Bernardo S. Buarque, Jascha Schmitz, Lea Weiß,
and Laura von Welczeck

Socio-Epistemic Networks: A Framework for History of Knowledge

Abstract: Focusing on methodologies such as network analysis, co-citation networks, and topic modelling, this paper analyses historical knowledge dynamics and evolution by means of the socio-epistemic networks (SENs) framework using computational methods. By applying the framework to two case studies (transnational scientific practices of Polish migrants and the evolution of general relativity and gravitation research) and integrating the social, semiotic/material, and semantic layers to analyse historical sources, the paper highlights the importance of studying interactions, material objects, and cognitive elements in combination in order to understand how knowledge systems develop over time.

Keywords: evolution of knowledge, historical network research, multi-layer networks, history of science, digital methods

1 Introduction

The advancement of technology has expanded the range of physical representations of knowledge and the ways in which we manage these. Digital archives, multimedia recordings, and virtual simulations offer new avenues for storing and studying knowledge, while digital workflows improve the accessibility of existing traditional archives. At the same time, we see the emergence of increasingly comprehensive and sophisticated computerised methods for processing these sources. New technologies thereby contribute to the exponential growth of records and sources available for study while at the same time expanding the ways in which they are handled. Historical research needs to adjust to this changing landscape if historians are to address the opportunities and new research questions presented by this situation. In this article, we present the framework of socio-epistemic networks (SENs), which aims to integrate large-scale exploration and analysis of historical sources using computational methods, thereby complementing traditional historical research.

The framework is intended to explore the intricate, multidimensional dynamics governing the formation and evolution of knowledge systems. It combines approaches of network analysis and digital methods with structural questions concerning knowledge production, formalisation, and dissemination, which are typically of interest to historians of knowledge. We envision that this framework will integrate and add to existing research methods, which will allow us to broaden and corroborate qualitative research outputs using a quantitative, structural approach.

1.1 Conceptual Framework

The ModelSEN project seeks to create a quantitative, network-inspired approach to the history of knowledge, which integrates micro-history with macro-history while accounting for global, transregional effects of knowledge processes.[1] While appreciating the breadth of research focusing on knowledge networks, the SENs framework presented here serves as a continuation of work initiated by Jürgen Renn and others in the early 2010s.[2] Renn et al. define knowledge as a "codified experience and potential for problem-solving".[3] Codification occurs through the formation of cognitive, material, and social structures. Examples of such structures include mental models, but also material representations of knowledge, or sign systems, all within a realm of interactions between social actors. Accordingly, cognitive, material, and social dimensions of knowledge emerge. We argue that these dimensions can be modelled by multi-layered, time-evolving SENs: the social, the semiotic/material, and the semantic (see Figure 1 for a schematic representation). In addition to these layers, however, we argue there are also constraints concerning knowledge-related interactions in and between each of these layers governing the formation of these structures.

---

[1] ModelSEN Project, "Theory", Socio-Epistemic Networks: Modelling Historical Knowledge Processes, 2021, https://modelsen.mpiwg-berlin.mpg.de/theory/.
[2] Jürgen Renn et al., "Netzwerke als Wissensspeicher", in *Die Zukunft der Wissensspeicher: Forschen, Sammeln und Vermitteln im 21. Jahrhundert* (Munich: UVK Verlagsgesellschaft Konstanz, 2016), 35–79, https://pure.mpg.de/pubman/faces/ViewItemOverviewPage.jsp?itemId=item_2347024. For other approaches to historical knowledge networks, see, for example, Kapil Raj, "Networks of Knowledge, or Spaces of Circulation? The Birth of British Cartography in Colonial South Asia in the Late Eighteenth Century", *Global Intellectual History* 2, no. 1 (2 January 2017): 49–66, https://doi.org/10.1080/23801883.2017.1332883; Emily Erikson, *Trade and Nation: How Companies and Politics Reshaped Economic Thought*, The Middle Range Series (New York: Columbia University Press, 2021), https://doi.org/10.7312/erik18434; Cécile Armand, Christian Henriot, and Huei-min Sun, *Knowledge, Power, and Networks: Elites in Transition in Modern China* (Leiden: Brill, 2022).
[3] Renn et al., "Netzwerke als Wissensspeicher", 36.

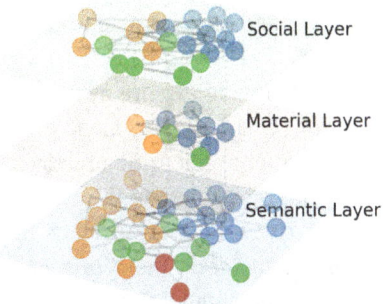

Figure 1: A schematic representation of the socio-epistemic network framework with social, material (also referred to as Semiotic), and semantic layers and both inter- and intra-layer links. For examples of nodes and edges in the different layers, see Table 1.

1.2 Case Studies and Research Questions

Before applying SENs, researchers must ask themselves if this framework is suitable for answering the research questions they wish to pursue. It is also vital to consider whether the available sources are sufficiently detailed to observe the changes in focus. As a framework, SENs are based on the conceptualisation that knowledge is culturally and physically embedded. It combines social networks, where a traditional approach of closely reading a large corpus might suffice, with networks of material outputs of that social network and the cognitive processes (represented by language) used to encode that output. The framework situates these in a temporally evolving multilayer frame.

Furthermore, this framework aims to uncover structural changes in the constructed networks and reflect on these changes from both quantitative and qualitative historical perspectives. This type of approach thereby forces historians to a) structurally think about the sources used and their relations, b) formulate their research hypothesis in this regard as well, and c) make their data and/or analysis reproducible and reusable for other scholars, which, unfortunately, is not always the case for quantitative research involving computer analysis.[4] In cases where software and data are produced, they should be findable, accessible, interoperable, and reusable (FAIR). Quantitative answers to questions related to historical

---

[4] For more on the replication crisis in the humanities, see Rik Peels, "Replicability and Replication in the Humanities", *Research Integrity and Peer Review* 4, no. 1 (9 January 2019): 2, https://doi.org/10.1186/s41073-018-0060-4.

phenomena are only truly reproducible when other researchers have access to both the data and the software used to obtain results and are thus able to check if they can arrive at the same results.

An example of a historical research question possible to explore by using the SEN framework is how the complex connections of Polish migrants along professional and geographical lines enabled their transnational scientific practices to function in the nineteenth century.[5] Which individuals or communities were important for developing ideas and practices, whose role might nevertheless have been unacknowledged until now due to the dominant "great men" or "centre-periphery" narratives? How was the knowledge they contributed circulated transnationally? And how did their work affect broader scientific debates? In the 1930s, Stanisław Zieliński, a Polish historian, independence activist, and editor, authored a few detailed compilations containing extensive lists of Polish intellectuals working abroad, along with their notable professional achievements and published works.[6] The data contained in Zieliński's compilation enables us to create a socio-epistemic network of Polish migrants working around the world in the nineteenth and early twentieth centuries. The social network reconstructed for the purposes of this case study connects the Polish migrants working around the world during the period 1830–1930. It is linked to the semantic network containing their professional achievements and expertise, which, in turn, is linked to the semiotic network of their publications and material outputs of their work, such as infrastructure projects to which they contributed. Such a SEN can be used to address the questions mentioned above in this paragraph.

Another question concerns the dynamics of scientific disciplinary formation, exemplified by applying the SEN framework to the so-called "Renaissance of General Relativity" in the field of general relativity and gravitation research (GRG).[7] In the social layer, an analysis of the networks of research centres and individual collaboration networks reveals how exchanges of personnel and the deliberate densification of relationships contributed to the emergence of the largest and

---

5 For more on this topic, see Aleksandra Kaye, "Mapping Transnational Knowledge Networks: Polish Scientific Professionals in Latin America, 1830–1889" (PhD diss., University College London, 2022).
6 Stanisław Zieliński, *Wybitne czyny Polaków na obczyźnie* (Wilno: Polska Drukarnia Artystyczna "Grafika", 1935); Stanisław Zieliński, *Bibljografia czasopism polskich zagranicą 1830–1934* (Warszawa: Drukarnia Społeczna, 1935); Stanisław Zieliński, *Mały słownik pionierów polskich kolonialnych i morskich: podróżnicy, odkrywcy, zdobywcy, badacze, eksploratorzy, emigranci – pamiętnikarze, działacze i pisarze migracyjni* (Warsaw: Instytut Wydawniczy Ligi Morskiej i Kolonialnej, 1933).
7 Roberto Lalli, Riaz Howey, and Dirk Wintergrün, "The Socio-Epistemic Networks of General Relativity, 1925–1970", in *The Renaissance of General Relativity in Context*, eds. Alexander S. Blum, Roberto Lalli, and Jürgen Renn, Einstein Studies (Cham: Springer International Publishing, 2020), 15–84, https://doi.org/10.1007/978-3-030-50754-1_2.

most stable component in the field of GRG, thus emphasising the role of active community-building in the formation of a scientific field (see section 2.1). The semiotic or material aspects of this formation can be seen in structural changes of citation patterns, such as co-citations, widely recognised as methods for identifying the emergence of research fields and routinely employed in scientometrics (see section 2.2). Lastly, the central topics of clusters in these co-cited papers and their structural positions serve to illustrate the semantic sphere over time, revealing conceptual shifts and the reorganisation of knowledge connected to the above-mentioned changes in the other two layers (see section 2.3). We argue that it is hardly possible to satisfactorily explain the phenomenon of the Renaissance of General Relativity or Polish contributions to scientific debates by only considering one of these layers. Additionally, an explanation that does not take into account large amounts of data over long periods of time is unlikely to fully account for this complexity.

2 Socio-Epistemic Networks in Practice

In this section, we illustrate the conceptual framework using the examples presented above. The section is structured by the different layers to highlight the relevant aspects of data gathering, network creation, and necessary steps in the analysis. Table 1 presents an at-a-glance summary of the different layers of SENs together with examples from the case studies presented in the text.

Table 1: Definition and examples of the layers of the socio-epistemic network framework.

Description	Nodes	Edges
Social layer		
Structures of social relations between individuals and/or groups	*General:* Individual people or groups of people (e.g., kinship unit, friendship/professional group)	*General:* Social relations (e.g., meetings, relationships, friendship bonds, professional ties, family ties)
	Polish Case Study: Polish migrants across the world in the nineteenth and early twentieth centuries	*Polish Case Study:* Acquaintanceship between migrants who worked together
	General Relativity Case Study: Scientists working in the field of GRG	*General Relativity Case Study:* Co-authorship, supervision relationships, working at the same institution at the same time

Table 1 (continued)

Description	Nodes	Edges
Semiotic/Material layer		
Structures of relations between material or formal representations of knowledge	*General:* Objects, artefacts, symbols, institutions (e.g., books, articles, journals, periodicals, instruments, images, buildings)	General: Semiotic relations (e.g., representation in the same object, citations, physical ties)
	Polish Case Study: Maps and publications by the migrants; infrastructure projects, such as the Trans-Andine Railway in Peru	*Polish Case Study:* Publishing in the same journal, using the same type of railway bridge truss in different viaducts, etc.
	General Relativity Case Study: Publications	*General Relativity Case Study:* (Co-)citations
Semantic layer		
Structures of semantic relations between knowledge elements	*General:* Cognitive elements (e.g., language entities, concepts, topics, keywords, theories, methods)	*General:* Semantic relations (e.g., co-occurrence, proximity in meaning, reuse of word groups)
	Polish Case Study: Areas of expertise of the migrants, such as oil exploration or railway construction	*Polish Case Study:* Similarity in terms of the focus of work (e.g., two migrants working on mapping oil fields regardless of geographical location)
	General Relativity Case Study: Topics of clusters of publications	*General Relativity Case Study:* Ties between topic clusters

2.1 The Social Layer of SEN

Social networks are networks whose nodes represent individual or collective actors and whose edges represent interactions between these actors. For examples of other types of nodes and edges that may be mapped in a social network, see Table 1. In the context of knowledge systems, these nodes and edges revolve around knowledge-related interactions (collaboration, teacher/student, master/apprentice, colleague, attending the same conference, supervisor/supervisee, etc.).

In the context of SENs, the social network is one of the three layers that need to be analysed in tandem with the semiotic/material and semantic networks discussed in the following sections. Formal social network analysis has a long "pre-history", which Linton C. Freeman traces back to the nineteenth century.[8] Using networks to understand the development of scientific knowledge can be observed as early as 1923.[9] Over the years, social network methods became more formalised and gained wider recognition among scholars across different disciplines. Phelps et al. have conducted a systematic review of research published in twelve management, psychology, sociology, and economics journals between 1970–2009, showing that an increasing amount of empirical research focused on "knowledge" centred around networks based on social ties.[10] Hence, it is perhaps not surprising that social network analysis concepts and methods are more familiar and thus more frequently chosen by scholars using network science in their historical research.[11] Furthermore, many programs and study resources have been developed to aid scholars in digital network analysis.[12]

For a social connection to exist, at the most basic level, two individuals are necessary. The interpersonal connections between a pair of individuals can be categorised in several different ways depending on the nature of the relationship; for instance, connections such as kinship, organisational and religious ties, etc. These interactions are subject to various constraints such as traditions, rules, conventions, and norms or, more broadly, by power dynamics and hierarchies that shape how these interactions unfold. To recreate a historical social network, it is necessary to use the sources to distil the relationships between individual historical actors or groups and to record this information in a structured way. This re-

---

[8] Linton C. Freeman, *The Development of Social Network Analysis: A Study in the Sociology of Science* (Vancouver, BC: Empirical Press, 2004).

[9] Giovanni Paoloni, "S for Scientometrics: Or How to Analyse and Measure Scientific Production", *Lettera Matematica – International Edition* 5, no. 2 (2017): 179.

[10] Corey Phelps, Ralph Heidl, and Anu Wadhwa, "Knowledge, Networks, and Knowledge Networks: A Review and Research Agenda", *Journal of Management* 38, no. 4 (1 July 2012): 1115–1166, doi:10.1177/0149206311432640.

[11] Lea Weiß, Laura von Welczeck, Malte Vogl, Marten Düring, Aleksandra Kaye, Jascha M. Schmitz, Raphael Schlattmann and Bernardo S. Buarque, "Past, Present, and Future of HNR: Reflections on the Practices and Methods in Historical Network Research Based on a Quantitative Survey" [Manuscript submitted for publication] (Berlin: Max Planck Institute for the History of Science, May 2024).

[12] For programs, see, for example, Mathieu Bastian, "Gephi – The Open Graph Viz Platform", accessed 1 April 2023, https://gephi.org/; Pim van Bree and Geert Kessels, "Nodegoat: a Web-based Data Management, Network Analysis & Visualisation Environment", accessed 8 May 2024, http://nodegoat.net. For tutorials teaching network science from scratch, as well as a list of network science software and a glossary, see the Archeological Networks website and accompanying textbook: Tom Brughmans, "Archaeological Networks", Archaeological Networks, accessed 9 October 2023, https://archaeologicalnetworks.wordpress.com/; Tom Brughmans and Matthew A. Peeples, *Network Science in Archaeology*, Cambridge Manuals in Archaeology (Cambridge: Cambridge University Press, 2023).

quires the researcher to make interpretative choices concerning who should be included in the network, how they would be represented by the nodes (individually or as groups), and which types of relations should be denoted by the edges. Furthermore, a researcher may choose to include the strength of the connections identified in a social network. Determining the strength of the ties frequently relies on participants reporting and rating the strength of their relationships. However, such information is not typically accessible for historians studying historical actors who are no longer alive. Should historians want to use weighted ties, they would need to consider which suitable proxies are available in the sources. For example, they may choose to weight family ties as stronger than friendships, even if that would not necessarily be true in all cases. These initial choices that go into the recreation of a historical social network will impact which sort of analysis may then be conducted. Even without knowing the directionality or strength of the connections, a lot can be learned about the structure of a network.

The position of an individual within a social network may provide clues regarding their importance for the generation of new ideas or the transfer of knowledge in this network. In social network analysis, betweenness-centrality and eigenvector-centrality are often employed to compare different individuals in the network and rank them by their importance: first, in terms of group cohesion and generating new ideas, and second, in terms of their significance for transmitting ideas between different groups in the network. The individuals scoring highly in the eigenvector-centrality measure may, for example, be conceptualised as influential or important for generating and developing ideas within the group. Here, we find the likes of Jan Sztolcman, who worked for many years in Latin America and, later among many roles, was the first director of the Branicki Museum in Warsaw between 1887 and 1919. As the network evolves and changes over time, different figures come to the fore. Hence, in the early twentieth century, we observe the increased importance of Polish editors working in the United States, such as W. Halicki at Detroit's *Dziennik Polski* (now *The Polish Weekly*). The ideas of these individuals would be influential and more likely to be accepted by others in the group. Those with high betweenness-centralities, on the other hand, are the ones who connect the most different individuals and communities in a network. Among Poles with the highest betweenness-centrality, we find expected figures, such as Joachim Lelewel, Władysław Czartoryski, or Ignacy Domejko, and the lesser-known such as Bronisław Antoni Szwarce. These individuals contribute significantly in terms of transferring knowledge from one community to another, and their removal would make the exchange of information more difficult and slower, as the number of steps required for information to travel between two distant individuals in the network would increase.[13] There are different reasons for why these individuals arrived at the privileged position of bridging different groups – Czartoryski, for example, was a Polish prince, closely associated with Hôtel Lambert (a Polish political salon in Paris) who worked on diplomatic missions in many countries, while Domejko, the rector of the University of Chile between 1867 and 1883, published profusely and corresponded widely with colleagues across Latin America and Europe. Questioning the idea of betweenness-centrality, Damon Centola proposes the concept of wide bridges, arguing that the presence of multiple shared social ties across communities is more important than individual brokers in terms of driving changes in ideas and behaviours.[14] Much can be gleaned from the structure of the network and the location of the individual nodes regarding the spread of knowledge within and between communities. Not least, important individuals who have hitherto been overshadowed by better-known colleagues come to the fore.

Using a network-based approach when studying historical migration shifts the focus from individual migrants towards their relationships with others in their communities, which, in turn, highlights that knowledge is a collaborative effort involving contributions from many individuals, not just a select celebrated few.[15] It is possible, for example, to use network methods to determine communities of practice within a network; that is, groups of people working closely together who develop joint expertise. In the Polish case studies, such communities include a group of Poles working with oil prospecting in Argentina in the 1880s or those working closely with Henryk Arctowski with regard to exploring Antarctica.[16] What is more, the evolution of the network structure can easily be observed. This is evident in the general relativity and gravitation research case study. With regard to the social networks of GRG, built by ties of collaboration and socio-institutional cooperation between actors, the late 1950s marked a crucial transformation. It went from a fragmented to a unified research network, driven mainly by the increasing mobility of postdoctoral researchers, and is re-

---

[13] The importance of such bridging individuals was observed by Ronald Burt when studying the significance of the different positions in the social capital network. He posited that a person acting as a mediator between two or more closely connected groups of people is in a privileged position to access novel information. For more, see Ronald S. Burt, "Structural Holes: The Social Structure of Competition", in *Structural Holes* (Cambridge, MA: Harvard University Press, 2009), doi:10.4159/9780674029095.

[14] Damon Centola, *How Behavior Spreads: The Science of Complex Contagions*, eds. Damon Centola, Karen S. Cook, and Peter Hedström (Princeton: Princeton University Press, 2018), https://doi.org/10.2307/j.ctvc7758p.

[15] Kaye, "Mapping Transnational Knowledge Networks".

[16] For more on Poles in Argentina, see Aleksandra Kaye, "Piecing Together 'Big Pictures' with Social Network Analysis and Digital Tools", *BJHS Themes* 9 (2024): 1–19, https://doi.org/10.1017/bjt.2024.5.

flected in the fusion of the largest components of the network. This shift towards greater connectivity and group integration occurred before key astrophysical discoveries, which supports the view that the gradual evolution of the field was actively pursued rather than being driven by research advancements, thereby supporting the findings of Blum et al.[17]

Despite its merits, exclusively analysing social networks can only offer a partial picture when studying the evolution of knowledge, which is why it needs to be supplemented with analysing the types of networks discussed in the following sections.

2.2 The Semiotic/Material Layer of SEN

Semiotic networks are networks whose nodes represent material objects or externalised representations and whose edges represent interactions or physical transformations between these objects. These may, for example, concern books in the same library or publications citing each other. These interactions are also subject to constraints such as citation conventions, archiving practices, or certain book production techniques. Semiotic networks mostly are the starting point for constructing the other levels of SENs, simply due to the fact that access to historical events frequently occurs via archival materials.

Written texts are intentionally produced manifestations of knowledge in the authors' minds. While approaches from psychology or neuroscience might pay more heed to the internal workings of the human mind, the physical representations of knowledge – be it written documents, recordings of conversations, paintings, scientific instruments, buildings, etc. – provide historians with rich evidence for the study of the outputs of human knowledge. Human knowledge is dynamic and constantly evolving, but physical representations freeze moments in time, thereby allowing us to observe the state of knowledge at specific points in history.

As an example, consider the question of the scientific history of a research organisation.[18] Using the publication output of the Max Planck Society generated in

---

[17] Alexander Blum, Roberto Lalli, and Jürgen Renn, "The Reinvention of General Relativity", *Isis* 106, no. 3 (2015): 598–620, https://doi.org/10.1086/683425; Alexander Blum, Roberto Lalli, and Jürgen Renn, "The renaissance of General Relativity", *Annalen der Physik* 528, no. 5 (2016): 344–349, https://doi.org/10.1002/andp.201600105; Alexander Blum, Roberto Lalli, and Jürgen Renn, "Gravitational waves and the long relativity revolution", *Nature Astronomy* 2, no. 7 (2018): 534–543, https://doi.org/10.1038/s41550-018-0472-6.
[18] For an in-depth online tutorial, see Malte Vogl, "The Max Planck Society and Its Scientific Context", ModelSEN, accessed 10 October 2023, https://modelsen.mpiwg-berlin.mpg.de/jupyterbooks/book/scigraph/.

all journals of the Springer/Nature publishing house between 1950 and 2005 as a corpus, we may create one realisation of a socio-epistemic network for each year with three different kinds of nodes. Authors are connected if they co-authored a publication while they are also connected to their respective publications. Publications are linked to the used word groups of length 2 ("2-gram" or more general "n-gram"). A scoring algorithm weights the link between a publication and the 2-gram.[19] In other words, the time-sliced multi-layer network thus has intra-layer links for the case of the author layer (authors are connected to co-authors) and inter-layer links between author, publication, and word layers (authors are connected to publications, and publications to 2-gram).

In order to find structural change in this set of essentially independent networks for each year, existing software such as the Infomap algorithm can be used.[20] This software enables finding communities in multilayer networks by applying concepts from information theory. A random walker traverses the network and records its path. The algorithm minimises the description of these paths by grouping nearby nodes into communities until an optimal description is found. It visualises these communities and their relations by connecting two communities in adjacent years if the majority of constituting nodes remain the same. The result (see Figure 2 for a static image) represents the starting point of a dialogue between the person building the SEN and a historian.[21] This dialogue may lead to a re-evaluation of the historian's hypotheses or a critical rebuilding of the networks.

The next example considers the following challenge often faced by historians of knowledge: how to create a useful sub-corpus for a specific research question from a larger corpus of literature without a useful classification with regard to the problem at hand?

For scientific literature, one approach is to define core papers, which, together with papers citing them and the references of these citing papers, thus make up the corpus to be analysed.[22] This approach typically requires detailed knowledge regarding the field at hand.[23]

---

19 Hidenao Abe and Shusaku Tsumoto, "Evaluating a Temporal Pattern Detection Method for Finding Research Keys in Bibliographical Data", in *Transactions on Rough Sets XIV*, eds. J.F. Peters et al. Lecture Notes in Computer Science, vol. 6600. (Berlin and Heidelberg: Springer, 2011).
20 Martin Rosvall and Carl T. Bergstrom, "Maps of Random Walks on Complex Networks Reveal Community Structure", *Proceedings of the National Academy of Sciences* 105, no. 4 (29 January 2008): 1118–1123, https://doi.org/10.1073/pnas.0706851105.
21 https://www.mapequation.org/alluvial/.
22 R. Sinatra et al., "A century of physics", *Nature Phys* 11 (2015): 791–796.
23 Lalli et al., "Socio-Epistemic Networks".

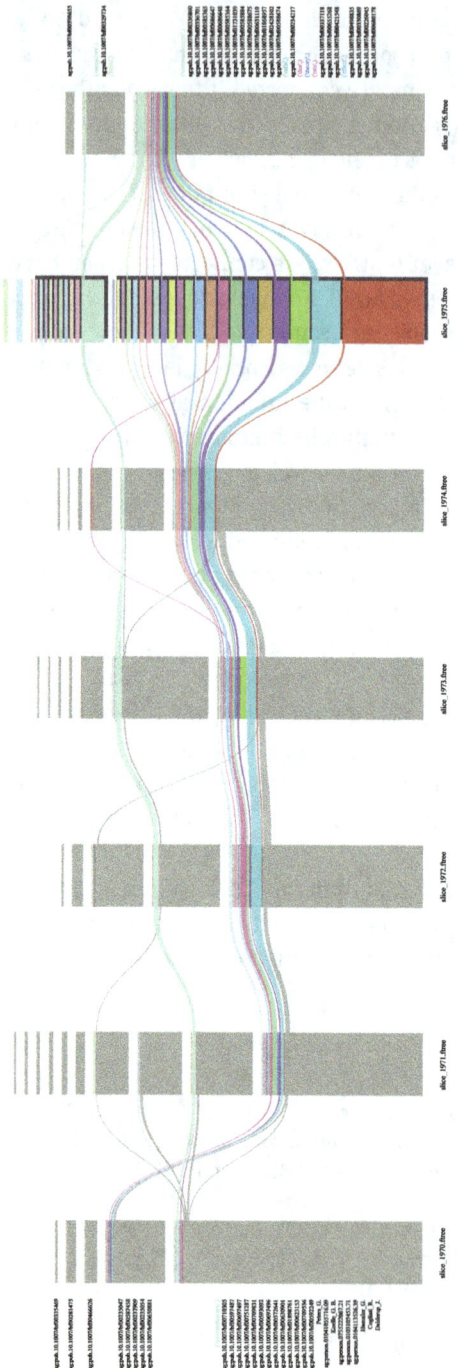

Figure 2: Flow between multilayer communities created from Max Planck Society publications in Springer/Nature during 1950–2005. The figure shows an excerpt from 1970–1976. Colours chosen so that nodes from communities in 1975 share the same colours in other years. The plot was created using Mapequations Alluvial Generator.

In the framework of SENs, a structure contained in the publications themselves can be used: their references. Using the notions of scientific fronts and the mainstream for each publication in each year, an edge entry is created between each referenced publication.[24] If the edge reoccurs in other publications, its weight is increased by one. This process is then repeated for each year. All referenced publications in the corpus must have stable and unique identifiers across the entire timespan. Due to its very nature, the resulting network is part of the semiotic layer of the SEN and contains a large number of nodes and edges. Furthermore, an edge in a given year, say 1950, can be created in this co-citation network between potentially much older literature. Hence, a co-citation is often interpreted as an expression of the authors of the publication finding that two other publications belong together to support an argument. While this may be contested given the different mechanisms of why publications are cited, such effects are negligible for larger corpora.

Existing software can also be used to retrieve information on structural changes in such a dense co-citation network. This time, the Leiden algorithm, which is an extension of the well-known Louvain algorithm, allows us to find communities in networks across temporal layers.[25] Just like the Louvain algorithm, this algorithm is also density-based, meaning that a density parameter must be determined so that nodes inside one community are more closely connected compared to nodes in other communities This necessitates another iteration cycle between the person building a SEN and a historian. The result of such an iteration is a list of publications grouped in communities for a range of years. To support the historical analysis, the software package semanticlayertools,[26] developed in the framework of the project ModelSEN, uses additional metadata related to the publications, such as authors and affiliations, and a fast topic modelling on the titles of each community as a reporting routine. After each iteration, the historian can decide which communities should remain part of the analysis and which are to be ignored. After several iteration cycles, the result is a more focused and narrower corpus in relation to the research question in conjunction with the researcher's interpretation. See Figure 3 for the example of astrophysics research literature related to the GRG case in the NASA Astrophysical Data System (ADS).[27]

---

[24] For more on the notions of scientific fronts and the mainstream, see: M. B. Synnestvedt, C. Chen, and J. H. Holmes, "CiteSpace II: Visualisation and knowledge discovery in bibliographic databases", *AMIA Annual Symposium Proceedings* (2005): 724–728.
[25] V.A. Traag, L. Waltman, and N.-J. Van Eck, "From Louvain to Leiden: Guaranteeing Well-connected Communities", *Scientific Reports* 9, no. 1 (2018): 5233.
[26] Malte Vogl, SemanticLayerTools (0.1.3). Zenodo (2022). https://doi.org/10.5281/zenodo.6401221.
[27] See "Astrophysics Data System", NASA/ADS, accessed 10 October 2023, https://ui.adsabs.harvard.edu/.

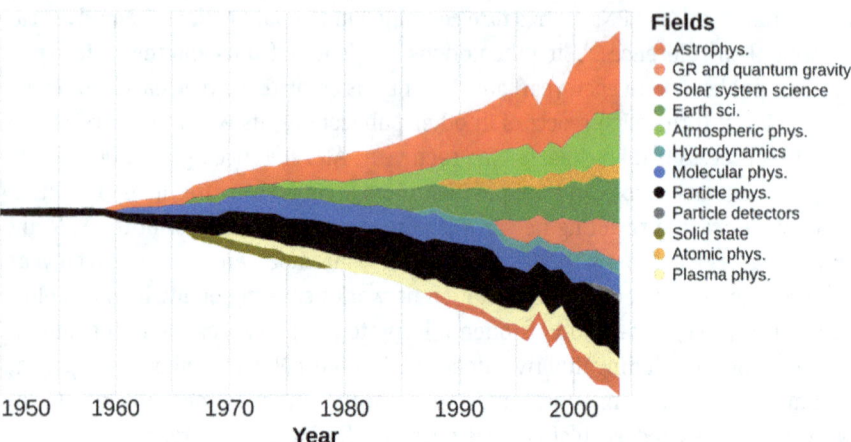

Figure 3: A streamgraph showing the temporal development of the size of co-citation clusters related to astrophysical research. The labelling was created manually by Roberto Lalli. Data retrieved from the NASA Astrophysical Data System, see main text.

For the GRG case, the analysis of co-citation networks highlights a dynamic evolution in the field. By examining the largest components, it can be observed that early periods underwent radical changes, which transitioned into stabilisation and the emergence of small-world network characteristics in later years. This transformation, demonstrated by long-term shifts in the largest components, points to a complex, two-phased (theoretical renaissance and astrophysical turn) but gradual development and consolidation of the field over the analysed decades rather than a sudden shift. This process is compatible with the community-building processes starting after World War II observed in the social layer and mentioned in section 2.1.

With regard to the Polish case study, the semiotic network highlights the changing interests and geographical distribution of the Polish diaspora. For example, a rise and decline of Polish political publications in the French language can be seen in the period between 1830 and 1870 – likely a reflection of the Great Emigration[28] – or an increase in Polish special-interest publications of Brazilian and Argentinian origin in the late nineteenth century and the later sharp rise of US-based publications in the early twentieth century as more and more Polish immigrants headed there. Linking the findings from this layer to the social layer through the different actors involved in the production of these periodicals allows

---

[28] In Polish historiography, the "Great Emigration" refers to the large-scale emigration of Poles following the November 1830 uprising and later failed uprisings. This migration wave ends roughly in the 1870s, the decade following the January 1863 uprising.

us to determine the importance of the different publications in terms of bringing together various professionals, while linking this layer to the semantic layer (see section 2.3) could clarify which periodicals were pioneering in terms of the content they published.

2.3 The Semantic Layer of SEN

Semantic networks comprise nodes representing cognitive elements, while the edges represent cognitive operations or interactions between these elements, which may be concepts, mental models, or other cognitive entities.[29] The significance here, as with the networks described above, concerns understanding the entire network as a carrier of knowledge compared to the individual elements. Institutionalisation or community-building processes are crucial for knowledge formation in social knowledge networks, while the ongoing reproduction and normalization of certain cognitive interactions are key for semantic knowledge structures. For example, continuously combining mental representations such as "negative charge", "particle", "spin" when dealing with the mental representation of "electron". In this regard, both processes are mirrored in systemic structures that can be represented by networks.

Unlike the other two types of networks, however, semantic networks are constructed more "indirectly" through language or other methods of culturally embedded, codified meaning, thereby making a mapping less tangible than, say, a social connection such as a record of a meeting between two individuals. In most cases in the history of knowledge, written texts are the foundation for constructing semantic networks, meaning that the process of extracting meaning in terms of concepts or similar structures is a complex one.[30] Adding a word to a sentence or even just a character may alter the whole meaning conveyed by this sentence. For instance, frequently co-occurring words (e.g., "energy", "level", "low", "high") may be seen as a rough operationalisation of a concept ("energy levels") but could convey very different meanings across different actors, contexts, or languages (e.g., physics, chemistry, sports, gaming, etc.). The example chosen is deliberately simplistic to highlight general difficulties that may be minimised by a clear definition of the realm of analysis and reflecting on the accuracy of the assumptions made, still permitting the construction of structurally useful approxi-

---

29 Renn et al., "Netzwerke als Wissensspeicher", 16.
30 Jürgen Renn, *The Evolution of Knowledge* (Princeton and Oxford: Princeton University Press, 2020), 324.

mations of semantic structures represented as networks. However, the level of abstraction is usually greater compared to the other layers.

Again, there are constraints for these interactions, which organise the development of these structures and are dynamic in nature. Examples include collective belief systems or systematisations such as the "scientific method"; in other words, underlying cognitive principles that govern or give order to these interactions, thus structuring cognitive elements into a system of knowledge.

The notion of semantic networks has been around for quite some time and has been utilised in various contexts such as psychology, linguistics, neuroscience, or computer science to model conceptual knowledge representation and organisation. They have been operationalised through various methods, such as word association tasks,[31] co-occurrence networks,[32] feature-based semantic networks,[33] semantic parsing,[34] or quantum semantics.[35] These approaches involve creating networks in which nodes represent either spoken or written words, phrases, or other n-grams, while edges represent associations, co-occurrences, proximity, shared features, or other semantic relationships. The specific method used depends on the research goals and the type of data being analysed.

For the GRG case, an example of a (semio-)semantic network is a network of topics built on top of a co-citation network.[36] The network formed from papers (nodes) of the subdiscipline general relativity and gravitation having been co-cited (edges) within a range of years (e.g., 1946–1975) has already been mentioned in section 2.2. The co-citation or, more generally, the network models underlying citation analysis are widely utilised and well-established across disciplines. The key assumption is simplified: nodes primarily represent a paper (semiotic/material layer) but also, secondly, certain topics (the content of the paper: semantic layer), while edges primarily represent a co-citation but also, secondly, a cognitive link between

---

31 Mark Steyvers and Joshua B. Tenenbaum, "The Large-Scale Structure of Semantic Networks: Statistical Analyses and a Model of Semantic Growth", *Cognitive Science* 29, no. 1 (2005): 41–78, https://doi.org/10.1207/s15516709cog2901_3.
32 Elad Segev, ed., *Semantic Network Analysis in Social Sciences* (London and New York: Routledge, 2021).
33 Ray Grondin, Stephen J. Lupker, and Ken McRae, "Shared Features Dominate Semantic Richness Effects for Concrete Concepts", *Journal of Memory and Language* 60, no. 1 (2009): 1–19, https://doi.org/10.1016/j.jml.2008.09.001.
34 Hoifung Poon and Pedro Domingos, "Unsupervised Semantic Parsing", *Proceedings of the 2009 Conference on Empirical Methods in Natural Language Processing*, 2009, 1–10.
35 Ismo Koponen and Ilona Södervik, "Lexicons of Key Terms in Scholarly Texts and Their Disciplinary Differences: From Quantum Semantics Construction to Relative-Entropy-Based Comparisons", *Entropy* 24, no. 8 (2022): 1058, https://doi.org/10.3390/e24081058.
36 Lalli et al., "Socio-Epistemic Networks".

these topics made by the authors who cited them. Many edges between two co-cited papers are then interpreted as topic proximity. These co-citation networks can be clustered using various methods (e.g., Louvain, Leiden, Girvan-Newman, etc.), and these clusters may be thought of as representing a specific topic mixture. There are several ways to extract them, one of which is to aggregate all texts (e.g., reduced to nouns or proper nouns) in a cluster and build a semantic network based on these texts.[37] For that, an ordered list of non-overlapping terms may be transformed into a semantic network representing the topic structure of the co-citation cluster. In this second-order network, each term is represented by a node, while edges link this term to other terms that co-occur within a specified window of terms around it, so that we get a co-occurrence network. The creation of links between nodes (terms) in the semantic network is determined by the window width. If it is set to 10, then an edge is created between two terms if they co-occur within a window of 10 terms. This is done for every cluster in the co-citation network so that a semantic network is created for each cluster. For these semantic networks, centrality measures such as eigenvector-centrality can then be calculated to find the most central words for every cluster, thus resulting in a list of words representing the encoded topics. Since these clusters are dynamic, this is done for all time slices of length x in the period of interest.

An analysis of this kind confirms the dynamic evolution in the GRG case, identifying clusters outlining the development and transformation of research topics from the late 1950s through to the early 1960s similar to the transition into a phase characterised by small-world networks mentioned in section 2.2. Notably, a significant cluster concerning general relativity marks a focused return to the foundational problems of the field, followed by the emergence of clusters related to astrophysical and cosmological topics, thus indicating a transition in research interests to relativistic astrophysics and the study of black holes.[38] This substantiates what we have seen in the semiotic layer: After World War II, GRG research initially experienced a refocusing on fundamental questions (theoretical renaissance), followed by a transition to astrophysical questions (astrophysical turn).

Two different semantic networks were created in the Polish case study: one focused specifically on narratives related to petroleum and one visualising the different forms of expertise of the migrants and how these changed over time. The first highlighted the change in petroleum being perceived as a medical curiosity through its application in kerosene lamps and later as a fuel for combustion engines, thereby allowing Polish Galician entrepreneurs to trade petroleum on

---

37 Lalli et al., "Socio-Epistemic Networks", 47.
38 Lalli et al., "Socio-Epistemic Networks".

the international markets until it transitioned into a commodity of national importance in relation to the war effort. The latter example enabled observing the shifts in contributions made by Polish migrants globally during the century between 1830 and 1930, thus suggesting avenues for further research.

Other methods used to extract and relate semantic information from groups of texts to other groups of text on a large scale include topic modelling and/or text embedding[39] or other information-theoretical techniques.[40] Unlike utilising second-order networks built from structures of another layer, these methods directly employ the underlying texts to create interpretable groups or clusters. Embeddings, for example, convert text into multidimensional numerical vectors that can be treated algebraically; for instance, similarities between words, sentences, paragraphs, and documents can easily be calculated. These techniques open up a strategy for responding to a wide array of intriguing questions. How does the context of the term "graviton" evolve over time? Or, in the Polish case study, how do the Poles conceptualise and write about petroleum and its applications? How do discourses change over time? Which topics are gaining popularity, which are dwindling, and which individuals or texts are driving these developments? Which publications in the year 2000 use language similar to the mainstream of their discipline as it looked in the 1950s, or how do those in 1910 compare to those in 1850?

Coupled with an iterative structural analysis of the social and semiotic/material layer, addressing these sorts of questions aims to systematise research across all dimensions of knowledge, thus offering broader perspectives and uncovering otherwise undiscovered correlations.

---

39 Maarten Grootendorst, "BERTopic: Neural topic modeling with a class-based TF-IDF procedure" (2022), http://arxiv.org/pdf/2203.05794v1; Adji B. Dieng, Francisco J. R. Ruiz, and David M. Blei, "Topic Modeling in Embedding Spaces," *Transactions of the Association for Computational Linguistics* 8 (2020), https://doi.org/10.1162/tacl_a_00325, https://aclanthology.org/2020.tacl-1.29/; Yuri Bizzoni et al., "Linguistic Variation and Change in 250 Years of English Scientific Writing: A Data-Driven Approach", *Frontiers in Artificial Intelligence* 3 (2020), https://doi.org/10.3389/frai.2020.00073, https://www.frontiersin.org/articles/10.3389/frai.2020.00073/full.
40 Stefania Degaetano-Ortlieb and Elke Teich, "Toward an Optimal Code for Communication: The Case of Scientific English", *Corpus Linguistics and Linguistic Theory* 18, no. 1 (2022), https://doi.org/10.1515/cllt-2018-0088, https://www.degruyter.com/document/doi/10.1515/cllt-2018-0088/html#j_cllt-2018-0088_ref_042.

3 Challenges, Limitations, and Rigour of Results

One of the greatest challenges linked to the broad implementation of the framework proposed in this chapter concerns the quality of the data available for analysis, from a complete lack of digitalisation to issues with digitised material, such as poor OCR or incorrect metadata. As a result, historians of knowledge interested in this method will need to invest significant time in data preparation tasks before they can embark on their analysis. While in many cases, the effort involved is worth the investment, as clean data can be used in many ways beyond just network analysis, scholars need to ask themselves if the knowledge they potentially gain justifies the effort involved in attaining it. A careful selection of methods and tools in the search for new knowledge is necessary. SENs may be one framework among many that scholars can use to better understand the evolution of knowledge rather than an ultimate means to an end. Before deriving conclusions from these networks, researchers should critically examine their hypothesis, data, and models. Indeed, as Albert-László Barabási and others write, "for any network, before attempting to model it, we need to understand the limitations of the data collection process and test their effect on the quantities of interest for us."[41]

When it comes to the case study on the Max Planck Society (see section 2.2), a critique of the result might be the missing historical interpretability of a community consisting of agglomerations of authors, publications, and words. While the rise and fall in the importance of one such community is hard to interpret, the structure of these changes may hint at where to direct traditional historical research. In this sense, as mentioned above, SENs do not constitute a method to an end but the combination of a certain perspective with certain methodologies in an iterative workflow between quantitative and qualitative analysis. Another criticism could be raised with regard to using publication time stamps to temporally order the publication material. It is well-known that the publication date is not the time of the creation of the semantic content, and a cut at each end of a calendar year when creating slices in the material is rather arbitrary (e.g., submission dates that are much earlier than publication dates). Statistics can mitigate data noise issues to some extent if the dataset used for the analysis is sufficiently large to identify relevant trends.

Other common challenges involve the biases encoded in source data and erroneous information on, for instance, authorship or time, as well as these resulting from the gaps and silences in the archival record. Furthermore, the need for elaborate

---

41 A. L. Barabási et al., "Evolution of the Social Network of Scientific Collaborations", *Physica A* 311, no. 3 (2002): 590–614, https://doi.org/10.1016/S0378-4371(02)00736-7.

tools or expertise to efficiently extract information, and the biases (often language-based) inherent in available tools and digital infrastructure are also challenging. These and similar challenges and limitations lead to a central question: how can a researcher quantify whether a historical analysis is rigorous?

Consider a scenario in which a researcher seeks to assess the impact of a particular variable on another. For example, they might want to learn how the historical number of oil wells in the region of Galicia (now Poland and Ukraine) affects its current air quality. Or they may want to measure the influence of Polish immigrants in Latin America on oil exploration across the continent. In other words, they want to test an existing hypothesis about the world. Hence, based on the relevant literature, they would need to construct a statistical test to address their specific questions. They would use the available data and methods to estimate whether oil wells lead to significantly worse air quality in Poland and Ukraine. But, after doing so, they would need to consider the robustness or reliability of the results from their test. Do the data and methods accurately represent the problem and theory in question? Could some other unaccounted third variable be impacting the results (e.g., the number of coal mines) and thus should be taken into consideration? If that is the case, they would need to perform the test again, this time including the third parameter. If so, what happens to the results? Does adding coal mines to the regression completely change it, or do the initial outputs still hold even after controlling for this aspect? Such an iterative process of refinement and modification is, in short, the core principle behind a robustness check.

With regard to the Polish case study, when conducting a social network analysis, one should ask whether the frequency of ties between Polish immigrants in a specific region is significantly greater than what would be expected by chance. To answer this question, a randomisation process, permutation analysis, or generative model could be applied. These are all tests commonly agreed upon and adopted throughout other research fields but not yet established in the fields of history of knowledge or history of science.

Researchers make inferences based on their assumptions about the world. Every mathematical model or statistical test is based on these assumptions – some explicitly, others not. Thus, researchers constantly need to remind themselves how changing these assumptions might influence the underlying results. This is the core logic behind robustness checks. For the emerging interdisciplinary research using digital sources in the history of knowledge, a coordinated toolkit of robustness checks that can be used to add greater confidence in the results thus far remains an urgent and much-needed desideratum.

4 Conclusion

This article illustrates the potential of SENs as a robust, interdisciplinary framework for examining the evolution of knowledge systems. By integrating social, semiotic/material, and semantic spheres, this framework takes into account the assumption that knowledge is inherently multidimensional. The computational aspects of this framework (i.e., multi-layered networks) underscore the necessity of addressing large-scale historical phenomena using a large-scale, structural approach. Knowledge systems can be represented as clearly defined (i.e., simplified), quantifiable/calculable, and reproducible structures, not only using networks but also other approaches of operationalisation, such as text embeddings. The principal argument is that knowledge is multidimensional and that large-scale developments require robust computational operationalisation to analyse structural changes. However, at this point in time, we believe that networks still represent the best way to accommodate this perspective, having reached a level of epistemic and methodological maturity enabling the realisation of these objectives. They capture the embeddedness and relationality of knowledge production and dissemination, while also offering tools to explore structural and temporal questions. As shown with the case studies presented, other computational methods such as topic modelling are necessary in order to complement the network approach. This further highlights the necessity of scrutinising the rigorousness of results by applying both digital source and tool criticism. The socio-epistemic networks framework then offers a structural approach to the evolution of knowledge systems that enables uncovering novel perspectives for the history of knowledge.

Aleksandra Kaye is a postdoctoral researcher at the Max Planck Institute of Geoanthropology in Jena. Her current research examines cross-regional interactions and the circulation of environmental knowledge in relation to forest stewardship and petroleum extraction. Her doctoral research traced the histories of Polish scientific professionals in Latin America in the nineteenth century. Recent publications include "Piecing together 'big pictures' with social network analysis and digital tools" in *BJHS Themes* (2024) and "Shaping Public Perception: Polish Illustrated Press and the Image of Polish Naturalists Working in Latin America, 1844–1885" in *Berichte zur Wissenschaftsgeschichte* (2023).

Raphael Schlattmann is a historian of science with a background in theoretical physics. His research centres on the history of gravitational research in the field of GDR during the Cold War. Methodologically, he specialises in computational history with a particular interest in historical network research and the application of natural language processing (NLP) in processes of knowledge evolution. He is currently developing new digital tools and methods to analyse trajectories of change within large text corpora at the Max Planck Institute of Geoanthropology in Jena.

Malte Vogl is a senior research fellow at the Max Planck Institute of Geoanthropology with a PhD in physics. Until recently, he worked as a research fellow and PI at the Max Planck Institute for the History of Science in projects ranging from digital humanities work on the ancient perception of time and space in the cluster of excellency TOPOI, building and evaluating research data infrastructures in the context of the DARIAH project, large-scale analysis of archival data for the history of the MPG project GMPG to the most recent, BMBF-funded work on developing methods for modelling knowledge evolution as a multilayered temporal network in the ModelSEN project.

Bernardo S. Buarque is a postdoctoral researcher at Te Punaha Matatini, New Zealand. Before moving to Wellington, he worked as a research scholar at the Max Planck Institute for the History of Science and earned his PhD from the University College Dublin. His research focuses on complex networks and dynamic systems modelling, particularly in the context of innovation and knowledge diffusion.

Jascha Schmitz is a PhD student at the digital history professorship of the Humboldt-University Berlin while also working there for Task Area 5 "Dataculture" of the NFDI4Memory – the national research data initiative for historical sciences. His research focuses include Anthropocene-centric historical research as well as the methodological and epistemological basis of digital historical methods, in particular simulation methods such as agent-based modelling. His PhD project concerns simulating the contexts and perspectives of individual mobility in a "modern" city (ca. 1920) before the advent of widespread individual car-use.

Lea Weiß is a student research assistant at the Max Planck Institute for the History of Science as part of the research project "Socio-epistemic Networks: Modelling Historical Knowledge Processes" (ModelSEN). With an interest in historical sociology, science studies, and computational social science, she wrote her bachelor's thesis on the social network positions of female scientists in twentieth-century physics and is currently studying the diversification of the methodological landscape in the field of historical network research.

Laura von Welczeck has previously served as a student research assistant at the Max Planck Institute for the History of Science and part of the ModelSEN team on modelling socio-epistemic networks for historical knowledge processes. There, she investigated the diversification of the methodological landscape in the field of historical network research. She studies sociology and information systems in Berlin.

Hampus Östh Gustafsson
R. S. Crane and the Invention of the Humanities: The Formation of Historical Narratives of Knowledge in the Mid-Twentieth Century

Abstract: Histories of knowledge have tended to be constructed and mobilized at times when the value of certain scholarly disciplines is being called into question. By investigating early examples of histories of the humanities in comparison to pioneering works in the history of science, this study sheds new light on the development of various fields in a broad sense concerned with the history of knowledge, emphasizing the need for studying the effects of histories of knowledge generated in the past. The article highlights a largely forgotten account by Ronald S. Crane that was said to form a unique genre while, in fact, reflecting a widespread controversy regarding the position of the humanities in mid-twentieth-century Western culture. The ambitious narratives of Crane and his colleagues at the University of Chicago and beyond contributed to the construction of long humanist traditions with the purpose of defining and making sense of their own scholarship at a time marked by political and social turmoil. These discursive interventions were embedded in wider processes of institutional reformation, as new study programs in the humanities were founded. Arguably, the novel historical narratives of knowledge thus contributed to the very "invention" of the modern US-American humanities.

Keywords: history of humanities, histories of knowledge, historical narratives, Ronald S. Crane, the Chicago School of Literary Criticism

---

Acknowledgements: This article was partly written during my stay as a research fellow at the Vossius Center for the History of Humanities and Sciences, University of Amsterdam. I am truly grateful for the generous support and warm welcome I received at the Vossius seminar, particularly from Rens Bod. Thanks also to Herman Paul, whose critical comments and advice were crucial for the completion of this article. I am also grateful to Erik Ahlenius, Isak Hammar, Johan Heilbron, the editors, and anonymous reviewers for useful comments. Finally, I wish to thank Åke Wibergs stiftelse for the generous funding I received for carrying out this project.

Introduction: A Unique Genre?

There is no name, I think, for the kind of humanistic scholar revealed in this collection from more than three decades of work by Ronald Crane. [. . .] What, for example, is the genre of the history of the humanities and how they were defined, from Vives, to the present, with which the book opens? [. . .] Of efforts to define the humanities there are many. But I know of nothing that is quite like this canvassing of our shortcomings and opportunities as humanists, done in the light of a historical construction of previous ideas about the humanities.[1]

In an introduction to *The Idea of the Humanities and Other Essays: Critical and Historical* by English professor and literary critic Ronald S. Crane (1886–1967), which was published the same year as the author passed away, Wayne C. Booth portrayed this account of the history of the humanities as highly original. Even though he may have been biased as a former student of Crane at the University of Chicago, Booth was not alone in his opinion. One review, for instance, stated that "many modern humanists, of all people, neglect the history and tradition of their field, not realizing that many insights of the past are still insights today."[2] Crane's historical narrative served to assist a larger project of reforming US-American higher education in the 1930s and 1940s, while also seeking to provide relevant historical knowledge to a war-torn world he believed had lost its course. Yet, despite its potential significance, this early history of the humanities has largely been forgotten.

Some fifty years later, however, we are seeing the emergence of *history of humanities* as a specific field of historical research.[3] While this field has been framed as a recent occurrence, first starting to become institutionalized in the twenty-first century, we should – keeping Crane's work in mind – question just how novel this type of historical inquiry actually is. Upon reviewing Rens Bod's formative monograph *A New History of the Humanities* (2013), Noel Malcolm indi-

---

[1] Wayne C. Booth, introduction to R. S. Crane, *The Idea of the Humanities and Other Essays: Critical and Historical*, vol. 1 (Chicago: University of Chicago Press, 1967), xiii, xxi.
[2] Everett Lee Hunt, "When are the 'Humanities' Humane?" *The Quarterly Journal of Speech* 53, no. 3 (1967): 285.
[3] Rens Bod, *A New History of the Humanities: The Search for Principles and Patterns from Antiquity to the Present* (Oxford: Oxford University Press, 2013); Rens Bod et al., "A New Field: History of Humanities," *History of Humanities* 1, no. 1 (2016): 1–8, DOI: https://doi.org/10.1086/685056; Isak Hammar and Hampus Östh Gustafsson, "Futures of the History of the Humanities: An Introduction," *History of Humanities* 8, no. 2 (2023): 177–187, DOI: https://doi.org/10.1086/726361; Herman Paul, "Introduction: What is the History of the Humanities?," in *Writing the History of the Humanities: Questions, Themes, Approaches*, ed. Herman Paul (London: Bloomsbury, 2023), 1–24.

cated that this was "the First History of its Kind."[4] This phrasing is curiously similar to the previous rhetoric used when characterizing Crane's narrative.

Over the years, scholars in the humanities have naturally reflected upon the collective history of their own disciplines, embedding historical narratives in attempts to articulate the value of the humanities. In most cases, however, this was done in passing or in fragmented ways, typically focusing on individual disciplines, institutions, or biographies.[5] Crane's endeavor stands out as an early and extraordinary attempt to systematically compile a comprehensive and systematic history of the humanities. As fractional historical perspectives still over the years informed so many reflections on the state of the humanities, it is remarkable that no specialized research field concerning the history of the humanities has emerged until now – in contrast to the history of science, with a much longer legacy. Historians of science, especially in the Anglo-American world, rarely include the humanities.[6] This is quite logical due to linguistic circumstances. In other contexts, however, such as those indebted to the German tradition of *Geisteswissenschaften*, intellectual history and the history of science have generally been broader in nature. Nevertheless, the recurring omission of the humanities has prompted proponents of the new history of humanities to advocate for a more inclusive stance, paired with an aspiration to establish an integrative history of knowledge that goes beyond any limitations imposed by the term "science."[7]

Writing Histories in Times of Crisis

In this article, I historicize the construction of histories of the humanities and their function in a larger scholarly and social context, touching upon questions such as: why do we need histories of the humanities or, indeed, histories of knowledge and

---

4 Noel Malcolm, "Masters of What? An Extraordinarily Ambitious Book, the First History of its Kind: But the Humanities Remain Hard to Define," *Times Literary Supplement*, 5801, June 6, 2014.
5 Cf. Lorraine Daston and Glenn W. Most, "History of Science and History of Philologies," *Isis* 106, no. 2 (2015): 385, DOI: https://doi.org/10.1086/681980.
6 Simone Lässig, "The History of Knowledge and the Expansion of the Historical Research Agenda," *Bulletin of the German Historical Institute* 59 (2016): 35.
7 For instance, Rens Bod, "How to Open Pandora's Box: A Tractable Notion of the History of Knowledge," *Journal for the History of Knowledge* 1, no. 1 (2020): 1–7, DOI: https://doi.org/10.5334/jhk.28. This would also include the history of the human and/or social sciences, which has been studied in new, sophisticated ways since at least the 1990s. See, for instance, Roger Smith, "What Is the History of the Human Sciences?," in *The Palgrave Handbook of the History of the Human Sciences*, ed. David McCallum (Singapore: Palgrave Macmillan, 2022), 3–28, DOI: 10.1007/978-981-16-7255-2_83. See also James Turner, *Philology: The Forgotten Origins of the Modern Humanities* (Princeton: Princeton University Press, 2014), xv.

scholarship at all? How do such narratives operate? And what does it mean to write them?

Crane's account not only serves as a past parallel to present-day histories of the humanities, but also as an example of how historical narratives of knowledge in a more general sense have been constructed in order to fulfill certain needs in the present. To this end, I study Crane's ventures in the context of broader US-American debates on the humanities. I also compare his narrative with other examples of grand histories of knowledge produced roughly at the same time, such as George Sarton's history of science. My scrutiny regarding such historiographic practices contributes to gaining a better understanding of the role of historical narratives related to the humanities – and possibly other forms of knowledge – also in our present day.

The recent formation of history of the humanities must be interpreted as a reaction to experiences of a strained situation for the humanities. As noted by Robert Proctor in 1988: "It is only with the so-called 'crisis of the humanities' that the question of defining and understanding the humanities historically becomes a relevant and useful one." In troubled times, Proctor found it urgent to look into the past, as the study of "the history of the humanities enables us to stand outside this disorder and confusion."[8] The present surge of histories of the humanities is clearly not the first occasion where we have seen historical narratives being used in the face of threats to the humanities – and society. In fact, the construction of such narratives in times of pressure has formed a recurring pattern, which is no surprise given that the humanities have tended to be seen as perpetually facing crises.[9]

In particular, this study looks into Crane's long essay "Shifting Definitions and Evaluations of the Humanities from the Renaissance to the Present," based on ten lectures at the University of Chicago in 1943 and eventually included in the aforementioned 1967 volume. The analysis also encompasses other programmatic texts, including works by other members of the early Chicago School of Literary Criticism founded by Crane in the 1930s. The literature on the Chicago School is relatively limited, and even more so when it comes to Crane and his works.[10] Previous scholarship has primarily focused on his contributions to literary theory.

---

[8] Robert Proctor, *Defining the Humanities: How Rediscovering a Tradition Can Improve our Schools* (Bloomington: Indiana University Press, 1998), 8, 87.

[9] Hampus Östh Gustafsson, "The Humanities in Crisis: Comparative Perspectives on a Recurring Motif," in *Writing the History of the Humanities: Questions, Themes, Approaches*, ed. Herman Paul (London: Bloomsbury 2023), 65–83; Paul Reitter and Chad Wellmon, *Permanent Crisis: The Humanities in a Disenchanted Age* (Chicago: University of Chicago Press, 2021).

[10] James Phelan, "The Chicago School: From Neo-Aristotelian Poetics to the Rhetorical Theory of Narrative," in *Theoretical Schools and Circles in the Twentieth-Century Humanities: Literary Theory, History, Philosophy*, eds. Marina Grishakova and Silvi Salupere (New York & London: Routledge, 2015), 133.

One exception is Anna-Dorothea Schneider's dissertation, even though it mainly focuses on the institutional context and Crane's significance in relation to US-American criticism.[11]

The main focus of this article is rather on how Crane and his fellow authors historicized the humanities and linked together various historical epochs, thus developing more synthetic claims in order to promote certain ends. What I try to emphasize is what they *did* (or attempted to do) through their constructions of historical narratives or traditions of knowledge within a wider discourse. Empirical studies of such narrative strategies are surprisingly scarce.[12] I here look upon the mobilization of histories of the humanities and/or knowledge as examples of how specific actors reacted to certain problems and sought to promote change by constructing historical narratives. Genealogical searches concerning the origins and traditions of scholarly branches either tend to pull up the roots in an emancipatory fashion or identify past examples that may reinvigorate current practices.[13] In such ways, histories of knowledge serve as discursive strategies with a legitimizing function. In the case of Crane, historical narratives were generated in order to make sense of, and preferably alter, a situation of socio-political turmoil and protracted debate by coming to terms with what the humanities actually were or should be – and what had to be done to secure their influence on higher education in modern America.

"What to do with the Humanities": The (American) Dream of a New Humanism

Crane obviously did not produce his history of the humanities in a vacuum. In fact, the first half of the twentieth century saw a great controversy over the fate of liberal education and humanism in America. This generated numerous discussions on the value and organization of the humanities, particularly during the in-

---

[11] Anna-Dorothea Schneider, *Humanities at the Crossroads: The Chicago Neo-Aristotelian Critics and the University of Chicago 1930–1950* (Baden-Baden: Nomos, 2019 [1991]). See also Asit Kr. Biswas, *Literary Criticism of R.S. Crane: Theory and Practice* (New Delhi: Atlantic, 2003).
[12] Stefan Berger and Chris Lorenz, "Analysing Historical Narratives: Concluding Remarks," in *Analysing Historical Narratives: On Academic, Popular and Educational Framings of the Past*, eds. Stefan Berger, Nicola Brauch, and Chris Lorenz, Making Sense of History 41 (New York: Berghahn Books, 2021), 334, 339.
[13] Cf. Herman Paul, "Genealogies of the Humanities: A Vision for the Field," *History of Humanities* 8, no. 2 (2023): 199–207.

terwar period. Classicist B. L. Ullman noted in *The Journal of Higher Education* (1946) that the "literature, so-called, on the humanities, also so-called" in the last decade had become so vast that: "Some persons seem to write books on the humanities as casually as they light a cigarette."[14]

Ullman's phrasing regarding the "so-called" humanities was not accidental. The English term *humanities* had its breakthrough in the US in the 1930s and 1940s. Obviously, it had circulated before (the explicit term was derived from the French *les humanités* in the late eighteenth century), but it was then typically tied to the classics or the curriculum established in relation to Renaissance humanism. Now, the term came to include broader connotations and was institutionalized as a common set of disciplines in higher education.[15] The University of Chicago played a significant part in this process by establishing a new Division of the Humanities. Several other universities followed suit, and more than thirty courses or programs in the humanities were launched in 1940. New ideas and definitions of the humanities thus materialized, and the new curricula cemented specific canons. Historical perspectives were crucial in relation to this conceptual and institutional formation, but there was no given legacy to draw from. Humanist traditions had to be traced in order to provide cultural guidance.[16] But why did it suddenly seem so urgent to dwell on the (historical) nature of the humanities?

One point of reference in numerous interwar debates was the literary scholar Irving Babbitt, who led the conservative movement of New Humanism in the early part of the century. Babbitt's call for a return to classical languages inspired later waves of humanist resistance against positivist pressure, but his project was

---

14 B. L. Ullman, "What Are the Humanities? An Appraisal of Current Definitions," *The Journal of Higher Education* 17, no. 6 (1946): 301.
15 Eric Adler, *The Battle of the Classics: How a Nineteenth-Century Debate Can Save the Humanities Today* (Oxford: Oxford University Press, 2020), 33; Steven Marcus, "Humanities from Classics to Cultural Studies: Notes Toward the History of an Idea," *Daedalus* 135, no. 2 (2006): 15–19; Robert E. Proctor, *Education's Great Amnesia: Reconsidering the Humanities from Petrarch to Freud with a Curriculum for Today's Students* (Bloomington: Indiana University Press, 1988), 7; Reitter and Wellmon, *Permanent Crisis*, 224; Jon H. Roberts and James Turner, *The Sacred and the Secular University* (Princeton: Princeton University Press, 2000), 75; Schneider, *Humanities at the Crossroads*, 26–27. See also Stefan Collini, "Seeing a Specialist: The Humanities as Academic Disciplines," *Past & Present* 229 (2015): 273; Anthony Grafton and Lisa Jardine, *From Humanism to the Humanities: Education and the Liberal Arts in Fifteenth- and Sixteenth-Century Europe* (London: Duckworth, 1986); Geoffrey Galt Harpham, *The Humanities and the Dream of America* (Chicago: University of Chicago Press, 2011); and cf. Julian Hamann, *The Making of the 'Geisteswissenschaften': A Case of Boundary Work?* FIW Working Papers 7 (Bonn: Rheinische Friedrich-Wilhelms-Universität Bonn, 2017).
16 Marcus, "Humanities," 17–19. See also Fabian Krämer, "What Are the Humanities? A Short History of Concepts and Classifications," in *Writing the History of the Humanities: Questions, Themes, Approaches*, ed. Herman Paul (London: Bloomsbury, 2023), 39.

heavily criticized for being reactionary.[17] Even though they shared some common ground, Babbitt's ideas inevitably clashed with those of John Dewey, whose pragmatism and vocationalism were foundational to US-American debates on education following the First World War. Concerns were raised that Dewey's program left no room for traditional humanities. As the system of higher education expanded, a need for drastic curricular reforms was identified in order to safeguard the academic subjects that soon ended up being jointly referred to as the humanities.[18]

The critique against the New Humanists thus reflected a greater struggle to accommodate an older heritage of humanistic practices to a new reality, marked by positivist specialization and democratization.[19] If humanism and the humanities were to have any future, they had to become increasingly legitimized by larger narratives framing them as socially relevant and guarantors of liberal-democratic values.[20] The edited volume, *Humanism and America: Essays on the Outlook of Modern Civilisation* (1930), is striking in this respect. This book most likely marked the height of the New Humanism movement as it sought to restore "value to human existence" – this in a century where America was expected "to set the pattern."[21]

The intensity of debates on the role of humanism and US-American humanities education clearly peaked in the 1930s and 1940s with the experiences of totalitarianism and the Second World War. One could say that the humanities and their history were invented to counter scientism and Nazism – sometimes regarded as two sides of the same coin.[22] Great works of literature and art were brought into light to reverse these currents that symbolized how modernity had gone astray.[23]

A series of lectures at Princeton University on "The Meaning of the Humanities" in 1938 in particular served as "a 'catalyst' for the articulation and success of

---

17 Irving Babbitt, *Literature and the American College: Essays in Defense of the Humanities* (Boston: Houghton Mifflin, 1908).
18 Reitter and Wellmon, *Permanent Crisis*, 227, 234; Schneider, *Humanities at the Crossroads*, 21–25, 31–33; Kipton Smilie, "Unthinkable Allies? John Dewey, Irving Babbit and 'the Menace of the Specialized Narrowness'," *Journal of Curriculum Studies* 48, no. 1 (2016): 113–135.
19 John Guillory, "Who's Afraid of Marcel Proust? The Failure of General Education in the American University," in *The Humanities and the Dynamics of Inclusion Since World War II*, ed. David A. Hollinger (Baltimore: Johns Hopkins University Press, 2006), 30–31.
20 For instance, Richard McKeon, "The Nature and Teaching of the Humanities," *The Journal of General Education* 3, no. 4 (1949): 303.
21 Norman Foerster, "Preface," in *Humanism and America: Essays on the Outlook of Modern Civilisation*, ed. Norman Foerster (New York: Farrar and Rinehart, 1930), x, xii.
22 See, for instance, Bernard Phillips, "The Humanities and the Idea of Man," *Journal of General Education* 2, no. 2 (1948): 129.
23 See Andrew Jewett, *Science under Fire: Challenges to Scientific Authority in Modern America* (Cambridge, M.A.: Harvard University Press, 2020), 121–123.

the humanities as an institutional and ideological force in US-American higher education," as noted by Paul Reitter and Chad Wellmon.[24] In the preface to the proceedings of these lectures, Princeton dean Robert Kilburn Root stressed the need to maintain some unity that, purportedly, would have been natural to humanists in the late Middle Ages and the Renaissance. The volume thus sought to outline a common "humanistic spirit."[25] In a similar fashion, a number of publications and lectures in these years, such as Crane's in 1943, contributed to the identification of humanist traditions in order to enable humanities scholars to bond.

An overview of initiatives made to improve the state of the humanities was published by Patricia Beesley in *The Revival of the Humanities in American Education* (1940). Noting that "some knowledge of the long history of humanism and the Humanities, of the varying meanings of these terms as they reflect changes in educational and philosophical ideas" seemed necessary in order to understand recent developments, Beesley suggested that educational reforms, not just at Princeton, but perhaps most importantly in Chicago, had played a significant role in providing such knowledge.[26] At the center of these activities was Ronald Crane. In an attempt to summarize ongoing debates, he claimed that "the problem of 'what to do with the humanities' (or for them) has become once more one of the critical questions of the day, not only for those whose vested interests are immediately involved but for the general public as well."[27]

"Anarchy within and Tyranny without": Crane, Chicago, and the World

Michigan-born Ronald Salmon Crane, who held a Ph.D. from the University of Pennsylvania (1911), became a full professor of English at the University of Chicago in 1924. He would remain in that position until his retirement in 1951, simultaneously serving as long-term editor of the journal *Modern Philology*. In his

---

24 Reitter and Wellmon, *Permanent Crisis*, 233.
25 Robert Kilburn Root, "Preface," in *The Meaning of the Humanities*, ed. Theodore Meyer Greene (Princeton: Princeton University Press, 1938), v–vii.
26 Patricia Beesley, *The Revival of the Humanities in American Education* (New York: Columbia University Press, 1940), 4, 7, 112, 128. Beesley also included a relatively ambitious history of the humanities of her own (c. 40 pages), ranging from Renaissance humanism (the typical starting point) to current controversies regarding literature versus science in the aftermath of the famous scuffle between Matthew Arnold and Thomas Huxley.
27 Ronald S. Crane, "Shifting Definitions and Evaluations of the Humanities from the Renaissance to the Present," in Crane, *Idea of the Humanities*, 16.

capacity as chairman of the Department of English (1936–1947), Crane, together with philosophy professor and dean Richard McKeon, played a crucial role in creating a separate division for the humanities.[28] The duo was also the driving force behind the first generation of the Chicago School. Sharing a conviction "that study of the methods of the earlier liberal arts would clarify inquiry concerning liberal arts for our times," the group was aiming for a re-Renaissance.[29] If the original Renaissance had "invented" humanism by reforming the liberal arts into the *studia humanitiatis*, the Chicago School contributed to the invention of modern humanities via numerous public lectures and articles, thereby highlighting what they saw as great humanistic practices and achievements of the past.

The influence of this particular Chicago School (there were a few) beyond its immediate local milieu was limited, but some of its long-term impact may have been overlooked. Today, the school is mostly known for representing a form of neo-Aristotelianism (particularly indebted to the Philosopher's *Poetics*), thus offering an alternative to the movement of New Criticism by prescribing more thorough historical – and philosophical – reflections, paired with systematic analyses of literary theories and the foundations of criticism. By writing longer and ambitious narratives of the history of literary study/humanities, they believed that contemporary scholarship could be remedied from an excessive historical disposition that risked getting lost in details. Hence, it was key for the Chicago School to engage with their own history as critics – an ambition fulfilled with the 1952 manifesto *Critics and Criticism*.[30]

This historicizing ambition was further manifested in Crane's 1967 volume on *The Idea of the Humanities*. After some hesitation, he was encouraged by Wayne Booth to finally publish this collection of texts, which – due to the delay – must have seemed somewhat untimely to readers as the intellectual atmosphere had obviously changed during the last couple of decades. The first volume contained a brief but formative essay called "The Idea of the Humanities."[31] This was fol-

---

28 Schneider, *Humanities at the Crossroads*, 57, 85–86, 90, 107, 116.
29 Richard McKeon, "Philosophy as a Humanism," in *Selected Writings of Richard McKeon: Philosophy, Science and Culture*, vol. 1, ed. Zahava K. McKeon and William G. Swenson (Chicago: University of Chicago Press, 1998), 32–33.
30 Robert D. Hume, "'What is Your Evidence?' R. S. Crane as Scholar, Critic, and Theorist of Methodology," *Modern Philology* 115, no. 4 (2018): 432; Ian Hunter, "The Mythos, Ethos, and Pathos of the Humanities," *History of European Ideas* 40, no. 1 (2014): 31; Tom Kindt and Hans-Harald Müller, *The Implied Author: Concept and Controversy* (Berlin: Walter de Gruyter, 2006), 18–37; Phelan, "Chicago School," 133, 142; Schneider, *Humanities at the Crossroads*, 91; René Wellek, *A History of Modern Criticism: 1750–1950*, vol. 6 (New Haven: Yale University Press, 1986), 64.
31 This 13-page essay was originally an address at Carleton College in 1953, first published in *Carleton College Bulletin*.

lowed by the far more extensive, over 150 pages long, overview on "Shifting Definitions and Evaluations of the Humanities from the Renaissance to the Present," which was based on his 1943 lectures but probably also derived from informal discussions with his Chicago peers.[32] Crane's history of the humanities should thus not be read in isolation from the local reform initiatives. The historical narratives emerged in symbiosis with the reorganization of liberal education in the 1930s and 1940s, as Crane believed that study programs should be informed by a fuller humanistic understanding in order to counter prevalent trends of positivist specialization.

Yet, Crane warned against letting the focus on such "external" factors steer the discussion away from the concrete practices of humanists: "For the most serious threats to the humanities, it seems to me, comes from within rather than from without."[33] Intellectual vices such as dogmatism and reductionism represented the most fatal foes. That meant that developing a solid methodological identity and epistemological foundation for the humanities was key to Crane's project.

Internal weaknesses notwithstanding, Crane still emphasized that debates on the humanities in the 1940s were conditioned by the circumstances of the Second World War. Society would "continue to be threatened by anarchy within and tyranny without until we have restored the ideals of reason and freedom which, because of the decline of the humanities, we have lost."[34] Crane thus placed an enormous weight on the humanities. They were the cause *and* the solution to world problems. A thorough understanding of their history would enable things to be set right again.

"But that is a Historical Problem": Historicizing the Repertory of the Humanities

What Crane set out to do in "Shifting Definitions" was to tackle current questions regarding the nature of the humanities and their place in Western culture. "But that is a historical problem," he maintained, "and we shall attempt to solve it (in a humanistic way) by tracing from the Renaissance [although his narrative started with

---

32 Schneider, *Humanities at the Crossroads*, 216, 219, 257.
33 Crane, "Idea of the Humanities," 13–14. See also the review by Everett Lee Hunt, "When Are the 'Humanities' Humane?" *The Quarterly Journal of Speech* 53, no. 3 (1967): 285.
34 Crane, "Shifting Definitions," 16; Ronald S. Crane, "The Idea of the Humanities," in Crane, *Idea of the Humanities*, 6.

ancient Rome], and chiefly, though not exclusively, in English literature, the successive steps of discussion that have preceded the controversies of the present day."[35]

By means of this historical survey, Crane chose another path for restoring the liberal arts compared to Babbitt. An educational program in the humanities should not be bound to the classics. Instead, Crane sought to focus more closely on the special means by which certain arts or disciplines were cultivated and which, in a wider sense, made us human. Such means were to be found in outstanding "human achievements" of the past. These achievements had to be made accessible, not least for students, in order to "nourish our minds, refine our sensibilities, or civilize our actions." Crane believed that the humanities were "in a very real sense, identical with these arts or disciplines" whose "proper cultivation" would "enable us to discover the distinctively humanistic values that inhere in the subject matters to which we apply them."[36] The "history of the humanities," as summarized in his essay "Ideas," constituted the "the story of how many philosophers, many rhetoricians, many logicians, many grammarians, philologists, critics, and historians have unconsciously cooperated in the discovery, formulation, and refinement of techniques of all sorts suited to the isolation and appreciation of the humanistic aspects of human achievements."[37]

True to these above definitions, the humanities should ideally be practiced as "normative arts" based on factual scholarly inquiry. However, Crane argued, they had never in their long history fully reached that potential. As he identified humanistic arts or disciplines as susceptible to occasional intellectual decline and corruption (thus "far from being a chronicle of cumulative advance"), Crane did not see the return to their past as an end in itself. The history of the humanities instead offered a prism through which their current state could be captured and improved. Despite historical flux, it was possible to connect to great traditions in the past. Past periods in the history of the humanities were used as "analogy" through great examples of how these disciplines had previously been adopted in successful ways – although never with perfection. This pragmatic use of history would hopefully illuminate "the direction in which we should wish them to go in the future."[38]

---

[35] Crane, "Shifting Definitions," 22.
[36] Crane, "Idea of the Humanities," 8–11. See also Richard McKeon, "The Nature and Teaching of the Humanities," *The Journal of General Education* 3 no. 4 [1949]: 290, 292.
[37] Crane, "Idea of the Humanities," 9.
[38] R. S. Crane, "Introduction," in *Critics and Criticism: Ancient and Modern*, eds. R. S. Crane et al. (Chicago: University of Chicago Press, 1952); Crane, "Shifting Definitions," 155, 168–170. See also Biswas, *Literary Criticism*, 59, 61.

The affiliates of the Chicago School united in a commitment to methodological pluralism, which easily invited accusations of eclecticism.³⁹ In line with this inclination, Crane's history of the humanities to a large extent sought to demonstrate the manifold potential of humanistic practices. By thoroughly revisiting the pluralistic past (and great achievements) of the humanities – which in Booth's interpretation was employed as "a living repertory of methods useful in solving modern problems" – contemporary imaginaries could be expanded.⁴⁰ Beyond all the many facets in the history of the humanities, however, Crane was able to distinguish some aggregated patterns. For instance, he argued that the humanities tended to end up impoverished as soon as "we neglect to employ as many as possible of the resources of analysis and appreciation which the long tradition of the humanities has made available to us."⁴¹ He traced this tradition to ancient Rome, primarily locating its origins in the writings of Cicero and Quintilian, whose distinctions and general vocabulary had formed a marked heritage focused on the perfection of humanity. According to Crane's narrative, these authors had set the contents and discussions of the humanities in a particular direction, putting the humanities in the service of practical or "humanizing" ends – a function that would thrive with the Renaissance humanists. As long as the humanities were true to this imperative of practical usefulness (understood in a broad sense), Crane was convinced that they would maintain their significance to society.⁴²

However, after the phase of prosperity during the Renaissance, Crane argued that the seventeenth century brought challenges to the humanities, as the systematic philosophies developed by Bacon and Descartes made the natural sciences foundational and seemingly more useful to society, thus lowering the intellectual position of the humanities. The seventeenth century was in that sense outlined as the start of a continuous struggle for the humanities not to be seen as inferior to the natural sciences or supposedly "real," "solid," or "useful" knowledge.⁴³ Yet another problem added to this exertion with the famous Quarrel of the Ancient and the Moderns. Crane, unsurprisingly, argued that the humanities were associated

---

39 Hume, "'What is Your Evidence?'," 440; Kindt and Müller, *Implied Author*, 29–31; Phelan, "Chicago School," 134; Schneider, *Humanities at the Crossroads*, 107, 110–111, 257. On Crane's pluralism, see Wayne C. Booth, "Ronald Crane and the Pluralism of Discrete Modes," in *Critical Understanding: The Powers and Limits of Pluralism* (Chicago: University of Chicago Press, 1979), 37–97.
40 Booth, introduction, xviii.
41 Crane, "Idea of the Humanities," 9–14. He based this long tradition on four principal categories of humanistic arts: 1) "language," 2) "analysis and appreciation of ideas," 3) "literary and artistic criticism," and 4) "knowledge and understanding of the particular historical situations and causes."
42 Crane, "Shifting Definitions," 27, 55, 156–158.
43 Crane, "Shifting Definitions," 28, 32, 56–67, 73.

with the Ancients – but now in a negative sense, as discourses on the future increasingly relied on the forces of science and technology; that is, the Moderns.[44] According to this narrative, the humanities began to lose their practical usefulness and future-generating capacity already in the early modern period. But despite the emergence of this reactive character of the humanities, Crane went on to depict the eighteenth century as yet another strong period, with particular reference to British humanists such as Gibbon and Hume. Thanks to an internal balance, achieved through a harmonious union between philosophical and literary strands, the humanities secured firm legitimacy externally. However, this meant that their main emphasis switched from practical ends to more general methodological and philosophical issues, which, in turn, would have critical long-term consequences. The typical character of scholars in the humanities also changed as philosophers, rather than rhetoricians and critics, became the main practitioners.[45]

When we come to the nineteenth century, Crane eventually highlighted a number of attacks on – and defenses of – the humanities, stating that "the history of the humanities in the nineteenth century in its main features [was] the reverse" of the previous century. Harmony was replaced by "separation and controversy," and the educational and cultural influence of the humanities was questioned as the natural and social sciences expanded, forcing the humanities into an apologetic mode. They were, for instance, accused of being unprogressive or ill-adapted to "the needs of the new democracy." While the scientific revolution seemed to come to its completion, Crane argued, the humanities failed to move on. As a consequence, they were unable to offer any foundation for modern civilization.[46]

Here, it is plain to see that Crane distinguished an oscillating pattern over the centuries with regard to the state of the humanities.[47] Moreover, it is evident that such historical narratives of knowledge depend on the geographical focus. Just like Patricia Beesley, Crane focused heavily on the trajectory of the English humanities. This selection determined the somewhat counterintuitive pattern of prosperity and decline. In contrast to many later histories of the humanities, which tend to emphasize the formation, or even "golden age," of the humanities in nineteenth-century Germany, Crane viewed the humanities as being a product of the (British) Enlight-

---

44 Crane, "Shifting Definitions," 74, 84–89.
45 Crane, "Shifting Definitions," 90, 102–103, 106, 122.
46 Crane, "Shifting Definitions," 123, 132, 137–138.
47 This is not an uncommon way of perceiving the history of the humanities. For instance, Proctor claims that: "The humanities have had a strangely cyclical history," oscillating between degeneration and renaissances. See Proctor, *Education's Great Amnesia*, 87.

enment rather than an offspring from Romanticism and German New Humanism.[48] Some elements that today seem canonized in Western histories of the humanities were strikingly absent in his narrative. This was also noted by René Wellek, who critically pointed out "a yawning gap," noting that the "name of Goethe is not even mentioned, and the whole phalanx of Germans (Winckelmann, Herder, Schiller, Wilhelm von Humboldt) who did so much to revive the idea of humanity and the humanities is ignored, an omission possibly explainable by the date of the original lectures."[49] As Crane aspired to put the history of the humanities at the service of Western liberal democracy circa 1943, there was, for obvious reasons, limited space for German traditions in his narrative.

Beneath the back-and-forth movement, however, Crane also identified internal, structural problems that the humanities had to grapple with. In particular, he pointed to the constant struggle to establish agreement regarding fundamental humanistic methods or principles – the harmonious eighteenth century being a notable exception. In the Renaissance (and, in fact, already in Quintilian's writings), Crane recognized a fundamental tension between, on the one hand, scholarly philologists (seemingly representing the application of historical methods in an ideal-typical fashion) and, on the other, literary critics or rhetoricians. He perceived this tension as still relevant in his own day, as it represented a division between the theoretical and practical aspects that Crane recommended integrating with one another. Claiming that most modern humanists still followed the practically oriented Roman tradition of conducting studies in the humanities for the pursuit of practical ends (which had grown particularly strong in the US-American context), he believed that the current humanities needed an injection of theoretical elements. To the above division, he also added philosophers as a major category of humanists, representing a third methodological approach. By way of conclusion, however, he did not look back at the philosophical prominence of eighteenth-century Britain as he sought to find historical sources of inspiration for the theoretical revitalization of the humanities. Instead, he sought to recall "the theoretical and philosophic spirit which the Greeks had."[50] Thus, the humanities had to transcend their own history, which had been outlined as beginning with the Romans. By constructing a specific humanistic tradition and then moving beyond it, Crane's history of the humanities laid out a potential route for re-invention – hopefully making the humanities relevant once again to a world in need of humanizing perspectives.

---

[48] The enlightenment tradition generally resonated well with the liberally minded Crane, who distanced himself from various forms of "romantic eccentricity" (e.g., associated with the New Critics). See Schneider, *Humanities at the Crossroads*, 332.
[49] Wellek, *Modern Criticism*, 66.
[50] Crane, "Shifting Definitions," 165–170.

Humanizing the Sciences: Bridging Competing Histories of Knowledge

As we know, not only histories of the humanities seemed relevant to bring forth in light of political events on the world stage in the 1930s and 1940s. If Crane made the case for internal unity among the humanities, while also adopting a rather conciliatory attitude toward the sciences, several actors explicitly pushed for an even more ambitious bridging of different forms of knowledge. Beesley, for instance, discussed the recent rise of "scientific humanism" in America and elsewhere. This movement held that the sciences and humanities were complementary parts of a larger unit, which can be seen as part of a more general surge to bond "the two cultures." When C. P. Snow thus published his famous lecture/book in 1959, it was actually not particularly original (which might explain its immense impact) in the sense that the humanities-science divide had already been widely acknowledged and debated on numerous occasions.[51] Histories of science (and the humanities) had for a number of decades repeatedly been invoked in attempts to address scholarly overspecialization.[52] The single project that stood out in line with such an ecumenic spirit, according to Beesley, was that of George Sarton, whose historiographical endeavor puts Crane's enterprise into further context.[53]

The first half of the twentieth century was a formative period for the history of science. In the US, Belgian-born Sarton founded the History of Science Society in 1924. However, even though it emerged as a study program after the First World War, it was primarily in the postwar period that it clearly materialized into a robust discipline. Narratives of the development of science, just like the humanities, became integral to progressive curricula at US-American liberal arts colleges and universities as they, via increasingly popular concepts such as "the scientific revolution," offered students novel ways of understanding long-term intellectual as well

---

[51] See Guy Ortolano, "The Literature and the Science of 'Two Cultures' Historiography," *Studies in History and Philosophy of Scieence* 39 (2008): 143–150, DOI: 10.1016/j.shpsa.2007.11.012, and Guy Ortolano, *The Two Cultures Controversy: Science, Literature and Cultural Politics in Postwar Britain* (Cambridge: Cambridge University Press, 2009), 5–6. Crane also referred to Snow, stating that if his essay should have been thoroughly revised, in order to be up to date in the 1960s, *The Two Cultures* controversy would have been the most obvious point of reference. See Crane, "Shifting Definitions," 16.
[52] Cf. Tore Frängsmyr, "Science or History: George Sarton and the Positivist Tradition in the History of Science," *Lychnos* (1973/1974): 125; Bert Theunissen, "Unifying Science and Human Culture: The Promotion of the History of Science by George Sarton and Frans Verdoorn," in *Pursuing the Unity of Science: Ideology and Scientific Practice from the Great War to the Cold War*, eds. Harmke Kammninga and Geert Somsen (Abingdon: Routledge, 2016), 190.
[53] Beesley, *Revival of the Humanities*, 56.

as social developments.⁵⁴ Many of these knowledge histories were fundamentally embedded in discourses on civilization, but they contained some ambivalence as to whether the humanities and sciences, respectively, should play the role of villains or heroes. Although Crane's back-and-forth pattern differed significantly from the positivist framework of accumulation and progress that was at the core of Sarton's account, the two authors made some similar synthetic claims. But they sided with different protagonists in their search for saviors. While Crane sought to revitalize humanist traditions in the face of scientism, Sarton's call to humanize science, primarily presented in *History of Science and the New Humanism* (1931, originally given as the 1930 Colver lectures at Brown University), echoed his conviction that science should lead the way to a better future world, where Western society would be remolded based on science. Old humanist traditions were seen as obstacles to this project, prompting Sarton to, in a more fundamental sense, champion a "New Humanism," cross-fertilized with scientism.

In this fashion, the twentieth century saw various attempts to define and launch new forms of genuine humanism, originating from the competition of various historical narratives of knowledge.⁵⁵ Sarton's New Humanism thus appeared as an opposite to the New Humanism associated with Babbitt, as he pushed for questions concerning the intellectual value of human life not to be monopolized by a limited group of men of letters, or "so-called humanists." To enable this change and to build bridges between the opposing cultures of knowledge, Sarton requested combined educational programs, including proper training in history for non-historians, as this could pave the way for a "double renaissance" for both scientists and humanists.⁵⁶ In Sarton's own account of the history of science, however, only marginal space was given to the humanities (the exceptions being linguistics and musicology).⁵⁷ Nonetheless, he maintained that a more comprehensive historiography was required: "With-

---

54 James Poskett, "Science in History," *The Historical Journal* 63, no. 2 (2020): 212; James A. Secord, "Inventing the Scientific Revolution," *Isis* 114, no. 1 (2023): 62. See also Arnold Thackray, "The Pre-History of an Academic Discipline: The Study of the History of Science in the United States, 1891–1941," *Minerva* 18, no. 3 (1980): 448–473.
55 Benjamin R. Cohen, "On the Historical Relationship Between the Sciences and the Humanities: A Look at Popular Debates That Have Exemplified Cross-Disciplinary Tension," *Bulletin of Science, Technology & Society* 21, no. 4 (2001): 287; Frängsmyr, "Science or History," 126; Lewis Pyenson, *The Passion of George Sarton: A Modern Marriage and Its Disciplines* (Philadelphia: American Philosophical Society, 2007), 449–450. See also Erik Ahlenius, "Vetenskapshistoriedisciplinens etiska rötter: Kulturkritik, idealism och dygdelära i George Sartons kamp om begreppet humanism" (Bachelor's thesis, Department of History of Science and Ideas, Uppsala University, 2017).
56 George Sarton, *The History of Science and the New Humanism* (New York: Henry Holt and Company, 1931), 8–9, 52, 69–72, 150, 174, 178.
57 Bod, *New History of the Humanities*, 3.

out history, scientific knowledge may become culturally dangerous; combined with history, tempered with reverence, it will nourish the highest culture."[58]

This perception was further enhanced in other, comparable accounts of the history of science (including the history of social science), such as Irish-British physicist John Desmond Bernal's *Science in History* (1954), written against the backdrop of totalitarianism and world wars and clearly sharing a similar civilizational vision as the guiding principle for the construction of historical narratives.[59] In a 1946 lecture at Birkbeck College, Bernal identified a need for epistemic balance in order to foster a democratic community and avoid the rise of Nazism in the future: "the union of science and the humanities is for us a condition of survival."[60] Taken together, these comparative outlooks indicate that pioneers of the history of (natural and social) science shared many concerns voiced by Crane and his Chicago colleagues in the 1930s and 1940s. They all united in a wish for a closer collaboration between "the two cultures." By better grasping the long histories of knowledge, it would be possible to set things right, as a historically informed – and humanized – scientific culture was seen as a (or perhaps even the greatest) source of hope in the twentieth century.[61]

This begs the question of why the postwar period did not see any institutionalization of the history of humanities, as in the case of the history of science. The limited influence of the Chicago School notwithstanding, one may wonder what would have happened had Crane published his lectures immediately in the 1940s – or linked his historical account to the two cultures controversy in the 1960s. Even if one should not exaggerate the importance of individual works or authorships for such institutional formations, could such (counterfactual) turns of events have given some impetus to further include the humanities in other histories of knowledge? This reflection is obviously speculative. A safer conclusion is that Crane's collected efforts, albeit leaving few direct traces in the humanist meta-discourse, in substantial ways contributed to the formation – and to some extent invention – of the US-American humanities in the mid-twentieth century. Seen from this perspective, his narrative efforts had some long-standing effects, but perhaps most notably through the introduction of novel curricula and the implementation of new organizational structures within the expanding field of higher education.

---

58 Sarton, *History of Science*, 69.
59 J. D. Bernal, *Science in History* (London: Watts, 1954). See also Anna K. Maier, "Setting Up a Discipline: Conflicting Agendas of the Cambridge History of Science Committee, 1936–1950," *Studies in History and Philosophy of Science Part A* 31, no. 4 (2000): 665–689.
60 John Desmond Bernal, "Science and the Humanities," 1946, available at Marxists Internet Archive, accessed August 3, 2023, https://www.marxists.org/archive/bernal/works/1940s/humsci.htm.
61 Cf. Secord, "Inventing the Scientific Revolution," 58, 71.

Conclusion: "The Humanities as They Have Been and as They Might Be"

The histories of knowledge examined in this article were typically aiming for change, generated as deliberate responses to the challenges facing academia and society at large. The US-American humanities – and their history – were constructed in the face of crisis sentiments in the mid-twentieth century. Various threats, ranging from dogmatism and reductionism to scientism and Nazism, prompted a restoration of the humanities with the purpose of bringing balance to a world seemingly torn apart by excessive modern forces.

The role of historical narratives in contexts of crisis would become perhaps even more salient in the postwar decades, as discourses of crisis in the humanities were segmented. In some national contexts, historical accounts of the humanities, packed with large, synthetic claims, have been identified as essential tools, or discursive strategies, for younger generations of humanists seeking to strengthen the legitimacy of their disciplines and contribute to radical changes in society.[62] While such a revolutionary spirit would have resonated well with historical materialists such as Bernal, Crane's history of the humanities was of a different nature, as it did not seek to break with the past by pulling up the roots. The final part of his essay "Shifting Definitions" was called "The Humanities as They Have Been and as They Might Be," indicating how the narrative was linked to the creation of something new, while still seeking to preserve the guiding power of tradition. Since the humanities, according to Crane's narrative, had lost their future-oriented, generative capacity, they required a re-renaissance to become relevant in the making of humanity's future.

In retrospect, it seems as if many of the defenses of the humanities in 1940s America, based on liberal-democratic values, were quite successful.[63] The humanities and their histories were indeed constructed and mobilized to meet certain practical ends (to borrow from Crane's terminology). The construction of new sets of historical traditions offered a solid identity, and the humanities developed into an epistemic nation in the expanding postwar world of higher education as humanists were able to gather around a relatively uniform purpose and history.

---

[62] Hampus Östh Gustafsson, "Mobilising the Outsider: Crises and Histories of the Humanities in the 1970s Scandinavian Welfare States," in *Histories of Knowledge in Postwar Scandinavia: Actors, Arenas, and Aspirations*, eds. Johan Östling, Niklas Olsen, and David Larsson Heidenblad (London: Routledge, 2020), 208–224.

[63] Claire Rydell Arcenas, "On the Purpose of Humanities Education: A Historical Perspective from the Mid-Twentieth-Century United States," in *Writing the History of the Humanities: Questions, Themes, Approaches*, ed. Herman Paul (London: Bloomsbury, 2023), 296.

As recently proposed, historians of science or knowledge need to reflect more carefully upon the *historical* status in their respective disciplines and what they actually do by producing historical narratives.[64] By highlighting past examples of histories of knowledge, this article encourages further reflection on the possible functions of such narratives. Apart from balancing the dominant history of science, what can we expect the novel forms of history of the humanities to achieve?[65] Perhaps they may serve as a reminder of a constant need to "reinvent" the humanities, informed by their complex history.

It is not uncommon that advocates of the humanities still assign their disciplines the role of being saviors – in line with a general inclination toward "overpromising."[66] But even if we must be wary of exaggerating the world-saving potential of the humanities, we might still argue that the twenty-first century also needs a stronger supply of historical, and perhaps even humanizing, perspectives. As French-born literary historian Gilbert Chinard pointed out in one of the Princeton lectures in 1938, the humanities were "attacked on every side," but their task was "not to fight their opponents with the weapons they are using, but to approach the problem in a humanistic, that is to say in a truly historical, spirit."[67]

About the Contributor

Hampus Östh Gustafsson is a researcher at Uppsala University and Lund University. After completing his PhD in history of science and ideas with a dissertation on the legitimacy of the humanities in the politics of knowledge in twentieth-century Sweden, his postdoctoral projects have concerned broader themes in the history of the humanities and the organization of modern universities. Recent publications include the edited volume *The Humanities and the Modern Politics of Knowledge* (together with Anders Ekström, Amsterdam University Press, 2022).

---

64 Poskett, "Science in History," 210–211, 237. See also Richard Bourke and Quentin Skinner, *History in the Humanities and Social Sciences* (Cambridge: Cambridge University Press, 2023); Michiel Leezenberg, *History and Philosophy of the Humanities: An Introduction* (Amsterdam: Amsterdam University Press, 2018), 16–17.
65 Cf. Suzanne Marchand, "What the History of the Humanities Can, and Cannot, Learn from the History of Science," *History of Humanities* 8, no. 2 (2023): 209–216.
66 Reitter and Wellmon, *Permanent Crisis*, 79.
67 Gilbert Chinard, "Literature and the Humanities," in Meyer Greene, *Meaning of the Humanities*, 153, 170.

HIC Conversation with Tiffany N. Florvil, Madalitso Zililo Phiri, and Vanessa D. Plumly, edited and introduced by Jana Weiß

Interrogating Epistemologies: Decolonizing Knowledge in Academia and Beyond

Abstract: This conversation discusses the need to and the challenges to decolonize knowledge in academia. The interviewed scholars reflect on their own academic journey and the knowledge hierarchies and structural racism they have encountered (and still do). In offering practices of "gate-opening" for underrepresented and minoritized communities, the exchange stresses the importance of non-disciplinary collaboration while reminding us to recognize quotidian intellectuals beyond the ivory tower and epistemic localities beyond the West.

Keywords: decolonizing knowledge, epistemicide, gatekeeping, (dis)empowerment

In 2014, Portuguese sociologist Boaventura de Sousa Santos urged us to seek global cognitive justice by introducing the term "epistemicide" to conceptualize colonial violence against indigenous knowledge.[1] Destructing, producing, and circulating knowledge is deeply embedded in colonial practices. Colonialism has left a legacy of suppressed and imposed knowledge (structures). It has also excluded indigenous forms of knowledge at universities, archives, and the public at large. The concept of the coloniality of knowledge questions the hegemony of white, Eurocentric systems and conceptions of knowledge.[2] It raises fundamental epistemological concerns (for some, also discomfort) regarding questions of power relations, the quest for supposed (Western) "truths," and objectivity (who creates what kind of knowledge, who is (dis)empowered).[3]

---

1 *Epistemologies of the South: Justice Against Epistemicide* (Boulder, CO: Paradigm Publishers, 2014). We would like to acknowledge that we are aware of the serious allegations of multiple instances of sexual harassment made against Boaventura de Sousa Santo.
2 Please note that calls to "decolonize" are not new and (under different names) date back to the 1950s (cf. Aníbal Quijano, "Coloniality of Power and Eurocentrism in Latin America," *International Sociology* 15, no. 2 (2000): 215–232; Achille Mbembe, "Future Knowledges and Their Implications for the Decolonisation Project," in *Decolonisation in Universities: The Politics of Knowledge*, ed. Jonathan D. Jansen (Johannesburg: Wits University Press, 2019), 239–254). For a critique, especially regarding generalizations related to Western epistemology, cf. Paul A. Chambers, "Epistemology and Domination: Problems with the Coloniality of Knowledge Thesis in Latin American Decolonial Theory," *Dados* 63, no. 4 (2020): 1–36.
3 Sarah L. Hoagland, "Aspects of the Coloniality of Knowledge," *Critical Philosophy of Race* 8, no. 1–2 (2020): 48–60; Daniel Bendix, Franziska Müller, and Aram Ziai, *Beyond the Master's*

In order to decolonize knowledge, it is crucial that we address the role of academia. Western scholars often impose their research categories and systems of thought on their non-Western subjects (e.g., what counts as knowledge, which processes of knowledge production are "legitimate," who is considered a "knowing subject," and, subsequently, whose knowledge counts as valid).[4] This has created a knowledge barrier, through which everything outside of Western conceptualizations is rendered inferior and pseudo-scientific.

Decolonizing research, administration, and curricula is only slowly entering (Western) academic discourse and has been met with resistance. Since the 2015 "Rhodes Must Fall" Campaign in Cape Town,[5] decolonizing academia has begun to spread, especially in British and U.S. universities while only slowly in other parts of the Western world. As scholars, it is key to ask ourselves which voices, epistemologies, and topics are represented in our syllabi and research. Shose Kessi, Zoe Marks, and Elelwani Ramugondo have put it more bluntly:

> Which indigenous or community knowledge systems are we listening to, elevating, or letting redefine our learning agenda? What is our purpose and whose future does our knowledge imagine? Across all of these categories: where is racial or ethnic, regional, gender, class, religious or ideological, and linguistic diversity? How do we account for historic hierarchies and systems of exclusion and erasure? Most university lecturers and professors have never been taught to ask these questions [. . .].[6]

This conversation cannot fully do justice to all the issues raised, but it seeks to engage with them from both a personal view and from an inter-disciplinary or rather, as Madalitso Zililo Phiri puts it below, *non-disciplinary* perspective. While the focus is on the field of Black German Studies, much of what is discussed applies across disciplines and to more general constellations.

The scholars participating in this conversation have lived and worked across the globe, in Brazil, Germany, Malawi, Mozambique, South Africa, the U.K., and the U.S. They all stress the importance of collaboration in order to make the invis-

---

Tools? Decolonizing Knowledge Orders, Research Methods and Teaching. Kilombo: International Relations and Colonial Questions (Lanham, MD: Rowman & Littlefield Publishers, 2020).

4 Hoagland, "Aspects," 53. See also the 2023 anthology by Kate Reed and Marcia C. Schenck, *The Right to Research. Historical Narratives by Refugee and Global South Researchers* (Montreal: McGill-Queen's University Press, 2023).

5 "Rhodes Must Fall" was a protest movement aimed at the statue of Cecil Rhodes at the University of Cape Town. It began in March 2015 and ignited a wider, global movement to decolonize education. Cf. Sabelo J. Ndlovu-Gatsheni, *Epistemic Freedom in Africa: Deprovincialization and Decolonization* (London: Routledge, 2018), esp. 221–242.

6 "Introduction: Decolonizing Knowledge Within and Beyond the Classroom," *Critical African Studies* 13, no. 1 (2021): 1–9, here 6.

ible visible, to center and empower marginalized scholarship, to "open" and not guard academic gates, as Tiffany N. Florvil emphasizes. They also reflect on and challenge us to navigate between scholarship and activism. Overcoming the long legacy of colonial violence and epistemicide is not a one-person job. Most importantly, as Vanessa Plumly aptly points out, we need to "listen more than speak, especially as a white person."

Introductions

Please briefly introduce yourself to our readers and describe how your work relates to the (de)coloniality of knowledge. Moreover, please reflect on your positionality within academia and your field in particular.

Tiffany N. Florvil: Greetings, I am excited to participate in this HIC conversation with these amazing scholars. I am an interdisciplinary Caribbean American scholar of modern European (German) history based in the United States, with an emphasis on the African/Black diaspora, Black internationalism, intellectualism, social movements, and women and gender. I specifically focus on Black German history and culture, mostly in the twentieth century. I study the resistance of Black German and other minoritized communities against anti-Black racism and their strategies and practices to address the (after)effects of chattel slavery, colonialism, and the Shoah/Holocaust in the nation. I also explore the contours of Black diasporic identity and transnational exchange. Indeed, all of my work, much of which has involved collaboration, foregrounds Black German histories and experiences while also emphasizing how building movements requires intellectual and affective efforts.

This work is inherently decolonial as it challenges white hegemonic frameworks by positioning Black Germans as intellectuals. I also push back against the idea that intellectuals should look one way (white, cisgendered, or male) or produce in a particular mode (high art or mainstream publications). I show that Black Germans have always been "Dichter und Denker." In fact, I coined the concept of "quotidian intellectual."[7] By using this concept, I argue that quotidian intellectuals used vernacular aesthetic cultural forms and styles such as spoken word poetry, graphic artwork, and hip-hop music to create a new lexicon and practices that led to the (re)formation of a vibrant Black public sphere. They intel-

---

7 Tiffany N. Florvil, *Mobilizing Black Germany: Afro-German Women and the Making of a Transnational Movement* (Chicago: University of Illinois Press, 2020), esp. 6–7.

lectualized the everyday in their works and brought the margins to the center. In essence, my research and teaching confront the notion of what Europe is and who may be defined as a European and who may be considered an intellectual. Hence, my entire research agenda and academic existence constitute an example of the decoloniality of knowledge in practice. In essence, my work examines the intellectual imprint of Black Germans across time and space, reorienting our perspectives to Black epistemologies in the German polity.

Madalitso Zilio Phiri: I am a critical pan-African sociologist whose research interests focus on three thematic areas: the political economy of racialized welfare in South Africa and Brazil, sociology of race, and Black political thought. As a post-doctoral fellow, my research interests have continued to build upon scholarly interests that were honed during my doctoral training as well as my lifelong pursuit to think across *non-disciplinary* perspectives through the Mafejean lenses in the social sciences and humanities.[8] I have often been reluctant to use the word decolonization as it has turned into a fad that lost its meaning. In my work, I mostly focus on epistemologies of Blackness, critical theorists of the African (Black) world who provide alternative imaginaries to the world of empire and institutionalized racism and violence.

My quest to decenter Eurocentrism is rooted in my own analysis of contradictory and oppressive social, epistemic, and political systems of societies that I have called "home" at various times in my social, spiritual, and intellectual formation (Malawi, Mozambique, and South Africa) and my study of Brazil as a problematic racial polity. My experiences across these settler colonial polities, whether in dialogue with texts, oppressed marginalized groups such as beneficiaries of social welfare programs, and intellectual traditions, confirm my observations that colonial violence has carved out these societies, which then pushes me to agitate for a new human project.

Sociology, the humanities, and the social sciences in general offer me a vocabulary as well as methodological tools to think about counter-hegemonic knowledge ecologies that critique Africa's positionality in a racialized and hierarchical knowledge ecology. There is no doubt, however, that sociology and all the bourgeois social sciences are predicated on exclusionary practices enmeshed with the world of empire.[9] I thus see the university as a site of struggle (obviously, forged

---

[8] Archie Mafeje, *The Theory and Ethnography of African Social Formations: The Case of the Interlacustrine Kingdoms* (Dakar: CODESRIA Book Series, 1991).

[9] Edward Said, *Orientalism* (London: Routledge & Keagan Paul Ltd., 1978); G. K. Bhambra & J. Holmwood, *Colonialism and Modern Social Theory* (Cambridge: Polity Press, 2021); Reiland Rabaka, *Against Epistemic Apartheid: W.E.B. Du Bois and the Disciplinary Decadence of Sociology* (Plymouth: Lexington Books, 2010); Reiland Rabaka, *Du Bois: A Critical Introduction* (Cambridge: Polity Press, 2021); Reiland Rabaka, "Return to the Source: Cabral, Fanon, the Dialectic of Revolu-

through Eurocentric violence), as I am bringing a liberatory praxis. Whether this exists in principle through the attainment of academic freedom is something open for debate. Knowledge is not only found in the university, as there are organic intellectuals throughout the ages having bequeathed world society with tools to challenge oppressive conditions as well as epistemic marginality. I am only but a piece in a large puzzle of effecting pan-African liberation praxis. My scholarship links quotidian experiences of being born and socialized in heteronormative, patriarchal, erstwhile colonized spaces and places. I was born in Malawi, where I lived until I was fifteen years old. I have also had the opportunity to live a greater part of my life in post-conflict Mozambique for fourteen years, and I try to make sense of Black joy, strivings, marginality, and sufferings in a settler colonial polity that I call "home": South Africa. I have also had the opportunity to travel and conduct research in Brazil, a country with the largest Black diaspora in the world. I dislike the idea that I am violently produced through the kernels of epistemicide and erasure. It was inevitable that my scholarship would pivot liberatory praxis that reifies the conditions of marginality for global Black life.

Vanessa D. Plumly: As an undergraduate, I studied German and history at a small liberal arts college called Bethany College in West Virginia. Ironically, or perhaps not so much given the content of this question and the awareness of an embedded coloniality in academia that motivates it, it was not until I saw Dr. Tyrone Parker give a talk at the American Council on the Teaching of Foreign Languages (ACTFL) conference in New York City in 2006 that I learned about the history of German colonization. This experience shook me out of my initial naïveté as a young white adult who grew up in the working class of rural Appalachia. Since then, I have endeavored to make visible what is all too often intentionally made invisible, the coloniality that pervades the very systems we all inhabit and our own minds.

My research from my undergraduate years to my doctoral work and to the present has always focused on minoritized populations and their cultural productions. I see my work, alongside that of countless others, as an imperative intervention into the discipline of German Studies, which continues to endorse a hegemonic white German canon. By focusing on both the knowledge and cultural production of Black Germans and challenging anti-Black racism in Germany and Europe, my scholarship centers on Black German voices and actions. Moreover, conducting research and working in collaboration with members of the Black German community disrupts Western academic standards of so-called "objectivity" and aligns my work with those who are immediately impacted by it.

---

tionary Decolonization/Revolutionary Re-Africanization, and the African Renaissance," *Journal of Black Studies* 53, no. 5: 419–440.

Academic Knowledge Hierarchies & Gatekeepers

Despite laudable claims that "the worldwide circulation of knowledge is now considered not just as a one-sided colonial or post-colonial diffusion process, but rather as an exchange of knowledge in which each side is active,"[10] *hierarchies do exist. Academia and archives are embedded in racial structures and thus replicate oppression and regulate access to knowledge. The list of potential gatekeepers of knowledge is long – many of us may have had experiences of gatekeeping but may also have served as gatekeepers ourselves.*

Vanessa D. Plumly: When I was an undergraduate student, one of my history professors told me that the number of Namibian children who were sent to East Germany during the Namibian War of Independence and the Cassinga Massacre was not sufficiently significant to merit a capstone research project. While I ended up completing the project for my German major instead, this represented a pivotal turning point for me away from history and toward German Studies. However, even as a graduate student in German Studies, I faced pushback on my dissertation proposal. One professor explicitly asked me if Black Germans were still only writing about racism (implicit in this statement was the notion that racism is somehow no longer an issue in Germany). This comment was dismissive of Black Germans and their political and aesthetic efforts. I was lucky to find extensive support and guidance within the Black German community to which I am indebted and which enabled me not only to acquire more sources for my project and to hone my topic but also kept me focused on what mattered.

Tiffany N. Florvil: My academic journey certainly reflects these dynamics as well as that of countless other PhD candidates of Color not mentioned. For instance, my PhD process at both the University of Wisconsin-Madison and the University of South Carolina-Columbia was extremely difficult, which was due to gatekeeping and structural racism. According to previous advisors, I was not a graduate student possessing the proper writing skills, nor was studying the African/Black diaspora in Europe seen as important. Underlining the latter idea was a belief that Black European history was not a "real" field that warranted study. However, I overcame these impositions and setbacks and eventually worked with an amazing advisor, Dr. Ann Johnson. She believed in me and knew that I could produce amazing work, and I did working with her. Furthermore, she never tried

---

[10] Jürgen Renn, "From the History of Science to the History of Knowledge – and Back," *Centaurus* 57, no. 1 (2015): 37–53, here 38.

to mold me in her academic image and respected that I was a scholar in my own right.

Moreover, my PhD is not from a well-known institution in the field of European history, and I work at a poor R-1 university in the Southwest also not well-known for European history. This has impacted me in ways that have resulted in limited opportunities, especially in terms of acquiring funding for my first single-authored monograph, *Mobilizing Black Germany: Afro-German Women and the Making of a Transnational Movement*.[11] Regardless, I worked hard and used my limited resources to conduct research in the United States and Germany. My research relied on the use of alternative archives (non-traditional and subcultural), which forced me to reimagine the importance of the quotidian as a site for intellectualism, memory, and history. A large number of my archival materials, including ephemera, came from Black German quotidian intellectuals who were key figures in the Black German movement of the 1980s and 1990s. I forged kinships with these quotidian intellectuals and reviewed their archival materials, and as a result, they helped me recognize their important intellectual efforts and contributions. I also visited subcultural lesbian and feminist archives in Berlin and Hamburg. Combined, these experiences helped me piece together an institutional and intellectual history of the modern Black German movement. These women showed me that archives and knowledge are legible in the everyday, while also demonstrating that political work involved intellectual labor. These ideas continue to shape my current intellectual biography on Black German poet and activist May Ayim.

In addition, I have unintentionally become a gatekeeper in the field as a result of the "Imagining Black Europe" book series launched in 2019 at Peter Lang, which I edit together with Vanessa Plumly, who also participates in this conversation. The series is the first to publish scholarship on Black European Studies. I will certainly do this again with the creation of a new series at another press in 2024. Teehee, stay tuned! Vanessa and I did not intend to prevent the publication of nuanced scholarship on Black European Studies when we established our series. Instead, we wanted it to be a space for critical interventions from scholars on both sides of the Atlantic. We had experienced institutional gatekeeping, especially in European Studies, with regard to our work, and we wanted to offer scholars opportunities to publish their work. Co-founding the Black Diaspora Studies Network at the German Studies Association in 2015, again with my collaborator Vanessa, represents another example of my aim to provide scholars at all levels with a space to present their work and forge links with other scholars. Building these networks entails decolonizing knowledge and knowledge production while affirming the work and ap-

---

11 Florvil, *Mobilizing Black Germany*.

proaches of underrepresented scholars – these scholars are our present and future. This all feels like what I refer to as "gate-opening" as it provides a space for underrepresented and minoritized communities while also privileging their forms of knowledge and knowledge production. This gate-opening work is an important part of my academic work institutionally, nationally, and internationally.

Vanessa D. Plumly: I too still recall when Tiffany and I initially decided to pursue the creation of a Black Diaspora Studies Network at the German Studies Association. We were told that it was probably not the place for such a network. We persisted despite this effort to deter us, and the panels each year hosted by our network are among the most attended at the conference.

As editors of the series "Imagining Black Europe," Tiffany and I have turned ourselves into gatekeepers of knowledge production in this field, but as Tiffany has pointed out, our goal with the series is a different one – to establish a venue for scholars in the field who may have difficulties finding an outlet for their work (often due to institutional gatekeeping) and which will accept and foster their critical interventions in productive and non-prohibitive ways.

Let me make one further note on gatekeeping in academia. As a professor at a private, small liberal arts college, I have personally witnessed talented students withdrawing from the institution as a result of not being able to pay their semester tuition. Until college in the United States becomes affordable and accessible to all, it will remain undemocratic and continue to reproduce the same inequities that permeate all spheres of our society.

Madalitso Zilio Phiri: One of the sad intellectual artifacts of colonialism is that it produced a regime of epistemic fear and terror. Indeed, both Aimé Cesaire and Frantz Fanon make poignant observations regarding the insecurities produced by colonialism.[12] Cesaire's criticism focuses on the ideology of imperial violence by dissecting the relationship between Adolf Hitler's fascism and imperial violence. Cesaire argues that what Europe hates in the fascist leader is that Hitler applied violent technologies reserved for the Africans (those racialized as Blacks), Coolies, and Indigenous peoples on European territory. Fanon, on the other hand, understands imperial violence through his training as a medical practitioner, psychiatrist, physician, and psychologist. His complete oeuvre is linked to the aesthetics of Black liberation. The distribution of violence as a global project gives us an understanding of the project of epistemicide.

---

[12] Aimé Cesaire, *Discourse on Colonialism* (New York: Monthly Review Press, 1972); Frantz Fanon, *The Wretched of the Earth* (London: Penguin, 1961).

We cannot have an understanding of gatekeeping if the regime of intellectual fear and terror is not centered. Both Cesaire and Fanon leave us with an appreciation that colonialism is a cancer spreading to kill life-producing cells. Europe never healed from the cancer it spread across the world through labeling, classification, eugenics, and racial hygiene. Europe's epistemological foundations produced the continent as a self-referential civilization, and Western knowledge production ecologies operate within this regime of epistemic fear and terror. Now, this self-referential civilization is oblivious to its intellectual poverty achieved by plundering other world civilizations. The regime of epistemic terror and fear produces a racist knowledge archive that is intolerant of alternative epistemic locales, archives, and points of reference. Furthermore, this regime of terror also jettisons dialogue with knowledge archives it is not familiar with.

For instance, I am currently a visiting fellow at the University of Cambridge's Centre of African Studies and a visiting college research associate at the Wolfson College, Cambridge. Over the past couple of months, I have had the opportunity to participate in the collegiate life of this medieval institution. Some of the older and more prestigious colleges such as Trinity, St. John's, Gonville and Caius, Magdalene, and King's valorize the idea of basing their epistemic traditions on the classics (i.e., the inclusion of Latin and Greek as a referential epistemic archive). These traditions become more overt, in rituals and symbolic formalities as seen across the Oxbridge traditions, at the recitation of formal dinner prayers in tune with these medieval practices. This, however, is not an indictment of the leading Oxbridge traditions – it is a Euro-American colonial practice par excellence. I have encountered this across all my travels to the United States, Canada, continental Europe, as well as the formerly colonized societies across Africa and Latin America.

The idea of the classics built on Greece and Rome is an epistemic historical fallacy. Disbanding the manichean colonial imaginary separating North Africa from sub-Saharan Africa, the continent witnessed university institutions before these emerged across medieval Europe. Two such institutions are the University of Al Quaraouiyine in Fez, Morocco and the University of Timbuktu. Al Quaraouiyine was originally founded as a mosque in 859, before becoming one of the leading spiritual and educational centers of the Islamic Golden Age. The University of Timbuktu was a hub of learning, polycentric exchanges, and pluriversal worldviews. Hundreds of thousands of manuscripts were written in Timbuktu. This university city published books and manuscripts primarily written in Arabic but also in local languages such as Fulfulde, Songhai, Soninke, and Bambara.The idea that negates dialectical links and contributions of the Islamic Golden Age to Europe's rediscovery of knowledge is the Eurocentric religious extremism that begins after the Reconquista. Given this colonial imaginary, the classics cannot be seen through the lenses of Arabic and Islamic contributions and exchange. The Greek and Latin references are part of the colonial, Eurocentric, and Renaissance imaginary of the classics, which has made its way into university practices due to the way they were institutionalized at the time in Europe and then taken across the world via colonialism. In other words – the "idea of the university" is very much based on these traditions. The problem is that these traditions were Eurocentric and colonial.

These questions animated pan-Africanists in the past century as well as those inside the European intellectual culture. Both traditions provide us with historical data that challenge colonial motifs highlighting evidence to the contrary. Would it make a difference if we viewed the classics as belonging to Black Egypt? I ask this rhetorically as the Eurocentric mind does not want to wrestle with this question. At no given point did these civilizations (Greece and Rome) see themselves as belonging to the so-called European knowledge archive.[13] Of course, such claims are pushed as pseudo-history, not scientific and thus not scholarly. In fact, Rome celebrates its one thousand years of existence under an African emperor.[14] The Eurocentric university pivots classical knowledge evolution from Greece and Rome as if these civilizations may be abstracted from Black Egypt. Indeed, the very thought that Egypt has existed as a Black civilization incenses some Eurocentric archaeologists, paleontologists, anthropologists, and Egyptologists alike.[15] The challenge at hand is that some scholars have built their careers around these problematic historical motifs positioning it as the only intellectual archive. This practice is informed by what I described above as meditated epistemic fear and terror. The abandonment of epistemic fear and terror opens the mind to possibilities beyond the traditional knowledge archives. This is what I see as a liberatory practice informed by a *non-disciplinary* approach to the academic project.

Black history is often excluded from traditional archives at museums, universities, government agencies, and historical societies. In your work as researcher and/or lecturer, how do you address under-documentation? A prominent example is The

---

[13] C. A. Diop, *The African Origin of Civilization: Myth or Reality* (Paris: Presence Africaine, 1974); Martin Bernal, *Black Athena: Afroasiatic Roots of Classical Civilization, Volume I: The Brication of Ancient Greece, 1785–1985* (New Brunswick, NJ: Rutgers University Press, 1987); Martin Bernal, *Black Athena: Afroasiatic Roots of Classical Civilization, Volume II: The Archaeological and Documentary Evidence* (New Brunswick, NJ: Rutgers University Press, 1991); Martin Bernal, *Black Athena: The Afroasiatic Roots of Classical Civilization, Volume III: The Linguistic Evidence* (New Brunswick, NJ: Rutgers University Press, 2006).
[14] M. Mamdani, *Define and Rule: Native as Political Identity* (Johannesburg: Wits University Press, 2012).
[15] Diop, *African Origin*.

Blackivists, a Chicago-based collective of trained African American archivists who stress the preservation of Black heritage.[16] *Have you come across any examples of best practices to protect and spread marginalized histories and artifacts? How do you think these have and will inspire your research and teaching in the past and future?*

Madalitso Zilio Phiri: There are some elements of Black history that remain hidden. There are also different dimensions of Black history that are celebrated. It is not all exclusionary practices. Eurocentrism, however, has publicly erased the intimate links between Africa's epistemic underdevelopment and racialization of knowledge. The Eurocentric concept of memorialization excludes Black memory culture through a neglected ontology, more especially when it comes to narratives of imperial force and violence. Now, I am not saying that Black life is defined by pain, it is also defined by aesthetics, joy, bounty, and plenty. In all my travels, I make it a point to visit museums and monuments that ameliorate, negate, or reify Black aesthetics and contributions. Marginality in Black history is informed by the shame and guilt of Eurocentrism. I have come across many museums and monuments across the Black Atlantic and the African continent confronting biases and marginalization of histories as well as Africa's contributions to world civilization. On the African continent, however, a major stumbling block in the endeavor to cement a memory culture has been the precarious economic and material conditions of what might be called custodianship of the past. This is largely informed by a hierarchical neoliberal approach to ordering life and society that valorizes pragmatic scholarship in the natural sciences and medicine to the detriment of the humanities and social sciences. Some of this is due to ideological extremism seeking to neglect the role of history in society and memory culture itself.

The erasure of historical figures, genderization of knowledge, and marginalization of intellectual cultures are reified when right-wing or extremist governments usurp certain histories to place their own at the center. If we follow this logic, then the violence of erasure in post-colonial Africa is connected to the Eurocentric civilization's cardinal sin of erasure. Exploring inter-connections of Black Atlantic and radical African intellectuals such as W. E. B. Du Bois, Kwame Nkrumah, Ifi Amadiume, Ida B. Wells, and Sylvia Wynter begins the long process of decentering Eurocentrism. These intellectuals give us conceptual as well as methodological vocabularies to think beyond tools that constitute the colonised global social sciences and humanities. Totalizing regimes of state-sanctioned violence and a racialized ordering of knowledge in African academia perpetuate the marginality of this scholarship. These figures may be reduced to activists and not nec-

---

16 https://www.theblackivists.com, last accessed June 29, 2023.

essarily pioneering interlocutors in the Eurocentric canon alongside realizations of liberatory praxis to understand the Black condition.

My intellectual duty is to center such marginalized scholarship, thereby encouraging the next generation of scholars who will excavate from both the physical and epistemic archives. Of course, the Black radical tradition is not sacrosanct to critique. The scholarly community needs to be introduced on how to read classical texts. Here, I agree with Scott's understanding of a classic. He argues that a classic, evidently, is a book one feels compelled to return to again and again, a book read by generation after generation, not because it offers us invaluable information or irrefutable facts, but because it tells a story that reflects back to us recognizable dimensions of a human spirit struggling against vicious odds to affirm, enhance, and expand the given boundaries of our common humanity.[17]

Recently, I finished working on a co-edited volume titled *Monuments and Memory in Africa*.[18] In this volume, we argue that the argument that archives are historically constituted, incomplete, and expressive of power relations is indisputable, yet it does not follow that the project of epistemic decolonization may dispense with the archive as such. Monuments and archives are obviously not just physical collections and libraries. They are equally a matter of how discourses are framed and what is regarded as belonging and not belonging to the sphere of possible and authoritative knowledge. Monuments are the embodiment of the life and spirit of those who have lived before any group of people. For it is in monuments that any people's philosophy and aesthetics are to be found, thereby providing foundational artifacts of spirituality, ontology, epistemology, and constitution into civilizational ecologies. The foreword in this aforementioned volume raises a question related to the theme we are exploring here. Sabelo J. Ndlovu-Gatsheni makes observations on decommissioning and demonumentalization. He rhetorically asks whether this revolution (memory culture) should be predicated on the reconciliation of different recollections of the past.[19] The answer is to be found in the suspension of colonial time, which provides the roadmap and political aesthetics of the new human project.

Tiffany N. Florvil: Indeed, Madalitso has offered us a very detailed account. Black women scholars, such as Darlene Clark Hine, Deborah Gray White, Marisa Fuentes, Robin Mitchell, Saidiya Hartman, and Deirdre Cooper Owens have long

---

17 D. Scott, "C. L. R. James's Radical Vision of Common Humanity," *Boston Review*, August 17, 2023, https://www.bostonreview.net/articles/c-l-r-jamess-radical-vision-of-common-humanity, accessed December 12, 2023.

18 John Sodiq Sanni and Madalitso Zililo Phiri, *Monuments and Memory in Africa: Reflections on Coloniality and Decoloniality* (London: Routledge, 2024).

19 S. Ndlovu-Gatsheni, "Foreword," in *Monuments and Memory in Africa: Reflections on Coloniality and Decoloniality* (London: Routledge, 2024).

recognized the violence, erasures, and absences in the archives.[20] I also think of scholars such as Tina M. Campt, Michelle M. Wright, and Fatima El-Tayeb who push us to reconsider Black European history and how it defies formal disciplinary boundaries.[21] In many ways, my work builds on these scholars by affirming the importance of Black experiences in Europe (Black Europe). In survey and specialized topics courses, I uncover and share knowledge regarding the existence of Black Europeans in various national and historical contexts. I expose students to the reality that Europe, especially Germany, was never a homogeneously white or Judeo-Christian place/space but was only constructed as such. I prompt them to interrogate their ideas and understandings of the continent through critical readings, assignments, and in-class exercises.

Decentering Eurocentric perspectives and re-narrating stories of Europe in my courses, I use diverse cultural texts, such as poetry, prose, autobiography, fiction, film, and music, particularly produced by and/or dealing with Black Europeans and other Communities of Color in Europe across different *spacetimes*.[22] I use the works of multiple European Communities of Color in my courses. Furthermore, I rely on the works of Black Germans such as May Ayim, Theodor Michael, Olumide Popoola, and Ika Hügel-Marshall, and I use them to show how their cultural productions challenge and complicate notions of identity, nation, and belonging. The works of these individuals also intentionally center race in larger discussions in the public sphere and in nuanced ways open up new spaces for the decolonization of the German literary canon. Indeed, their writing does not relegate Black Germans to a perpetual state of marginality or victimhood, instead viewing them as empowered citizen subjects in the writing and curating of their

---

20 Darlene Clark Hine, *Hine Sight: Black Women and the Re-Construction of American History* (Bloomington, IN: Indiana University Press, 1997); Deborah Gray White, "Mining the Forgotten: Manuscript Sources for Black Women's History," *Journal of American History* 74, no. 1 (June 1987): 237–42; Marisa Fuentes, *Dispossessed Lives: Enslaved Women, Violence, and the Archive* (Philadelphia: University of Pennsylvania Press, 2016); Robin Mitchell, *Vénus Noire: Black Women and Colonial Fantasies in Nineteenth-Century France* (Athens, GA: University of Georgia Press, 2020); Saidiya Hartman, "Venus in Two Acts," *Small Axe* 26, vol. 12, no. 2 (June 2008): 1–14; Deirdre Cooper Owens, *Medical Bondage: Race, Gender, and the Origins of American Gynecology* (Athens, GA: University of Georgia Press, 2017).
21 Tina M. Campt, *Image Matters: Archive, Photography and the African Diaspora in Europe* (Durham, NC: Duke University Press, 2012); Fatima El-Tayeb, "Undisciplined Knowledge: Intersectional Black European Studies," *New German Critique* 150, vol. 50, no. 3 (November 2023): 37; and Fatima El-Tayeb, "The Future of Black German Studies Cannot Be Within Academia Alone," Forum on Black German Studies, *German Quarterly* 95, no. 4 (November 2022): 412–14.
22 Michelle M. Wright, *Physics of Blackness: Beyond the Middle Passage Epistemology* (Minneapolis: University of Minnesota Press, 2015).

own histories, which, in turn, restores their agential voices. This pedagogical practice serves as a corrective, challenging the silencing of discussions on race and racial diversity as well as the normalization of racial erasure in Europe. Basically, I stress the heterogeneity and historicity of Black Europe in my teaching and research.

Vanessa D. Plumly: During my first year at my university, I gave a talk on Fasia Jansen to interested students, faculty, and staff as part of our Martin Luther King Jr.'s legacy and Black History Month events. Our university president attended the presentation and conversation, and his comment at the end was that he knew about the U.S. civil rights movement but did not know all that much about how such movements transpired on a global scale, in places such as Germany, and were indeed interconnected. Jansen is a great example of under-documentation in the sense of publications and writings on her work. Her life and legacy remain mostly invisible and unknown, even in Germany. Exceptions are Tina M. Campt's early historical monograph on Black German experiences during the Third Reich and Marina Achenbach's biography.[23]

What is significant is that Jansen and her life partner Ellen Diederich kept their own archive of their activism and organizing in the women's movement and in the anti-nuclear movement in West Germany and beyond, recognizing that no one else was doing so at the time. Nevertheless, one of the points I made during my lecture on Jansen was that her songs remain more or less inaccessible to non-German speakers (hence the significance of knowing another language, which is addressed in the next section) as only a few have been translated into English. The materials I provided to students who came to the talk were my own translations of her songs. Moving forward, I would like to make more of these kinds of resources connected to Black German history available to a wider public and more accessible through translation. In conducting research on Jansen for a project in progress, one of the difficulties I encountered was that her archives are housed in many different locations, are not yet fully cataloged, and that some parts of the archive are still held in her partner's home. The benefit of this is that you are forced to seek engagement with those who are in the know, meaning an active involvement in the community and those materially tied to the history. This type of research, the active work of uncovering that which has been forcibly hidden or undocumented by those in power, continues to inspire the work I do on a daily basis.

---

[23] Tina Campt, *Other Germans: Black Germans and the Politics of Race, Gender, and Memory in the Third Reich* (Ann Arbor, MI: The University of Michigan Press, 2004).

Ashley D. Farmer has called for an "archival reckoning" asking what it would mean not only to curate and write about the past but to actually confront it.[24] How is decolonization at your universities related to stories of resistance (e.g., "Rhodes Must Fall")? How have student activists served as agents of colonial change on campus and beyond?

Tiffany N. Florvil: UNM has a strong legacy of dealing with colonialism and racism but with mixed results, which is often the case when it comes to social movements. Campus student activists rallying, in turn, led to the creation of Women Studies, Africana Studies, and Chicano/a Studies at the university, even though the latter is a more recent development. Much of this activism had roots in the late 1960s and 1970s and was even supported by local Black Panther and Students for a Democratic Society or SDS groups. Student activism has also led to increased awareness concerning Title IX and sexual harassment. All of this does not mean that students (and their parents) still cannot uphold the status quo, espouse racist views, affirm right-wing populism, and hamper freedom of speech. Certainly, both types of students are visible in the aftermath of the Hamas attack in Palestine/Israel on October 7 across U.S. campuses. While the protests in support of Palestinians have grown, so too has the right-wing agitation against those students, professors, and others. Right-wing discourses and politics have also resulted in an uptick in antisemitic, anti-Islamic, and anti-Black violence, allowing people to practice exclusion and harm in everyday life. Unfortunately, we are living at a scary moment in time that will continue to be challenging unless we push back against it. Decolonizing history and the past represents one step in that direction.

I must also add that I see my scholarly and intellectual work as a form of "archival reckoning" in both Black German and Black European Studies/History. The retrieval and excavation of Black diasporic narratives, voices, and actions simply overturns the belief that they exhibited no significant presence on the European continent. For Germany, it is important to reorient people's gaze toward Black abundance rather than absence.

Vanessa D. Plumly: My campus has an organization called Concerned Black Students that issued demands in 1969 and staged a walkout. That walkout continues to date, and the list of demands remains a staple of the annual walkout.[25] Some of the demands in 2022 included a call for an increase in the Black student population, communication concerning issues on campus, hiring more diverse, and specifically

---

[24] Ashley D. Farmer et al., "Toward an Archival Reckoning," *The American Historical Review* 127, no. 2 (2022): 799–829.

[25] https://www.wittenberg.edu/student-life/multicultural/cbs-walkout-2022, last accessed July 12, 2024.

Black, faculty and staff, a Black mental health counselor, more diverse and Black-oriented courses, disarming campus police, and mandatory, annual diversity training. This is a clear indicator that confronting the past also means confronting the persistence of that past into the present. Recently, I also learned that the existence of the McClain Center for Diversity on our campus was the result of student activism following from a racial slur being spraypainted on the fountain at the heart of our campus and which remained there for well over a week. One of our Martin Luther King Jr. convocation speakers this year, Moses Mbeseha (Class of '13), was a student leader at that time who made the current space and its administrators into a reality by forcing the administration and campus to account for the presence and persistence of anti-Black racism and to address this issue through action.

Madalitso Zilio Phiri: The South African student community has always been linked to the struggle for justice and anti-colonial organizing. This goes back to student activism across all the multifaceted social movements and political organizations in South Africa since the early 1900s (Pixley Seme, Nelson Mandela, Walter Sisulu, Charlotte Maxexe), the Unity Movement, and Steve Biko's Black Consciousness Movement, which culminated in the Soweto 1976 mass mobilization. The past decade saw continued resistance that was manifested in the #RhodesMustFall, #FeesMustFall, and #FeesMustFall2.0 campaigns. The temporal links in two different eras are intimately linked as both material and epistemic marginalities have created conditions reproducing colonial violence. Some of these contemporary fallist movements were diffused by state-sanctioned espionage, erasure, and a ludicrous mission to lure activists into the luxuries of crass materialism. Such contemporary movements however, were connecting as well as challenging tropes of cumulative historical epistemic and material marginalisations that continue to facilitate conditions of domination. These movements also reverberated across the Black Atlantic to remind us that the aesthetics of oppression, suppression, depression, and visibility of Black life on the African continent and Black diaspora are inter-connected.

There were some pitfalls in these movements. Material inequalities in South African academia are also widely connected to the struggle of workers such as cleaners, catering staff, and bus drivers, who occupy a gendered and racialized hierarchical racialised political economy. We inhabit and orbit a racialized political economy that valorizes capital over investing in workers' benefits, which has led to the casualization as well as informality of work. This is a process that began in the 1970s rooted in the so-called market fundamentalist revolution. Casualization of work in South African academia became real when the language of managerialism and corporatization was deployed in the early 2000s. Student movements constitute a transitory community that may be exploited by powerful ideological forces, thereby abandoning the mission of what Amilcar Cabral coined as class suicide.[26] Agitations for a decolonized curriculum are intimately linked to gatekeeping practices entrenched by a hegemonic white subject in the South African academe. This is not to say that "all" Black voices in the South African academe aspire toward epistemic justice. Black conservative voices are hijacked by Eurocentric bent academe to derail processes of epistemic justice. Yet, this is still informed by discourses that are steeped in academic cultures of white supremacy and epistemic marginality. Some Black "progressive" voices even resort to nativism and narrow ethno-nationalism, which perpetuates colonial and violent tropes under the guise of decolonising the South African academe. Removing statues as well as demanding a decolonized curriculum does not jettison the material and epistemic marginalities produced historically. Eurocentric social science and humanities convinced the world that there are no alternatives to their canon. However, the very same Eurocentric canon produced visible epistemic marginalities that are evident in the contemporary modern world. Our challenge is to engage Blackness as a living archive, a zone of epistemic possibility. This is a tradition bequeathed to us by Black radical thinkers, who provided alternative imaginaries to the world of empire, epistemic marginalisation, and violence.

Beyond Western Canons & Language(s) of Knowledge

Decolonizing the curriculum and publishing practices has been a central tenet. Frequently, theoretical contributions of racialized and indigenous scholars are reduced to mere experiences or "stories."[27] *At the same time, decolonization does not involve a total rejection of all things Western. Who gets canonized, who is considered "foundational" in your respective field and how have you made space for diverse voices? How can we seek and ensure a plurality and inclusivity of knowledge (and thus epistemic justice) in our research and curricula?*

Madalitso Zilio Phiri: The quest for epistemic justice should never be about inclusion so that we feel better about ourselves. Such approaches constitute what I call the "violence of inclusion." Black radical theorists have always offered imaginaries outside of epistemicide and empire. As mentioned above, in saying this, I do not sub-

---

26 A. Cabral, "The Weapon of Theory." Address delivered to the first Tricontinental Conference of the Peoples of Asia, Africa and Latin America held in Havana in January 1966. Available on https://www.marxists.org/subject/africa/cabral/1966/weapon-theory.htm, last accessed July 12, 2024.
27 Shana Almeida, "Race-Based Epistemologies: The Role of Race and Dominance in Knowledge Production," *Wagadu* 13 (2015): 79–105, esp. 88, 90–92.

scribe to the idea that the Black intellectual archive should be sacrosanct to critique, especially when we revisit classical texts in the Black radical tradition. No scholarship stands the eternality of time in the same breath that those who come after us will stand back and subject our contributions to intellectual scrutiny. However, decentering Eurocentrism taps into the intellectual archive of Africa and the Black diaspora as an ontological space and a zone of epistemic possibility. I have already intimated that sociology as a discipline fails to overcome epistemicide. One possibility toward epistemic justice is to think of *sociology as worldmaking* or rather *humanities and social sciences as worldmaking*. Such an approach opens up the canon wider than the Eurocentric disciplines. It is vital to tear down the idea of a world society through mono-discipline. This is what made twentieth-century Black theorists such as C. L. R. James, Kwame Nkrumah, Cheik Anta Diop, W. E. B. Du Bois, Archie Mafeje, Ida B. Wells, Audre Lorde, and Sylvia Wynter different. They theorized based on their conditions and in doing so developing multiplicities of existence. Their ontological locations thereby deployed potent vocabularies that explained world society, erasure, violence, and possibilities. Their empirical, methodological, and conceptual frameworks provide us with alternative canons to engage in *non-disciplinary* studies.

Vanessa D. Plumly: I have had the privilege of crafting my own curricula at every institution where I have worked. This was no doubt part of the draw to each of these places and programs. As the sole professor in German at Wittenberg University in Ohio, I determine the course materials taught within our existing curricular structure. This is one benefit of running your own German program. One way in which I seek to dismantle the flattening of experiences of racialized and indigenous scholars and their work, as well as the experiences of those alongside whom I conduct research, is to invite them to my campus to talk virtually or in person with my students. This often takes the form of a guest lecture, but it can also occur in the form of invited teaching via an online platform. This allows students not only to learn from me, but also from scholars, artists, and activists who produce or analyze the very discourses we are seeking to comprehend and who embody the identity categories with which we are engaged in the classroom.

Beyond my campus, Tiffany and I have created spaces for Black scholars who carry out research in German Studies by launching the above-mentioned Black Diaspora Studies Network at the German Studies Association and through our founding of the book series "Imagining Black Europe" published by Peter Lang International. In the collaborative work on our edited volumes, we have sought to ensure that a plurality of positionalities and interdisciplinary forms of knowledge breaking-down traditional Western paradigms, are represented. This does not, however, mean that we have always been successful in this endeavor.

Tiffany N. Florvil: In the history department at UNM, I cannot change the entire undergraduate or graduate curricula to reflect more antiracist or decolonial histories and knowledge. But what I can do is decolonize my teaching, and I do this by including at least 60 percent of work from Black, Indigenous, and People of Color (BIPOC) scholars in all my syllabi. By doing this, I reorient perspectives and decenter whiteness in my European history courses. For example, in my "Modern Germany" or "Black Europe" courses, I include materials from Black communities in Europe such as Claudia Jones, Hazel Carby, Gloria Wekker, Frantz Fanon, and Stuart Hall. I also include lesser-known figures such as Ricky Reiser, Una Marson, or Olive Morris, to name a few. Doing so offers students a degree of epistemic justice.

In terms of the issue of canonization, I thought that Black German writer May Ayim had reached that level. But in October 2023, I was disappointed. After a colleague inquired about editing a special issue on Ayim in a prominent German journal, *Text+Kritik*, an editor responded that Ayim was mostly known as an activist and had no literary significance. Ayim's literary and political work were intricably linked and not separate pursuits. I named the journal because they should be called out for this absurd take. Beyond enraging me, this response made me realize that I no longer want Ayim to be in the German literary canon per se; I want to disrupt the canon. I want to pursue what Venkat Mani proposed in his 2023 piece in the *New German Critique*: "In other words, decolonization should be understood as the disarrangement of any linear progression of thought that privileges majoritarian stances, but decolonization must also be critical of any fetishization of minoritarian works under the umbrella term *inclusion*. Effective decolonization [. . .] is a desideratum to explore and apply readerly curiosity to account for the critical work that literary imagination can generate in social life."[28] I want Ayim and other minoritized writers to be considered "an inherent and crucial part of the literatures and languages of" the German nation; they must not be afterthoughts. This is why decolonization has to be a critical method enabling scholars across the globe to advocate for concrete change and not engage in the performative acts of Diversity, Equity, and Inclusion (DEI) and exclusivity. Currently, we are witnessing a backlash against DEI, decolonization, postcolonialism, "wokeness," critical race theory, and so much more in the United States and Germany. At the moment, censorship is also particularly egregious in Germany with regard to people who support Palestine. Fascist legislation in Florida, Texas, Louisiana, and Georgia continues to prohibit basic human and civil rights. While it will take some time to recover from this re-

---

28 B. Venkat Mani, "Decolonizing Reading Publics, Decompartmentalizing German Studies," *New German Critique* 150, vol. 50, no. 3 (November 2023): 119–131, esp. 122.

gressive and illiberal moment, I know that the classroom represents one way of pushing for some change.

As already briefly mentioned above, epistemic hierarchies, knowledge, and language mutually enforce one another. The English language reigns supreme as the "language of science." Drawing on the experience of two universities, Makerere University and the University of Dar es Salaam, Mahmood Mamdani criticizes the idea of a university based on a single, colonial language.[29] In your opinion, how can we overcome language barriers in academia?

Madalitso Zilio Phiri: Linguicide exists on the African continent as the imposition of Eurocentrism killed the possibility of an African philosophy and thereby linguistic pluralism and memory culture. The task of language recognition is the unfinished business of what Dani Nabudere refers to as *Afrikology*. The two different approaches for overcoming epistemicide continue to animate and polarize public and scholarly debates on the role of language and literature in Africa. One position favors abandoning European languages, while the other favors a hybridization of language. Each position pushes for epistemic orders that challenge epistemicide while acknowledging colonial trappings. My contribution, however, in terms of forging a new path from these diverging views should pivot the African civilizational discourse that centers Africa's spirituality in the philosophy of language. This was articulated by Nabudere, who notes that *Afrikology* draws its scientificity and uniqueness from the fact that it is based on an all-embracing philosophy of humankind originating in Egypt and updated by the lived experiences of all humanity, which still draws on its deep-rooted wisdom. It is based on a philosophy that is conscious of itself, conscious of its own existence as thought and which, although originally based on myth, was able to move itself from myth to concept within its own development.[30] William Blyden, the early twentieth-century pan-Africanist, and Marcus Garvey may be credited for coining the term *African personality*. It is in thinking along the lines of the African personality that a new humanhood, spirituality, and linguistic locales emerge.

Tiffany N. Florvil: As an associate professor who teaches at a majority-minority university, many of my students can speak another language. This means that my students come into the classroom with embodied knowledge shaping how they

---

[29] Mahmood Mamdani, "Decolonising Universities," in *Decolonisation in Universities: The Politics of Knowledge*, ed. Jonathan D. Jansen (Johannesburg: Wits University Press, 2019), 15–28, esp. 15–16, 24–26.

[30] Dani Wadada Nabudere, "Towards an Afrokology of Knowledge Production and African Regeneration," *International Journal of African Renaissance Studies* 1, vol. 1 (2006): 7–32, esp. 20.

approach historical subjects. I find that this is definitely an asset. However, as many of my students lack German proficiency, I need to provide them with translated (German-English) texts so that they can understand the German context. I wish that many more German texts were translated. I wish that I could teach Raja Lubinetzki's poetry or Noah Sow's detective novel in my "Gender in the Modern World/Sex in the City" course. I also wish that Ayim's complete collected works were published so that I could assign her in my graduate seminars. This is all to say that translation is extremely important, but it is also costly in some immeasurable ways. We need more translated works to help facilitate cross-cultural understanding in and beyond the classroom. This is one of the reasons why I wanted to publish my 2020 book in German last year (2023). I wanted to expose my scholarship to a German audience so that they can see the richness of their own Black history.

Moreover, multilingual scholars are already engaged in this work. They examine sources in multiple languages, which offers them diverse perspectives on a range of topics. Their work provides tangible models for overcoming monolingualism.[31] They also show us that reading beyond our fields and borders shapes rather than hinders our thinking. In fact, crossing borders geographically and methodologically can be generative and affirming. Even though the United States does not privilege multilingualism, this does not mean that scholars across a wide array of disciplines do the same.

Vanessa D. Plumly: This past semester, I taught a translation course for the first time. It was a challenge for me, but the result of the course was that it forced my students to have a reckoning with language, knowledge, power, and the making of meaning. Teaching this course enabled me to articulate how language and the interpretation thereof in any given cultural context (its original context and its newly attained context) is always and may remain a barrier to understanding. Something that my students and I discussed was that collaborative work is imperative in any hermeneutic undertaking and that the presence of multiple languages adds to the layers of meaning that one may derive from any given text, while also complicating it in productive ways, preventing us from ever knowing whether we fully understand. This in and of itself is a decolonial act as it refutes Western claims to absolute knowledge and supremacy. It undoes the hierarchical structures of one dominant language, instead placing languages in a relational and co-dependent meaning-making and rhizomic structure. This is what Catherine Walsh refers to as "decolonial insurgency" when writing: "insurgency urges, puts forth, and advances from

---

[31] See, for example, Yuliya Komska, Michelle Moyd, and David Gramling, *Linguistic Disobedience: Restoring Power to Civic Language* (New York: Palgrave, 2018).

the ground up and from the margins, other imaginaries, visions, knowledges, modes of thought, other ways of being, becoming, and living in relation."[32] So, instead of overcoming language barriers, I find it more powerful to produce more and more of these in an ongoing insurgent act of decoloniality across which differences must be navigated, understood, and acknowledged.

Empowerment & Resistance

Some scholars such as Liberian academic and activist Robtel Neajai Pailey have argued that decolonization cannot occur in a "political vacuum."[33] To what extent is the scholarly "decolonial turn" divorced from daily struggles?

Vanessa D. Plumly: I think that the answer to this question to a great extent depends on the discipline as well as the scholars and work to which one is oriented in that discipline or even who one is. For example, Black scholars working in Black German Studies cannot be divorced from daily struggles as their bodies literally constitute a political terrain. On the other hand, there are plenty of white scholars who claim to be participants in the decolonial turn in German Studies who are removed from daily struggles and who are apolitical and not active beyond their scholarly contributions to the ivory tower.

Madalitso Zilio Phiri: The link between the political and epistemic is an intimate one. I agree with Pailey that decolonization cannot occur in a political vacuum. We should always define the political. Sometimes, the quest to decolonize has become a fad in academia so that the project becomes a fruitless intellectual exercise in the confines of the academy by disembodied interlocutors divorced from the gendered and racialised poor. Global struggles waged by workers, peasants, and the racialized poor remind us that a racialized hierarchical political economy continues to order and govern global power and social relations. The global economy is predicated on anti-Black racism, dominance, and erasure. The knowledge that materially produced our contemporary world is still imperial. Linking the epistemic to the material conditions of the erstwhile colonized is what will make

---

32 Catherine Walsh, "The Decolonial For: Resurgences, Shifts, and Movements," in *On Decoloniality: Concepts, Analytics, Praxis*, eds. Walter Mignolo and Catherine Walsh (Durham, NC: Duke University Press, 2018), p. 34.

33 Robtel Neajai Pailey, "How to Truly Decolonise the Study of Africa," *Al Jazeera*, June 10, 2019, https://www.aljazeera.com/opinions/2019/6/10/how-to-truly-decolonise-the-study-of-africa, last accessed June 29, 2023.

the realization of a world not predicated on domination possible. We should imagine a development without imperial imaginaries.

In my work, I am wrestling with the idea of "thinking about development as reparations". This I argue, is a challenge of the present and not the future. This is because those racialized as Blacks were aborted from the teleological goal of colonial modernity, which is why the future remains illusory. Yet, there cannot be global justice without epistemic justice. Material inequalities linked to the tropes of intersectionality such as gender, race, class, and geography in the present are real. I have my own definition of development as reparations: a process and current moment of attainment and a reversal of imperial violence to achieve a distribution of tangible material, spiritual, and metaphysical benefits of classic and contemporary Black liberatory aesthetics into the ecological, social, political, economic, and psychological milieu not dictated by whiteness, empire, racism as totalizing ontological categories of ordering global power and social relations.[34] Again, our duty as scholars is to suspend colonial time, which enables the dismantling of the cumulative material disadvantages that define the formerly colonized peoples.

Tiffany N. Florvil: Much like intersectionality, the new iteration of the decolonial turn, especially post-BLM in 2020, has become rather capacious and meaningless. Many scholars sought to decolonize curricula, disciplines, and universities without truly understanding the meaning of the word or recognizing that such work is arduous. As a result, the word has in many ways become depoliticized, and it is seen as a destination or product.

Yet, some minoritized communities do not have the luxury of divorcing their daily struggles from their scholarly work; there is never a clear divide between theory and praxis for them. The two are intertwined and inform one another. Their intellectual work is activism, and their activism is intellectual work. They make sure that there is no "political vacuum." Nowhere is this more evident than in the work of recent scholarship on Haiti, Sudan, and Palestine. For scholars in and from these countries, the political is not only personal but epistemic.

Closely related, Fatima El-Tayeb has recently (and repeatedly) pointed out that the future of Black German Studies is not to be found in academia alone. In contrast to Ethnic or African American Studies, Black German Studies is rooted "in traditional, elitist, exclusionary academia rather than in activism."[35] How can we overcome

---

[34] M. Z. Phiri, "The Idea of development as reparations: Another world is possible," *European Journal of Development Research* (forthcoming, special issue on Race and Development).
[35] "Forum: On Black German Studies – The Future of Black German Studies Cannot Be Within Academia Alone," *The German Quarterly* 95, no. (2022): 412–414, here 413.

"practice[s] of transgressive resistance" as this is not only the case for Black German Studies?[36]

Vanessa D. Plumly: El-Tayeb is right to call out the necessity of a collaboration and institutionalization of Black German Studies in Germany that is rooted in the community and its activism. Black German Studies has existed long before it came to the academy in places and spaces that operate outside of the confines of Western institutions of knowledge (e.g., in the homes of members of the movement), and it will continue to exist beyond the academy since Black Germans as knowledge producers and agents of change constitute the very foundation from which any such discipline can ever exist. El-Tayeb's demand echoes Pailey's critique of decolonization existing in a political vacuum, as the field cannot be devoid of the voices to which it claims to speak and work with and for.

Tiffany N. Florvil: On the one hand, Fatima El-Tayeb is correct. Indeed, much of the work of Black German and Black European Studies is done outside of activist circles. On the other hand, she is not entirely correct, as Vanessa also notes. Black German Studies originated in grassroots activism, outside the confines of the ivory towers of academia, and it still to this day takes shape outside academia. In the past, Black German quotidian intellectuals decolonized knowledge and offered an "archival reckoning"; they proved that intellectual work was not the purview of white academics alone. They opened up spaces for knowing and learning of the past in the present. When Black German women, such as May Ayim and Katharina Oguntoye, worked together and edited *Farbe bekennen: Afro-deutsche Frauen auf den Spuren ihrer Geschichte* (*Showing Our Colors*), they made significant political, cultural, and intellectual interventions turning Black German Studies into a viable form of inquiry.[37] Ayim's senior thesis, which provided the foundation for *Farbe bekennen*, normalized alternative epistemologies and frameworks that challenged white or Western knowledge and histories. Her 1990 thesis on speech pathology at the Freie Universität Berlin also accomplished this. To this day, her thesis remains the only one to tackle issues of ethnocentrism and gendered stereotypes in the area of speech therapy. Contemporary Black German writings and cultural productions from Philipp Khabo Koepsell, Josephine Apraku, Emila Roig, and Alice Hasters con-

---

[36] Peggy Piesche, Eric Otieno, and Maisha Auma, "'Reclaiming Our Time' in African Studies: Conversations from the Perspective of the Black Studies Movement in Germany," *Critical African Studies* 12, no. 3 (2020): 330–353, here 343.

[37] Katharina Oguntoye, May Opitz/Ayim, and Dagmar Schultz, eds., *Farbe bekennen: Afro-deutsche Frauen auf den Spuren ihrer Geschichte* (1986; Berlin: Orlanda, 2006) and May Opitz, Katharina Oguntoye, and Dagmar Schultz, eds. *Showing Our Colors: Afro-German Women Speak Out*, trans. Anne Adama (Amherst, MA: University of Massachusetts Press, 1992).

tinue to serve in this capacity. The efforts of Black German quotidian intellectuals demonstrate that the political and the epistemic undergird what they do in both the streets and in the lecture halls then and now.

Madalitso Zilio Phiri: Of late I have been thinking about the role of art, knowledge production, and Black aesthetics. Sometimes, artists produce materials that are publicly consumed without commodification. This is more reified for those who write intellectual biographies of artists, poets, musicians, and scholar activists. The artifacts left behind may be compiled by a scholar whose research initiatives enrich our intellectual archives to the detriment of material benefits to the artists themselves. I am particularly thinking about the African context whereby artists orbit a zone of precarity as well as material deprivations. This observation may also be true globally. The process of knowledge curation and development on the producers of art however, benefits university presses and publishing companies, which curate this knowledge in books and journal articles. The artists do not stand to benefit from this consumption. This cross-pollination of exchange enables transgressive resistance.

Our consumption of decommodified art opens up to possibilities of resistance. In fact, it opens us up to possibilities of generosity and exchange. This is how we should view these disciplines. Being committed to transgressive resistance is a possibility when we are invited to stand outside the decommodified knowledge community. Black aesthetics invites us to positions of surrender and vulnerability where the disciplines are not king. Surrendering Eurocentric disciplines, approaches and methodologies enables possibilities of commitments of non-disciplinarity.

Arguably, globalization and digitalization enhance the transformation from knowledge-consuming to knowledge-producing societies in the Global South. How do you assess the role of open access to empowerment and the recognition of indigenous knowledge? What are the risks?

Tiffany N. Florvil: Yes, open access is an important and necessary step to ensure a wider dissemination of BIPOC works to broader audiences (lay or otherwise). However, it is both costly and difficult for some scholars to pursue. For instance, I have no funding resources at UNM that would help me publish my materials in the form of open access.

In addition, digital spaces such as Twitter (now called X), Facebook, and blogs have enabled the circulation of alternative knowledge and knowledge forms, thus enabling the otherwise or other worlds. These spaces also show us that knowledge is not only produced in academic circles. Sadly, it has also led to ideas and work being stolen and/or BIPOC not being credited. I am not sure how to reconcile this at the moment. More of us need to engage with additional scholarship on digital humanities to understand which solutions are available. Open access and digital spaces help democratize knowledge in ways that matter even more so now.

Madalitso Zilio Phiri: The regime that governs Eurocentric knowledge production is enmeshed in the hierarchical commodified knowledge production value chain. Open access seeks to challenge this marginality. This, however, is just the beginning. I think that we should imagine a world whereby we abandon the intellectual property regime and the commodification of what is considered knowledge. As scholars, we obviously benefit from the regime producing this value chain. This is enabled by the ranking of journals, books, and university presses. If we start to think of knowledge as a global commons, our perspectives on what constitutes indigenous knowledge will also change. Indeed, the binary relationship between "indigenous knowledge" and "real knowledge" reinforces the colonial logics in which Eurocentric traditions are valorized.

Vanessa D. Plumly: The role of open access with regard to empowerment means disseminating knowledge beyond the classroom and in venues open to the public. There is always a risk that this knowledge is co-opted and used against the very communities that create it, thereby furthering extractivist conditions in a capitalist and neoliberal world order.

Critique of "Decolonization"

The use of the term "decolonization" has grown exponentially over the past couple of years. For some scholars, it has become conflated, turned into an impossible political project that risks denying agency to former colonized countries and/or reducing the complexity of the issues at hand. At the same time, there is a conceived "gap between high theory in decolonization writings and the practicalities of 'making decolonization work' on the ground."[38] As practitioners, how do we avoid falling into the trap of reproducing the norms of Eurocentric disciplinary knowledge economies?

Madalitso Zilio Phiri: As long as the world is predicated on colonial logics, there will always be a need to rethink the world from those who have been ejected from the project of modernity. Scholars and society at large may disagree on the deployment of discourses and vocabularies, which make these imaginaries and

---

[38] Jonathan D. Jansen, "Making Sense of Decolonsation in Universities," in Jansen, Decolonisation in Universities, 7.

futures possible. I have already argued that these are realities of the future as of the present. I agree that decolonization has become a fad over the past decade. Some scholars enmeshed in their denialism and conceptual decadence of Eurocentric theoretical tools have even started writing against decolonization. My intellectual journey, however, is to tap into the Black radical archive to make sense of the present toward the liberation of those globally racialized as black. This is what animated pan-Africanists of the past century whose efforts aimed at the promotion of the political, socio-economic, cultural unity and self-reliance of Africa and its Diaspora. This journey has assisted me in developing a taxonomy of diverse texts that need to be excavated to understand contemporary epistemic shifts. However, this process was kickstarted by my intellectual ancestors who theorized the Black condition from alternative perspectives. Blackness is not only defined by the existence of a sole epistemic locale. A recognition of multiple epistemic localities can assist in opening up alternative knowledge archives in order to challenge mono-disciplinarity.

Vanessa D. Plumly: I am not sure that we can ever actually get around that trap as we are implicated in it. Rather, we must continually work in and against it given where (at least speaking on behalf of Tiffany and I) we are located geographically. What I mean by this is that I am working in the United States and not in Germany, but this does not mean that the decolonization efforts of Black Germans are not applicable to the United States or to my classroom and my teaching and that it cannot have an impact here.

Decolonization is not an impossible political project, and anyone who claims otherwise does not wish to imagine and work to create this world in another way than as it already exists. Indeed, decolonization has been transpiring for decades among colonized and affected communities and affinity groups. This process requires constant action and vigilance in every sphere of our lives and a commitment to listen more than speak, especially as a white person.

Tiffany N. Florvil: Vanessa is correct. The trap of replicating Eurocentric narratives and frameworks is a difficult one to completely avoid. I find that many white scholars have a hard time seeing the possibility of other worlds and perspectives not entangled in whiteness (Vanessa is an exception here). I work through and against Eurocentric narratives by centering minoritized and/or Blackened knowledge in my own scholarly work. Again, I believe that Black feminist scholars such as Sylvia Wynter, Christina Sharpe, Régine Michelle Jean-Charles, bell hooks, Patrica Hill Collins, Audre Lorde, M. Jacqui Alexander, May Ayim, and others and their works model what alternative worldmaking and Black feminist praxes look like. For me, this entails going back to their texts and grounding my intellectual work in these Black feminist traditions. Is it an easy task? Oh, heavens no. But Black feminism offers me an ethics of care and a pathway forward in my scholarship on Black Germany and Black Europe.

Tiffany N. Florvil is an associate professor of twentieth-century European women's and gender history at the University of New Mexico, Albuquerque. She specializes in the histories of post-1945 Europe, the African/Black diaspora, Black internationalism, and gender and sexuality. She has published *Mobilizing Black Germany: Afro-German Women and the Making of a Transnational Movement* (University of Illinois Press 2020) and its German translation, *Black Germany-Schwarz, deutsch, feministisch-die Geschichte einer Bewegung* (Ch. Links Verlag, 2023). Her book won the Waterloo Centre for German Studies First Book Prize in 2021, in addition to other honors. This past academic year, she served as the Joy Foundation Fellow at Harvard's Radcliffe Institute, where she worked on an intellectual biography of Black German poet May Ayim.

Madalitso Zililo Phiri is a post-doctoral fellow in the South Africa United Kingdom Bilateral Research Chair in Political Theory, University of the Witwatersrand, South Africa. He was until recently a visiting fellow at the University of Cambridge's Centre of African Studies, visiting college research associate, Wolfson College, University of Cambridge, and Carnegie Corporation Fellow (2014–2017) through the Next Generation of Social Science in Africa, Social Science Research Council, New York, United States. He is co-author of *Monuments and Memory in Africa: Reflections on Coloniality and Decoloniality* (New York: Routledge, 2024). Phiri's publications include book chapters and refereed journal articles in publications such as *Critical Sociology* and *Monthly Review*. His ongoing research interests include political economy of racialized welfare (South Africa and Brazil), sociology of race, and Black political thought.

Vanessa D. Plumly is an assistant professor of German at Wittenberg University. Her scholarly work centers on interdisciplinary analyses of Black German cultural productions, ranging from theater and hip-hop to crime novels and autobiographies. Recent publications include "Black German Orientational *Heimat Archi-textures* in Noah Sow's *Die Schwarze Madonna: Afrodeutscher Heimatkrimi* (2019)" in the volume *Heimat and Migration: Reimagining the Regional and the Global in the 21st Century* (2023), "'Racial Hauntings' and the Complexities of Afro-German Women's Kin(d)ship" in the volume *The Global History of Black Girlhood* (2022), and "*Auf den Spuren ihrer Geschichte*: Black German Detectives and the Cases of Anaïs Schmitz and Fatou Fall," *Seminar. A Journal of Germanic Studies* 57, no. 4 (2021): 402–423.

Contributors

Katherine Arens is a professor of Germanic Studies at the University of Texas at Austin. Her work focuses on the history and epistemology of the humanities since 1750 and particularly on intellectual migration and the need to disambiguate regional germanophone cultures. Her most recent books are a volume (edited with Robert Dassanowsky) on *Interwar Salzburg* (2024) and *Vienna's Dreams of Europe: Thinking Beyond the Nation State* (2015), alongside essays on the foundation of art history as a human science, on anglophone historiography on Habsburg Austria, and on J. F. Herbart, J. G. Herder, and Robert Zimmerman as creating an inductive approach to the human sciences, especially the modern social sciences, that need to be set apart from traditional accounts of German Idealism as a coherent body of thought.

Adam Bisno is an independent scholar in Stockholm. He is the author of *Big Business and the Crisis of German Democracy: Liberalism and the Grand Hotels of Berlin, 1875–1933* (Cambridge University Press, 2024), a case study in the failure of German liberalism. From the vantage of grand hotels, the book also accounts for the ironies in liberal ideology that made it no match for the fascist onslaught. Between 2020 and 2022, Bisno served as the official historian of the U.S. Patent and Trademark Office.

Bernardo S. Buarque is a postdoctoral researcher at Te Punaha Matatini, New Zealand. Before moving to Wellington, he worked as a research scholar at the Max Planck Institute for the History of Science in Berlin and earned his PhD from the University College Dublin. His research focuses on complex networks and dynamic systems modelling, particularly in the context of innovation and knowledge diffusion.

Rasmus Fleischer is a researcher in economic history at Stockholm University focusing on cultural economy, media history and the critique of economic statistics. His current focus is on the measurement of inflation: the mostly implicit valuations made when statisticians decide to compare the prices of qualitatively different products in the Consumer Price Index. Together with Daniel Berg, he has recently published the monograph *Varors värde: Kvalitetsvärderingar i konsumentprisindex under 1900-talet* (2023). Previously, he has been involved in an interdisciplinary project examining the streaming service Spotify, co-authoring the book *Spotify Teardown* (MIT Press, 2019).

Tiffany N. Florvil is an associate professor of twentieth-century European women's and gender history at the University of New Mexico, Albuquerque. She specializes in the histories of post-1945 Europe, the African/Black diaspora, Black internationalism, and gender and sexuality. She has published *Mobilizing Black Germany: Afro-German Women and the Making of a Transnational Movement* (University of Illinois Press, 2020) and its German translation, *Black Germany: Schwarz, deutsch, feministisch – die Geschichte einer Bewegung* (Ch. Links Verlag, 2023). Her book won the Waterloo Centre for German Studies First Book Prize in 2021, in addition to other honors. This past academic year, she served as the Joy Foundation Fellow at Harvard's Radcliffe Institute, where she worked on an intellectual biography of Black German poet May Ayim.

Tomás Irish is an associate professor of modern history at Swansea University, Wales. He has published on the cultural history of Europe during the First World War and the interwar period, with a focus on universities and intellectual life. His most recent book, *Feeding the Mind*:

Humanitarianism *and the Reconstruction of European Intellectual Life, 1919–1933*, was published in 2023.

Aleksandra Kaye is a postdoctoral researcher at the Max Planck Institute of Geoanthropology in Jena. Her current research examines cross-regional interactions and the circulation of environmental knowledge in relation to forest stewardship and petroleum extraction. Her doctoral research traced the histories of Polish scientific professionals in Latin America in the nineteenth century. Recent publications include "Piecing together 'big pictures' with social network analysis and digital tools" in *BJHS Themes* (2024) and "Shaping Public Perception: Polish Illustrated Press and the Image of Polish Naturalists Working in Latin America, 1844–1885" in *Berichte zur Wissenschaftsgeschichte* (2023).

Anne Kwaschik is a professor of contemporary history at Konstanz University with a special focus on the history of knowledge. Her research focuses on knowledge cultures and scientization processes such as the scientization of colonialism, the epistemology of health feminism, and the history of social experiments. Recent publications include "Reconstructing Colonial Sociology," *Social Science History* 48, no. 1 (2024), "'We Witches': Knowledge Wars, Experience and Spirituality in the Women's Movement in the 1970s," *NTM* 31 (2023).

Charlotte A. Lerg is senior assistant professor of North-American History at Ludwig-Maximilian University Munich and managing director of the Lasky Center for Transatlantic Studies. She has also taught at the Universities of Münster, Jena, and Bochum. Her research focuses on the cultural history of knowledge, visual media, and historical theory. Publications include *Universitätsdiplomatie: Prestige und Wissenschaft in den transatlantischen Beziehungen 1890–1920* (2019) and numerous articles on nineteenth and twentieth century transatlantic history. In her current project, funded by the German Research Foundation (DFG), she examines documentary drawing as part of the U.S. media landscape in the twentieth century.

Alina Marktanner is a postdoctoral researcher at the Chair for Modern History (C19–21) with its Knowledge and Technology Cultures, RWTH Aachen University. In her dissertation titled *Behördenconsulting*, she investigated the emergence of management consulting in the German public sector after the 1970s. Her second book project focuses on the history of pest control in German East Africa and British India around 1900. Her research interests include the history of science, knowledge and technology, political and administrative history and global and colonial history.

Victoria Van Orden Martínez is a researcher at Linköping University and Lund University in Sweden. Her current research focuses on how survivors of Nazi persecution who came to Sweden as refugees during and after the Second World War and the Holocaust were involved in various social and political processes in the early postwar period, with a focus on the role of gender and other differences. Recent publications include "Witnessing the Suffering of Others in Watercolor and Pencil: Jadwiga Simon-Pietkiewicz's Holocaust Art Exhibited in Sweden, 1945–46" in *Holocaust and Genocide Studies* (2023), "Monuments Cast Shadows: Remembering and Forgetting the 'Dead Survivors' of Nazi Persecution in Swedish Cemeteries," co-authored with Malin Thor Tureby, in *Fallen Monuments and Contested Memorials* (2023), and her Ph.D. thesis, *Afterlives: Jewish and Non-Jewish Polish Survivors of Nazi Persecution in Sweden Documenting Nazi Atrocities, 1945–1946* (2023).

Gilberto Mazzoli is a post-doctoral researcher in North American environmental history at the University of Konstanz tied to the ERC project "Off the Road: The Environmental Aesthetics of Early

Automobility." His research focuses on the merging of environmental history with migration and urban histories in the nineteenth and twentieth centuries. His recent publications include "Italianness in the United States between migrants' informal gardening practices and agricultural diplomacy, 1880–1912," *Modern Italy* 26, no. 2 (2021).

Hampus Östh Gustafsson is a researcher at Uppsala University and Lund University. After completing his PhD in history of science and ideas with a dissertation on the legitimacy of the humanities in the politics of knowledge in twentieth-century Sweden, his postdoctoral projects have concerned broader themes in the history of the humanities and the organization of modern universities. Recent publications include the edited volume *The Humanities and the Modern Politics of Knowledge* (together with Anders Ekström, Amsterdam University Press, 2022).

Johan Östling is Professor of History, Director of the Lund Centre for the History of Knowledge (LUCK), and Wallenberg Academy Fellow. His research is mainly devoted to the history of knowledge, but he has a more general interest in the intellectual, political, and cultural history of modern Europe. His recent publications comprise the trilogy *Circulation of Knowledge* (2018), *Forms of Knowledge* (2020), and *Knowledge Actors* (2023) as well as the introductory book *The History of Knowledge* (2023).

Vanessa D. Plumly is an assistant professor of German at Wittenberg University. Her scholarly work centers on interdisciplinary analyses of Black German cultural productions, ranging from theater and hip-hop to crime novels and autobiographies. Recent publications include "Black German Orientational *Heimat Archi-textures* in Noah Sow's *Die Schwarze Madonna: Afrodeutscher Heimatkrimi* (2019)" in the volume *Heimat and Migration: Reimagining the Regional and the Global in the 21st Century* (2023), "'Racial Hauntings' and the Complexities of Afro-German Women's Kin(d)ship" in the volume *The Global History of Black Girlhood* (2022), and *"Auf den Spuren ihrer Geschichte*: Black German Detectives and the Cases of Anaïs Schmitz and Fatou Fall," *Seminar. A Journal of Germanic Studies* 57, no. 4 (2021): 402–423.

Anne-Sophie Reichert is a cultural anthropologist interested in somatic and affective forms of knowledge, bodily learning, habits, and skills. She studied political science, political theory, and anthropology in Berlin, Chicago, Davis and Berkeley and received her PhD from the University of Chicago with a dissertation on motion and perception skills in dance practice. She is a co-founder of ALASKA-Studio for Feelings, an arts education initiative creating immersive environments, interactive sculptures, and hosting workshops on bodily and emotional literacy. She teaches anthropology of body and mind, anthropological theory, and feminist science studies and collaborates with artists and scientists.

Claudia Roesch is a post-doctoral researcher at the University of Konstanz affiliated with the history of knowledge working group. Her research interests include the history of knowledge and technology, North American history, gender and the family, and migration history. Her current research project "Utopian Engineering" investigates the role of science and engineering knowledge in social reform projects in the nineteenth-century Atlantic world. Her most recent publication is "Owen and the Engineers: Cross-Fertilization between Engineering and Early Socialism in the Owenite Tradition," *Global Intellectual History* (2023): 1–16.

Raphael Schlattmann is a historian of science with a background in theoretical physics. His research centres on the history of gravitational research in the field of GDR during the Cold War. Methodologically, he specialises in computational history with a particular interest in historical network research and the application of natural language processing (NLP) in processes of knowledge evolution. He is currently developing new digital tools and methods to analyse trajectories of change within large text corpora at the Max Planck Institute of Geoanthropology in Jena.

Jascha Schmitz is a PhD student at the digital history professorship of the Humboldt-University Berlin while also working there for Task Area 5 "Dataculture" of the NFDI4Memory – the national research data initiative for historical sciences. His research focuses include Anthropocene-centric historical research as well as the methodological and epistemological basis of digital historical methods, in particular simulation methods such as agent-based modelling. His PhD project concerns simulating the contexts and perspectives of individual mobility in a "modern" city (ca. 1920) before the advent of widespread individual car-use.

Isabelle Strömstedt is a lecturer at the Department of Science and Technology, Linköping University. Her research focuses on narratology, communication, visual culture, and popular culture. Strömstedt's dissertation was published in 2023 and is a microhistorical study of the Swedish Intellectual Property Office's fiftieth anniversary in 1941. The dissertation examines how the patent office presented itself to the public by positioning itself in master narratives of the independent inventor and Swedish inventiveness but also established a narrative of the patent office as effective and bureaucratic.

Malte Vogl is a senior research fellow at the Max Planck Institute of Geoanthropology in Jena with a PhD in physics. Until recently, he worked as a research fellow and PI at the Max Planck Institute for the History of Science in projects ranging from digital humanities work on the ancient perception of time and space in the cluster of excellency TOPOI, building and evaluating research data infrastructures in the context of the DARIAH project, large-scale analysis of archival data for the history of the MPG project GMPG to the most recent, BMBF-funded work on developing methods for modelling knowledge evolution as a multilayered temporal network in the ModelSEN project.

Jana Weiß is DAAD Associate Professor at the University of Texas at Austin. With a focus on U.S. and transatlantic history, her research interests include nineteenth and twentieth century immigration, knowledge, and religious history as well as the history of racism. Recently, she has co-edited the special issue on the "International Knowledge Transfer and Circulation within the Brewing Industry" in the 2024 *Economic History Yearbook* (with Nancy Bodden) and launched a student-miniseries on "Texas Germans' Migration and Knowledge" on the *Migrant Knowledge* blog of the German Historical Institute in Washington, D.C.

Lea Weiß is a student research assistant at the Max Planck Institute for the History of Science in Berlin as part of the research project "Socio-epistemic Networks: Modelling Historical Knowledge Processes" (ModelSEN). With an interest in historical sociology, science studies, and computational social science, she wrote her bachelor's thesis on the social network positions of female scientists in twentieth-century physics and is currently studying the diversification of the methodological landscape in the field of historical network research.

Laura von Welczeck has previously served as a student research assistant at the Max Planck Institute for the History of Science and part of the ModelSEN team on modelling socio-epistemic networks for historical knowledge processes. There, she investigated the diversification of the methodological landscape in the field of historical network research. She studies sociology and information systems in Berlin.

Madalitso Zililo Phiri is a post-doctoral fellow in the South Africa United Kingdom Bilateral Research Chair in Political Theory, University of the Witwatersrand, South Africa, visiting fellow at the University of Cambridge's Centre of African Studies. He was until recently a visiting fellow at the University of Cambridge's Centre of African Studies, visiting college research associate, Wolfson College, University of Cambridge, and Carnegie Corporation Fellow (2014–2017) through the Next Generation of Social Science in Africa, Social Science Research Council, New York, United States. He is co-author of *Monuments and Memory in Africa: Reflections on Coloniality and Decoloniality* (New York: Routledge, 2024). Phiri's publications include book chapters and refereed journal articles in publications such as *Critical Sociology* and *Monthly Review*. His ongoing research interests include political economy of racialized welfare (South Africa and Brazil), sociology of race, and Black political thought.

www.ingramcontent.com/pod-product-compliance
Lightning Source LLC
Chambersburg PA
CBHW051349290426
44108CB00015B/1945